Economics/IS 13 - Global Economy

Custom Edition for UC Irvine/Prof George Sarraf

William A. McEachern | Robert J. Carbaugh | Lee R. Dlabay |
James Calvert Scott

CENGAGE
Learning·

Australia • Brazil • Japan • Korea • Mexico • Singapore • Spain • United Kingdom • United States

Economics/IS 13 - Global Economy: Custom Edition for UC Irvine/Prof George Sarraf

Macroeconomics: A Contemporary Introduction, 9th Edition
William A. McEachern

© 2012 Cengage Learning. All rights reserved.

International Economics, 13th Edition
Robert Carbaugh

© 2011 Cengage Learning. All rights reserved.

International Business, 4th Edition
Lee R. Dlabay |
James Calvert Scott

© 2011 Cengage Learning. All rights reserved.

Executive Editors:
 Maureen Staudt
 Michael Stranz

Senior Project Development Manager:
 Linda deStefano

Marketing Specialist:
 Courtney Sheldon

Senior Production/Manufacturing Manager:
 Donna M. Brown

PreMedia Manager:
 Joel Brennecke

Sr. Rights Acquisition Account Manager:
 Todd Osborne

Cover Image:
Getty Images*

*Unless otherwise noted, all cover images used by Custom Solutions, a part of Cengage Learning, have been supplied courtesy of Getty Images with the exception of the Earthview cover image, which has been supplied by the National Aeronautics and Space Administration (NASA).

For product information and technology assistance, contact us at
Cengage Learning Customer & Sales Support, 1-800-354-9706

For permission to use material from this text or product,
submit all requests online at **cengage.com/permissions**
Further permissions questions can be emailed to
permissionrequest@cengage.com

This book contains select works from existing Cengage Learning resources and was produced by Cengage Learning Custom Solutions for collegiate use. As such, those adopting and/or contributing to this work are responsible for editorial content accuracy, continuity and completeness.

Compilation © 2012 Cengage Learning
ISBN-13: 978-1-133-68923-2

ISBN-10: 1-133-68923-X

Cengage Learning
5191 Natorp Boulevard
Mason, Ohio 45040
USA
Cengage Learning is a leading provider of customized learning solutions with office locations around the globe, including Singapore, the United Kingdom, Australia, Mexico, Brazil, and Japan. Locate your local office at:
international.cengage.com/region.

Cengage Learning products are represented in Canada by Nelson Education, Ltd.
For your lifelong learning solutions, visit **www.cengage.com/custom.**
Visit our corporate website at **www.cengage.com.**

Printed in the United States of America

Brief Custom Contents

The Art and Science of Economic Analysis

Sin Stafford/Getty Images

○ Why are comic-strip and TV characters like Foxtrot, the Simpsons, and the Family Guy missing a finger on each hand?

○ Why do the kids on South Park have hands that look like mittens? And where is Dilbert's mouth?

○ Why does Japan have nearly 10 times more vending machines per capita than does Europe?

○ In what way are people who pound on vending machines relying on theory?

○ Why is a good theory like a California Closet?

○ What's the big idea with economics?

○ Finally, how can it be said that in economics "what goes around comes around"?

These and other questions are answered in this chapter, which introduces the art and science of economic analysis.

You have been reading and hearing about economic issues for years—unemployment, inflation, poverty, recessions, federal deficits, college tuition, airfares, stock prices, computer prices, gas prices. When explanations of such issues go into any depth, your eyes may glaze over and you may tune out, the same way you do when a weather forecaster tries to provide an in-depth analysis of high-pressure fronts colliding with moisture carried in from the coast.

What many people fail to realize is that economics is livelier than the dry accounts offered by the news media. Economics is about making choices, and you make economic choices every day—choices about whether to get a part-time job or focus on your studies, live in a dorm or off campus, take a course in accounting or one in history, get married or stay single, pack a lunch or buy a sandwich. You already know much more about economics than you realize. You bring to the subject a rich personal experience, an experience that will be tapped throughout the book to reinforce your understanding of the basic ideas.

Topics discussed in this chapter include:

- The economic problem
- Marginal analysis
- Rational self-interest

- Scientific method
- Normative versus positive analysis
- Pitfalls of economic thinking

The Economic Problem: Scarce Resources, Unlimited Wants

Would you like a new car, a nicer home, better meals, more free time, a more interesting social life, more spending money, more leisure, more sleep? Who wouldn't? But even if you can satisfy some of these desires, others keep popping up. *The problem is that, although your wants, or desires, are virtually unlimited, the resources available to satisfy these wants are scarce.* A resource is *scarce* when it is not freely available—that is, when its price exceeds zero. Because resources are scarce, you must choose from among your many wants, and whenever you choose, you must forgo satisfying some other wants. The problem of scarce resources but unlimited wants exists to a greater or lesser extent for each of the 6.9 billion people on earth. Everybody—cab driver, farmer, brain surgeon, dictator, shepherd, student, politician—faces the problem. For example, a cab driver uses time and other scarce resources, such as the taxi, knowledge of the city, driving skills, and gasoline, to earn income. That income, in turn, buys housing, groceries, clothing, trips to Disney World, and thousands of other goods and services that help satisfy some of the driver's unlimited wants. **Economics** examines how people use their scarce resources to satisfy their unlimited wants. Let's pick apart the definition, beginning with resources, then goods and services, and finally focus on the heart of the matter—economic choice, which arises from scarcity.

Resources

Resources are the inputs, or factors of production, used to produce the goods and services that people want. *Goods and services are scarce because resources are scarce.* Resources sort into four broad categories: labor, capital, natural resources, and entrepreneurial ability. **Labor** is human effort, both physical and mental. Labor includes the effort of the cab driver and the brain surgeon. Labor itself comes from a more fundamental resource: *time.* Without time we can accomplish nothing. We allocate our time to alternative uses: We can *sell* our time as labor, or we can *spend* our time doing other things, like sleeping, eating, studying, playing sports, going online, attending class, watching TV, or just relaxing with friends.

  Capital includes all human creations used to produce goods and services. Economists often distinguish between physical capital and human capital. *Physical capital* consists

economics
The study of how people use their scarce resources to satisfy their unlimited wants

resources
The inputs, or factors of production, used to produce the goods and services that people want; resources consist of labor, capital, natural resources, and entrepreneurial ability

labor
The physical and mental effort used to produce goods and services

capital
The buildings, equipment, and human skills used to produce goods and services

of factories, tools, machines, computers, buildings, airports, highways, and other human creations used to produce goods and services. Physical capital includes the cab driver's taxi, the surgeon's scalpel, and the building where your economics class meets (or, if you are taking this course online, your computer and online connectors). *Human capital* consists of the knowledge and skill people acquire to increase their productivity, such as the cab driver's knowledge of city streets, the surgeon's knowledge of human anatomy, and your knowledge of economics.

Natural resources include all *gifts of nature,* such as bodies of water, trees, oil reserves, minerals, even animals. Natural resources can be divided into renewable resources and exhaustible resources. A *renewable resource* can be drawn on indefinitely if used conservatively. Thus, timber is a renewable resource if felled trees are replaced to regrow a steady supply. The air and rivers are renewable resources if they are allowed sufficient time to cleanse themselves of any pollutants. More generally, biological resources like fish, game, livestock, forests, rivers, groundwater, grasslands, and soil are renewable if managed properly. An *exhaustible resource*—such as oil or coal—does not renew itself and so is available in a limited amount. Once burned, each barrel of oil or ton of coal is gone forever. The world's oil and coal deposits are exhaustible.

A special kind of human skill called **entrepreneurial ability** is the talent required to dream up a new product or find a better way to produce an existing one. This special skill comes from an entrepreneur. An **entrepreneur** is a profit-seeking decision maker who starts with an idea, organizes an enterprise to bring that idea to life, and then assumes the risk of operation. An entrepreneur pays resource owners for the opportunity to employ their resources in the firm. Every firm in the world today, such as Ford, Microsoft, Google, and Dell, began as an idea in the mind of an entrepreneur.

Resource owners are paid **wages** for their labor, **interest** for the use of their capital, and **rent** for the use of their natural resources. Entrepreneurial ability is rewarded by **profit**, which equals the *revenue* from items sold minus the *cost* of the resources employed to make those items. The word *profit* comes from the Latin *proficere*, which means "to benefit." The entrepreneur benefits from what's left over after paying other resource suppliers. Sometimes the entrepreneur suffers a loss. Resource earnings are usually based on the *time* these resources are employed. Resource payments therefore have a time dimension, as in a wage of $10 *per hour,* interest of 6 percent *per year,* rent of $600 *per month,* or profit of $10,000 *per year.*

Goods and Services

Resources are combined in a variety of ways to produce goods and services. A farmer, a tractor, 50 acres of land, seeds, and fertilizer combine to grow the good: corn. One hundred musicians, musical instruments, chairs, a conductor, a musical score, and a music hall combine to produce the service: Beethoven's *Fifth Symphony.* Corn is a **good** because it is something you can see, feel, and touch; it requires scarce resources to produce; and it satisfies human wants. The book you are now holding, the chair you are sitting in, the clothes you are wearing, and your next meal are all goods. The performance of the *Fifth Symphony* is a **service** because it is intangible, yet it uses scarce resources to satisfy human wants. Lectures, movies, concerts, phone service, broadband connections, yoga lessons, dry cleaning, and haircuts are all services.

Because goods and services are produced using scarce resources, they are themselves scarce. *A good or service is scarce if the amount people desire exceeds the amount available at a zero price.* Because we cannot have all the goods and services we would like, we must continually choose among them. We must choose among more pleasant living quarters, better meals, nicer clothes, more reliable transportation, faster computers, and so on. Making choices in a world of **scarcity** means we must pass up some goods and

---

natural resources
All gifts of nature used to produce goods and services; includes renewable and exhaustible resources

entrepreneurial ability
The imagination required to develop a new product or process, the skill needed to organize production, and the willingness to take the risk of profit or loss

entrepreneur
A profit-seeking decision maker who starts with an idea, organizes an enterprise to bring that idea to life, and assumes the risk of the operation

wages
Payment to resource owners for their labor

interest
Payment to resource owners for the use of their capital

rent
Payment to resource owners for the use of their natural resources

profit
Reward for entrepreneurial ability; sales revenue minus resource cost

good
A tangible product used to satisfy human wants

service
An activity, or intangible product, used to satisfy human wants

scarcity
Occurs when the amount people desire exceeds the amount available at a zero price

services. But not everything is scarce. In fact some things we would prefer to have less of. For example, we would prefer to have less garbage, less spam email, and less pollution. Things we want none of even at a zero price are called *bads*, the opposite of goods.

A few goods and services seem *free* because the amount available at a zero price exceeds the amount people want. For example, air and seawater often seem free because we can breathe all the air we want and have all the seawater we can haul away. Yet, despite the old saying "The best things in life are free," most goods and services are scarce, not free, and even those that appear to be free come with strings attached. For example, *clean* air and *clean* seawater have become scarce. *Goods and services that are truly free are not the subject matter of economics. Without scarcity, there would be no economic problem and no need for prices.*

Sometimes we mistakenly think of certain goods as free because they involve no apparent cost to us. Napkins seem to be free at Starbucks. Nobody stops you from taking a fistful. Supplying napkins, however, costs the company millions each year and prices reflect that cost. Some restaurants make special efforts to keep napkin use down—such as packing them tightly into the dispenser or making you ask for them.

You may have heard the expression "There is no such thing as a free lunch." There is no free lunch because all goods and services involve a cost to someone. The lunch may seem free to you, but it draws scarce resources away from the production of other goods and services, and whoever provides a free lunch often expects something in return. A Russian proverb makes a similar point but with a bit more bite: "The only place you find free cheese is in a mousetrap." Albert Einstein once observed, "Sometimes one pays the most for things one gets for nothing."

Economic Decision Makers

There are four types of decision makers in the economy: households, firms, governments, and the rest of the world. Their interaction determines how an economy's resources are allocated. *Households* play the starring role. As consumers, households demand the goods and services produced. As resource owners, households supply labor, capital, natural resources, and entrepreneurial ability to firms, governments, and the rest of the world. *Firms, governments,* and *the rest of the world* demand the resources that households supply and then use these resources to supply the goods and services that households demand. The rest of the world includes foreign households, foreign firms, and foreign governments that supply resources and products to U.S. markets and demand resources and products from U.S. markets.

Markets are the means by which buyers and sellers carry out exchange. By bringing together the two sides of exchange, markets determine price, quantity, and quality. Markets are often physical places, such as supermarkets, department stores, shopping malls, or yard sales. But markets also include other mechanisms by which buyers and sellers communicate, such as classified ads, radio and television ads, telephones, bulletin boards, online sites, and face-to-face bargaining. These market mechanisms provide information about the quantity, quality, and price of products offered for sale. Goods and services are bought and sold in **product markets**. Resources are bought and sold in **resource markets**. The most important resource market is the labor, or job, market. Think about your own experience looking for a job, and you'll already have some idea of that market.

A Simple Circular-Flow Model

Now that you have learned a bit about economic decision makers, consider how they interact. Such a picture is conveyed by the **circular-flow model**, which describes the flow of resources, products, income, and revenue among economic decision makers.

market
A set of arrangements by which buyers and sellers carry out exchange at mutually agreeable terms

product market
A market in which a good or service is bought and sold

resource market
A market in which a resource is bought and sold

circular-flow model
A diagram that traces the flow of resources, products, income, and revenue among economic decision makers

EXHIBIT   1   The Simple Circular-Flow Model for Households and Firms

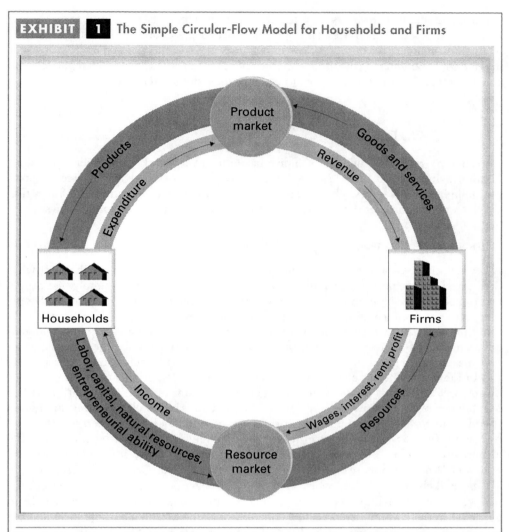

Households earn income by supplying resources to the resource market, as shown in the lower portion of the model. Firms demand these resources to produce goods and services, which they supply to the product market, as shown in the upper portion of the model. Households spend their income to demand these goods and services. This spending flows through the product market as revenue to firms.

The simple circular-flow model focuses on the primary interaction in a market economy—that between households and firms. Exhibit 1 shows households on the left and firms on the right; please take a look.

Households supply labor, capital, natural resources, and entrepreneurial ability to firms through resource markets, shown in the lower portion of the exhibit. In return, households demand goods and services from firms through product markets, shown on the upper portion of the exhibit. Viewed from the business end, firms demand labor, capital, natural resources, and entrepreneurial ability from households through resource markets, and firms supply goods and services to households through product markets.

The flows of resources and products are supported by the flows of income and expenditure—that is, by the flow of money. So let's add money. The demand and supply of resources come together in resource markets to determine what firms pay for resources. These resource prices—wages, interest, rent, and profit—flow as *income* to households. The demand and supply of products come together in product markets to determine what households pay for goods and services. These product prices of goods and services flow as *revenue* to firms. Resources and products flow in one direction—in this case, counterclockwise— and the corresponding payments flow in the other direction—clockwise. What goes around comes around. Take a little time now to trace the logic of the circular flows.

The Art of Economic Analysis

An economy results as millions of individuals attempt to satisfy their unlimited wants. Because their choices lie at the heart of the economic problem—coping with scarce resources but unlimited wants—these choices deserve a closer look. Learning about the forces that shape economic choice is the first step toward mastering the art of economic analysis.

Rational Self-Interest

A key economic assumption is that individuals, in making choices, rationally select what they perceive to be in their best interests. By *rational,* economists mean simply that people try to make the best choices they can, given the available time and information. People may not know with certainty which alternative will turn out to be the best. They simply select the alternatives they *expect* will yield the most satisfaction and happiness. In general, **rational self-interest** means that each individual tries to maximize the expected benefit achieved with a given cost or to minimize the expected cost of achieving a given benefit.

Rational self-interest should not be viewed as blind materialism, pure selfishness, or greed. We all know people who are tuned to radio station WIIFM (What's In It For Me?). For most of us, however, self-interest often includes the welfare of our family, our friends, and perhaps the poor of the world. Even so, our concern for others is influenced by the personal cost of that concern. We may readily volunteer to drive a friend to the airport on Saturday afternoon but are less likely to offer a ride if the plane leaves at 6:00 A.M. When we donate clothes to an organization such as Goodwill Industries, they are more likely to be old and worn than brand new. People tend to give more to charities when their contributions are tax deductible and when contributions garner social approval in the community (as when contributor names are made public or when big donors get buildings named after them). TV stations are more likely to donate airtime for public-service announcements during the dead of night than during prime time (in fact, 80 percent of such announcements air between 11:00 P.M. and 7:00 A.M.[1]). In Asia some people burn money to soothe the passage of a departed loved one. But they burn fake money, not real money. The notion of self-interest does not rule out concern for others; it simply means that concern for others is influenced by the same economic forces that affect other economic choices. *The lower the personal cost of helping others, the more help we offer.* We don't like to think that our behavior reflects our self-interest, but it usually does. As Jane Austen wrote in *Pride and Prejudice,* "I have been a selfish being all my life, in practice, though not in principle."

Choice Requires Time and Information

Rational choice takes time and requires information, but time and information are scarce and therefore valuable. If you have any doubts about the time and information needed to make choices, talk to someone who recently purchased a home, a car, or a personal

rational self-interest
Each individual tries to maximize the expected benefit achieved with a given cost or to minimize the expected cost of achieving a given benefit

net 📖 bookmark
To make good use of the Internet, you need Adobe Acrobat Reader. You can download it from http://get .adobe.com/reader/. An economic question is: Why does Adobe give its Reader away free?

---

1.   Sally Goll Beatty, "Media and Agencies Brawl Over Do-Good Advertising," *Wall Street Journal,* 29 September 1997.

computer. Talk to a corporate official trying to decide whether to introduce a new product, sell online, build a new factory, or buy another firm. Or think back to your own experience in choosing a college. You probably talked to friends, relatives, teachers, and guidance counselors. You likely used school catalogs, college guides, and Web sites. You may have visited some campuses to meet the admissions staff and anyone else willing to talk. The decision took time and money, and it probably involved aggravation and anxiety.

Because information is costly to acquire, we are often willing to pay others to gather and digest it for us. College guidebooks, stock analysts, travel agents, real estate brokers, career counselors, restaurant critics, movie reviewers, specialized Web sites, and *Consumer Reports* magazine attest to our willingness to pay for information that improves our choices. As we'll see next, *rational decision makers continue to acquire information as long as the additional benefit expected from that information exceeds the additional cost of gathering it.*

Economic Analysis Is Marginal Analysis

Economic choice usually involves some adjustment to the existing situation, or status quo. Amazon.com must decide whether to add an additional line of products. The school superintendent must decide whether to hire another teacher. Your favorite jeans are on sale, and you must decide whether to buy another pair. You are wondering whether to carry an extra course next term. You just finished lunch and are deciding whether to order dessert.

Economic choice is based on a comparison of the *expected marginal benefit* and the *expected marginal cost* of the action under consideration. **Marginal** means incremental, additional, or extra. Marginal refers to a change in an economic variable, a change in the status quo. *A rational decision maker changes the status quo if the expected marginal benefit from the change exceeds the expected marginal cost.* For example, Amazon .com compares the marginal benefit expected from adding a new line of products (the additional sales revenue) with the marginal cost (the additional cost of the resources required). Likewise, you compare the marginal benefit you expect from eating dessert (the additional pleasure or satisfaction) with its marginal cost (the additional money, time, and calories).

Typically, the change under consideration is small, but a marginal choice can involve a major economic adjustment, as in the decision to quit school and find a job. For a firm, a marginal choice might mean building a plant in Mexico or even filing for bankruptcy. By focusing on the effect of a marginal adjustment to the status quo, the economist is able to cut the analysis of economic choice down to a manageable size. Rather than confront a bewildering economic reality head-on, the economist begins with a marginal choice to see how this choice affects a particular market and shapes the economic system as a whole. Incidentally, to the noneconomist, *marginal* usually means relatively inferior, as in "a movie of marginal quality." Forget that meaning for this course and instead think of *marginal* as meaning incremental, additional, or extra.

marginal
Incremental, additional, or extra; used to describe a change in an economic variable

Microeconomics and Macroeconomics

Although you have made thousands of economic choices, you probably seldom think about your own economic behavior. For example, why are you reading this book right now rather than doing something else? **Microeconomics** is the study of your economic behavior and the economic behavior of others who make choices about such matters as how much to study and how much to party, how much to borrow and how much to save, what to buy and what to sell. Microeconomics examines individual economic choices and how markets coordinate the choices of various decision makers. Microeconomics explains how price and quantity are determined in individual markets—the market for breakfast cereal, sports equipment, or used cars, for instance.

microeconomics
The study of the economic behavior in particular markets, such as that for computers or unskilled labor

You have probably given little thought to what influences your own economic choices. You have likely given even less thought to how your choices link up with those made by millions of others in the U.S. economy to determine economy-wide measures such as total production, employment, and economic growth. **Macroeconomics** studies the performance of the economy as a whole. Whereas microeconomics studies the individual pieces of the economic puzzle, as reflected in particular markets, macroeconomics puts all the pieces together to focus on the big picture.

The national economy usually grows over time, but along the way it sometimes stumbles, experiencing *recessions* in economic activity, as reflected by a decline in production, employment, and other aggregate measures. **Economic fluctuations** are the rise and fall of economic activity relative to the long-term growth trend of the economy. These fluctuations, or *business cycles,* vary in length and intensity, but they usually involve the entire nation and often other nations too. For example, the U.S. economy now produces more than four times as much as it did in 1960, despite experiencing eight recessions since then, including the painful recession of 2007–2009.

To Review: The art of economic analysis focuses on how people use their scarce resources in an attempt to satisfy their unlimited wants. Rational self-interest guides individual choice. Choice requires time and information, and involves a comparison of the expected marginal benefit and the expected marginal cost of alternative actions. Microeconomics looks at the individual pieces of the economic puzzle; macroeconomics fits the pieces together to form the big picture.

macroeconomics
The study of the economic behavior of entire economies, as measured, for example, by total production and employment

economic fluctuations
The rise and fall of economic activity relative to the long-term growth trend of the economy; also called business cycles

The Science of Economic Analysis

Economists use scientific analysis to develop theories, or models, that help explain economic behavior. An **economic theory**, or **economic model**, is a simplification of economic reality that *is used to make predictions about the real world.* A theory, or model, such as the circular-flow model, captures the important elements of the problem under study but need not spell out every detail and interrelation. In fact, adding more details may make a theory more unwieldy and, therefore, less useful. For example, a wristwatch is a model that tells time, but a watch festooned with extra features is harder to read at a glance and is therefore less useful as a time-telling model. The world is so complex that we must simplify it to make sense of things. Store mannequins simplify the human form (some even lack arms and heads). Comic strips and cartoons simplify characters—leaving out fingers or a mouth, for instance. You might think of economic theory as a stripped-down, or streamlined, version of economic reality.

A good theory helps us understand a messy and confusing world. Lacking a theory of how things work, our thinking can become cluttered with facts, one piled on another, as in a messy closet. You could think of a good theory as a closet organizer for the mind. A good theory offers a helpful guide to sorting, saving, and understanding information.

economic theory, or economic model
A simplification of reality used to make predictions about cause and effect in the real world

The Role of Theory

Most people don't understand the role of theory. Perhaps you have heard, "Oh, that's fine in theory, but in practice it's another matter." The implication is that the theory in question provides little aid in practical matters. People who say this fail to realize that they are merely substituting their own theory for a theory they either do not believe or do not understand. They are really saying, "I have my own theory that works better."

All of us employ theories, however poorly defined or understood. Someone who pounds on the Pepsi machine that just ate a quarter has a crude theory about how that machine works. One version of that theory might be "The quarter drops through a series of *whatchamacallits,* but sometimes it gets stuck. *If* I pound on the machine, *then* I can free up the quarter and send it on its way." Evidently, this theory is widespread enough that people continue to pound on machines that fail to perform (a real problem for the vending machine industry and one reason newer machines are fronted with glass). Yet, if you were to ask these mad pounders to explain their "theory" about how the machine works, they would look at you as if you were crazy.

The Scientific Method

To study economic problems, economists employ a process of theoretical investigation called the *scientific method,* which consists of four steps, as outlined in Exhibit 2.

Step One: Identify the Question and Define Relevant Variables

The scientific method begins with curiosity: Someone wants to answer a question. Thus, the first step is to identify the economic question and define the variables relevant to a solution. For example, the question might be "What is the relationship between the price of Pepsi and

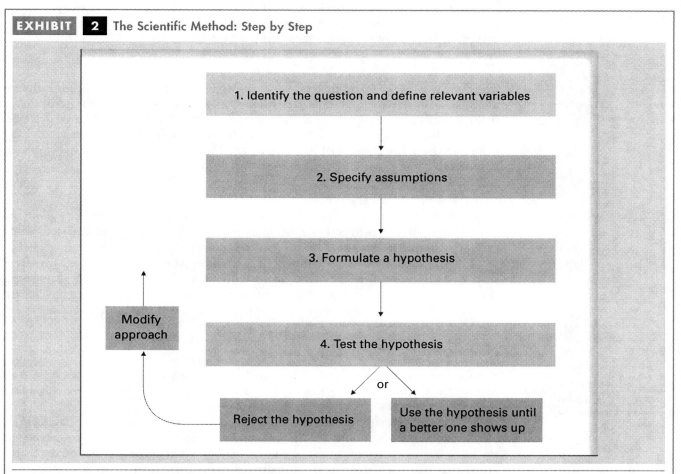

EXHIBIT   2   The Scientific Method: Step by Step

1. Identify the question and define relevant variables

2. Specify assumptions

3. Formulate a hypothesis

4. Test the hypothesis

Modify approach

or

Reject the hypothesis

Use the hypothesis until a better one shows up

The steps of the scientific method are designed to develop and test hypotheses about how the world works. The objective is a theory that predicts outcomes more accurately than the best alternative theory. A hypothesis is rejected if it does not predict as accurately as the best alternative. A rejected hypothesis can be modified or reworked in light of the test results.

the quantity of Pepsi purchased?" In this case, the relevant variables are price and quantity. A **variable** is a measure that can take on different values at different times. The variables of concern become the elements of the theory, so they must be selected with care.

variable

A measure, such as price or quantity, that can take on different values at different times

Step Two: Specify Assumptions

The second step is to specify the assumptions under which the theory is to apply. One major category of assumptions is the **other-things-constant assumption**—in Latin, the *ceteris paribus* assumption. The idea is to identify the variables of interest and then focus exclusively on the relationships among them, assuming that nothing else important changes—that other things remain constant. Again, suppose we are interested in how the price of Pepsi influences the amount purchased. To isolate the relation between these two variables, we assume that there are no changes in other relevant variables such as consumer income, the average temperature, or the price of Coke.

other-things-constant assumption

The assumption, when focusing on the relation among key economic variables, that other variables remain unchanged; in Latin, *ceteris paribus*

We also make assumptions about how people behave; these are called **behavioral assumptions**. The primary behavioral assumption is rational self-interest. Earlier we assumed that each decision maker pursues self-interest rationally and makes choices accordingly. Rationality implies that each consumer buys the products expected to maximize his or her level of satisfaction. Rationality also implies that each firm supplies the products expected to maximize the firm's profit. These kinds of assumptions are called behavioral assumptions because they specify how we expect economic decision makers to behave—what makes them tick, so to speak.

behavioral assumption

An assumption that describes the expected behavior of economic decision makers, what motivates them

Step Three: Formulate a Hypothesis

The third step in the scientific method is to formulate a **hypothesis**, which is a theory about how key variables relate to each other. For example, one hypothesis holds that if the price of Pepsi goes up, other things constant, then the quantity purchased declines. The hypothesis becomes a prediction of what happens to the quantity purchased if the price increases. *The purpose of this hypothesis, like that of any theory, is to help make predictions about cause and effect in the real world.*

hypothesis

A theory about how key variables relate

Step Four: Test the Hypothesis

In the fourth step, by comparing its predictions with evidence, we test the validity of a hypothesis. To test a hypothesis, we must focus on the variables in question, while carefully controlling for other effects assumed not to change. The test leads us either to (1) reject the hypothesis, or theory, if it predicts worse than the best alternative theory or (2) use the hypothesis, or theory, until a better one comes along. If we reject the hypothesis, we can go back and modify our approach in light of the results. Please spend a moment now reviewing the steps of the scientific method in Exhibit 2.

Normative Versus Positive

Economists usually try to explain how the economy works. Sometimes they concern themselves not with how the economy *does* work but how it *should* work. Compare these two statements: "The U.S. unemployment rate is 9.7 percent." and "The U.S. unemployment rate should be lower." The first, called a **positive economic statement**, is an assertion about economic reality that can be supported or rejected by reference to the facts. Positive economics, like physics or biology, attempts to understand the world around us. The second, called a **normative economic statement**, reflects an opinion. And an opinion is merely that—it cannot be shown to be true or false by reference to the facts. Positive statements concern what *is*; normative statements concern what, in someone's opinion, *should be*. Positive statements need not necessarily be true, but

positive economic statement

A statement that can be proved or disproved by reference to facts

normative economic statement

A statement that reflects an opinion, which cannot be proved or disproved by reference to the facts

they must be subject to verification or refutation by reference to the facts. Theories are expressed as positive statements such as "If the price of Pepsi increases, then the quantity demanded decreases."

Most of the disagreement among economists involves normative debates—such as the appropriate role of government—rather than statements of positive analysis. To be sure, many theoretical issues remain unresolved, but economists generally agree on most fundamental theoretical principles—that is, about positive economic analysis. For example, in a survey of 464 U.S. economists, only 6.5 percent disagreed with the statement "A ceiling on rents reduces the quantity and quality of housing available." This is a positive statement because it can be shown to be consistent or inconsistent with the evidence. In contrast, there was much less agreement on normative statements such as "The distribution of income in the United States should be more equal." Half the economists surveyed "generally agreed," a quarter "generally disagreed," and a quarter "agreed with provisos."[2]

Normative statements, or value judgments, have a place in a policy debate such as the proper role of government, provided that statements of opinion are distinguished from statements of fact. In such policy debates, you are entitled to your own opinion, but you are not entitled to your own facts.

Economists Tell Stories

Despite economists' reliance on the scientific method for developing and evaluating theories, economic analysis is as much art as science. Formulating a question, isolating the key variables, specifying the assumptions, proposing a theory to answer the question, and devising a way to test the predictions all involve more than simply an understanding of economics and the scientific method. Carrying out these steps requires good intuition and the imagination of a storyteller. Economists explain their theories by telling stories about how they think the economy works. To tell a compelling story, an economist relies on case studies, anecdotes, parables, the personal experience of the listener, and supporting data. Throughout this book, you'll hear stories that bring you closer to the ideas under consideration. The stories, such as the one about the Pepsi machine, breathe life into economic theory and help you personalize abstract ideas. As another example, here is a case study on the popularity of vending machines in Japan.

CASE STUDY

WORLD OF BUSINESS

A Yen for Vending Machines   Japan faces a steady drop in the number of working-age people. Here are three reasons why: (1) Japan's birthrate has dropped to a record low, (2) Japan allows little immigration, and (3) Japan's population is aging. As a result, unemployment has usually been lower in Japan than in other countries. For example, Japan's unemployment rate in 2010 was only about half that of the United States and Europe. Because labor is relatively scarce in Japan, it is relatively costly. To sell products, Japanese retailers rely more on physical capital, particularly vending machines, which obviously eliminate the need for sales clerks.

Japan has more vending machines per capita than any other country on the planet—twice as many as the United States and nearly 10 times as many as Europe. And vending machines in Japan sell a wider range of products than elsewhere, including beer, sake, whiskey, rice, fresh eggs, beef, vegetables, pizza, entire meals, fried foods, fresh flowers, clothes, toilet paper, fishing supplies including bait, video

e activity
Do you want to see more pictures of unusual vending machines in Japan? Go to http://www.toxel.com/tech and scroll down to find the search box. Enter "14 Cool Vending Machines from Japan." In the search results, click on the link for Read Full Post.

2.   Richard M. Alston et al., "Is There a Consensus Among Economists in the 1990s?" *American Economic Review*, 82 (May 1992): 203–209, Table 1.

games, software, ebooks, toys, DVDs, mobile phone recharging, and even X-rated comic books. Japan's vending machines are also more sophisticated. Newer models come with video monitors and touch-pad screens. Wireless chips alert vendors when supplies run low. Some cigarette and liquor machines have artificial vision that reportedly are better at estimating age than are nightclub bouncers. Sanyo makes a giant machine that sells up to 200 different items at three different temperatures. Some cold-drink dispensers automatically raise prices in hot weather. Thousands of machines allow cell phone users to pay by pressing a few buttons on their phones.

As noted earlier, it is common practice in the United States to shake down vending machines that malfunction. Such abuse increases the probability the machines will fail again, leading to a cycle of abuse. Vending machines in Japan are less abused, in part because they are more sophisticated and more reliable and in part because the Japanese generally have greater respect for private property and, consequently, a lower crime rate (e.g., Japan's theft rate is about half the U.S. rate).

Forty percent of all soft-drink sales in Japan are through vending machines, compared to only 12 percent of U.S. sales. Japanese sales per machine are double the U.S. rate. Research shows that most Japanese consumers prefer an anonymous machine to a salesperson. Despite the abundance of vending machines in Japan, more growth is forecast, spurred on by a shrinking labor pool, technological innovations, and wide acceptance of machines there.

Sources: "Machines That Can See," *The Economist*, 5 March 2009; Hiroko Tabuchi, "Beef Bowl Economics," *New York Times*, 30 January 2010; and Trends in Japan at http://web-japan.org/trends/lifestyle/lif060720.html. For a photo gallery of vending machines in Japan go to http://www.photomann.com/japan/machines/.

This case study makes two points. First, producers combine resources in a way that conserves, or economizes on, the resource that is more costly—in this case, labor. Second, the customs and conventions of the marketplace can differ across countries, and this variance can result in different types of economic arrangements, such as the more extensive use of vending machines in Japan.

Predicting Average Behavior

The goal of an economic theory is to predict the impact of an economic event on economic choices and, in turn, the effect of these choices on particular markets or on the economy as a whole. Does this mean that economists try to predict the behavior of particular consumers or producers? Not necessarily, because a specific individual may behave in an unpredictable way. But the unpredictable actions of numerous individuals tend to cancel one another out, so the *average behavior* of groups can be predicted more accurately. For example, if the federal government cuts personal income taxes, certain households may decide to save the entire tax cut. On average, however, household spending increases. Likewise, if Burger King cuts the price of Whoppers, the manager can better predict how much sales will increase than how a specific customer coming through the door will respond. *The random actions of individuals tend to offset one another, so the average behavior of a large group can be predicted more accurately than the behavior of a particular individual.* Consequently, economists tend to focus on the average, or typical, behavior of people in groups—for example, as average taxpayers or average Whopper consumers—rather than on the behavior of a specific individual.

Some Pitfalls of Faulty Economic Analysis

Economic analysis, like other forms of scientific inquiry, is subject to common mistakes in reasoning that can lead to faulty conclusions. Here are three sources of confusion.

The Fallacy That Association Is Causation

In the last two decades, the number of physicians specializing in cancer treatment increased sharply. At the same time, the incidence of some cancers increased. Can we conclude that physicians cause cancer? No. To assume that event A caused event B simply because the two are associated in time is to commit the **association-is-causation fallacy**, a common error. The fact that one event precedes another or that the two events occur simultaneously does not necessarily mean that one causes the other. Remember: Association is not necessarily causation.

association-is-causation fallacy
The incorrect idea that if two variables are associated in time, one must necessarily cause the other

The Fallacy of Composition

Perhaps you have been to a rock concert where everyone stands to get a better view. At some concerts, most people even stand on their chairs. But even standing on chairs does not improve the view if others do the same, unless you are quite tall. Likewise, arriving early to buy game tickets does not work if many have the same idea. These are examples of the **fallacy of composition**, which is an erroneous belief that what is true for the individual, or the part, is also true for the group, or the whole.

fallacy of composition
The incorrect belief that what is true for the individual, or part, must necessarily be true for the group, or the whole

The Mistake of Ignoring the Secondary Effects

In many cities, public officials have imposed rent controls on apartments. The primary effect of this policy, the effect policy makers focus on, is to keep rents from rising. Over time, however, fewer new apartments get built because renting them becomes less profitable. Moreover, existing rental units deteriorate because owners have plenty of customers anyway. Thus, the quantity and quality of housing may decline as a result of what appears to be a reasonable measure to keep rents from rising. The mistake was to ignore the **secondary effects**, or the unintended consequences, of the policy. Economic actions have secondary effects that often turn out to be more important than the primary effects. Secondary effects may develop more slowly and may not be immediately obvious, but good economic analysis tries to anticipate them and take them into account.

secondary effects
Unintended consequences of economic actions that may develop slowly over time as people react to events

If Economists Are So Smart, Why Aren't They Rich?

Why aren't economists rich? Well, some are, earning over $25,000 per appearance on the lecture circuit. Others top $2 million a year as consultants and expert witnesses.[3] Economists have been appointed to federal cabinet posts, such as secretaries of commerce, defense, labor, state, and treasury, and to head the U.S. Federal Reserve System. Economics is the only social science and the only business discipline for which the prestigious Nobel Prize is awarded, and pronouncements by economists are reported in the media daily. *The Economist*, a widely respected news weekly from London, has argued that economic ideas have influenced policy "to a degree that would make other social scientists drool."[4]

The economics profession thrives because its models usually do a better job of making economic sense out of a confusing world than do alternative approaches. But not all economists are wealthy, nor is personal wealth the goal of the discipline. In a similar vein, not all doctors are healthy (some even smoke), not all carpenters live in perfectly built homes, not all marriage counselors are happily married, and not all

---

3. As reported by George Anders, "An Economist's Courtroom Bonanza," *Wall Street Journal*, 19 March 2007.
4. "The Puzzling Failure of Economics," *Economist*, 23 August 1997, p. 11.

child psychologists have well-adjusted children. Still, those who study economics do reap financial rewards, as discussed in this closing case study, which looks at the link between a college major and annual earnings.

THE INFORMATION ECONOMY

College Major and Annual Earnings   Earlier in the chapter, you learned that economic choice involves comparing the expected marginal benefit and the expected marginal cost. Surveys show that students go to college because they believe a college diploma is the ticket to better jobs and higher pay. Put another way, for nearly two-thirds of U.S. high school graduates, the expected marginal benefit of college apparently exceeds the expected marginal cost. The cost of college will be discussed in the next chapter; the focus here is on the benefits of college, particularly expected earnings.

Among college graduates, all kinds of factors affect earnings, such as general ability, effort, occupation, college attended, college major, and highest degree earned. PayScale .com collected real time information on annual pay from its 10 million users. The site focused on the 20 popular college majors where most graduates go into the private sector (this excluded public sector majors such as education and social work, where pay is relatively low). To isolate the effects of a college major on earnings, only workers with a bachelor's as their highest degree were included in the results. Exhibit 3 shows the median earnings in 2008 by major for two groups of college graduates: (1) those with zero to five years of job experience and (2) those with 10 to 20 years of job experience. Majors are listed from the top down by the median annual pay of those with between zero and five years experience, indentified by the light green bars. The top pay of $60,500 went to those majoring in computer engineering; indeed, the top five slots went to engineering and computer graduates. Economics ranked sixth out of twenty majors with a median pay of $48,100, or 20 percent below the top pay. Criminal justice majors held the bottom spot of $34,200, which was 44 percent below the top pay.

The dark green bars show the median pay by major for those with 10 to 20 years of job experience. Those majoring in computer engineering still lead the field with $104,000, an increase of 72 percent over the pay of newer graduates with that degree. Economics majors with 10 to 20 years of job experience saw a 100 percent pay increase to $96,200. While economics majors with zero to five years experience were paid 20 percent less than the top paying major, among those with at least a decade of job experience, the median pay for economics majors moved up to within 7 percent of the top pay. In fact, economics majors saw their median pay grow more both in dollar terms and in percentage terms than did any other major. This suggests that those who study economics acquire skills that appreciate with experience.

The bump in median pay based on experience for the 19 other majors averaged 67 percent. Criminal justice remained the lowest paying major among those with 10 to 20 years of experience. Note that the majors ranked toward the top of the list tend to be more quantitative and analytical. The selection of a relatively more challenging major such as economics may send a favorable signal to future employers.

Remember, the survey was limited to those whose highest degree was the baccalaureate, so it excluded the many economics majors who went on to pursue graduate studies in law, business administration, economics, public administration, journalism, and other fields (a different study found that lawyers with undergraduate degrees in economics earned more on average than lawyers with other majors).

© Amy Etra/Photo Edit

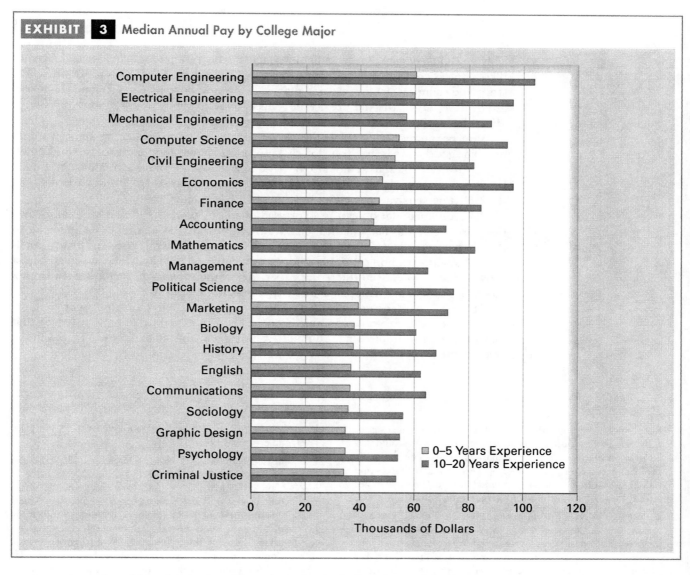

EXHIBIT 3 Median Annual Pay by College Major

A number of world leaders majored in economics, including three of the last seven U.S. presidents, Chile's president and billionaire, Sabastian Pinera (who earned a Ph.D. in economics from Harvard), Turkey's first female prime minister, Tansu Ciller (who earned a Ph.D. in economics from the University of Connecticut), U.S. Supreme Court justices Steven Breyer and Anthony Kennedy, and former justice Sandra Day O'Connor. Other notable economics majors include billionaire Donald Trump, former eBay president (and billionaire) Meg Whitman, Microsoft chief executive officer (and billionaire) Steve Ballmer, CNN founder (and billionaire) Ted Turner, Intel president Paul Otellini, NFL Patriot's coach Bill Belichick, Governor Arnold Schwarzenegger, and Scott Adams, creator of Dilbert, the mouthless wonder.

Sources: Kurt Badenhausen, "Most Lucrative College Major," *Forbes.com*, 18 June 2008 at http://www.forbes .com/2008/06/18/college-majors-lucrative-lead-cx_kb_0618majors.html. "The World's Billionaires," *Forbes*, 11 March 2010; and R. Kim Craft and Joe Baker, "Do Economists Make Better Lawyers?, "*Journal of Economic Education,*" 34 (Summer 2003): 263–281. For a survey of employment opportunities, go to the U.S. Labor Department's *Occupational Outlook Handbook* at http://www.bls.gov/oco/.

Conclusion

This textbook describes how economic factors affect individual choices and how all these choices come together to shape the economic system. Economics is not the whole story, and economic factors are not always the most important. But economic considerations have important and predictable effects on individual choices, and these choices affect the way we live.

Sure, economics is a challenging discipline, but it is also an exciting and rewarding one. The good news is that you already know a lot about economics. To use this knowledge, however, you must cultivate the art and science of economic analysis. You must be able to simplify the world to formulate questions, isolate the relevant variables, and then tell a persuasive story about how these variables relate.

An economic relation can be expressed in words, represented as a table of quantities, described by a mathematical equation, or illustrated as a graph. The appendix to this chapter introduces graphs. You may find this unnecessary. If you are already familiar with relations among variables, slopes, tangents, and the like, you can probably just browse. But if you have little recent experience with graphs, you might benefit from a more careful reading with pencil and paper in hand.

The next chapter introduces key tools of economic analysis. Subsequent chapters use these tools to explore economic problems and to explain economic behavior that may otherwise seem puzzling. You must walk before you can run, however, and in the next chapter, you take your first wobbly steps.

Summary

1. Economics is the study of how people choose to use their scarce resources to produce, exchange, and consume goods and services in an attempt to satisfy unlimited wants. The economic problem arises from the conflict between scarce resources and unlimited wants. If wants were limited or if resources were not scarce, there would be no need to study economics.

2. Economic resources are combined in a variety of ways to produce goods and services. Major categories of resources include labor, capital, natural resources, and entrepreneurial ability. Because economic resources are scarce, only a limited number of goods and services can be produced with them. Therefore, goods and services are also scarce so choices must be made.

3. Microeconomics focuses on choices made in households, firms, and governments and how these choices affect particular markets, such as the market for used cars. Choice is guided by rational self-interest. Choice typically requires time and information, both of which are scarce and valuable.

4. Whereas microeconomics examines the individual pieces of the puzzle, macroeconomics steps back to consider the big picture—the performance of the economy as a whole as reflected by such measures as total production, employment, the price level, and economic growth.

5. Economists use theories, or models, to help understand the effects of an economic change, such as a change in price or income, on individual choices and how these choices affect particular markets and the economy as a whole. Economists employ the scientific method to study an economic problem by (a) formulating the question and identifying relevant variables, (b) specifying the assumptions under which the theory operates, (c) developing a theory, or hypothesis, about how the variables relate, and (d) testing that theory by comparing its predictions with the evidence. A theory might not work perfectly, but it is useful as long as it predicts better than competing theories do.

6. Positive economics aims to discover how the economy works. Normative economics is concerned more with how, in someone's opinion, the economy should work. Those who are not careful can fall victim to the fallacy that association is causation, to the fallacy of composition, and to the mistake of ignoring secondary effects.

Key Concepts

Economics 2
Resources 2
Labor 2
Capital 2
Natural resources 3
Entrepreneurial ability 3
Entrepreneur 3
Wages 3
Interest 3

Questions for Review

1. **DEFINITION OF ECONOMICS**   What determines whether or not a resource is scarce? Why is the concept of scarcity important to the definition of economics?

2. **RESOURCES**   To which category of resources does each of the following belong?

   a. A taxi
   b. Computer software
   c. One hour of legal counsel
   d. A parking lot
   e. A forest
   f. The Mississippi River
   g. An individual introducing a new way to market products on the Internet

3. **GOODS AND SERVICES**   Explain why each of the following would *not* be considered "free" for the economy as a whole:

   a. Food vouchers
   b. U.S. aid to developing countries
   c. Corporate charitable contributions
   d. Noncable television programs
   e. Public high school education

4. **ECONOMIC DECISION MAKERS**   Which group of economic decision makers plays the leading role in the economic system? Which groups play supporting roles? In what sense are they supporting actors?

5. **MICRO VERSUS MACRO**   Determine whether each of the following is primarily a microeconomic or a macroeconomic issue:

   a. What price to charge for an automobile
   b. Measuring the impact of tax policies on total consumer spending in the economy
   c. A household's decisions about what to buy
   d. A worker's decision regarding how much to work each week
   e. Designing a government policy to increase total employment

6. **MICRO VERSUS MACRO**   Some economists believe that to really understand macroeconomics, you must first understand microeconomics. How does microeconomics relate to macroeconomics?

7. **NORMATIVE VERSUS POSITIVE ANALYSIS**   Determine whether each of the following statements is normative or positive:

   a. The U.S. unemployment rate was below 10.0 percent in 2010.
   b. The inflation rate in the United States is too high.
   c. The U.S. government should increase the minimum wage.
   d. U.S. trade restrictions cost consumers $40 billion annually.

8. **ROLE OF THEORY**   What good is economic theory if it can't predict the behavior of a specific individual?

Problems and Exercises

9. **RATIONAL SELF-INTEREST**   Discuss the impact of rational self-interest on each of the following decisions:

   a. Whether to attend college full time or enter the workforce full time
   b. Whether to buy a new textbook or a used one
   c. Whether to attend a local college or an out-of-town college

10. **RATIONAL SELF-INTEREST**   If behavior is governed by rational self-interest, why do people make charitable contributions of time and money?

11. **MARGINAL ANALYSIS**   The owner of a small pizzeria is deciding whether to increase the radius of delivery area by one mile. What considerations must be taken into account if such a decision is to increase profitability?

12. **TIME AND INFORMATION**   It is often costly to obtain the information necessary to make good decisions. Yet your own interests can be best served by rationally weighing all options available to you. This requires informed decision making. Does this mean that making uninformed decisions is irrational? How do you determine how much information is the right amount?

13. *Case Study: A Yen for Vending Machines*   Do vending machines conserve on any resources other than labor? Does your answer offer any additional insight into the widespread use of vending machines in Japan?

14. *Case Study: A Yen for Vending Machines*   Suppose you had the choice of purchasing identically priced lunches from a vending machine or at a cafeteria. Which would you choose? Why?

15. PITFALLS OF ECONOMIC ANALYSIS   Review the discussion of pitfalls in economic thinking in this chapter. Then identify the fallacy, or mistake in thinking, in each of the following statements:

    a. Raising taxes always increases government revenues.
    b. Whenever there is a recession, imports decrease. Therefore, to stop a recession, we should increase imports.
    c. Raising the tariff on imported steel helps the U.S. steel industry. Therefore, the entire economy is helped.
    d. Gold sells for about $1,000 per ounce. Therefore, the U.S. government could sell all the gold in Fort Knox at $1,000 per ounce and reduce the national debt.

16. ASSOCIATION VERSUS CAUSATION   Suppose I observe that communities with lots of doctors tend to have relatively high rates of illness. I conclude that doctors cause illness. What's wrong with this reasoning?

17. *Case Study: College Major and Career Earnings*   Because some college majors pay nearly twice as much as others, why would students pursuing their rational self-interest choose a lower paying major?

Global Economic Watch Exercises

Login to www.cengagebrain.com and access the Global Economic Watch to do these exercises.

18. GLOBAL ECONOMIC WATCH   Go to the Global Economic Crisis Resource Center. Select Global Issues in Context. In the Basic Search box at the top of the page, enter the phrase "selfish." On the Results page, scroll down to the Magazines section. Choose the red link to View All. Scroll down to click on the link for the December 8, 2008, article "Going Green for Selfish Reasons." Are the companies described acting out of rational self-interest?

19. GLOBAL ECONOMIC WATCH   Go to the Global Economic Crisis Resource Center. Select Global Issues in Context. In the Basic Search box at the top of the page, enter either the term "microeconomic" or the term "macroeconomic." Choose one of the resources and write a summary in your own words. Especially emphasize how the resource is an example of microeconomics or macroeconomics.

Appendix

Understanding Graphs

Take out a pencil and a blank piece of paper. Go ahead. Put a point in the middle of the paper. This is your point of departure, called the **origin**. With your pencil at the origin, draw a straight line off to the right. This line is called the **horizontal axis**. The value of the variable *x* measured along the horizontal axis increases as you move to the right of the origin. Now mark off this line from 0 to 20, in increments of 5 units each. Returning to the origin, draw another line, this one straight north. This line is called the **vertical axis**. The value of the variable *y* measured along the vertical axis increases as you move north of the origin. Mark off this line from 0 to 20, in increments of 5 units each.

Within the space framed by the two axes, you can plot possible combinations of the variables measured along each axis. Each point identifies a value measured along the horizontal, or *x,* axis *and* a value measured along the vertical, or *y,* axis. For example, place point *a* in your graph to reflect the combination where *x* equals 5 units and *y* equals 15 units. Likewise, place point *b* in your graph to reflect 10 units of *x* and 5 units of *y*. Now compare your results with points shown in Exhibit 4.

A **graph** is a picture showing how variables relate, and a picture can be worth a thousand words. Take a look at Exhibit 5, which shows the U.S. annual unemployment rate since 1900. The year is measured along the horizontal axis and the unemployment rate is measured as a percentage along the vertical axis. Exhibit 5 is a *time-series graph,* which shows the value of a variable, in this case the percent of the labor force unemployed, over time. If you had to describe the information presented in Exhibit 5 in words, the explanation could take many words. The picture shows not only how one year compares to the next but also how one decade compares to another and how the unemployment rate trends over time. The sharply higher unemployment rate during the Great Depression of the 1930s is unmistakable. *Graphs convey information in a compact and efficient way.*

This appendix shows how graphs express a variety of possible relations among variables. Most graphs of interest in this book reflect the relationship between

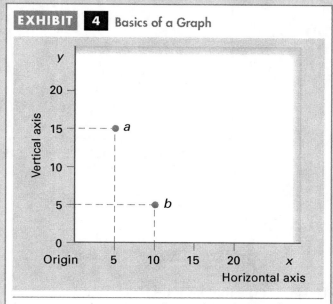

EXHIBIT 4 Basics of a Graph

Any point on a graph represents a combination of particular values of two variables. Here point *a* represents the combination of 5 units of variable *x* (measured on the horizontal axis) and 15 units of variable *y* (measured on the vertical axis). Point *b* represents 10 units of *x* and 5 units of *y*.

two economic variables, such as the unemployment rate and the year, the price of a product and the quantity demanded, or the price of production and the quantity supplied. Because we focus on just two variables at a time, we usually assume that other relevant variables remain constant.

One variable often depends on another. The time it takes you to drive home depends on your average speed. Your weight depends on how much you eat. The amount of Pepsi you buy depends on the price. A *functional relation* exists between two variables when the value of one variable *depends* on the value of another variable. The value of the **dependent variable** depends on the value of the **independent variable**. The task of the economist is to isolate economic relations and determine the direction of causality, if any. Recall that one of the pitfalls of economic

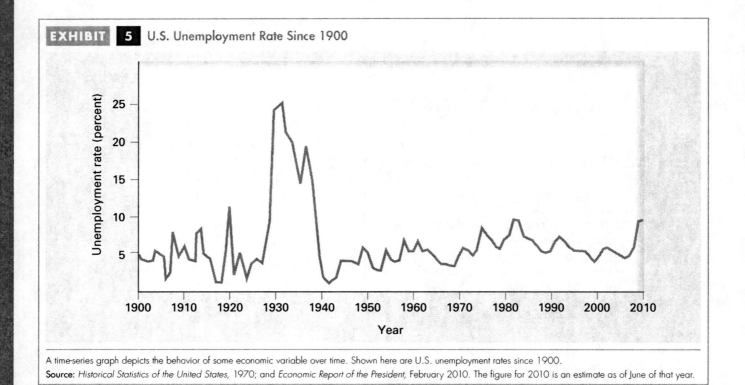

EXHIBIT **5** U.S. Unemployment Rate Since 1900

A time-series graph depicts the behavior of some economic variable over time. Shown here are U.S. unemployment rates since 1900.

Source: *Historical Statistics of the United States,* 1970; and *Economic Report of the President,* February 2010. The figure for 2010 is an estimate as of June of that year.

thinking is the erroneous belief that association is causation. We cannot conclude that, simply because two events relate in time, one causes the other. There may be no relation between the two events.

Drawing Graphs

Let's begin with a simple relation. Suppose you are planning to drive across country and want to figure out how far you will travel each day. You plan to average 50 miles per hour. Possible combinations of driving time and distance traveled per day appear in Exhibit 6. One column lists the hours driven per day, and the next column lists the number of miles traveled per day, assuming an average speed of 50 miles per hour. The distance traveled, the *dependent* variable, depends on the number of hours driven, the *independent* variable. Combinations of hours driven and distance traveled are shown as *a, b, c, d,* and *e.* Each combination is represented by a point in Exhibit 7. For example, point *a* shows that if you drive for 1 hour, you travel 50 miles. Point *b* indicates that if you drive for 2 hours, you travel 100 miles. By connecting the points, or possible combinations, we create a

EXHIBIT **6** Schedule Relating Distance Traveled to Hours Driven

	Hours Driven per Day	Distance Traveled per Day (miles)
a	1	50
b	2	100
c	3	150
d	4	200
e	5	250

The distance traveled per day depends on the number of hours driven per day, assuming an average speed of 50 miles per hour. This table shows combinations of hours driven and distance traveled. These combinations are shown as points in Exhibit 7.

line running upward and to the right. This makes sense, because the longer you drive, the farther you travel. Assumed constant along this line is your average speed of 50 miles per hour.

Types of relations between variables include the following:
1. As one variable increases, the other increases—as in Exhibit 7; this is called a **positive,** or **direct, relation** between the variables.

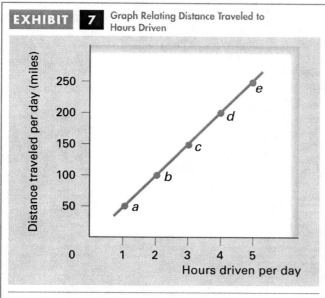

EXHIBIT 7 Graph Relating Distance Traveled to Hours Driven

Points *a* through *e* depict different combinations of hours driven per day and the corresponding distances traveled. Connecting these points creates a graph.

2. As one variable increases, the other decreases; this is called a **negative, or inverse, relation.**

3. As one variable increases, the other remains unchanged; the two variables are said to be *independent, or unrelated.*

One of the advantages of graphs is that they easily convey the relation between variables. We do not need to examine the particular combinations of numbers; we need only focus on the shape of the curve.

The Slopes of Straight Lines

A more precise way to describe the shape of a curve is to measure its slope. The **slope of a line** indicates how much the vertical variable changes for a given increase in the horizontal variable. Specifically, the slope between any two points along any straight line is the vertical change between these two points divided by the horizontal increase, or

$$\text{Slope} = \frac{\text{Change in the vertical distance}}{\text{Increase in the horizontal distance}}$$

Each of the four panels in Exhibit 8 indicates a vertical change, given a 10-unit increase in the horizontal variable. In panel (a), the vertical distance increases by 5 units when the horizontal distance increases by 10 units.

The slope of the line is therefore 5/10, or 0.5. Notice that the slope in this case is a positive number because the relation between the two variables is positive, or direct. This slope indicates that for every 1-unit increase in the horizontal variable, the vertical variable increases by 0.5 units. The slope, incidentally, does not imply causality; the increase in the horizontal variable does not necessarily *cause* the increase in the vertical variable. The slope simply measures the relation between an increase in the horizontal variable and the associated change in the vertical variable.

In panel (b) of Exhibit 8, the vertical distance declines by 7 units when the horizontal distance increases by 10 units, so the slope equals −7/10, or −0.7. The slope in this case is a negative number because the two variables have a negative, or inverse, relation. In panel (c), the vertical variable remains unchanged as the horizontal variable increases by 10, so the slope equals 0/10, or 0. These two variables are not related. Finally, in panel (d), the vertical variable can take on any value, although the horizontal variable remains unchanged. Again, the two variables are not related. In this case, any change in the vertical measure, for example a 10-unit change, is divided by 0, because the horizontal value does not change. Any change divided by 0 is mathematically undefined, but as the line tilts toward vertical, its slope gets incredibly large. For practical purposes, we will assume that the slope of this line is not undefined but infinitely large.

The Slope, Units of Measurement, and Marginal Analysis

The mathematical value of the slope depends on the units measured on the graph. For example, suppose copper tubing costs $1 a foot. Graphs depicting the relation between total cost and quantity purchased are shown in Exhibit 9. In panel (a), the total cost increases by $1 for each 1-foot increase in the amount of tubing purchased. Thus, the slope equals 1/1, or 1. If the cost per foot remains the same but units are measured not in *feet* but in *yards,* the relation between total cost and quantity purchased is as depicted in panel (b). Now total cost increases by $3 for each 1-*yard* increase in output, so the slope equals 3/1, or 3. Because different units are used to measure the copper tubing, the two panels reflect different slopes, even though the cost is $1 per foot in each panel. Keep in mind that *the slope depends in part on the units of measurement.*

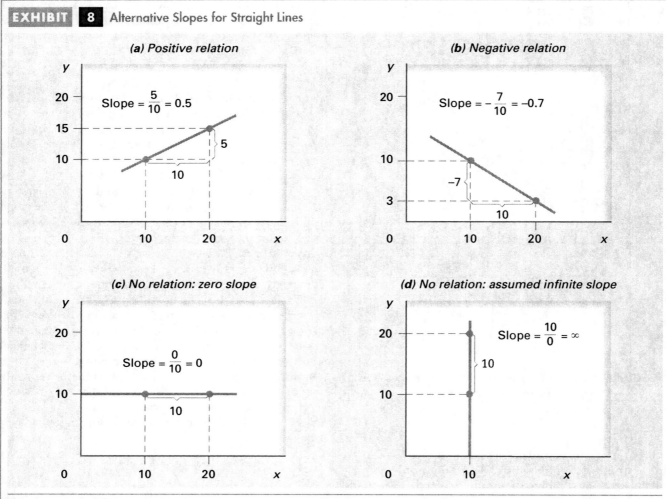

EXHIBIT 8   Alternative Slopes for Straight Lines

(a) Positive relation

Slope = $\dfrac{5}{10}$ = 0.5

(b) Negative relation

Slope = $-\dfrac{7}{10}$ = −0.7

(c) No relation: zero slope

Slope = $\dfrac{0}{10}$ = 0

(d) No relation: assumed infinite slope

Slope = $\dfrac{10}{0}$ = ∞

The slope of a line indicates how much the vertically measured variable changes for a given increase in the variable measured along the horizontal axis. Panel (a) shows a positive relation between two variables; the slope is 0.5, a positive number. Panel (b) depicts a negative, or inverse, relation. When the x variable increases, the y variable decreases; the slope is −0.7, a negative number. Panels (c) and (d) represent situations in which two variables are unrelated. In panel (c), the y variable always takes on the same value; the slope is 0. In panel (d), the x variable always takes on the same value; the slope is mathematically undefined but we simplify by assuming the slope is infinite.

Economic analysis usually involves *marginal analysis,* such as the marginal cost of one more unit of output. The slope is a convenient device for measuring marginal effects because it reflects the change in total cost, measured along the vertical axis, for each 1-unit change in output, measured along the horizontal axis. For example, in panel (a) of Exhibit 9, the marginal cost of another *foot* of copper tubing is $1, which also equals the slope of the line. In panel (b), the marginal cost of another *yard* of tubing is $3, which again is the slope of that line. Because of its applicability to marginal analysis, the slope has special relevance in economics.

The Slopes of Curved Lines

The slope of a straight line is the same everywhere along the line, but the slope of a curved line differs along the curve, as shown in Exhibit 10. To find the slope of a curved line at a particular point, draw a straight line that just touches the curve at that point but does not cut or cross the curve. Such a line is called a tangent to the curve at that point. The slope of the **tangent** gives the slope of the curve at that point. Look at line A, which is tangent to the curve at point *a*. As the horizontal value increases from 0 to 10, the vertical value drops along A from

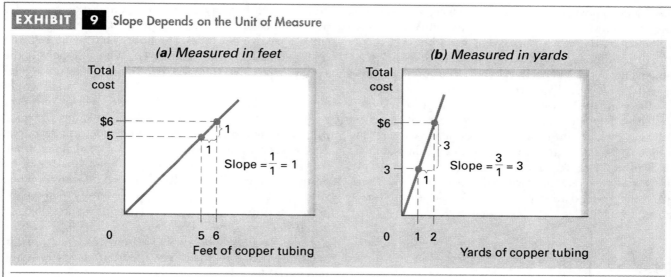

EXHIBIT 9   Slope Depends on the Unit of Measure

(a) Measured in feet

(b) Measured in yards

The value of the slope depends on the units of measure. In panel (a), output is measured in feet of copper tubing; in panel (b), output is measured in yards. Although the cost is $1 per foot in each panel, the slope is different in the two panels because copper tubing is measured using different units.

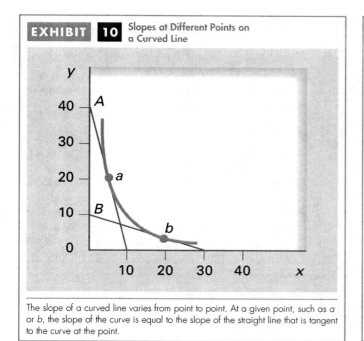

EXHIBIT 10   Slopes at Different Points on a Curved Line

The slope of a curved line varies from point to point. At a given point, such as a or b, the slope of the curve is equal to the slope of the straight line that is tangent to the curve at the point.

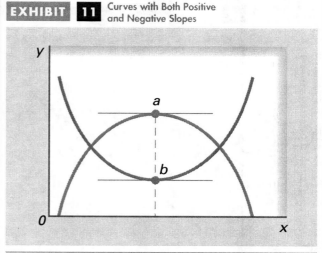

EXHIBIT 11   Curves with Both Positive and Negative Slopes

Some curves have both positive and negative slopes. The hill-shaped curve (in red) has a positive slope to the left of point a, a slope of 0 at point a, and a negative slope to the right of that point. The U-shaped curve (in blue) starts off with a negative slope, has a slope of 0 at point b, and has a positive slope to the right of that point.

40 to 0. Thus, the vertical change divided by the horizontal change equals $-40/10$, or -4, which is the slope of the curve at point a. This slope is negative because the vertical value decreases as the horizontal value increases. Line B, a line tangent to the curve at point b, has the slope $-10/30$, or -0.33. As you can see, the curve depicted in Exhibit 10 gets flatter as the

horizontal variable increases, so the value of its slope approaches zero.

Other curves, of course, will reflect different slopes as well as different changes in the slope along the curve. Downward-sloping curves have negative slopes, and upward-sloping curves, positive slopes. Sometimes curves, such as those in Exhibit 11, are more complex, having both positive and negative ranges, depending on the horizontal value. In the hill-shaped curve, for small values of *x*, there is a positive relation between *x* and *y*, so the slope is positive. As the value of *x* increases, however, the slope declines and eventually becomes negative. We can divide the curve into two segments: (1) the segment between the origin and point *a*, where the slope is positive; and (2) the segment of the curve to the right of point *a*, where the slope is negative. The slope of the curve at point *a* is 0. The U-shaped curve in Exhibit 11 represents the opposite relation: *x* and *y* are negatively related until point *b* is reached; thereafter, they are positively related. The slope equals 0 at point *b*.

Line Shifts

Let's go back to the example of your cross-country trip, where we were trying to determine how many miles you would travel per day. Recall that we measured

hours driven per day on the horizontal axis and miles traveled per day on the vertical axis, assuming an average speed of 50 miles per hour. That same relation is shown as line *T* in Exhibit 12. What happens if the average speed is 40 miles per hour? The entire relation between hours driven and distance traveled would change, as shown by the shift to the right of line *T* to *T'*. With a slower average speed, any distance traveled per day now requires more driving time. For example, 200 miles traveled requires 4 hours of driving when the average speed is 50 miles per hour (as shown by point *d* on curve *T*), but 200 miles takes 5 hours when your speed averages 40 miles per hour (as shown by point *f* on curve *T'*). Thus, *a change in the assumption about average speed changes the relationship between the two variables observed.* This changed relationship is expressed by a shift of the line that shows how the two variables relate.

That ends our once-over of graphs. Return to this appendix when you need a review.

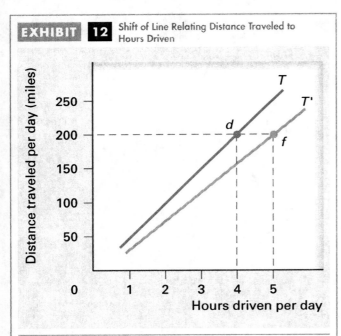

EXHIBIT 12 Shift of Line Relating Distance Traveled to Hours Driven

Line *T* appeared originally in Exhibit 7 to show the relation between hours driven and distance traveled per day, assuming an average speed of 50 miles per hour. If the average speed is only 40 miles per hour, the entire relation shifts to the right to *T'*, indicating that any given distance traveled requires more driving time. For example, 200 miles traveled takes 4 hours of driving at 50 miles per hour but 5 hours at 40 miles per hour. This figure shows how a change in assumptions, in this case, the average speed assumed, can shift the entire relationship between two variables.

Appendix Questions

1. **UNDERSTANDING GRAPHS** Look at Exhibit 5 and answer the following questions:

   a. In what year (approximately) was the unemployment rate the highest? In what year was it the lowest?

   b. In what decade, on average, was the unemployment rate highest? In what decade was it lowest?

   c. Between 1950 and 1980, did the unemployment rate generally increase, decrease, or remain about the same?

2. **DRAWING GRAPHS** Sketch a graph to illustrate your idea of each of the following relationships. Be sure to label each axis appropriately. For each relationship, explain under what circumstances, if any, the curve could shift:

   a. The relationship between a person's age and height

   b. Average monthly temperature in your home town over the course of a year

   c. A person's income and the number of hamburgers consumed per month

   d. The amount of fertilizer added to an acre and the amount of corn grown on that land in one growing season

   e. An automobile's horsepower and its gasoline mileage (in miles per gallon)

3. SLOPE   Suppose you are given the following data on wage rates and number of hours worked:

Point	Hourly Wage	Hours Worked per Week
a	$0	0
b	5	0
c	10	30
d	15	35
e	20	45
f	25	50

a. Construct and label a set of axes and plot these six points. Label each point a, b, c, and so on. Which variable do you think should be measured on the vertical axis, and which variable should be measured on the horizontal axis?

b. Connect the points. Describe the resulting curve. Does it make sense to you?

c. Compute the slope of the curve between points a and b. Between points b and c. Between points c and d. Between points d and e. Between points e and f. What happens to the slope as you move from point a to point f?

Economic Tools and Economic Systems

○ Why are you reading this book right now rather than doing something else?

○ What is college costing you?

○ Why will you eventually major in one subject rather than continue to take courses in different ones?

○ Why is fast food so fast?

○ Why is there no sense crying over spilt milk?

These and other questions are addressed in this chapter, which introduces some tools of economic analysis—some tools of the trade.

Chapter 1 introduced the idea that scarcity forces us to make choices, but the chapter said little about how to make economic choices. This chapter develops a framework for evaluating economic alternatives. First, we consider the cost involved in selecting one alternative over others. Next, we develop tools to explore the choices available to individuals and to the economy as a whole. Finally, we examine the questions that different economies must answer—questions about what goods and services to produce, how to produce them, and for whom to produce them.

Topics discussed include:

- Opportunity cost
- Comparative advantage
- Specialization
- Division of labor

- Production possibilities frontier
- Economic systems
- Three economic questions
- Capitalism and command system

© 2010 Digital Vision/JupiterImages Corporation

Choice and Opportunity Cost

Think about a choice you just made: the decision to begin reading this chapter right now rather than use your time to study for another course, play sports, watch TV, go online, get some sleep, hang with friends, or do something else. Suppose it's late and your best alternative to reading right now is getting some sleep. The cost of reading is passing up the opportunity of sleep. Because of scarcity, whenever you make a choice, you must pass up another opportunity; you must incur an *opportunity cost.*

Opportunity Cost

opportunity cost
The value of the best alternative forgone when an item or activity is chosen

What do we mean when we talk about the cost of something? Isn't it what we must give up—must forgo—to get that thing? The **opportunity cost** of the chosen item or activity is *the value of the best alternative that is forgone.* You can think of opportunity cost as the *opportunity lost.* Sometimes opportunity cost can be measured in terms of money, although, as we shall see, money is usually only part of opportunity cost.

How many times have you heard people say they did something because they "had nothing better to do"? They actually mean they had nothing else going on. Yet, according to the idea of opportunity cost, people *always* do what they do because they have nothing better to do. The choice selected seems, at the time, preferable to any other possible alternative. You are reading this chapter right now because you have nothing better to do. In fact, you are attending college for the same reason: College appears more attractive than your best alternative, as discussed in the following case study.

e activity
Is college a sensible investment for you? Find out by reading "Sure You Should Go to College?" by Marty Nemko at http://www.martynemko.com/articles/sure-you-should-go-college_id1412.

BRINGING THEORY TO LIFE

The Opportunity Cost of College   What is your opportunity cost of attending college full time this year? What was the best alternative you gave up? If you held a full-time job, you would have some idea of the income you gave up to attend college. Suppose you expected to earn $20,000 a year, after taxes, from a full-time job. As a full-time college student, you plan to work part time during the academic year and full time during the summer, earning a total of $10,000 after taxes (about 40 percent of college students hold jobs during the academic year). Thus, by attending college this year, you gave up after-tax earnings of $10,000 (= $20,000 − $10,000).

What about the direct cost of college itself? Suppose you are paying $6,000 this year for in-state tuition, fees, and books at a public college (paying out-of-state rates would tack on $6,000 to that, and attending a private college would add about $15,000). *The opportunity cost of paying for tuition, fees, and books is what you and your family could otherwise have purchased with that money.*

How about room and board? Expenses for room and board are not necessarily an opportunity cost because, even if you were not attending college, you would still need to live somewhere and eat something, though these could differ from your college costs. Likewise, whether or not you attended college, you would still buy goods such as CDs, clothes, and toiletries, and services such as laundry, haircuts, and mobile service. Your spending for such products is not an opportunity cost of attending college but the personal cost that arises regardless of what you do. So for simplicity, assume that room, board, and personal expenses are the same whether or not you attend college. The forgone earnings of $10,000 plus the $6,000 for tuition, fees, and books yield an opportunity cost of $16,000 this year for a student paying in-state rates at a public college. Opportunity cost jumps to about $22,000 for students paying out-of-state rates and to about $31,000 for those at private colleges. Scholarships, but not loans, would reduce your opportunity cost (why not loans?).

This analysis assumes that other things remain constant. But if, in your view, attending college is more of a pain than you expected your best alternative to be, then the opportunity cost of college is even higher. In other words, if you are one of those people who find college difficult, often boring, and in most ways more unpleasant than a full-time job, then the money cost understates your opportunity cost, because your best alternative offers a more enjoyable quality of life. If, on the other hand, you believe the wild and crazy life of a college student is more enjoyable than a full-time job would be, then the dollar figures overstate your opportunity cost, because your best alternative involves a less satisfying quality of life.

Apparently, you view college as a good investment in your future, even though it's costly and perhaps even painful. College graduates on average earn about twice as much per year as high school graduates, a difference that exceeds $1 million over a lifetime. These pay-gains from college prompt some college students to pile up debts to finance their education. Among those earning a bachelor's degrees at public four-year institutions in 2008, 38 percent graduated without education debt, but 6 percent were more than $40,000 in debt. One medical school graduate accumulated an education debt of $550,000 (counting unpaid interest and default charges).

Still, college is not for everyone. Some find the opportunity cost too high. For example, Bill Gates and Paul Allen dropped out of college to cofound Microsoft (both are now among the richest people on earth). Tiger Woods, once an economics major at Stanford, dropped out after two years to earn a fortune in professional golf. And Paula Creamer, who skipped college to play golf, won her first $1 million sooner than any LPGA player in tour history. High school basketball players who believed they were ready for the pros, such as Kobe Bryant and LeBron James, also skipped college (now players can't enter the pros until reaching 19 years of age and out of high school at least a year), as do most tennis pros. Many actors even dropped out of high school to follow their dreams, including Jim Carrey, Russell Crowe, Tom Cruise, Johnny Depp, Robert DeNiro, Cameron Diaz, Colin Farrell, Nicole Kidman, Jude Law, Lindsay Lohan, Demi Moore, Keanu Reeves, Kiefer Sutherland, Hilary Swank, Charlize Theron, and Kate Winslet.

Sources: Elyse Ashburn, "Why Do Students Drop Out? Because They Must Work at Jobs Too," *Chronicle of Higher Education,* 9 December 2009; Mary Pilon, "The $550,000 Student Loan Burden," *Wall Street Journal,* 13 February 2010; "The World's Billionaires," *Forbes,* 11 March 2010; and "College Board Connect to College Success" at http://www.collegeboard.com/.

Opportunity Cost Is Subjective

Like beauty, opportunity cost is in the eye of the beholder. It is subjective. Only the individual making the choice can identify the most attractive alternative. But the chooser seldom knows the actual value of what was passed up, because that alternative is "the road not taken." If you give up an evening of pizza and conversation with friends to work on a research paper, you will never know exactly what you gave up. You know only what you *expected*. Evidently, you expected the benefit of working on that paper to exceed the benefit of the best alternative. (Incidentally, focusing on the best alternative forgone makes all other alternatives irrelevant.)

Calculating Opportunity Cost Requires Time and Information

Economists assume that people rationally choose the most valued alternative. This does not mean you exhaustively assess the value of all possibilities. You assess alternatives as long as the expected marginal benefit of gathering more information about your options exceeds the expected marginal cost (even if you are not aware of making such conscious calculations). In other words, you do the best you can for yourself.

Because learning about alternatives is costly and time consuming, some choices are based on limited or even wrong information. Indeed, some choices may turn out badly (you went for a picnic but it rained; the movie you rented stunk; your new shoes pinch; your new exercise equipment gets no exercise; the stock you bought tanked). Regret about lost opportunities is captured in the common expression "coulda, woulda, shoulda." At the time you made the selection, however, you thought you were making the best use of all your scarce resources, including the time required to gather and evaluate information about your choices.

Time: The Ultimate Constraint

The Sultan of Brunei is among the richest people on earth, worth billions based on huge oil revenues that flow into his tiny country. He and his royal family (which has ruled since 1405) live in a palace with 1,788 rooms, 257 bathrooms, and a throne room the size of a football field. The family owns hundreds of cars, including dozens of Rolls-Royces; he can drive any of these or pilot one of his seven planes, including the 747 with gold-plated furniture. Supported by such wealth, the Sultan would appear to have overcome the economic problem of scarcity. Though he can buy just about whatever he wants, he lacks the time to enjoy his stuff. If he pursues one activity, he cannot at the same time do something else. Each activity involves an opportunity cost. Consequently, the Sultan must choose from among the competing uses of his scarcest resource, time. Although your alternatives are less exotic, you too face a time constraint, especially as the college term winds down.

Opportunity Cost Varies With Circumstance

Opportunity cost depends on your alternatives. This is why you are more likely to study on a Tuesday night than on a Saturday night. The opportunity cost of studying is lower on a Tuesday night, because your alternatives are less attractive than on a Saturday night, when more is going on. Suppose you go to a movie on Saturday night. Your opportunity cost is the value of your best alternative forgone, which might be attending a college game. For some of you, studying on Saturday night may rank well down the list of possibilities—perhaps ahead of reorganizing your closet but behind doing your laundry.

Opportunity cost is subjective, but in some cases, money paid for goods and services is a reasonable approximation. For example, the opportunity cost of the new DVD player you bought is the benefit from spending that $100 on the best forgone alternative. The money measure may leave out some important elements, however, particularly the value of the time involved. For example, watching the latest hit movie costs you not only the $10 admission price but also the time needed to get there, watch the movie, and return home.

Even religious practices are subject to opportunity cost. For example, about half the U.S. population attends religious services at least once a month. In some states, so-called blue laws prohibit retail activity on Sunday. Some states have repealed these laws in recent years, thus raising the opportunity cost of church attendance. Researchers have found that when a state repeals its blue laws, religious attendance declines as do church donations. These results do not seem to be linked to any decline in religiosity before the repeal.[1]

Sunk Cost and Choice

Suppose you have just finished grocery shopping and are wheeling your cart toward the checkout counters. How do you decide which line to join? Easy. You pick the one with the shortest expected wait. Suppose that barely moves for 10 minutes, when you notice that a cashier has opened a new line and invites you to check out. Do you switch to the open cashier, or do you think, "Since I've already spent 10 minutes in this line, I'm staying put"? The 10 minutes you waited represents a **sunk cost**, which is a cost that has already been incurred and cannot be recovered, regardless of what you do next. You should ignore sunk costs in making economic choices. Hence, you should switch. *Economic decision makers should consider only those costs that are affected by the choice. Sunk costs have already been incurred and are not affected by the choice, so they are irrelevant.* Likewise, you should walk out on a bad movie, even if you spent $10 to get in. Your $10 is gone, and sitting through that stinker only makes you worse off. The irrelevance of sunk costs is underscored by proverbs such as "Don't throw good money after bad," "Let bygones be bygones," "That's water over the dam," and "There's no sense crying over spilt milk." The milk has already spilled, so whatever you do now cannot change that. Or, as Tony Soprano would say, "Fuhgeddaboudit!"

Now that you have some idea about opportunity cost, let's see how it helps solve the economic problem.

sunk cost
A cost that has already been incurred, cannot be recovered, and thus is irrelevant for present and future economic decisions

Comparative Advantage, Specialization, and Exchange

Suppose you live in a dormitory. You and your roommate have such tight schedules that you each can spare only about an hour a week for mundane tasks like ironing shirts and typing papers (granted, in reality you may not iron shirts or type papers, but this example will help you understand some important principles). Each of you must turn in a typed three-page paper every week, and you each prefer ironed shirts when you have the time. Let's say it takes you a half hour to type a handwritten paper. Your roommate

---

1. See Jonathan Gruber and Daniel Hungerman, "The Church vs. the Mall: What Happens When Religion Faces Increased Secular Competition?" *Quarterly Journal of Economics*, 123 (May 2008): 831–862.

is from the hunt-and-peck school and takes about an hour. But your roommate is a talented ironer and can iron a shirt in 5 minutes flat (or should that be, iron it flat in 5 minutes?). You take twice as long, or 10 minutes, to iron a shirt.

During the hour set aside each week for typing and ironing, typing takes priority. If you each do your own typing and ironing, you type your paper in a half hour and iron three shirts in the remaining half hour. Your roommate spends the entire hour typing the paper, leaving no time for ironing. Thus, if you each do your own tasks, the combined output is two typed papers and three ironed shirts.

The Law of Comparative Advantage

law of comparative advantage
The individual, firm, region, or country with the lowest opportunity cost of producing a particular good should specialize in that good

Before long, you each realize that total output would increase if you did all the typing and your roommate did all the ironing. In the hour available for these tasks, you type both papers and your roommate irons 12 shirts. As a result of specialization, total output increases by 9 shirts! You strike a deal to exchange your typing for your roommate's ironing, so you each end up with a typed paper and 6 ironed shirts. Thus, *each of you is better off as a result of specialization and exchange.* By specializing in the task that you each do better, you rely on the **law of comparative advantage**, which states that the individual with the lower opportunity cost of producing a particular output should specialize in that output. You face a lower opportunity cost of typing than does your roommate, because in the time it takes to type a paper, you could iron 3 shirts whereas your roommate could iron 12 shirts. And if you face a lower opportunity cost of typing, your roommate must face a lower opportunity cost of ironing (try working that out).

Absolute Advantage Versus Comparative Advantage

absolute advantage
The ability to make something using fewer resources than other producers use

The gains from specialization and exchange so far are obvious. A more interesting case is if you are faster at both tasks. Suppose the example changes only in one respect: Your roommate takes 12 minutes to iron a shirt compared with your 10 minutes. You now have an *absolute advantage* in both tasks, meaning each task takes you less time than it does your roommate. More generally, having an **absolute advantage** means making something using fewer resources than other producers require.

Does your absolute advantage in both activities mean specialization is no longer a good idea? Recall that the law of comparative advantage states that the individual with *the lower opportunity cost* of producing a particular good should specialize in that good. You still take 30 minutes to type a paper and 10 minutes to iron a shirt, so your opportunity cost of typing the paper remains at three ironed shirts. Your roommate takes an hour to type a paper and 12 minutes to iron a shirt, so your roommate could iron five shirts in the time it takes to type a paper. Your opportunity cost of typing a paper is ironing three shirts; for your roommate, it's ironing five shirts. *Because your opportunity cost of typing is lower than your roommate's, you still have a comparative advantage in typing.* Consequently, your roommate must have a comparative advantage in ironing (again, try working this out to your satisfaction). Therefore, you should do all the typing and your roommate, all the ironing. Although you have an absolute advantage in both tasks, your **comparative advantage** calls for specializing in the task for which you have the lower opportunity cost—in this case, typing.

comparative advantage
The ability to make something at a lower opportunity cost than other producers face

If neither of you specialized, you could type one paper and iron three shirts. Your roommate could still type just the one paper. Your combined output would be two papers and three shirts. If you each specialized according to comparative advantage, in an hour you could type both papers and your roommate could iron five shirts. Thus, specialization increases total output by two ironed shirts. Even though you are better at both tasks than your roommate, you are comparatively better at typing. Put another way, your roommate, although worse at both tasks, is not quite as bad at ironing as at typing.

Don't think that this is just common sense. Common sense would lead you to do your own ironing and typing, because you are better at both. *Absolute advantage focuses on who uses the fewest resources, but comparative advantage focuses on what else those resources could produce—that is, on the opportunity cost of those resources.* Comparative advantage is the better guide to who should do what.

The law of comparative advantage applies not only to individuals but also to firms, regions of a country, and entire nations. Individuals, firms, regions, or countries with the lowest opportunity cost of producing a particular good should specialize in producing that good. Because of such factors as climate, workforce skills, natural resources, and capital stock, certain parts of the country and certain parts of the world have a comparative advantage in producing particular goods. From Washington State apples to Florida oranges, from software in India to hardware in Taiwan—*resources are allocated most efficiently across the country and around the world when production and trade conform to the law of comparative advantage.*

Specialization and Exchange

In the previous example, you and your roommate specialized and then exchanged output. No money was involved. In other words, you engaged in **barter**, where products are traded directly for other products. Barter works best in simple economies with little specialization and few traded goods. But for economies with greater specialization, *money* facilitates exchange. Money—coins, bills, checks, and debit cards—is a *medium of exchange* because it is the one thing that everyone accepts in return for goods and services.

barter
The direct exchange of one product for another without using money

Because of specialization and comparative advantage, most people consume little of what they produce and produce little of what they consume. Each individual specializes, then exchanges that product for money, which in turn is exchanged for other products. Did you make anything you are wearing? Probably not. Think about the degree of specialization that went into your cotton shirt. A farmer in a warm climate grew the cotton and sold it to someone who spun it into thread, who sold it to someone who wove it into fabric, who sold it to someone who sewed the shirt, who sold it to a wholesaler, who sold it to a retailer, who sold it to you. Many specialists in the chain of production created that shirt.

Evidence of specialization is all around us. Shops at the mall specialize in products ranging from luggage to lingerie. Restaurants range from subs to sushi. Or let your fingers do the walking through the help-wanted ads or *Yellow Pages,* where you will find thousands of specializations. Without moving a muscle, you can observe the division of labor within a single industry by watching the credits roll at the end of a movie. The credits list scores of specialists—from gaffer (lighting electrician) to assistant location scout. As an extreme example, more than 3,000 specialists helped create the movie *Avatar.*[2] Even a typical TV drama, such as *Grey's Anatomy* or *CSI: Miami*, requires hundreds of specialists.

Some specialties may seem odd. For example, professional mourners in Taiwan are sometimes hired by grieving families to scream, wail, and otherwise demonstrate the deep grief befitting a proper funeral. The sharp degree of specialization is perhaps most obvious online, where the pool of potential customers is so vast that individual sites

2.   As reported in Hendrik Hertzberg, "And the Oscar Goes To," *The New Yorker*, 15 & 22 February 2010, p. 46.

become finely focused. For example, you can find sites specializing in musical bowls, tongue studs, toe rings, brass knuckles, mouth harps, ferret toys, and cat bandannas—just to name a few of the hundreds of thousands of specialty sites. You won't find such precise specialization at the mall. Adam Smith said the degree of specialization is limited by the extent of the market. Online sellers draw on the broadest customer base in the world to find a market niche.

Division of Labor and Gains From Specialization

division of labor
Breaking down the production of a good into separate tasks

Picture a visit to McDonald's: "Let's see, I'll have a Big Mac, an order of fries, and a chocolate shake." Less than a minute later your order is ready. It would take you much longer to make a homemade version of this meal. Why is the McDonald's meal faster, cheaper, and—for some people—tastier than one you could make yourself? Why is fast food so fast? McDonald's takes advantage of the gains resulting from the **division of labor**. Each worker, rather than preparing an entire meal, specializes in separate tasks. This division of labor allows the group to produce much more.

How is this increase in productivity possible? First, the manager can assign tasks according to *individual preferences and abilities*—that is, according to the law of comparative advantage. The worker with the friendly smile and pleasant personality can handle the customers up front; the one with the strong back but few social graces can handle the heavy lifting out back. Second, a worker who performs the same task again and again gets better at it (experience is a good teacher). The worker filling orders at the drive-through, for example, learns to deal with special problems that arise. As another example, consider the experience gained by someone screening bags at airport security. Experience helps the screener distinguish the harmful from the harmless. Third, specialization means no time is lost moving from one task to another. Finally,

specialization of labor
Focusing work effort on a particular product or a single task

and perhaps most importantly, the **specialization of labor** allows for the introduction of more sophisticated production techniques—techniques that would not make sense on a smaller scale. For example, McDonald's large shake machine would be impractical in the home. *Specialized machines make each worker more productive.*

To summarize: The specialization of labor (a) takes advantage of individual preferences and natural abilities, (b) allows workers to develop more experience at a particular task, (c) reduces the need to shift between different tasks, and (d) permits the introduction of labor-saving machinery. Specialization and the division of labor occur not only among individuals but also among firms, regions, and indeed entire countries. The cotton shirt mentioned earlier might involve growing cotton in one country, turning it into cloth in another, making the shirt in a third, and selling it in a fourth.

We should also acknowledge the downside of specialization. Doing the same thing all day can become tedious. Consider, for example, the assembly line worker whose sole task is to tighten a particular bolt. Such a monotonous job could drive that worker bonkers or lead to repetitive motion injury. Thus, the gains from dividing production into individual tasks must be weighed against any problems caused by assigning workers to repetitive, tedious, and potentially harmful jobs. Fortunately, many routine tasks, particularly on assembly lines, can be turned over to robots.

The Economy's Production Possibilities

The focus to this point has been on how individuals choose to use their scarce resources to satisfy their unlimited wants or, more specifically, how they specialize based on comparative advantage. This emphasis on the individual has been appropriate because the economy is shaped by the choices of individual decision makers, whether they are consumers, producers, or public officials. Just as resources are scarce for the individual, they are also scarce for the economy as a whole (no fallacy of composition here). An economy has millions of different resources that can be combined in all kinds of ways to produce millions of different goods and services. This section steps back from the immense complexity of the real economy to develop another simple model, which explores the economy's production options.

Efficiency and the Production Possibilities Frontier, or PPF

Let's develop a model to get some idea of how much an economy can produce with the resources available. What are the economy's production capabilities? Here are the model's assumptions:

1. To simplify matters, output is limited to just two broad classes of products: consumer goods and capital goods.
2. The focus is on production during a given period—in this case, a year.
3. The economy's resources are fixed in both quantity and quality during that period.
4. Society's knowledge about how these resources combine to produce output—that is, the available *technology*—does not change during the year.
5. Also assumed fixed during the period are the "rules of the game" that facilitate production and exchange. These include such things as the legal system, property rights, tax laws, patent laws, and the manners, customs, and conventions of the market.

The point of these simplifying assumptions is to freeze in time the economy's resources, technology, and rules of the game so we can focus on the economy's production options. Otherwise, the production possibilities of the economy would be a moving target.

Given the resources, technology, and rules of the game available in the economy, the **production possibilities frontier**, or **PPF**, identifies possible combinations of the two types of goods that can be produced when all available resources are employed efficiently. *Resources are employed efficiently when there is no change that could increase the production of one good without decreasing the production of the other good.* **Efficiency** involves getting the most from available resources.

The economy's PPF for consumer goods and capital goods is shown by the curve *AF* in Exhibit 1. Point *A* identifies the amount produced per year if all the economy's resources are used efficiently to produce consumer goods. Point *F* identifies the amount produced per year if all the economy's resources are used efficiently to produce capital goods. Points along the curve between *A* and *F* identify possible combinations of the two goods that can be produced when all the economy's resources are used efficiently.

Inefficient and Unattainable Production

Points inside the PPF, such as *I* in Exhibit 1, identify combinations that do not employ resources efficiently. Note that *C* yields more consumer goods and no fewer capital goods than *I*. And *E* yields more capital goods and no fewer consumer goods than *I*. Indeed, any point along the PPF between *C* and *E*, such as *D*, yields both more consumer goods and more capital goods than *I*. Hence, combination *I* is *inefficient*. By using resources more efficiently, the economy can produce more of at least one good without reducing the production of the other good. Points outside the PPF, such as *U* in Exhibit 1, identify *unattainable* combinations, given the availability of resources, technology, and rules of the game. Thus, *the PPF not only shows efficient combinations of production but also serves as the boundary between inefficient combinations inside the frontier and unattainable combinations outside the frontier.*

Production possibilities frontier (PPF)
A curve showing alternative combinations of goods that can be produced when available resources are used efficiently; a boundary line between inefficient and unattainable combinations

efficiency
The condition that exists when there is no way resources can be reallocated to increase the production of one good without decreasing the production of another; getting the most from available resources

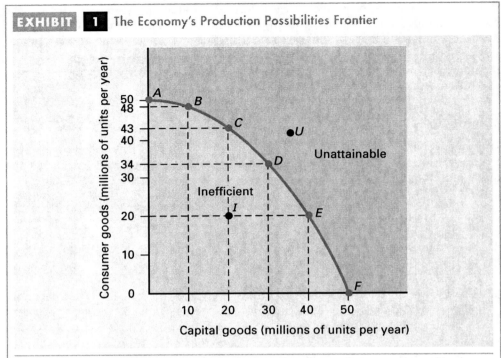

EXHIBIT 1 The Economy's Production Possibilities Frontier

If the economy uses its available resources and technology efficiently to produce consumer goods and capital goods, that economy is on the production possibilities frontier, *AF*. The PPF is bowed out to reflect the law of increasing opportunity cost; the economy must sacrifice more and more units of consumer goods to produce an additional increment of capital goods. Note that more consumer goods must be given up in moving from *E* to *F* than in moving from *A* to *B*, although in each case the gain in capital goods is 10 million units. Points inside the PPF, such as *I*, represent inefficient use of resources. Points outside the PPF, such as *U*, represent unattainable combinations.

The Shape of the Production Possibilities Frontier

Any movement along the PPF involves producing less of one good to produce more of the other. Movements down along the curve indicate that the opportunity cost of more capital goods is fewer consumer goods. For example, moving from point *A* to point *B* *increases* capital production from none to 10 million units but *reduces* consumer units from 50 million to 48 million. Increasing capital goods to 10 million reduces consumer goods only a little. Capital production initially employs resources (such as heavy machinery used to build factories) that add few consumer units but are quite productive in making capital.

As shown by the dashed lines in Exhibit 1, each additional 10 million units of capital produced reduce consumer goods by successively larger amounts. The resources used to produce more capital are increasingly better suited to producing consumer goods. *The opportunity cost of making more capital goods increases, because resources in the economy are not all perfectly adaptable to the production of both types of goods.* The shape of the production possibilities frontier reflects the **law of increasing opportunity cost**. If the economy uses all resources efficiently, the law of increasing opportunity cost states that each additional increment of one good requires the economy to sacrifice successively larger and larger increments of the other good.

The PPF derives its bowed-out shape from the law of increasing opportunity cost. For example, whereas the first 10 million units of capital have an opportunity cost of only

law of increasing opportunity cost

To produce more of one good, a successively larger amount of the other good must be sacrificed

2 million consumer units, the final 10 million units of capital—that is, the increase from *E* to *F*—have an opportunity cost of 20 million consumer units. Notice that the slope of the PPF shows the opportunity cost of an increment of capital. As the economy moves down the curve, the curve becomes steeper, reflecting the higher opportunity cost of capital goods in terms of forgone consumer goods. The law of increasing opportunity cost also applies when shifting from capital goods to consumer goods. Incidentally, if resources were perfectly adaptable to the production of both consumer goods and capital goods, the PPF would be a straight line, reflecting a constant opportunity cost along the PPF.

What Can Shift the Production Possibilities Frontier?

Any production possibilities frontier assumes the economy's resources, technology, and rules of the game are fixed during the period under consideration. Over time, however, the PPF may shift if resources, technology, or the rules of the game change. **Economic growth** is an expansion in the economy's production possibilities as reflected by an outward shift of the PPF.

economic growth
An increase in the economy's ability to produce goods and services; reflected by an outward shift of the economy's production possibilities frontier

Changes in Resource Availability

If people decide to work longer hours, the PPF shifts outward, as shown in panel (a) of Exhibit 2. An increase in the size or health of the labor force, an increase in the skills of the labor force, or an increase in the availability of other resources, such as new oil discoveries, also shifts the PPF outward. In contrast, a decrease of resources shifts the PPF inward, as depicted in panel (b). For example, in 1990 Iraq invaded Kuwait, setting oil fields ablaze and destroying much of Kuwait's physical capital. In West Africa, the encroaching sands of the Sahara destroy thousands of square miles of farmland each year. And in northwest China, a rising tide of wind-blown sand has claimed grasslands, lakes, and forests, and swallowed entire villages, forcing tens of thousands of people to flee.

The new PPFs in panels (a) and (b) appear to be parallel to the original ones, indicating that the resources that changed could produce both capital goods and consumer goods. For example, an increase in electrical power can enhance the production of both, as shown in panel (a). If a resource such as farmland benefits just consumer goods, then increased availability or productivity of that resource shifts the PPF more along the consumer goods axis, as shown in panel (c). Panel (d) shows the effect of an increase in a resource such as construction equipment that is suited only to capital goods.

Increases in the Capital Stock

An economy's PPF depends in part on the stock of human and physical capital. The more capital an economy produces one period, the more output can be produced the next period. Thus, producing more capital goods this period (for example, more machines in the case of physical capital or more education in the case of human capital) shifts the economy's PPF outward the next period.

Technological Change

A technological discovery that employs resources more efficiently could shift the economy's PPF outward. Some discoveries enhance the production of both consumer goods and capital goods, as shown in panel (a) of Exhibit 2. For example, the Internet has increased each firm's ability to find available resources. A technological discovery that benefits consumer goods only, such as more disease-resistant crops, is reflected by a rotation outward of the PPF along the consumer goods axis, as shown in panel (c).

EXHIBIT 2   Shifts of the Economy's Production Possibilities Frontier

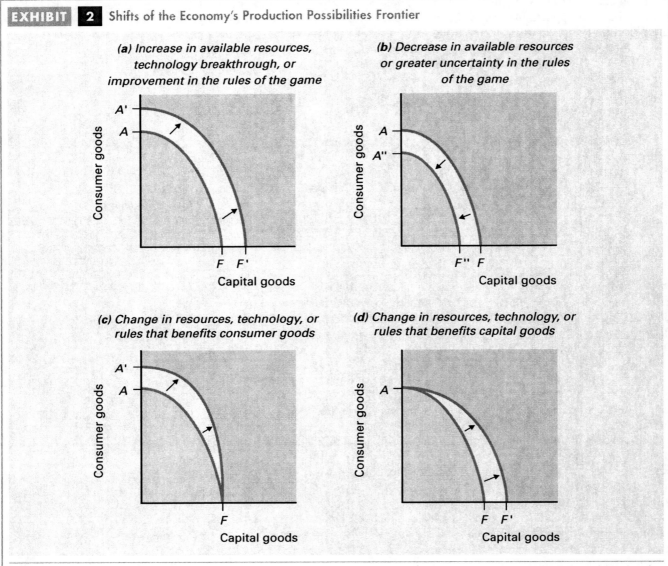

(a) Increase in available resources, technology breakthrough, or improvement in the rules of the game

(b) Decrease in available resources or greater uncertainty in the rules of the game

(c) Change in resources, technology, or rules that benefits consumer goods

(d) Change in resources, technology, or rules that benefits capital goods

When the resources available to an economy change, the PPF shifts. If more resources become available, if technology improves, or if the rules of the game improve, the PPF shifts outward, as in panel (a), indicating that more output can be produced. A decrease in available resources or an upheaval in the rules causes the PPF to shift inward, as in panel (b). Panel (c) shows a change affecting consumer goods production. More consumer goods can now be produced at any given level of capital goods. Panel (d) shows a change affecting capital goods production.

Note that point *F* remains unchanged because the breakthrough does not affect the production of capital goods. Panel (d) shows a technological advance in the production of capital goods, such as better software for designing heavy machinery.

Improvements in the Rules of the Game

The **rules of the game** are the formal and informal institutions that support the economy—the laws, customs, manners, conventions, and other institutional underpinnings that encourage people to pursue productive activity. A more stable political environment and more reliable property rights increase the incentive to work and to invest, and thus help the economy grow. For example, people have more incentive to work if taxes claim less of their paychecks. People have more incentive to invest if they are confident that their investment will not be appropriated by government, stolen by thieves, destroyed by civil unrest, or blown up by terrorists. Improvements in the rules of the game shift the economy's PPF outward. On the other hand, greater uncertainty about the rules of the game reduces the economy's productive capacity as reflected by an inward shift of the PPF. The following case study underscores the importance of the rules of the game.

PUBLIC POLICY

CASE STUDY

Rules of the Game and Economic Development Rules of the game can affect the PPF by either nurturing or discouraging economic development. Businesses supply jobs, tax revenue, and consumer products, but owning and operating a business is risky even in the best of times. How hard is it for an entrepreneur to start a business, import products for sale, comply with tax laws, and settle business disputes? The World Bank, a nonprofit international organization, has developed a composite measure that rolls answers to all these questions into a single measure and ranks 183 countries from best to worst based on their ease of doing business. Exhibit 3 lists the best 10 and the worst 10 countries in terms of the ease of doing business. The countries with the friendliest business climate all have a high standard of living and a sophisticated economy. The United States ranks fourth best, behind Singapore, New Zealand, and Hong Kong. The 10 most difficult countries all have a low standard of living, a poor economy, and nine are in Africa.

Consider, for example, the burden facing a business that wants to sell an imported product. No business in the African country of Burundi makes bicycles, so a shop selling bicycles there must import them. Bicycles are shipped to Burundi via a port in Tanzania. In all, it takes the shop owner at least 10 documents and at least 71 days to get the bicycles from the port in Tanzania to the bicycle shop. Contrast this with 3 documents, and 5 days needed to import products in Denmark. Burundi is one of the poorest countries on earth, based on per capita income. Denmark is among the richest, with a per capita income about 120 times that of Burundi.

How does the burden imposed by business taxes differ across countries? In Burundi, businesses are subject to a tax rate totalling 279 percent of profit. So all business profits and much more are eaten up by taxes, in the process destroying the primary reason to even open a business. Meanwhile, a business in Hong Kong pays a tax rate amounting to only 24 percent of profit.

Of course, some level of business regulation and taxation is necessary to ensure public health and safety and to nurture market competition. Few would argue, however, that the world's most prosperous economies have allowed businesses to go wild. But why would a country impose taxes and regulations so severe as to kill business development, thereby choking off the jobs, taxes, and consumer products that go with it? One possible explanation is that many countries with the worst business climate were once under colonial rule and have not yet developed the ability to operate

e activity
You can see how difficult it is to do business in 183 countries by examining the rankings in the annual report on Doing Business. Find this and previous reports on other topics at the World Bank Group's Web site at http://www.doingbusiness.org.

ALESSANDRO DELLA BELLA/KEYSTONE/landov

EXHIBIT 3	Best 10 and Worst 10 Among 183 Countries Based on Ease of Doing Business

Best 10	Worst 10
1. Singapore	174. Niger
2. New Zealand	175. Eritrea
3. Hong Kong, China	176. Burundi
4. United States	177. Venezuela
5. United Kingdom	178. Chad
6. Denmark	179. Republic of Congo
7. Ireland	180. São Tomé and Principe
8. Canada	181. Guinea-Bissau
9. Australia	182. Democratic Republic of Congo
10. Norway	183. Central African Republic

Source: *Doing Business in 2010: Reforming Through Difficult Times,* (World Bank Publications, 2010) at http://www.doingbusiness.org/documents/fullreport/2010/DB10-full-report.pdf.

government efficiently. Another possibility is that governments in poor countries usually offer the most attractive jobs around. Politicians create government jobs for friends, relatives, and supporters. Overseeing bureaucratic regulations gives all these people something to do, and high tax rates are needed to pay the salaries of all these political cronies.

Perhaps the darkest explanation for the bad business climate in some countries is that business regulations and tax laws provide government bureaucrats with more opportunities for graft and corruption. For example, the more government documents needed to execute a business transaction, the more opportunities to seek bribes. In other words, obstacles are put in the way of business so that government bureaucrats can demand bribes to circumvent those obstacles. Even Irish rocker Bono, a long-time supporter of aid to Africa, has called for "advances in fighting the evils of corruption in Africa." Regardless of the explanation, poor countries are poor in part because they have not yet developed the rules of the game that nurture a prosperous economy.

Source: *Doing Business in 2010: Reforming Through Difficult Times,* (World Bank Publications, 2010) also available at http://www.doingbusiness.org/documents/fullreport/2010/DB10-full-report.pdf; and Bono, "A Time for Miracles," *Time,* 2 April 2007.

What We Learn From the PPF

The PPF demonstrates several ideas introduced so far. The first is *efficiency:* The PPF describes efficient combinations of output, given the economy's resources, technology, and rules of the game. The second idea is *scarcity:* Given the resources, technology, and rules of the game, the economy can produce only so much output per period. The PPF slopes downward, because more of one good means less of the other good, thus demonstrating *opportunity cost.* The PPF's bowed-out shape reflects the *law of increasing opportunity cost,* which arises because some resources are not perfectly adaptable to the production of each type of good. And a shift outward in the PPF reflects *economic growth.*

Finally, because society must somehow select a specific combination of output—a single point—along the PPF, the PPF also underscores the need for *choice*. Selecting a particular combination determines not only consumer goods available this period, but also the capital stock available next period. One thing the PPF does not tell us is which combination to choose. The PPF tells us only about the costs, not the benefits, of the two goods. To make a selection, we need to know about both costs *and* benefits. How society goes about choosing a particular combination depends on the nature of the economic system, as you will see next.

Economic Systems

Each point along the economy's production possibilities frontier is an efficient combination of outputs. Whether the economy produces efficiently and how the economy selects the most preferred combination depends on the decision-making rules employed. But regardless of how decisions are made, each economy must answer three fundamental questions.

Three Questions Every Economic System Must Answer

What goods and services are to be produced? How are they to be produced? And for whom are they to be produced? An **economic system** is the set of mechanisms and institutions that resolve the *what, how,* and *for whom* questions. Some criteria used to distinguish among economic systems are (1) who owns the resources, (2) what decision-making process is used to allocate resources and products, and (3) what types of incentives guide economic decision makers.

economic system
The set of mechanisms and institutions that resolve the what, how, and for whom questions

What Goods and Services Are to Be Produced?

Most of us take for granted the incredible number of choices that go into deciding what gets produced—everything from which new kitchen appliances are introduced, which roads get built, to which of the 10,000 movie scripts purchased by U.S. studios each year get to be among the 500 movies made.[3] Although different economies resolve these and millions of other questions using different decision-making rules and mechanisms, all economies must somehow make such choices.

How Are Goods and Services to Be Produced?

The economic system must determine how output gets produced. Which resources should be used, and how should they be combined to make stuff? How much labor should be used and at what skill levels? What kinds of machines should be used? What new technology should be incorporated into the latest video games? Should the office complex be built in the city or closer to the interstate highway? Millions of individual decisions determine which resources are employed and how these resources are combined.

For Whom Are Goods and Services to Be Produced?

Who will actually consume the goods and services produced? The economic system must determine how to allocate the fruits of production among the population. Should everyone receive equal shares? Should the weak and the sick get more? Should those

3. As reported in Ian Parker, "The Real McKee," *New Yorker*, 20 October 2003.

willing to wait in line get more? Should goods be allocated according to height? Weight? Religion? Age? Gender? Race? Looks? Strength? Political connections? The value of resources supplied? The question "For whom are goods and services to be produced?" is often referred to as the *distribution question*.

Although the three economic questions were discussed separately, they are closely related. The answer to one depends on the answers to the others. For example, an economy that distributes goods and services uniformly to all will, no doubt, answer the what-will-be-produced question differently than an economy that somehow allows more personal choice. As we have seen, laws about resource ownership and the role of government determine the "rules of the game"—the set of conditions that shape individual incentives and constraints. Along a spectrum ranging from the freest to the most regimented types of economic systems, *pure capitalism* would be at one end and the *pure command system* at the other.

Pure Capitalism

pure capitalism
An economic system characterized by the private ownership of resources and the use of prices to coordinate economic activity in unregulated markets

private property rights
An owner's right to use, rent, or sell resources or property

net ⓜ bookmark

The Center for International Comparisons at the University of Pennsylvania at http://pwt .econ.upenn.edu/ is a good source of information on the performance of economies around the world.

Under **pure capitalism,** the rules of the game include the private ownership of resources and the market distribution of products. Owners have *property rights* to the use of their resources and are therefore free to supply those resources to the highest bidder. **Private property rights** allow individual owners to use resources or to charge others for their use. Any income derived from supplying labor, capital, natural resources, or entrepreneurial ability goes to the individual resources owners. Producers are free to make and sell whatever they think will be profitable. Consumers are free to buy whatever goods they can afford. All this voluntary buying and selling is coordinated by unrestricted markets, where buyers and sellers make their intentions known. Market prices guide resources to their most productive use and channel goods and services to the consumers who value them the most.

Under pure capitalism, markets answer the what, how, and for whom questions. That's why capitalism is also referred to as a *market system*. Markets transmit information about relative scarcity, provide individual incentives, and distribute income among resource suppliers. No individual or small group coordinates these activities. Rather, it is the voluntary choices of many buyers and sellers responding only to their individual incentives and constraints that direct resources and products to those who value them the most.

According to Adam Smith (1723–1790), market forces allocate resources as if by an "invisible hand"—an unseen force that harnesses the pursuit of self-interest to direct resources where they earn the greatest reward. According to Smith, *although each individual pursues his or her self-interest, the "invisible hand" of market forces promotes the general welfare.* Capitalism is sometimes called *laissez-faire;* translated from the French, this phrase means "to let do," or to let people do as they choose without government intervention. Thus, under capitalism, voluntary choices based on rational self-interest are made in unrestricted markets to answer the questions what, how, and for whom.

As we will see in later chapters, pure capitalism has its flaws. The most notable market failures are:

1. No central authority protects property rights, enforces contracts, and otherwise ensures that the rules of the game are followed.
2. People with no resources to sell could starve.
3. Some producers may try to monopolize markets by eliminating the competition.

4. The production or consumption of some goods involves side effects that can harm or benefit people not involved in the market transaction.
5. Private firms have no incentive to produce so-called *public goods,* such as national defense, because private firms cannot prevent nonpayers from enjoying the benefits of public goods.

Because of these limitations, countries have modified pure capitalism to allow some role for government. Even Adam Smith believed government should play a role. The United States is among the most market-oriented economies in the world today.

Pure Command System

In a **pure command system**, resources are directed and production is coordinated not by market forces but by the "command," or central plan, of government. In theory at least, instead of private property, there is public, or *communal,* ownership of property. That's why central planning is sometimes called *communism.* Government planners, as representatives of all the people, answer the three questions through *central plans* spelling out how much steel, how many cars, and how much housing to produce. They also decide how to produce these goods and who gets them.

In theory, the pure command system incorporates individual choices into collective choices, which, in turn, are reflected in the central plans. In fact, command economies often have names that focus on collective choice, such as the People's Republic of China and the Democratic People's Republic of Korea (North Korea). In practice, the pure command system also has flaws, most notably:

1. Running an economy is so complicated that some resources are used inefficiently.
2. Because nobody in particular owns resources, each person has less incentive to employ them in their highest-valued use, so some resources are wasted.
3. Central plans may reflect more the preferences of central planners than those of society.
4. Because government is responsible for all production, the variety of products tends to be more limited than in a capitalist economy.
5. Each individual has less personal freedom in making economic choices.

Because of these limitations, countries have modified the pure command system to allow a role for markets. North Korea is perhaps the most centrally planned economy in the world today.

Mixed and Transitional Economies

No country on earth exemplifies either type of economic system in its pure form. Economic systems have grown more alike over time, with the role of government increasing in capitalist economies and the role of markets increasing in command economies. The United States represents a **mixed system**, with government directly accounting for a little more than one-third of all economic activity. What's more, U.S. governments at all levels regulate the private sector in a variety of ways. For example, local zoning boards determine lot sizes, home sizes, and the types of industries allowed. Federal bodies regulate workplace safety, environmental quality, competitive fairness, food and drug quality, and many other activities.

Although both ends of the spectrum have moved toward the center, capitalism has gained the most converts in recent decades. Perhaps the benefits of markets are no better illustrated than where a country, as a result of war or political upheaval, became

pure command system
An economic system characterized by the public ownership of resources and centralized planning

mixed system
An economic system characterized by the private ownership of some resources and the public ownership of other resources; some markets are regulated by government

divided by ideology into a capitalist economy and a command economy, such as with Taiwan and China or South Korea and North Korea. In each case, the economies began with similar human and physical resources, but once they went their separate ways, economic growth diverged sharply, with the capitalist economies outperforming the command economies. For example, Taiwan's production per capita in 2010 was four times that of China's, and South Korea's production per capita was 15 times that of North Korea's.

Consider the experience of the pilgrims in 1620 while establishing Plymouth Colony. They first tried communal ownership of the land. That turned out badly. Crops were neglected and food shortages developed. After three years of near starvation, the system was changed so that each family was assigned a plot of land and granted the fruits of that plot. Yields increased sharply. The pilgrims learned that people take better care of what they own individually; common ownership often leads to common neglect.

Recognizing the incentive power of property rights and markets, some of the most die-hard central planners are now allowing a role for markets. For example, about one-fifth of the world's population lives in China, which grows more market oriented each day, even going so far as to give private property constitutional protection on a par with state property. In a poll of Chinese citizens, 74 percent agreed that "the free enterprise system is the best system on which to base the future of the world." Among Americans polled, 71 percent agreed with that statement.[4] Two decades ago, the former Soviet Union dissolved into 15 independent republics; most converted state-owned enterprises into private firms. From Moscow to Beijing, from Hungary to Mongolia, the transition to mixed economies now underway in former command economies will shape the world for decades to come.

Economies Based on Custom or Religion

Finally, some economic systems are molded largely by custom or religion. For example, caste systems in India and elsewhere restrict occupational choices. Charging interest is banned under Islamic law. Family relations also play significant roles in organizing and coordinating economic activity. Even in the United States, some occupations are still dominated by women, others by men, largely because of tradition. Your own pattern of consumption and choice of occupation may be influenced by some of these considerations.

Conclusion

Although economies can answer the three economic questions in a variety of ways, this book focuses primarily on the mixed market system, such as exists in the United States. This type of economy blends *private choice,* guided by the price system in competitive markets, with *public choice,* guided by democracy in political markets. The study of mixed market systems grows more relevant as former command economies try to develop markets. The next chapter focuses on the economic actors in a mixed economy and explains why and how government gets into the act.

---

4. As reported in "Capitalism, Comrade," *Wall Street Journal,* 18 January 2006.

Summary

1. Resources are scarce, but human wants are unlimited. Because you cannot satisfy all your wants, you must choose, and whenever you choose, you must forgo some option. Choice involves an opportunity cost. The opportunity cost of the selected option is the value of the best alternative forgone.

2. The law of comparative advantage says that the individual, firm, region, or country with the lowest opportunity cost of producing a particular good should specialize in that good. Specialization according to the law of comparative advantage promotes the most efficient use of resources.

3. The specialization of labor increases efficiency by (a) taking advantage of individual preferences and natural abilities, (b) allowing each worker to develop expertise and experience at a particular task, (c) reducing the need to shift between different tasks, and (d) allowing for the introduction of more specialized machines and large-scale production techniques.

4. The production possibilities frontier, or PPF, shows the productive capabilities of an economy when all resources are used efficiently. The frontier's bowed-out shape reflects the law of increasing opportunity cost, which arises because some resources are not perfectly adaptable to the production of different goods. Over time, the PPF can shift in or out as a result of changes in the availability of resources, in technology, or in the rules of the game. The PPF demonstrates several economic concepts, including efficiency, scarcity, opportunity cost, the law of increasing opportunity cost, economic growth, and the need for choice.

5. All economic systems, regardless of their decision-making processes, must answer three basic questions: What is to be produced? How is it to be produced? And for whom is it to be produced? Economies answer the questions differently, depending on who owns the resources and how economic activity is coordinated. Economies can be directed by market forces, by the central plans of government officials, or, in most cases, by a mix of the two.

Key Concepts

Opportunity cost   28

Sunk cost   31

Law of comparative advantage   32

Absolute advantage   32

Comparative advantage   32

Barter   33

Division of labor   34

Specialization of labor   34

Production possibilities frontier (PPF)   35

Efficiency   35

Law of increasing opportunity cost   36

Economic growth   37

Economic system   41

Pure capitalism   42

Private property rights   42

Pure command system   43

Mixed system   43

Questions for Review

1. OPPORTUNITY COST   Discuss the ways in which the following conditions might affect the opportunity cost of going to a movie tonight:
   a. You have a final exam tomorrow.
   b. School will be out for one month starting tomorrow.
   c. The same movie will be on TV next week.
   d. The Super Bowl is on TV.

2. OPPORTUNITY COST   Determine whether each of the following statements is true, false, or uncertain. Explain your answers:
   a. The opportunity cost of an activity is the total value of all the alternatives passed up.
   b. Opportunity cost is an objective measure of cost.
   c. When making choices, people carefully gather all available information about the costs and benefits of alternative choices.
   d. A decision maker seldom knows the actual value of a forgone alternative and therefore must make decisions based on expected values.

3. COMPARATIVE ADVANTAGE   "You should never buy precooked frozen foods because the price you pay includes the labor costs of preparing food." Is this conclusion always valid, or can it be invalidated by the law of comparative advantage?

4. SPECIALIZATION AND EXCHANGE   Explain how the specialization of labor can lead to increased productivity.

5. PRODUCTION POSSIBILITIES   Under what conditions is it possible to increase production of one good without decreasing production of another good?

6. PRODUCTION POSSIBILITIES   Under what conditions would an economy be operating inside its PPF? On its PPF? Outside its PPF?

7. SHIFTING PRODUCTION POSSIBILITIES   In response to an influx of undocumented workers, Congress made it a federal offense to hire them. How do you think this measure affected the U.S. production possibilities frontier? Do you think all industries were affected equally?

8. **PRODUCTION POSSIBILITIES** "If society decides to use its resources efficiently (that is, to produce *on* its production possibilities frontier), then future generations will be worse off because they will not be able to use these resources." If this assertion is true, full employment of resources may not be a good thing. Comment on the validity of this assertion.

9. **ECONOMIC QUESTIONS** What basic economic questions must be answered in a barter economy? In a primitive economy? In a capitalist economy? In a command economy?

10. **ECONOMIC SYSTEMS** What are the major differences between a pure capitalist system and a pure command system? Is the United States closer to a pure capitalist system or to a pure command system?

Problems and Exercises

11. Case Study: The Opportunity Cost of College During the Vietnam War, colleges and universities were overflowing with students. Was this bumper crop of students caused by a greater expected return on a college education or by a change in the opportunity cost of attending college? Explain.

12. **SUNK COST AND CHOICE** Suppose you go to a restaurant and buy an expensive meal. Halfway through, despite feeling quite full, you decide to clean your plate. After all, you think, you paid for the meal, so you are going to eat all of it. What's wrong with this thinking?

13. **OPPORTUNITY COST** You can either spend spring break working at home for $80 per day for five days or go to Florida for the week. If you stay home, your expenses will total about $100. If you go to Florida, the airfare, hotel, food, and miscellaneous expenses will total about $700. What's your opportunity cost of going to Florida?

14. **ABSOLUTE AND COMPARATIVE ADVANTAGE** You have the following information concerning the production of wheat and cloth in the United States and the United Kingdom:

Labor Hours Required to Produce One Unit

	United Kingdom	United States
Wheat	2	1
Cloth	6	5

a. What is the opportunity cost of producing a unit of wheat in the United Kingdom? In the United States?
b. Which country has an absolute advantage in producing wheat? In producing cloth?
c. Which country has a comparative advantage in producing wheat? In producing cloth?
d. Which country should specialize in producing wheat? In producing cloth?

15. **SPECIALIZATION** Provide some examples of specialized markets or retail outlets. What makes the Web so conducive to specialization?

16. **SHAPE OF THE PPF** Suppose a production possibilities frontier includes the following combinations:

Cars	Washing Machines
0	1,000
100	600
200	0

a. Graph the PPF, assuming that it has no curved segments.
b. What is the cost of producing an additional car when 50 cars are being produced?

c. What is the cost of producing an additional car when 150 cars are being produced?
d. What is the cost of producing an additional washing machine when 50 cars are being produced? When 150 cars are being produced?
e. What do your answers tell you about opportunity costs?

17. **PRODUCTION POSSIBILITIES** Suppose an economy uses two resources (labor and capital) to produce two goods (wheat and cloth). Capital is relatively more useful in producing cloth, and labor is relatively more useful in producing wheat. If the supply of capital falls by 10 percent and the supply of labor increases by 10 percent, how will the PPF for wheat and cloth change?

18. **PRODUCTION POSSIBILITIES** There's no reason why a production possibilities frontier could not be used to represent the situation facing an individual. Imagine your own PPF. Right now—today—you have certain resources—your time, your skills, perhaps some capital. And you can produce various outputs. Suppose you can produce combinations of two outputs, call them studying and partying.

a. Draw your PPF for studying and partying. Be sure to label the axes of the diagram appropriately. Label the points where the PPF intersects the axes, as well as several other points along the frontier.
b. Explain what it would mean for you to move upward and to the left along your personal PPF. What kinds of adjustments would you have to make in your life to make such a movement along the frontier?
c. Under what circumstances would your personal PPF shift outward? Do you think the shift would be a "parallel" one? Why, or why not?

19. **SHIFTING PRODUCTION POSSIBILITIES** Determine whether each of the following would cause the economy's PPF to shift inward, outward, or not at all:

a. An increase in average length of annual vacations
b. An increase in immigration
c. A decrease in the average retirement age
d. The migration of skilled workers to other countries

20. Case Study: Rules of the Game and Economic Development Why is the standard of living higher in countries where doing business is easier? Why do governments collect any taxes or impose any regulations at all?

21. **ECONOMIC SYSTEMS** The United States is best described as having a mixed economy. What are some elements of command in the U.S. economy? What are some elements of tradition?

Global Economic Watch Exercises

Login to www.cengagebrain.com and access the Global Economic Watch to do these exercises.

22. GLOBAL ECONOMIC WATCH Go to the Global Economic Crisis Resource Center. Select Global Issues in Context. In the Basic Search box at the top of the page, enter the phrase "Build Ontario's economy." On the Results page, scroll down to the Global Viewpoints section. Click on the link for the December 8, 2009, article "Build Ontario's economy on battle-tested financial sector." Use your understanding of opportunity cost to explain the idea that the Canadian province of Ontario has a comparative advantage in the financial sector.

23. GLOBAL ECONOMIC WATCH   Go to the Global Economic Crisis Resource Center. Select Global Issues in Context. In the Basic Search box at the top of the page, enter the term "capitalism." Find one resource that supports capitalism and one that criticizes. Write a summary of the viewpoints in your own words.

Demand, Supply, and Markets

○ Why do roses cost more on Valentine's Day than during the rest of the year?

○ Why do TV ads cost more during the Super Bowl ($3.0 million for 30 seconds in 2010) than during *Nick at Nite* reruns?

○ Why do Miami hotels charge more in February than in August?

○ Why do surgeons earn more than butchers?

○ Why do basketball pros earn more than hockey pros?

○ Why do economics majors earn more than most other majors?

Answers to these and most economic questions boil down to the workings of demand and supply—the subject of this chapter.

This chapter introduces demand and supply and shows how they interact in competitive markets. *Demand and supply are the most fundamental and the most powerful of all economic tools*—important enough to warrant a chapter. Indeed, some believe that if you program a computer to answer "demand and supply" to every economic question, you could put many economists out of work. An understanding of the two ideas will take you far in mastering the art and science of economic analysis. This chapter uses more graphs, so you may need to review the Chapter 1 appendix as a refresher.

Topics discussed include:

- Demand and quantity demanded
- Movement along a demand curve
- Shift of a demand curve
- Supply and quantity supplied
- Movement along a supply curve
- Shift of a supply curve
- Markets and equilibrium
- Disequilibrium

Demand

How many six packs of Pepsi will people buy each month at a price of $4? What if the price is $3? What if it's $5? The answers reveal the relationship between the price of a six pack and the quantity of Pepsi demanded. Such a relationship is called the *demand* for Pepsi. **Demand** indicates the quantity consumers are both *willing and able* to buy at each possible price during a given time period, other things constant. Because demand pertains to a specific period—a day, a week, a month—think of demand as the *amounts purchased per period* at each possible price. Also, notice the emphasis on *willing and able*. You may be *able* to buy a new Harley-Davidson Sportster Forty-Eight for $10,500 because you can afford one, but you may not be *willing* to buy one if motorcycles don't interest you.

demand
A relation between the price of a good and the quantity that consumers are willing and able to buy per period, other things constant

The Law of Demand

In 1962, Sam Walton opened his first store in Rogers, Arkansas, with a sign that read: "Wal-Mart Discount City. We sell for less." Wal-Mart now sells more than any other retailer in the world because prices there are among the lowest around. As a consumer, you understand why people buy more at a lower price. Sell for less, and the world will beat a path to your door. Wal-Mart, for example, sells on average over 20,000 pairs of shoes *an hour*. This relation between the price and the quantity demanded is an economic law. The **law of demand** says that quantity demanded varies inversely with price, other things constant. Thus, the higher the price, the smaller the quantity demanded; the lower the price, the greater the quantity demanded.

law of demand
The quantity of a good that consumers are willing and able to buy per period relates inversely, or negatively, to the price, other things constant

Demand, Wants, and Needs

Consumer demand and consumer wants are not the same. As we have seen, wants are unlimited. You may want a new Mercedes-Benz SL600 Roadster convertible, but the $139,100 price tag is likely beyond your budget (that is, the quantity you demand at that price is zero). Nor is demand the same as need. You may need a new muffler for your car, but a price of $300 is just too high for you right now. If, however, the price drops enough—say, to $200—then you become both willing and able to buy one.

The Substitution Effect of a Price Change

What explains the law of demand? Why, for example, is more demanded at a lower price? The explanation begins with unlimited wants confronting scarce resources. Many goods and services could satisfy particular wants. For example, you can satisfy your hunger with pizza, tacos, burgers, chicken, or hundreds of other foods. Similarly, you can satisfy your desire for warmth in the winter with warm clothing, a home-heating system, a trip to Hawaii, or in many other ways. Clearly, some alternatives have more appeal than others (a trip to Hawaii is more fun than warm clothing). In a world without scarcity, everything would be free, so you would always choose the most attractive alternative. Scarcity, however, is a reality, and the degree of scarcity of one good relative to another helps determine each good's relative price.

substitution effect of a price change
When the price of a good falls, that good becomes cheaper compared to other goods so consumers tend to substitute that good for other goods

Notice that the definition of *demand* includes the other-things-constant assumption. Among the "other things" assumed to remain constant are the prices of other goods. For example, if the price of pizza declines while other prices remain constant, pizza becomes relatively cheaper. Consumers are more *willing* to purchase pizza when its relative price falls; they substitute pizza for other goods. This principle is called the **substitution effect of a price change**. On the other hand, an increase in the price of pizza, other things constant, increases the opportunity cost of pizza—that is, the amount of other goods you must give up to buy pizza. This higher opportunity cost causes consumers to substitute other goods for the now higher-priced pizza, thus reducing their quantity of pizza demanded. Remember that *it is the change in the relative price—the price of one good relative to the prices of other goods—that causes the substitution effect.* If all prices changed by the same percentage, there would be no change in relative prices and no substitution effect.

The Income Effect of a Price Change

A fall in the price of a good increases the quantity demanded for a second reason. Suppose you earn $30 a week from a part-time job, so $30 is your money income. **Money income** is simply the number of dollars received per period, in this case, $30 per week. Suppose you spend all that on pizza, buying three a week at $10 each. What if the price drops to $6? At the lower price, you can now afford five pizzas a week. Your money income remains at $30 per week, but the decrease in the price has increased your **real income**—that is, your income measured in terms of what it can buy. The price reduction, other things constant, increases the purchasing power of your income, thereby increasing your ability to buy pizza. The quantity of pizza you demand will likely increase because of this **income effect of a price change**. You may not increase your quantity demanded to five pizzas, but you could. If you decide to purchase four pizzas a week when the price drops to $6, you would still have $6 remaining to buy other stuff. Thus, the income effect of a lower price increases your real income and thereby increases your ability to purchase all goods, making you better off. The income effect is reflected in Wal-Mart's slogan, which trumpets low prices: "Save money. Live better." Because of the income effect, consumers typically increase their quantity demanded when the price declines.

Conversely, an increase in the price of a good, other things constant, reduces real income, thereby reducing your *ability* to purchase all goods. Because of the income effect, consumers typically reduce their quantity demanded when the price increases. Again, note that money income, not real income, is assumed to remain constant along a demand curve. A change in price changes your real income, so real income varies along a demand curve. The lower the price, the greater your real income.

The Demand Schedule and Demand Curve

Demand can be expressed as a *demand schedule* or as a *demand curve*. Panel (a) of Exhibit 1 shows a hypothetical demand schedule for pizza. In describing demand, we must specify the units measured and the period considered. In our example, the unit is a 12-inch regular pizza and the period is a week. The schedule lists possible prices, along with the quantity demanded at each price. At a price of $15, for example, consumers demand 8 million pizzas per week. As you can see, the lower the price, other things constant, the greater the quantity demanded. Consumers substitute pizza for other foods. And as the price falls, real income increases, causing consumers to increase the quantity of pizza they demand. If the price drops as low as $3, consumers demand 32 million per week.

The demand schedule in panel (a) appears as a **demand curve** in panel (b), with price measured on the vertical axis and the quantity demanded per week on the horizontal axis. Each price-quantity combination listed in the demand schedule in the left panel becomes a point in the right panel. Point *a*, for example, indicates that if the price is $15, consumers demand 8 million pizzas per week. Connecting points forms the demand curve for pizza, labeled *D*. (By the way, some demand curves are straight lines, some are curved lines, and some are even jagged lines, but they all are called demand *curves*.)

money income
The number of dollars a person receives per period, such as $400 per week

real income
Income measured in terms of the goods and services it can buy; real income changes when the price changes

income effect of a price change
A fall in the price of a good increases consumers' real income, making consumers more able to purchase goods; for a normal good, the quantity demanded increases

demand curve
A curve showing the relation between the price of a good and the quantity consumers are willing and able to buy per period, other things constant

EXHIBIT   **1**   The Demand Schedule and Demand Curve for Pizza

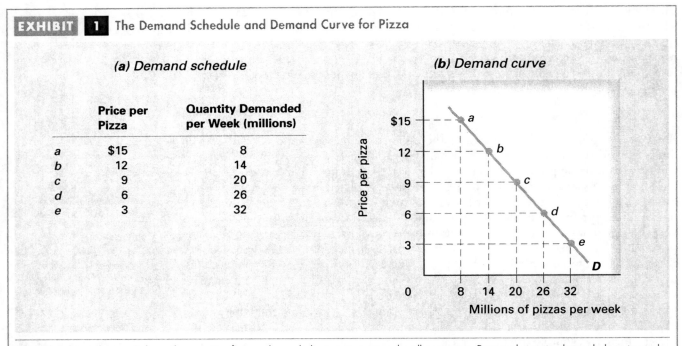

(a) Demand schedule

	Price per Pizza	Quantity Demanded per Week (millions)
a	$15	8
b	12	14
c	9	20
d	6	26
e	3	32

(b) Demand curve

The market demand curve *D* shows the quantity of pizza demanded, at various prices, by all consumers. Price and quantity demanded are inversely related.

A demand curve slopes downward, reflecting the *law of demand:* Price and quantity demanded are inversely related, other things constant. Besides money income, also assumed constant along the demand curve are the prices of other goods. Thus, along the demand curve for pizza, the price of pizza changes *relative to the prices of other goods.* The demand curve shows the effect of a change in the *relative price* of pizza—that is, relative to other prices, which do not change.

Take care to distinguish between *demand* and *quantity demanded.* The *demand* for pizza is not a specific amount, but rather the *entire relationship* between price and quantity demanded—represented by the demand schedule or the demand curve. An individual point on the demand curve indicates the **quantity demanded** at a particular price. For example, at a price of $12, the quantity demanded is 14 million pizzas per week. If the price drops from $12 to, say, $9, this is shown in Exhibit 1 by *a movement along the demand curve*—in this case from point *b* to point *c*. Any movement along a demand curve reflects a *change in quantity demanded,* not a change in demand.

The law of demand applies to the millions of products sold in grocery stores, department stores, clothing stores, shoe stores, drugstores, music stores, bookstores, hardware stores, other retailers, travel agencies, and restaurants, as well as through mail-order catalogs, the *Yellow Pages,* classified ads, online sites, stock markets, real estate markets, job markets, flea markets, and all other markets. The law of demand applies even to choices that seem more personal than economic, such as whether or not to own a pet. For example, after New York City passed an anti-dog-litter law, law-abiding owners had to follow their dogs around the city with scoopers, plastic bags—whatever would do the job. Because the law in effect raised the personal cost of owning a dog, the

quantity demanded

The amount of a good consumers are willing and able to buy per period at a particular price, as reflected by a point on a demand curve

quantity of dogs demanded decreased. Some dogs were abandoned, increasing strays in the city. The number of dogs left at animal shelters doubled. The law of demand predicts this inverse relation between cost, or price, and quantity demanded.

It is useful to distinguish between **individual demand**, which is the demand of an individual consumer, and **market demand**, which is the sum of the individual demands of all consumers in the market. In most markets, there are many consumers, sometimes millions. Unless otherwise noted, when we talk about demand, we are referring to market demand, as shown in Exhibit 1.

individual demand
The relation between the price of a good and the quantity purchased by an individual consumer per period, other things constant

market demand
The relation between the price of a good and the quantity purchased by all consumers in the market during a given period, other things constant; sum of the individual demands in the market

Shifts of the Demand Curve

A demand curve isolates the relation between the price of a good and quantity demanded when other factors that could affect demand remain unchanged. What are those other factors, and how do changes in them affect demand? Variables that can affect market demand are (1) the money income of consumers, (2) prices of other goods, (3) consumer expectations, (4) the number or composition of consumers in the market, and (5) consumer tastes. How do changes in each affect demand?

Changes in Consumer Income

Exhibit 2 shows the market demand curve D for pizza. This demand curve assumes a given level of money income. Suppose consumer income increases. Some consumers are then willing and able to buy more pizza at each price, so market demand increases. The demand curve shifts to the right from D to D'. For example, at a price of $12,

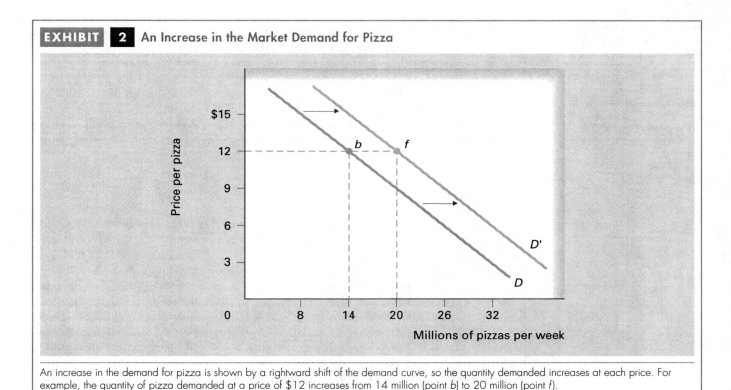

EXHIBIT 2 An Increase in the Market Demand for Pizza

An increase in the demand for pizza is shown by a rightward shift of the demand curve, so the quantity demanded increases at each price. For example, the quantity of pizza demanded at a price of $12 increases from 14 million (point *b*) to 20 million (point *f*).

the amount of pizza demanded increases from 14 million to 20 million per week, as indicated by the movement from point *b* on demand curve *D* to point *f* on demand curve *D'*. In short, *an increase in demand—that is, a rightward shift of the demand curve—means that consumers are willing and able to buy more pizza at each price.*

Goods are classified into two broad categories, depending on how consumers respond to changes in money income. The demand for a **normal good** increases as money income increases. Because pizza is a normal good, its demand curve shifts rightward when money income increases. Most goods are normal. In contrast, demand for an **inferior good** actually decreases as money income increases, so the demand curve shifts leftward. Examples of inferior goods include bologna sandwiches, used furniture, and used clothes. As money income increases, consumers tend to switch from these inferior goods to normal goods (such as roast beef sandwiches, new furniture, and new clothes).

Changes in the Prices of Other Goods

Again, the prices of other goods are assumed to remain constant along a given demand curve. Now let's bring these other prices into play. Consumers have various ways of trying to satisfy any particular want. Consumers choose among substitutes based on relative prices. For example, pizza and tacos are substitutes, though not perfect ones. An increase in the price of tacos, other things constant, reduces the quantity of tacos demanded along a given taco demand curve. An increase in the price of tacos also increases the demand for pizza, shifting the demand curve for pizza to the right. Two goods are considered **substitutes** if an increase in the price of one shifts the demand for the other rightward and, conversely, if a decrease in the price of one shifts demand for the other leftward.

Goods used in combination are called **complements**. Examples include Coke and pizza, milk and cookies, computer software and hardware, and airline tickets and rental cars. Two goods are considered **complements** if an increase in the price of one decreases the demand for the other, shifting that demand curve leftward. For example, an increase in the price of pizza shifts the demand curve for Coke leftward. But most pairs of goods selected at random are *unrelated*—for example, pizza and housing, or milk and gasoline. Still, an increase in the price of an unrelated good reduces the consumers' real income and can reduce the demand for pizza and other goods. For example, a sharp increase in housing prices reduces the amount of income remaining for other goods, such as pizza.

Changes in Consumer Expectations

Another factor assumed constant along a given demand curve is consumer expectations about factors that influence demand, such as incomes or prices. A change in consumers' *income expectations* can shift the demand curve. For example, a consumer who learns about a pay raise might increase demand well before the raise takes effect. A college senior who lands that first real job may buy a new car even before graduation. Likewise, a change in consumers' *price expectations* can shift the demand curve. For example, if you expect the price of pizza to jump next week, you may buy an extra one today for the freezer, shifting this week's demand for pizza rightward. Or if consumers come to believe that home prices will climb next year, some will increase their demand for housing now, shifting this year's demand for housing rightward. On the other hand, if housing prices are expected to fall next year, some consumers will postpone purchases, thereby shifting this year's housing demand leftward.

---

normal good
A good, such as new clothes, for which demand increases, or shifts rightward, as consumer income rises

inferior good
A good, such as used clothes, for which demand decreases, or shifts leftward, as consumer income rises

substitutes
Goods, such as Coke and Pepsi, that relate in such a way that an increase in the price of one shifts the demand for the other rightward

complements
Goods, such as milk and cookies, that relate in such a way that an increase in the price of one shifts the demand for the other leftward

Changes in the Number or Composition of Consumers

As mentioned earlier, the market demand curve is the sum of the individual demand curves of all consumers in the market. If the number of consumers changes, the demand curve will shift. For example, if the population grows, the demand curve for pizza will shift rightward. Even if total population remains unchanged, demand could shift with a change in the composition of the population. For example, an increase over time in the teenage population could shift pizza demand rightward. A baby boom would shift rightward the demand for car seats and baby food. A growing Latino population would affect the demand for Latino foods.

Changes in Consumer Tastes

Do you like anchovies on your pizza? How about sauerkraut on your hot dogs? Are you into tattoos and body piercings? Is music to your ears more likely to be rock, country, hip-hop, reggae, R&B, jazz, funk, Latin, gospel, new age, or classical? Choices in food, body art, music, clothing, books, movies, TV—indeed, all consumer choices—are influenced by consumer tastes. **Tastes** are nothing more than your likes and dislikes as a consumer. What determines tastes? Your desires for food when hungry and drink when thirsty are largely biological. So too is your desire for comfort, rest, shelter, friendship, love, status, personal safety, and a pleasant environment. Your family background affects some of your tastes—your taste in food, for example, has been shaped by years of home cooking. Other influences include the surrounding culture, peer pressure, and religious convictions. So economists can say a little about the origin of tastes, but they claim no special expertise in understanding how tastes develop and change over time. Economists recognize, however, that tastes have an important impact on demand. For example, although pizza is popular, some people just don't like it and those who are lactose intolerant can't stomach the cheese topping. Thus, most people like pizza but some don't.

In our analysis of consumer demand, *we will assume that tastes are given and are relatively stable.* Tastes are assumed to remain constant along a given demand curve. A change in the tastes for a particular good would shift that good's demand curve. For example, a discovery that the tomato sauce and cheese combination on pizza promotes overall health could change consumer tastes, shifting the demand curve for pizza to the right. But because a change in tastes is so difficult to isolate from other economic changes, we should be reluctant to attribute a shift of the demand curve to a change in tastes. We try to rule out other possible reasons for a shift of the demand curve before accepting a change in tastes as the explanation.

That wraps up our look at changes in demand. Before we turn to supply, you should remember the distinction between a **movement along a given demand curve** and a **shift of a demand curve**. A change in *price*, other things constant, causes a *movement along a demand curve,* changing the quantity demanded. A change in one of the determinants of demand other than price causes a *shift of a demand curve,* changing demand.

Supply

Just as demand is a relation between price and quantity demanded, supply is a relation between price and quantity supplied. **Supply** indicates how much producers are *willing* and *able* to offer for sale per period at each possible price, other things constant. The **law of supply** states that the quantity supplied is usually directly related to its price,

---

tastes
Consumer preferences; likes and dislikes in consumption; assumed to remain constant along a given demand curve

movement along a demand curve
Change in quantity demanded resulting from a change in the price of the good, other things constant

shift of a demand curve
Movement of a demand curve right or left resulting from a change in one of the determinants of demand other than the price of the good

supply
A relation between the price of a good and the quantity that producers are willing and able to sell per period, other things constant

law of supply
The amount of a good that producers are willing and able to sell per period is usually directly related to its price, other things constant

other things constant. Thus, the lower the price, the smaller the quantity supplied; the higher the price, the greater the quantity supplied.

The Supply Schedule and Supply Curve

supply curve
A curve showing the relation between price of a good and the quantity producers are willing and able to sell per period other things constant

Exhibit 3 presents the market *supply schedule* and market **supply curve** S for pizza. Both show the quantities supplied per week at various possible prices by the thousands of pizza makers in the economy. As you can see, price and quantity supplied are directly, or positively, related. Producers offer more at a higher price than at a lower price, so the supply curve slopes upward.

There are two reasons why producers offer more for sale when the price rises. First, as the price increases, other things constant, a producer becomes more *willing* to supply the good. Prices act as signals to existing and potential suppliers about the rewards for producing various goods. A higher pizza price attracts resources from lower-valued uses. *A higher price makes producers more willing to increase quantity supplied.*

Higher prices also increase the producer's *ability* to supply the good. The law of increasing opportunity cost, as noted in Chapter 2, states that the opportunity cost of producing more of a particular good rises as output increases—that is, the *marginal cost* of production increases as output increases. Because producers face a higher marginal cost for additional output, they need to get a higher price for that output to be *able* to increase the quantity supplied. *A higher price makes producers more able to increase quantity supplied.* As a case in point, a higher price for gasoline increases oil companies' ability to extract oil from tar sands, to drill deeper, and to explore in less accessible areas, such as the remote jungles of the Amazon, the stormy waters of the North Sea, and the frozen tundra above the Arctic Circle. For example, at a market

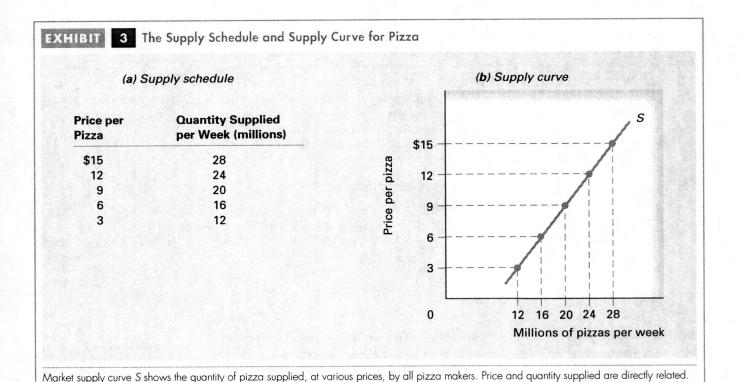

EXHIBIT 3 The Supply Schedule and Supply Curve for Pizza

(a) Supply schedule

Price per Pizza	Quantity Supplied per Week (millions)
$15	28
12	24
9	20
6	16
3	12

(b) Supply curve

Market supply curve S shows the quantity of pizza supplied, at various prices, by all pizza makers. Price and quantity supplied are directly related.

price of $50 per barrel, extracting oil from tar sands is unprofitable, but at price of $55 per barrel, producers are able to supply millions of barrels per month from tar sands.

Thus, a higher price makes producers more *willing* and more *able* to increase quantity supplied. Producers are more *willing* because production becomes more attractive than other uses of the resources involved. Producers are more *able* because they can afford to cover the higher marginal cost that typically results from increasing output.

On the other hand, a lower price makes production less attractive, so suppliers are less willing and less able to offer the good. For example, a mining company "reacted quickly to steep copper price declines in 2008 by curbing production at its North American sites and implementing layoffs at its mines and corporate headquarters."[1]

As with demand, we distinguish between *supply* and *quantity supplied*. *Supply* is the entire relationship between prices and quantities supplied, as reflected by the supply schedule or supply curve. **Quantity supplied** refers to a particular amount offered for sale at a particular price, as reflected by a point on a given supply curve. We also distinguish between **individual supply**, the supply of an individual producer, and **market supply**, the sum of individual supplies of all producers in the market. Unless otherwise noted, the term *supply* refers to market supply.

quantity supplied
The amount offered for sale per period at a particular price, as reflected by a point on a given supply curve

individual supply
The relation between the price of a good and the quantity an individual producer is willing and able to sell per period, other things constant

market supply
The relation between the price of a good and the quantity all producers are willing and able to sell per period, other things constant

Shifts of the Supply Curve

The supply curve isolates the relation between the price of a good and the quantity supplied, other things constant. Assumed constant along a supply curve are the determinants of supply other than the price of the good, including (1) the state of technology, (2) the prices of resources, (3) the prices of other goods, (4) producer expectations, and (5) the number of producers in the market. Let's see how a change in each affects the supply curve.

Changes in Technology

Recall from Chapter 2 that the state of technology represents the economy's knowledge about how to combine resources efficiently. Along a given supply curve, technology is assumed to remain unchanged. If a better technology is discovered, production costs will fall; so suppliers will be more willing and able to supply the good at each price. For example, new techniques helped Marathon Oil cut drilling time for a new well from 56 days in 2006 to only 24 days in 2009.[2] Consequently, supply will increase, as reflected by a rightward shift of the supply curve. For example, suppose a new, high-tech oven that costs the same as existing ovens bakes pizza in half the time. Such a breakthrough would shift the market supply curve rightward, as from *S* to *S'* in Exhibit 4, where more is supplied at each possible price. For example, at a price of $12, the amount supplied increases from 24 million to 28 million pizzas, as shown in Exhibit 4 by the movement from point *g* to point *h*. In short, *an increase in supply—that is, a rightward shift of the supply curve—means that producers are willing and able to sell more pizza at each price.*

1. Andrew Johnson, "Freeport Outsourcing Will Cut 60 Valley Jobs," *Arizona Republic*, 23 February 2010.
2. Ben Casselman, "Oil Industry Boom—in North Dakota," *Wall Street Journal*, 26 February 2010.

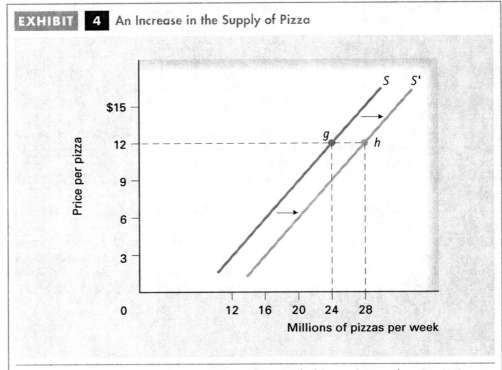

EXHIBIT   4   An Increase in the Supply of Pizza

An increase in the supply of pizza is reflected by a rightward shift of the supply curve, from *S* to *S'*. Quantity supplied increases at each price level. For example, at a price of $12, the quantity of pizza supplied increases from 24 million pizzas (point *g*) to 28 million pizzas (point *h*).

Changes in the Prices of Resources

The prices of resources employed to make the good affect the cost of production and therefore the supply of the good. For example, suppose the price of mozzarella cheese falls. This reduces the cost of making pizza, so producers are more willing and better able to supply it. The supply curve for pizza shifts rightward, as shown in Exhibit 4. On the other hand, an increase in the price of a resource reduces supply, meaning a shift of the supply curve leftward. For example, a higher price of mozzarella increases the cost of making pizza. Higher production costs decrease supply, as reflected by a leftward shift of the supply curve.

Changes in the Prices of Other Goods

Nearly all resources have alternative uses. The labor, building, machinery, ingredients, and knowledge needed to run a pizza business could produce other goods instead. A drop in the price of one of these other goods, with the price of pizza unchanged, makes pizza production more attractive. For example, if the price of Italian bread declines, some bread makers become pizza makers so the supply of pizza increases, shifting the supply curve of pizza rightward as in Exhibit 4. On the other hand, if the price of Italian bread increases, supplying pizza becomes relatively less attractive compared to supplying Italian bread. As resources shift from pizza to bread, the supply of pizza decreases, or shifts to the left.

Changes in Producer Expectations

Changes in producer expectations can shift the supply curve. For example, a pizza maker expecting higher pizza prices in the future may expand his or her pizzeria now, thereby shifting the supply of pizza rightward. When a good can be easily stored (crude oil, for example, can be left in the ground), expecting higher prices in the future might prompt some producers to *reduce* their current supply while awaiting the higher price. Thus, an expectation of higher prices in the future could either increase or decrease current supply, depending on the good. More generally, any change affecting future profitability, such as a change in business taxes, could shift the supply curve now.

Changes in the Number of Producers

Because market supply sums the amounts supplied at each price by all producers, market supply depends on the number of producers in the market. If that number increases, supply will increase, shifting supply to the right. If the number of producers decreases, supply will decrease, shifting supply to the left. As an example of increased supply, the number of gourmet coffee bars has more than quadrupled in the United States since 1990 (think Starbucks), shifting the supply curve of gourmet coffee to the right.

Finally, note again the distinction between a **movement along a supply curve** and a **shift of a supply curve**. A change in *price,* other things constant, causes *a movement along a supply curve,* changing the quantity supplied. A change in one of the determinants of supply other than price causes a *shift of a supply curve,* changing supply.

You are now ready to bring demand and supply together.

movement along a supply curve
Change in quantity supplied resulting from a change in the price of the good, other things constant

shift of a supply curve
Movement of a supply curve left or right resulting from a change in one of the determinants of supply other than the price of the good

Demand and Supply Create a Market

Demanders and suppliers have different views of price. Demanders pay the price and suppliers receive it. Thus, a higher price is bad news for consumers but good news for producers. As the price rises, consumers reduce their quantity demanded along the demand curve and producers increase their quantity supplied along the supply curve. How is this conflict between producers and consumers resolved?

Markets

Markets sort out differences between demanders and suppliers. A *market,* as you know from Chapter 1, includes all the arrangements used to buy and sell a particular good or service. Markets reduce **transaction costs**—the costs of time and information required for exchange. For example, suppose you are looking for a summer job. One approach might be to go from employer to employer looking for openings. But this could have you running around for days or weeks. A more efficient strategy would be to pick up a copy of the local newspaper or go online and look for openings. Classified ads and Web sites, which are elements of the job market, reduce the transaction costs of bringing workers and employers together.

The coordination that occurs through markets takes place not because of some central plan but because of Adam Smith's "invisible hand." For example, the auto dealers in your community tend to locate together, usually on the outskirts of town, where land is cheaper. The dealers congregate not because they all took an economics course or because they like one another's company but because grouped together they become a more attractive destination for car buyers. A dealer who makes the mistake of locating

transaction costs
The costs of time and information required to carry out market exchange

away from the others misses out on a lot of business. Similarly, stores locate together so that more shoppers will be drawn by the call of the mall. From Orlando theme parks to Broadway theaters to Las Vegas casinos, suppliers congregate to attract demanders. Some groupings can be quite specialized. For example, shops in Hong Kong that sell dress mannequins cluster along Austin Road. And diamond merchants in New York City congregate within a few blocks.

Market Equilibrium

To see how a market works, let's bring together market demand and market supply. Exhibit 5 shows the market for pizza, using schedules in panel (a) and curves in panel (b). Suppose the price initially is $12. At that price, producers supply 24 million

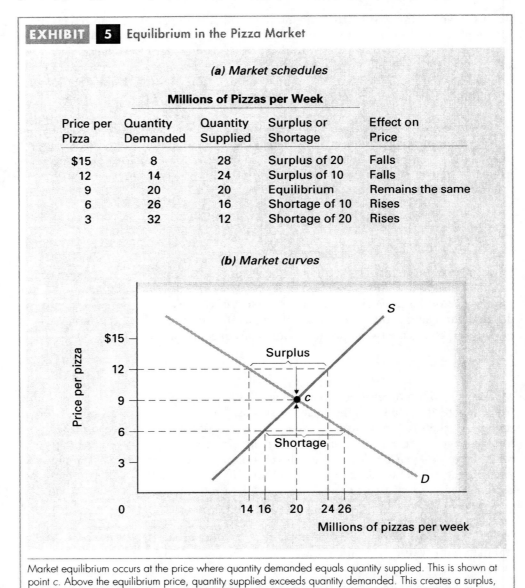

EXHIBIT 5   Equilibrium in the Pizza Market

(a) Market schedules

Millions of Pizzas per Week

Price per Pizza	Quantity Demanded	Quantity Supplied	Surplus or Shortage	Effect on Price
$15	8	28	Surplus of 20	Falls
12	14	24	Surplus of 10	Falls
9	20	20	Equilibrium	Remains the same
6	26	16	Shortage of 10	Rises
3	32	12	Shortage of 20	Rises

(b) Market curves

Market equilibrium occurs at the price where quantity demanded equals quantity supplied. This is shown at point c. Above the equilibrium price, quantity supplied exceeds quantity demanded. This creates a surplus, which puts downward pressure on the price. Below the equilibrium price, quantity demanded exceeds quantity supplied. The resulting shortage puts upward pressure on the price.

pizzas per week, but consumers demand only 14 million, resulting in an *excess quantity supplied,* or a **surplus,** of 10 million pizzas per week. Suppliers don't like getting stuck with unsold pizzas. Their desire to eliminate the surplus puts downward pressure on the price, as shown by the arrow pointing down in the graph. As the price falls, producers reduce their quantity supplied and consumers increase their quantity demanded. The price continues to fall as long as quantity supplied exceeds quantity demanded.

Alternatively, suppose the price initially is $6. You can see from Exhibit 5 that at that price consumers demand 26 million pizzas but producers supply only 16 million, resulting in an *excess quantity demanded,* or a **shortage,** of 10 million pizzas per week. Producers quickly notice they have sold out and those customers still demanding pizzas are grumbling. Profit-maximizing producers and frustrated consumers create market pressure for a higher price, as shown by the arrow pointing up in the graph. As the price rises, producers increase their quantity supplied and consumers reduce their quantity demanded. The price continues to rise as long as quantity demanded exceeds quantity supplied.

Thus, *a surplus creates downward pressure on the price, and a shortage creates upward pressure.* As long as quantity demanded differs from quantity supplied, this difference forces a price change. Note that a shortage or a surplus depends on the price. There is no such thing as a general shortage or a general surplus, only a shortage or a surplus at a particular price.

A market reaches equilibrium when the quantity demanded equals quantity supplied. In **equilibrium,** the independent plans of buyers and sellers exactly match, so market forces exert no pressure for change. In Exhibit 5, the demand and supply curves intersect at the *equilibrium point,* identified as point *c.* The *equilibrium price* is $9 per pizza, and the *equilibrium quantity* is 20 million per week. At that price and quantity, the market *clears.* Because there is no shortage or surplus, there is no pressure for the price to change. The demand and supply curves form an "x" at the intersection. The equilibrium point is found where "x" marks the spot.

A market finds equilibrium through the independent actions of thousands, or even millions, of buyers and sellers. In one sense, the market is personal because each consumer and each producer makes a personal decision about how much to buy or sell at a given price. In another sense, the market is impersonal because it requires no conscious communication or coordination among consumers or producers. The price does all the talking. *Impersonal market forces synchronize the personal and independent decisions of many individual buyers and sellers to achieve equilibrium price and quantity.* Prices reflect relative scarcity. For example, to rent a 26-foot truck one-way from San Francisco to Austin, U-Haul recently charged $3,236. Its one-way charge for that same truck from Austin to San Francisco was just $399. Why the difference? Far more people wanted to move from San Francisco to Austin than vice versa, so U-Haul had to pay its own employees to drive the empty trucks back from Texas. Rental rates reflected that extra cost.

surplus
At a given price, the amount by which quantity supplied exceeds quantity demanded; a surplus usually forces the price down

shortage
At a given price, the amount by which quantity demanded exceeds quantity supplied; a shortage usually forces the price up

equilibrium
The condition that exists in a market when the plans of buyers match those of sellers, so quantity demanded equals quantity supplied and the market clears

Changes in Equilibrium Price and Quantity

Equilibrium occurs when the intentions of demanders and suppliers exactly match. Once a market reaches equilibrium, that price and quantity prevail until something happens to demand or supply. A change in any determinant of demand or supply usually changes equilibrium price and quantity in a predictable way, as you'll see.

net ⊙ bookmark
The Inomics search engine at http://www.inomics.com/cgi/show is devoted solely to economics. Use it to investigate topics related to demand and supply and to other economic models.

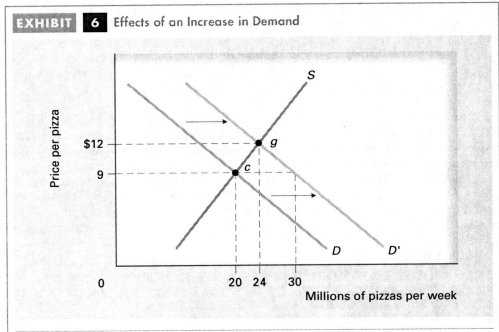

EXHIBIT 6 Effects of an Increase in Demand

An increase in demand is shown by a shift of the demand curve rightward from *D* to *D'*. Quantity demanded exceeds quantity supplied at the original price of $9 per pizza, putting upward pressure on the price. As the price rises, quantity supplied increases along supply curve *S*, and quantity demanded decreases along demand curve *D'*. When the new equilibrium price of $12 is reached at point *g*, quantity demanded once again equals quantity supplied.

Shifts of the Demand Curve

In Exhibit 6, demand curve *D* and supply curve *S* intersect at point *c* to yield the initial equilibrium price of $9 and the initial equilibrium quantity of 20 million 12-inch regular pizzas per week. Now suppose that one of the determinants of demand changes in a way that increases demand, shifting the demand curve to the right from *D* to *D'*. Any of the following could shift the demand for pizza rightward: (1) an increase in the money income of consumers (because pizza is a normal good); (2) an increase in the price of a substitute, such as tacos, or a decrease in the price of a complement, such as Coke; (3) a change in consumer expectations that causes people to demand more pizzas now; (4) a growth in the number of pizza consumers; or (5) a change in consumer tastes—based, for example, on a discovery that the tomato sauce on pizza has antioxidant properties that improve overall health.

After the demand curve shifts rightward to *D'* in Exhibit 6, the amount demanded at the initial price of $9 is 30 million pizzas, which exceeds the amount supplied of 20 million by 10 million pizzas. This shortage puts upward pressure on the price. As the price increases, the quantity demanded decreases along the new demand curve *D'*, and the quantity supplied increases along the existing supply curve *S* until the two quantities are equal once again at equilibrium point *g*. The new equilibrium price is $12, and the new equilibrium quantity is 24 million pizzas per week. Thus, given an upward-sloping supply curve, an increase in demand increases both equilibrium price and quantity. A decrease in demand would lower both equilibrium price and quantity.

These results can be summarized as follows: *Given an upward-sloping supply curve, a rightward shift of the demand curve increases both equilibrium price and quantity and a leftward shift decreases both equilibrium price and quantity.*

Shifts of the Supply Curve

Let's now consider shifts of the supply curve. In Exhibit 7, as before, we begin with demand curve *D* and supply curve *S* intersecting at point *c* to yield an equilibrium price of $9 and an equilibrium quantity of 20 million pizzas per week. Suppose one of the determinants of supply changes, increasing supply from *S* to *S'*. Changes that could shift the supply curve rightward include (1) a technological breakthrough in pizza ovens; (2) a reduction in the price of a resource such as mozzarella cheese; (3) a decline in the price of another good such as Italian bread; (4) a change in expectations that encourages pizza makers to expand production now; or (5) an increase in the number of pizzerias.

After the supply curve shifts rightward in Exhibit 7, the amount supplied at the initial price of $9 increases from 20 million to 30 million, so producers now supply 10 million more pizzas than consumers demand. This surplus forces the price down. As the price falls, the quantity supplied declines along the new supply curve and the quantity demanded increases along the existing demand curve until a new equilibrium point *d* is established. The new equilibrium price is $6, and the new equilibrium quantity is 26 million pizzas per week. In short, an increase in supply reduces the price and increases the quantity. On the other hand, a decrease in supply increases the price but decreases the quantity. Thus, *given a downward-sloping demand curve, a rightward shift of the supply curve decreases price but increases quantity, and a leftward shift increases price but decreases quantity.*

EXHIBIT   7   Effects of an Increase in Supply

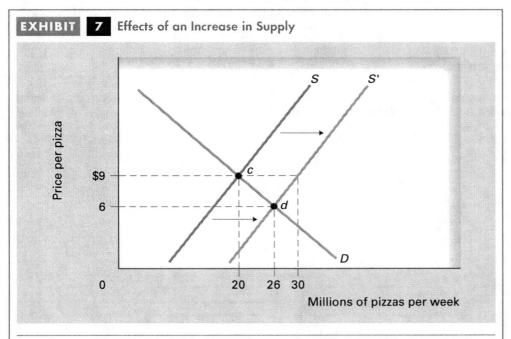

An increase in supply is shown by a shift of the supply curve rightward, from *S* to *S'*. Quantity supplied exceeds quantity demanded at the original price of $9 per pizza, putting downward pressure on the price. As the price falls, quantity supplied decreases along supply curve *S'*, and quantity demanded increases along demand curve *D*. When the new equilibrium price of $6 is reached at point *d*, quantity demanded once again equals quantity supplied.

Simultaneous Shifts of Demand and Supply Curves

As long as only one curve shifts, we can say for sure how equilibrium price and quantity will change. If both curves shift, however, the outcome is less obvious. For example, suppose both demand and supply increase, or shift rightward, as in Exhibit 8. Note that in panel (a), demand shifts more than supply, and in panel (b), supply shifts more than demand. In both panels, equilibrium quantity increases. The change in equilibrium price, however, depends on which curve shifts more. If demand shifts more, as in panel (a), equilibrium price increases. For example, between 1995 and 2005, the demand for housing increased more than the supply, so both price and quantity increased. But if supply shifts more, as in panel (b), equilibrium price decreases. For example, in the last decade, the supply of personal computers has increased more than the demand, so price has decreased and quantity increased.

Conversely, if both demand and supply decrease, or shift leftward, equilibrium quantity decreases. But, again, we cannot say what will happen to equilibrium price unless we examine relative shifts. (You can use Exhibit 8 to consider decreases in demand and supply by viewing D' and S' as the initial curves.) If demand shifts more, the price will fall. If supply shifts more, the price will rise.

If demand and supply shift in opposite directions, we can say what will happen to equilibrium price. Equilibrium price will increase if demand increases and supply decreases. Equilibrium price will decrease if demand decreases and supply increases. Without reference to particular shifts, however, we cannot say what will happen to equilibrium quantity.

These results are no doubt confusing, but Exhibit 9 summarizes the four possible combinations of changes. Using Exhibit 9 as a reference, please take the time right now to work through some changes in demand and supply to develop a feel for the results. Then, in the following case study, evaluate changes in the market for professional basketball.

EXHIBIT   8   Indeterminate Effect of an Increase in Both Demand and Supply

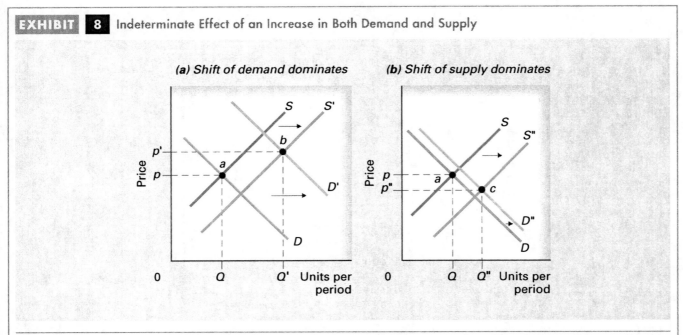

When both demand and supply increase, the equilibrium quantity also increases. The effect on price depends on which curve shifts more. In panel (a), the demand curve shifts more, so the price rises. In panel (b), the supply curve shifts more, so the price falls.

EXHIBIT **9** Effects of Shifts of Both Demand and Supply

	Change in demand	
Change in supply	**Demand increases**	**Demand decreases**
Supply increases	Equilibrium price change is indeterminate. Equilibrium quantity increases.	Equilibrium price falls. Equilibrium quantity change is indeterminate.
Supply decreases	Equilibrium price rises. Equilibrium quantity change is indeterminate.	Equilibrium price change is indeterminate. Equilibrium quantity decreases.

When the demand and supply curves shift in the same direction, equilibrium quantity also shifts in that direction. The effect on equilibrium price depends on which curve shifts more. If the curves shift in opposite directions, equilibrium price will move in the same direction as demand. The effect on equilibrium quantity depends on which curve shifts more.

WORLD OF BUSINESS

CASE STUDY

e activity
HoopsHype hosts a current salary list for top NBA players at http://hoopshype.com/salaries.htm.

The Market for Professional Basketball   Toward the end of the 1970s, the NBA seemed on the brink of collapse. Attendance had sunk to little more than half the capacity. Some teams were nearly bankrupt. Championship games didn't even merit prime-time television coverage. But in the 1980s, three superstars turned things around. Michael Jordan, Larry Bird, and Magic Johnson added millions of fans and breathed new life into the sagging league. Successive generations of stars, including Dwayne Wade, Kevin Durant, and LeBron James, continue to fuel interest.

Since 1980 the league has expanded from 22 to 30 teams and attendance has more than doubled. More importantly, league revenue from broadcast rights jumped nearly *50-fold* from $19 million per year in the 1978–1982 contract to $930 million per year in the current contract, which runs to 2016. Popularity also increased around the world as international players, such as Dirk Nowitzki of Germany and Yao Ming of China, joined the league (basketball is now the most widely played team sport in China). NBA rosters now include more than 80 international players. The NBA formed marketing alliances with global companies such as Coca-Cola and McDonald's, and league playoffs are now televised in more than 200 countries in 45 languages to a potential market of 3 billion people.

What's the key resource in the production of NBA games? Talented players. Exhibit 10 shows the market for NBA players, with demand and supply in 1980 as D_{1980} and S_{1980}. The intersection of these two curves generated an average pay in 1980 of $170,000, or $0.17 million, for the 300 or so players then in the league. Since 1980, the talent pool expanded somewhat, so the supply curve in 2010 was more like S_{2010} (almost

by definition, the supply of the top few hundred players in the world is limited). But demand exploded from D_{1980} to D_{2010}. With supply relatively fixed, the greater demand boosted average pay to $6.0 million by 2010 for the 450 or so players in the league. Such pay attracts younger and younger players. Stars who entered the NBA right out of high school include Kobe Bryant, Kevin Garnett, and LeBron James. (After nine players entered the NBA draft right out of high school in 2005, the league, to stem the flow, required draft candidates to be at least 19 years old and out of high school at least one year. So talented players started turning pro after their first year of college; in 2008, for example, 12 college freshman were drafted including five of the top seven picks.)

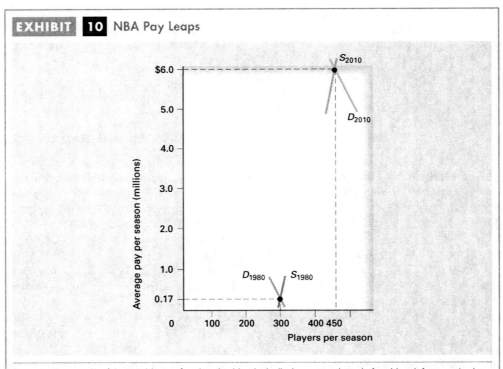

EXHIBIT 10 NBA Pay Leaps

Because the supply of the world's top few hundred basketball players is relatively fixed by definition, the big jump in the demand for such talent caused average league pay to explode. Average pay increased from $170,000 in 1980 to $6,000,000 in 2010. Because the number of teams in the NBA increased, the number of players in the league grew from about 300 to about 450.

Sources: Howard Beck, "Falk Says NBA and Players Headed for Trouble," *New York Times*, 13 February 2010; Jonathan Abrams, "NBA's Shrinking Salary Cap Could Shake Up 2010 Free Agency," *New York Times*, 8 July 2010; and U.S. Census Bureau, *Statistical Abstract of the United States*: 2010 at http://www.census.gov/compendia/statab/.

But rare talent alone does not command high pay. Top rodeo riders, top bowlers, and top women basketball players also possess rare talent, but the demand for their talent is not sufficient to support pay anywhere near NBA levels. NBA players earn on average nearly 100 times more than WNBA players. For example, Diana Taurasi, a great University of Connecticut player, earned only $40,800 her first WNBA season. Some sports aren't even popular enough to support professional leagues.

NBA players are now the highest-paid team athletes in the world—earning at least double that of professionals in baseball, football, and hockey. Both demand *and* supply determine average pay. But the NBA is not without its problems. In 2010 NBA players received 57 percent of all team revenue. Some team owners say they have been losing money, so they want to cut the share of revenue going to players. To cut costs, some teams, such as the Detroit Pistons, have traded their highest paid players.

Disequilibrium

A surplus exerts downward pressure on the price, and a shortage exerts upward pressure. Markets, however, don't always reach equilibrium quickly. During the time required to adjust, the market is said to be in disequilibrium. **Disequilibrium** is usually temporary as the market gropes for equilibrium. But sometimes, often as a result of government intervention, disequilibrium can last a while, perhaps decades, as we will see next.

disequilibrium
The condition that exists in a market when the plans of buyers do not match those of sellers; a temporary mismatch between quantity supplied and quantity demanded as the market seeks equilibrium

Price Floors

Sometimes public officials set prices above their equilibrium levels. For example, the federal government regulates some agriculture prices in an attempt to ensure farmers a higher and more stable income than they would otherwise earn. To achieve higher prices, the government sets a **price floor**, or a *minimum* selling price that is above the equilibrium price. Panel (a) of Exhibit 11 shows the effect of a $2.50 per gallon price floor for milk. At that price, farmers supply 24 million gallons per week, but consumers demand only 14 million gallons, yielding a surplus of 10 million gallons. This surplus milk will pile up on store shelves, eventually souring. To take it off the market, the government usually agrees to buy the surplus milk. The federal government, in fact, has spent billions buying and storing surplus agricultural products. Note, to have an impact, a price floor must be set *above* the equilibrium price. A price floor set at or below the equilibrium price wouldn't matter (how come?). Price floors distort markets and reduce economic welfare.

price floor
A minimum legal price below which a product cannot be sold; to have an impact, a price floor must be set above the equilibrium price

Price Ceilings

Sometimes public officials try to keep a price below the equilibrium level by setting a **price ceiling**, or a *maximum* selling price. Concern about the rising cost of rental housing in some cities prompted city officials to impose rent ceilings. Panel (b) of Exhibit 11 depicts the demand and supply of rental housing. The vertical axis shows monthly rent, and the horizontal axis shows the quantity of rental units. The equilibrium, or market-clearing, rent is $1,000 per month, and the equilibrium quantity is 50,000 housing units. Suppose city officials set a maximum rent of $600 per month. At that ceiling price, 60,000 rental units are demanded, but only 40,000 supplied, resulting in a housing shortage of 20,000 units. Because of the price ceiling, the rental price no longer rations housing to those who value it most. Other devices emerge to ration housing,

price ceiling
A maximum legal price above which a product cannot be sold; to have an impact, a price ceiling must be set below the equilibrium price

EXHIBIT 11 Price Floors and Price Ceilings

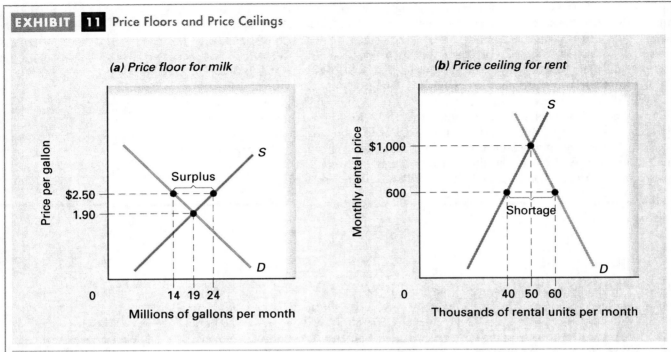

A price floor set above the equilibrium price results in a surplus, as shown in panel (a). A price floor set at or below the equilibrium price has no effect. A price ceiling set below the equilibrium price results in a shortage, as shown in panel (b). A price ceiling set at or above the equilibrium price has no effect.

such as long waiting lists, personal connections, and the willingness to make under-the-table payments, such as "key fees," "finder's fees," high security deposits, and the like. To have an impact, a price ceiling must be set *below* the equilibrium price. A price ceiling set at or above the equilibrium level wouldn't matter. Price floors and ceilings distort markets and reduce economic welfare. Let's take a closer look at rent ceilings in New York City in the following case study.

CASE STUDY

e activity

The New York State Division of Housing and Community Renewal features a number of fact sheets on rent control, stabilization, rent adjustments, special rights programs, and much more, at their Web site. Visit the site to see what kinds of problems exist with services, utilities, and other issues, at http://www.dhcr.state.ny.us/Rent/FactSheets/.

BRINGING THEORY TO LIFE

Rent Ceilings in New York City   New York City rent controls began after World War II, when greater demand for rental housing threatened to push rents higher. To keep rents from rising to their equilibrium level, city officials imposed rent ceilings. Since the quantity demanded at the ceiling rent exceeded the quantity supplied, a housing shortage resulted, as was sketched out in panel (b) of Exhibit 11. Thus, the perverse response to a tight housing market was a policy that reduced the supply of housing over time. The city-wide vacancy rate was recently just 3 percent.

Prior to rent controls, builders in New York City completed about 30,000 housing units a year and 90,000 units in the peak year. After rent controls, new construction dropped sharply. To stimulate supply, the city periodically promised rent-ceiling exemptions for new construction. But three times the city broke that promise after the housing was built. So builders remain understandably wary. During the peak year of the last decade only about 10,000 new housing units were built.

The excess demand for housing in the rent-controlled sector spilled into the free-market sector, increasing demand there. This greater demand raised rents in the free-market sector, making a rent-controlled apartment that much more attractive.

New York City rent regulations now cover about 70 percent of the 2.1 million rental apartments in the city.

Tenants in rent-controlled apartments are entitled to stay until they die, and with a little planning, they can pass the apartment to their heirs. Rent control forces tenants into housing choices they would not otherwise make. After the kids have grown and one spouse has died, the last parent standing usually remains in an apartment too big for one person but too much of a bargain to give up. An heir will often stay for the same reason. Some people keep rent-controlled apartments as weekend retreats for decades after they have moved from New York. All this wastes valuable resources and worsens the city's housing shortage.

Since there is excess quantity demanded for rent-controlled apartments, landlords have less incentive to maintain apartments in good shape. A survey found that about 30 percent of rent-controlled housing in the United States was deteriorating versus only 8 percent of free-market housing. Similar results have been found for England and France. Sometimes the rent is so low that owners simply abandon their property. During one decade, owners abandoned a third of a million units in New York City. So rent controls reduce both the quality and the quantity of housing available.

You would think that rent control benefits the poor most, but it hasn't worked out that way. Henry Pollakowski, an MIT housing economist, concludes that tenants in low- and moderate-income areas get little or no benefit from rent control. But some rich people living in a rent-controlled apartment in the nicest part of town get a substantial windfall. Someone renting in upscale sections of Manhattan might pay only $1,000 a month for a three-bedroom apartment that would rent for $12,000 a month on the open market. According to a recent study, more than 87,000 New York City households with incomes exceeding $100,000 a year benefited from rent control by paying below-market rents.

Once a tenant leaves a rent-controlled apartment, landlords can raise the rent on the next tenant and under some circumstances can escape rent controls entirely. With so much at stake, landlords under rent control have a strong incentive to oust a tenant. Some landlords have been known to pay $5,000 bounties to doormen who report tenants violating their lease (for example, the apartment is not the tenant's primary residence or the tenant is illegally subletting). Landlords also hire private detectives to identify lease violators. And landlords use professional "facilitators" to negotiate with tenants about moving out. Many tenants end up getting paid hundreds of thousands of dollars for agreeing to move. Some have been paid more than $1 million. Facilitators can often find tenants a better apartment in the free-market sector along with enough cash to cover the higher rent for, say, 10 years. Since the rental market is in disequilibrium, other markets, such as the market for buying out tenants, kick in.

Sources: Edward Glaeser and Erzo Luttmer, "The Misallocation of Housing Under Rent Control," *American Economic Review*, 93 (September 1993): 1027–1046; Henry Pollakowski, "Who Really Benefits from New York City's Rent Regulation System?" *Civic Report* 34 (March 2003) at http://manhattan-institute.org/pdf/cr_34.pdf. Janny Scott, "Illegal Sublets Put Private Eyes on the Cast," *New York Times*, 27 January 2007; and Eileen Norcross, "Rent Control Is the Real New York Scandal," *Wall Street Journal*, September 13, 2008. The New York City Rent Guideline Board's Web site is at http://www.housingnyc.com/html/resources/dhcr/dhcr1.html.

Government intervention is not the only source of market disequilibrium. Sometimes, when new products are introduced or when demand suddenly changes, it takes a while to reach equilibrium. For example, popular toys, best-selling books, and chart-busting CDs sometimes sell out. On the other hand, some new products attract few customers and pile up unsold on store shelves, awaiting a "clearance sale."

Conclusion

Demand and supply are the building blocks of a market economy. Although a market usually involves the interaction of many buyers and sellers, few markets are consciously designed. Just as the law of gravity works whether or not we understand Newton's principles, market forces operate whether or not participants understand demand and supply. These forces arise naturally, much the way car dealers cluster on the outskirts of town to attract more customers.

Markets have their critics. Some observers may be troubled, for example, that an NBA star like Kevin Garnett earns a salary that could pay for 500 new schoolteachers, or that corporate executives, such as the head of Goldman Sachs, a financial firm, earns enough to pay for 1,000 new schoolteachers, or that U.S. consumers spend over $40 billion on their pets. On your next trip to the supermarket, notice how much shelf space goes to pet products—often an entire aisle. PetSmart, a chain store, sells over 12,000 different pet items. Veterinarians offer cancer treatment, cataract removal, root canals, even acupuncture. Kidney dialysis for a pet can cost over $75,000 per year.

In a market economy, consumers are kings and queens. Consumer sovereignty rules, deciding what gets produced. Those who don't like the market outcome usually look to government for a solution through price ceilings and price floors, regulations, income redistribution, and public finance more generally.

Summary

1. Demand is a relationship between the price of a product and the quantity consumers are willing and able to buy per period, other things constant. According to the law of demand, quantity demanded varies negatively, or inversely, with the price, so the demand curve slopes downward.

2. A demand curve slopes downward for two reasons. A price decrease makes consumers (a) more *willing* to substitute this good for other goods and (b) more *able* to buy the good because the lower price increases real income.

3. Assumed to remain constant along a demand curve are (a) money income, (b) prices of other goods, (c) consumer expectations, (d) the number or composition of consumers in the market, and (e) consumer tastes. A change in any of these could shift, or change, the demand curve.

4. Supply is a relationship between the price of a good and the quantity producers are willing and able to sell per period, other things constant. According to the law of supply, price and quantity supplied are usually positively, or directly, related, so the supply curve typically slopes upward.

5. The supply curve slopes upward because higher prices make producers (a) more *willing* to supply this good rather than supply other goods that use the same resources and (b) more *able* to cover the higher marginal cost associated with greater output rates.

6. Assumed to remain constant along a supply curve are (a) the state of technology; (b) the prices of resources used to produce the good; (c) the prices of other goods that could be produced with these resources; (d) supplier expectations; and (e) the number of producers in this market. A change in any of these could shift, or change, the supply curve.

7. Demand and supply come together in the market for the good. A market provides information about the price, quantity, and quality of the good. In doing so, a market reduces the transaction costs of exchange—the costs of time and information required for buyers and sellers to make a deal. The interaction of demand and supply guides resources and products to their highest-valued use.

8. Impersonal market forces reconcile the personal and independent plans of buyers and sellers. Market equilibrium, once established, will continue unless there is a change in a determinant that shapes demand or supply. Disequilibrium is usually temporary while markets seek equilibrium, but sometimes

disequilibrium lasts a while, such as when government regulates the price.

9. A price floor is the minimum legal price below which a particular good or service cannot be sold. The federal government imposes price floors on some agricultural products to help farmers achieve a higher and more stable income than would be possible with freer markets. If the floor price is set above the market clearing price, quantity supplied exceeds quantity demanded. Policy makers must figure out some way to prevent this surplus from pushing the price down.

10. A price ceiling is a maximum legal price above which a particular good or service cannot be sold. Governments sometimes impose price ceilings to reduce the price of some consumer goods such as rental housing. If the ceiling price is below the market clearing price, quantity demanded exceeds the quantity supplied, creating a shortage. Because the price system is not allowed to clear the market, other mechanisms arise to ration the product among demanders.

Key Concepts

Questions for Review

1. **LAW OF DEMAND**   What is the law of demand? Give two examples of how you have observed the law of demand at work in the "real world." How is the law of demand related to the demand curve?

2. **CHANGES IN DEMAND**   What variables influence the demand for a normal good? Explain why a reduction in the price of a normal good does not increase the demand for that good.

3. **SUBSTITUTION AND INCOME EFFECTS**   Distinguish between the substitution effect and income effect of a price change. If a good's price increases, does each effect have a positive or a negative impact on the quantity demanded?

4. **DEMAND**   Explain the effect of an increase in consumer income on the demand for a good.

5. **INCOME EFFECTS**   When moving along the demand curve, income must be assumed constant. Yet one factor that can cause a change in the quantity demanded is the "income effect." Reconcile these seemingly contradictory facts.

6. **DEMAND**   If chocolate is found to have positive health benefits, would this lead to a shift of the demand curve or a movement along the demand curve?

7. **SUPPLY**   What is the law of supply? Give an example of how you have observed the law of supply at work. What is the relationship between the law of supply and the supply curve?

8. **CHANGES IN SUPPLY**   What kinds of changes in underlying conditions can cause the supply curve to shift? Give some examples and explain the direction in which the curve shifts.

9. **SUPPLY**   If a severe frost destroys some of Florida's citrus crop, would this lead to a shift of the supply curve or a movement along the supply curve?

10. **MARKETS**   How do markets coordinate the independent decisions of buyers and sellers?

11. *Case Study: The Market for Professional Basketball*   In what sense can we speak of a market for professional basketball? Who are the demanders and who are the suppliers? What are some examples of how changes in supply or demand conditions have affected this market?

Problems and Exercises

12. **SHIFTING DEMAND** Using demand and supply curves, show the effect of each of the following on the market for cigarettes:

    a. A cure for lung cancer is found.
    b. The price of cigars increases.
    c. Wages increase substantially in states that grow tobacco.
    d. A fertilizer that increases the yield per acre of tobacco is discovered.
    e. There is a sharp increase in the price of matches, lighters, and lighter fluid.
    f. More states pass laws restricting smoking in restaurants and public places.

13. **SUBSTITUTES AND COMPLEMENTS** For each of the following pair of goods, determine whether the goods are substitutes, complements, or unrelated:

    a. Peanut butter and jelly
    b. Private and public transportation
    c. Coke and Pepsi
    d. Alarm clocks and automobiles
    e. Golf clubs and golf balls

14. **EQUILIBRIUM** "If a price is not an equilibrium price, there is a tendency for it to move to its equilibrium level. Regardless of whether the price is too high or too low to begin with, the adjustment process will increase the quantity of the good purchased." Explain, using a demand and supply diagram.

15. **EQUILIBRIUM** Assume the market for corn is depicted as in the table that appears below.

    a. Complete the table below.
    b. What market pressure occurs when quantity demanded exceeds quantity supplied? Explain.
    c. What market pressure occurs when quantity supplied exceeds quantity demanded? Explain.
    d. What is the equilibrium price?
    e. What could change the equilibrium price?
    f. At each price in the first column of the table, how much is sold?

16. **MARKET EQUILIBRIUM** Determine whether each of the following statements is true, false, or uncertain. Then briefly explain each answer.

    a. In equilibrium, all sellers can find buyers.
    b. In equilibrium, there is no pressure on the market to produce or consume more than is being sold.

    c. At prices above equilibrium, the quantity exchanged exceeds the quantity demanded.
    d. At prices below equilibrium, the quantity exchanged is equal to the quantity supplied.

17. **DEMAND AND SUPPLY** How do you think each of the following affected the world price of oil? (Use demand and supply analysis.)

    a. Tax credits were offered for expenditures on home insulation.
    b. The Alaskan oil pipeline was completed.
    c. The ceiling on the price of oil was removed.
    d. Oil was discovered in the North Sea.
    e. Sport utility vehicles and minivans became popular.
    f. The use of nuclear power declined.

18. **DEMAND AND SUPPLY** What happens to the equilibrium price and quantity of ice cream in response to each of the following? Explain your answers.

    a. The price of dairy cow fodder increases.
    b. The price of beef decreases.
    c. Concerns arise about the fat content of ice cream. Simultaneously, the price of sugar (used to produce ice cream) increases.

19. **EQUILIBRIUM** Consider the following graph in which demand and supply are initially D and S, respectively. What are the equilibrium price and quantity? If demand increases to D', what are the new equilibrium price and quantity? What happens if the government does not allow the price to change when demand increases?

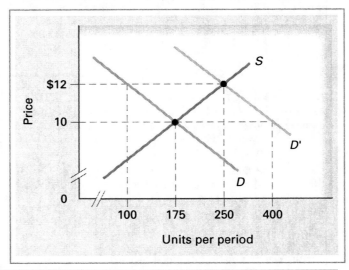

Price per Bushel ($)	Quantity Demanded (millions of bushels)	Quantity Supplied (millions of bushels)	Surplus/ Shortage	Will Price Rise or Fall?
1.80	320	200	_____	_____
2.00	300	230	_____	_____
2.20	270	270	_____	_____
2.40	230	300	_____	_____
2.60	200	330	_____	_____
2.80	180	350	_____	_____

20. CHANGES IN EQUILIBRIUM What are the effects on the equilibrium price and quantity of steel if the wages of steelworkers rise and, simultaneously, the price of aluminum rises?

21. PRICE FLOOR There is considerable interest in whether the minimum wage rate contributes to teenage unemployment. Draw a demand and supply diagram for the unskilled labor market, and discuss the effects of a minimum wage. Who is helped and who is hurt by the minimum wage?

22. Case Study: Rent Ceilings in New York City Suppose the demand and supply curves for rental housing units have the typical shapes and that the rental housing market is in equilibrium. Then, government establishes a rent ceiling below the equilibrium level.

   a. What happens to the quantity of housing available?
   b. What happens to the quality of housing and why?
   c. Who benefits from rent control?
   d. Who loses from rent control?
   e. How do landlords of rent-controlled apartments try to get tenants to leave?

Global Economic Watch Exercises

Login to www.cengagebrain.com and access the Global Economic Watch to do these exercises.

23. GLOBAL ECONOMIC WATCH Go to the Global Economic Crisis Resource Center. Select Global Issues in Context. In the Basic Search box at the top of the page, enter the phrase "Law of Supply, Demand." On the Results page, go to the Global Viewpoints section. Click on the link for the November 21, 1984, article "Law of Supply, Demand Applies to Everyone." Did the article describe a surplus of supply or a shortage of supply?

24. GLOBAL ECONOMIC WATCH Go to the Global Economic Crisis Resource Center. Select Global Issues in Context. Go to the menu at the top of the page and click on the tab for Browse Issues and Topics. Choose Business and Economy. Click on the link for Oil Prices. Find an article from the past 12 months. Compare and contrast the information about oil prices in the article from Problem 23 and in the current article. Use *demand*, *supply*, and *equilibrium* in your analysis.

Tracking the U.S. Economy

○ How do we keep track of the most complex economy in world history?

○ What's gross about the gross domestic product?

○ What's domestic about it?

○ If you make yourself a tuna sandwich, how much does your effort add to the gross domestic product?

○ Because prices change over time, how can we compare the economy's production in one year with that in other years?

Answers to these and other questions are addressed in this chapter, which introduces an economic scorecard for a $14 trillion U.S. economy. That scorecard is the national income accounting system, which reduces a huge network of economic activity to a few aggregate measures.

As you will see, aggregate output is measured either by the spending on that output or by the income derived from producing it. We examine each approach and learn why they are equivalent. The major components and important equalities built into the national income accounts are offered here as another way of understanding how the economy works—not as a foreign language to be mastered before the next exam. The emphasis is more on economic intuition than on accounting precision. The body of the chapter provides the background you need for later chapters.

Some details about the national income accounts are offered in the appendix.

Topics discussed in this chapter include:

- National income accounts
- Expenditure approach to GDP
- Income approach to GDP
- Circular flow of income and expenditure

- Leakages and injections
- Limitations of national income accounting
- Consumer price index
- GDP price index

The Product of a Nation

How do we measure the economy's performance? During much of the 17th and 18th centuries, when the dominant economic policy was mercantilism, many thought that economic prosperity was best measured by the *stock* of precious metals a nation accumulated in the public treasury. Mercantilism led to restrictions on international trade, with the unintended consequence of reducing the gains from comparative advantage. In the latter half of the 18th century, François Quesnay became the first to measure economic activity as a *flow*. In 1758 he published his *Tableau Économique*, which described the *circular flow* of output and income through different sectors of the economy. His insight was likely inspired by his knowledge of blood's circular flow in the body—Quesnay was court physician to King Louis XV of France.

Rough measures of national income were developed in England two centuries ago, but detailed calculations built up from microeconomic data were refined in the United States during the Great Depression. The resulting *national income accounting system* organizes huge quantities of data collected from a variety of sources across America. These data were summarized, assembled into a coherent framework, and reported by the federal government. The conception and implementation of these accounts have been hailed as one of the greatest achievements of the 20th century. The U.S. national income accounts are the most widely copied and most highly regarded in the world and earned their developer, Simon Kuznets, the Nobel Prize in 1971 for "giving quantitative precision to economic entities."

National Income Accounts

How do the national income accounts keep track of the economy's incredible variety of goods and services, from hiking boots to Pilates classes? The *gross domestic product,* or GDP, measures the market value of all final goods and services produced during a year by resources located in the United States, regardless of who owns the resources. For example, GDP includes production in the United States by foreign firms, such as a Toyota plant in Kentucky, but excludes foreign production by U.S. firms, such as a Ford plant in Mexico.

GDP estimates are computed each quarter by the Bureau of Economic Analysis in Washington, D.C. On computation day, staff members follow a process that dates back half a century. The office is in "lockup." Communications with the outside are shut down—no cell phones, land lines, or Internet connections. Office drapes are drawn. Only certain people are allowed in and out. To estimate GDP, they review more than 10,000 streams of data describing economic activity. Nobody speaks the final GDP estimate aloud for fear that it could be overheard and exploited in securities markets. Once they estimate GDP and its components, they write a press release, make hundreds of copies, then lock all but one in a safe for distribution to the media the next morning at 8:30 A.M. Eastern Time. The single copy not locked away is delivered to the head of the president's Council of Economic Advisors, who could give the president a heads-up.

The national income accounts are based on the simple fact that *one person's spending is another person's income.* GDP can be measured either by total spending on U.S. production or by total income received from that production. The **expenditure approach** adds up spending on all final goods and services produced during the year. The **income approach** adds up earnings during the year by those who produce all that output. In the *double-entry bookkeeping system* used to track the economy, spending on aggregate output is recorded on one side of the ledger and income from producing that aggregate output is recorded on the other side.

Gross domestic product includes only **final goods and services,** which are goods and services sold to the final, or end, user. A toothbrush, a pair of contact lenses, and a bus ride are examples of final goods and services. Whether a sale is to the final user depends on who buys the product. When you buy chicken for dinner, that's reflected in GDP. When KFC buys chicken, however, that's not counted in GDP because KFC is not the final consumer. Only after the chicken is cooked and sold by KFC is the transaction counted in GDP.

Intermediate goods and services are those purchased for additional processing and resale, like KFC's chicken. This change may be imperceptible, as when a grocer buys canned goods to restock shelves. Or the intermediate goods can be dramatically altered, as when a painter transforms a $100 canvas and $30 in oils into a work of art that sells for $5,000. Sales of intermediate goods and services are excluded from GDP to avoid the problem of **double counting,** which is counting an item's value more than once. For example, suppose the grocer buys a can of tuna for $1.00 and sells it for $1.50. If GDP counted both the intermediate transaction of $1.00 and the final transaction of $1.50, the recorded value of $2.50 would exceed its final value by $1.00. Hence, GDP counts only the market value of the final sale. As another example, in a recent year Wal-Mart paid $287 billion for products it sold for $375 billion. If GDP counted both Wal-Mart's intermediate transactions and final transactions, Wal-Mart's impact on GDP would be $287 billion too high. GDP also ignores most of the secondhand value of used goods, such as existing homes, used cars, and used textbooks. These goods were counted in GDP when they were produced. But just as the services provided by the grocer and by Wal-Mart are captured in GDP, so are the services provided by real estate agents, used-car dealers, and used-book sellers.

GDP Based on the Expenditure Approach

As noted already, one way to measure GDP is to add up spending on all final goods and services produced in the economy during the year. The easiest way to understand the spending approach is to sort aggregate expenditure into its components: consumption, investment, government purchases, and net exports. **Consumption,** or more specifically, *personal consumption expenditures,* consists of purchases of final goods and services by households during the year. Consumption is the largest spending category, averaging 70 percent of U.S. GDP during this past decade. Along with *services* like dry cleaning, haircuts, and air travel, consumption includes *nondurable goods*, like soap and soup,

expenditure approach to GDP
Calculating GDP by adding up spending on all final goods and services produced in the nation during the year

income approach to GDP
Calculating GDP by adding up all earnings from resources used to produce output in the nation during the year

final goods and services
Goods and services sold to final, or end, users

intermediate goods and services
Goods and services purchased by firms for further reprocessing and resale

double counting
The mistake of including both the value of intermediate products and the value of final products in calculating gross domestic product; counting the same production more than once

consumption
Household purchases of final goods and services, except for new residences, which count as investment

investment
The purchase of new plants, new equipment, new buildings, and new residences, plus net additions to inventories

physical capital
Manufactured items used to produce goods and services; includes new plants and new equipment

residential construction
Building new homes or dwelling places

inventories
Producers' stocks of finished and in-process goods

government purchases
Spending for goods and services by all levels of government; government outlays minus transfer payments

net exports
The value of a country's exports minus the value of its imports

aggregate expenditure
Total spending on final goods and services in an economy during a given period, usually a year

aggregate income
All earnings of resource suppliers in an economy during a given period, usually a year

and *durable goods*, like furniture and kitchen appliances. Durable goods are expected to last at least three years.

Investment, or more specifically, *gross private domestic investment*, consists of spending on new capital goods and on net additions to inventories. The most important investment is **physical capital,** such as new buildings and new machinery. Investment also includes new **residential construction.** Although it fluctuates from year to year, investment averaged 16 percent of U.S. GDP this past decade. More generally, investment consists of spending on current production that is not used for current consumption. A net increase to inventories also counts as investment because it represents current production not used for current consumption. **Inventories** are stocks of goods in process, such as computer parts, and stocks of finished goods, such as new computers awaiting sale. Inventories help manufacturers cope with unexpected changes in the supply of their resources or in the demand for their products.

Although investment includes purchasing a new residence, it excludes purchases of *existing* buildings and machines and purchases of financial assets, such as stocks and bonds. Existing buildings and machines were counted in GDP when they were produced. Stocks and bonds are not investments themselves but simply indications of ownership.

Government purchases, or more specifically, *government consumption and gross investment,* include government spending for goods and services—from clearing snowy roads to clearing court dockets, from buying library books to paying librarians. Government purchases averaged 19 percent of U.S. GDP during the last decade. Government purchases, and therefore GDP, exclude transfer payments, such as Social Security, welfare benefits, and unemployment insurance. Such payments are not true purchases by the government or true earnings by the recipients.

The final spending component, net exports, reflects international trade in goods and services. Goods, or *merchandise* traded, include physical items such as bananas and HDTVs (stuff you can load on a ship). Services, or so-called *invisibles,* include intangible items, such as European tours and online customer service from India. Foreign purchases of U.S. goods and services are counted as part of U.S. GDP. But U.S. purchases of foreign goods and services are subtracted from U.S. GDP. **Net exports** equal the value of U.S. exports of goods and services minus the value of U.S. imports of goods and services. U.S. imports have exceeded U.S. exports nearly every year since the 1960s, meaning U.S. net exports have been negative. During the last decade, net exports averaged a negative 5 percent of GDP.

With the expenditure approach, the nation's **aggregate expenditure** sums consumption, C; investment, I; government purchases, G; and net exports, which is the value of exports, X, minus the value of imports, M, or $(X - M)$. Summing these yields aggregate expenditure, or GDP:

$$C + I + G + (X - M) = \text{Aggregate expenditure} = \text{GDP}$$

GDP Based on the Income Approach

The expenditure approach sums, or aggregates, spending on production. The income approach sums, or aggregates, income arising from that production. Again, double-entry bookkeeping ensures that the value of aggregate output equals the aggregate income paid for resources used to produce that output: the wages, interest, rent, and profit arising from production. The price of a Hershey Bar reflects the income earned by resource suppliers along the way. **Aggregate income** equals the sum of all the income earned by resource suppliers in the economy. Thus, we can say that

$$\text{Aggregate expenditure} = \text{GDP} = \text{Aggregate income}$$

EXHIBIT 1 Computing Value Added for a New Desk

Stage of Production	(1) Sale Value	(2) Cost of Intermediate Goods	(3) Value Added (3) = (1) − (2)
Logger	$ 20	—	$20
Miller	50	$ 20	30
Manufacturer	120	50	70
Retailer	200	120	80
		Market value of final good	**$200**

The value added at each stage of production is the sale price at that stage minus the cost of intermediate goods, or column (1) minus column (2). The values added at each stage sum to the market value of the final good, shown at the bottom of column (3).

A product usually goes through several stages involving different firms on its way to the consumer. A wooden desk, for example, starts as raw timber, which is typically cut by one firm, milled by another, made into a desk by a third, and retailed by a fourth. We avoid double counting either by including only the market value of the desk when sold to the final user or by *summing the value added at each stage of production.* The **value added** by each firm equals that firm's selling price minus payments for inputs from other firms. The value added at each stage is the income earned by resource suppliers at that stage. *The value added at all stages sums to the market value of the final good, and the value added for all final goods sums to GDP based on the income approach.* For example, suppose you buy a wooden desk for $200. This final market value gets added directly into GDP. Consider the history of that desk. Suppose the tree that gave its life for your studies was cut into a log and sold to a miller for $20, who converted the log to lumber that sold for $50 to a desk maker, who made the desk and sold it for $120 to a retailer, who sold it to you for $200.

Column (1) of Exhibit 1 lists the selling price at each stage of production. If all these transactions were added up, the sum of $390 would exceed the $200 market value of the desk. To avoid double counting, we include only the value added at each stage, listed in column (3) as the difference between the purchase price and the selling price at that stage. Again, *the value added at each stage equals the income earned by those who supply their resources at that stage.* For example, the $80 in value added by the retailer consists of income to resource suppliers at that stage, from the salesperson to the janitor who cleans the showroom to the trucker who provides "free delivery" of your desk. The value added at all stages totals $200, which is both the final market value of the desk and the total income earned by all resource suppliers along the way.

To reinforce your understanding of the equality of income and spending, let's return to something introduced in the first chapter, the circular-flow model.

value added
At each stage of production, the selling price of a product minus the cost of intermediate goods purchased from other firms

Circular Flow of Income and Expenditure

The model in Exhibit 2 outlines the circular flow of income and spending in the economy for not only households and firms, as was the case in Chapter 1, but governments and the rest of the world. The main stream flows clockwise around the circle, first as income from firms to households (in the lower half of the circle), and then as spending from households back to firms (in the upper half of the circle). For each flow of money, there is an equal and opposite flow of products or resources. Here we follow the money.

EXHIBIT 2 Circular Flow of Income and Expenditure

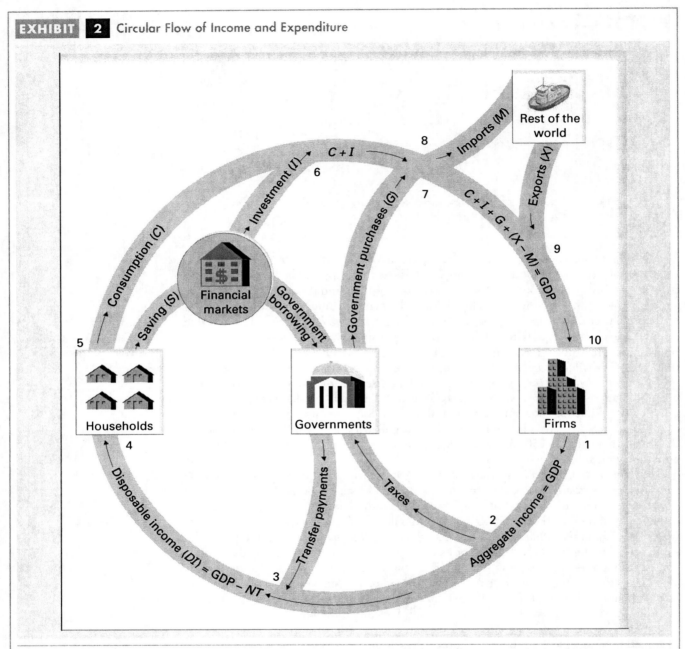

The circular-flow model captures important relationships in the economy. The bottom half depicts the income arising from production. At juncture (1), GDP equals aggregate income. Taxes leak from the flow at (2), but transfer payments enter the flow at (3). Taxes minus transfers equals net taxes, *NT*. Aggregate income minus net taxes equals disposable income, *DI*, which flows to households at juncture (4). The top half of the model shows the flow of expenditure. At (5), households either spend disposable income or save it. Consumption enters the spending flow directly. Saving leaks from the spending flow into financial markets, where it is channeled to borrowers. At (6), investment enters the spending flow. At (7), government purchases enter the spending flow. At (8), imports leak from the spending flow, and at (9), exports enter the spending flow. Consumption plus investment plus government purchases plus net exports add up to the aggregate expenditure on GDP received by firms at (10).

Income Half of the Circular Flow

To develop a circular flow of income and spending, we must make some simplifying assumptions. Specifically, by assuming that physical capital does not wear out (i.e., no capital depreciation) and that firms pay out all profits to firm owners (i.e., firms retain no earnings), we can say that *GDP equals aggregate income*. The circular flow is a continuous process, but the logic of the model is clearest if we begin at juncture (1) in Exhibit 2, where U.S. firms make production decisions. After all, production must occur before output can be sold and income earned. As Henry Ford explained, "It is not the employer who pays the wages—the employer only handles the money. It is the product that pays wages." Households supply their labor, capital, natural resources, and entrepreneurial ability to make products that sell to pay wages, interest, rent, and profit. Production of aggregate output, or GDP, gives rise to an equal amount of aggregate income.

Thus, at juncture (1), aggregate output equals aggregate income. But not all that income is available to spend. At juncture (2), governments collect taxes. Some of these tax dollars return as transfer payments to the income stream at juncture (3). By subtracting taxes and adding transfers, we transform aggregate income into **disposable income, DI,** which flows to households at juncture (4). Disposable income is take-home pay, which households can spend or save.

The bottom half of this circular flow is the *income half* because it focuses on the income arising from production. Aggregate income is the total income from producing GDP, and disposable income is the income remaining after taxes are subtracted and transfers added. To simplify the discussion, we define **net taxes, NT,** as taxes minus transfer payments. So *disposable income equals GDP minus net taxes.* Put another way, we can say that aggregate income equals disposable income plus net taxes:

$$GDP = \text{Aggregate income} = DI + NT$$

At juncture (4), firms have produced output and have paid resource suppliers; governments have collected taxes and made transfer payments. With the resulting disposable income in hand, households now decide how much to spend and how much to save. Because firms have already produced the output and have paid resource suppliers, firms wait to see how much consumers want to spend. Any unsold production gets added to firm inventories.

Expenditure Half of the Circular Flow

Disposable income splits at juncture (5). Part is spent on consumption, *C*, and the rest is saved, *S*. Thus,

$$DI = C + S$$

Consumption remains in the circular flow and is the biggest aggregate expenditure, about 70 percent of the total. Household saving flows to **financial markets,** which consist of banks and other financial institutions that link savers to borrowers. For simplicity, Exhibit 2 shows households as the only savers, though governments, firms, and the rest of the world could save as well (for example, savings from China finance U.S. borrowers). The primary borrowers are firms and governments, but households borrow too, particularly for new homes, and the rest of the world also borrows. In reality, financial markets should be connected to all four economic decision makers, but we have simplified the flows to keep the model from looking like a plate of spaghetti.

In our simplified model, firms pay resource suppliers an amount equal to the entire value of output. With nothing left for investment, firms must borrow to finance purchases of physical capital plus any increases in their inventories. Households also borrow to

disposable income (DI)
The income households have available to spend or to save after paying taxes and receiving transfer payments

net taxes (NT)
Taxes minus transfer payments

financial markets
Banks and other financial institutions that facilitate the flow of funds from savers to borrowers

purchase new homes. Therefore, investment, *I*, consists of spending on new capital by firms, including inventory changes, plus spending on residential construction. Investment enters the circular flow at juncture (6), so aggregate spending at that point totals *C* + *I*.

Governments must also borrow whenever they incur deficits, that is, whenever their total *outlays*—transfer payments plus purchases of goods and services—exceed their revenues. Government purchases of goods and services, represented by *G*, enter the spending stream in the upper half of the circular flow at juncture (7). Remember that *G excludes* transfer payments, which already entered the stream as income at juncture (3).

Some spending by households, firms, and governments goes for imports. Because spending on imports flows to foreign producers, spending on imports, *M*, leaks from the circular flow at juncture (8). But the rest of the world buys U.S. products, so foreign spending on U.S. exports, *X*, enters the spending flow at juncture (9). Net exports, the impact of the *rest of the world* on aggregate expenditure, equal exports minus imports, *X* − *M*, which can be positive, negative, or zero. In recent decades, net exports have been negative.

The upper half of the circular flow, the *expenditure half*, tracks the four components of aggregate expenditure: consumption, *C*; investment, *I*; government purchases, *G*; and net exports, *X* − *M*. Aggregate expenditure flows into firms at juncture (10). Aggregate expenditure equals the market value of aggregate output, or GDP. In short,

$$C + I + G + (X - M) = \text{Aggregate expenditure} = \text{GDP}$$

Leakages Equal Injections

Let's step back now to view the big picture. In the upper half of the circular flow, aggregate expenditure is total spending on U.S. output. In the lower half, aggregate income is the income arising from that spending. This is the first accounting identity. Aggregate expenditure (spending by each sector) equals aggregate income (disposable income plus net taxes), or

$$C + I + G + (X - M) = DI + NT$$

Because disposable income equals consumption plus saving, we can substitute *C* + *S* for *DI* in the above equation to yield

$$C + I + G + (X - M) = C + S + NT$$

After subtracting *C* from both sides and adding *M* to both sides, the equation reduces to

$$I + G + X = S + NT + M$$

injection

Any spending other than by households or any income other than from resource earnings; includes investment, government purchases, exports, and transfer payments

leakage

Any diversion of income from the domestic spending stream; includes saving, taxes, and imports

Note that **injections** into the main stream occur at various points around the circular flow. Investment, *I*, government purchases, *G*, and exports, *X*, are *injections* of spending into the circular flow. At the same time, some of the circular flow leaks from the main stream. Saving, *S*, net taxes, *NT*, and imports, *M*, are **leakages** from the circular flow. As you can see from the equation, *injections into the circular flow equal leakages from the flow*. This injections-leakages equality demonstrates a second accounting identity based on double-entry bookkeeping.

Limitations of National Income Accounting

Imagine the difficulty of developing an accounting system that must capture such a complex and dynamic economy. In the interest of clarity and simplicity, certain features get neglected. In this section, we examine some limitations of the national income accounting system, beginning with production not captured by GDP.

Some Production Is Not Included in GDP

With some minor exceptions, GDP includes only those products that are sold in markets. This ignores all do-it-yourself production—child care, meal preparation, house cleaning, family laundry, and home maintenance and repair. Thus, an economy in which householders are largely self-sufficient has a lower GDP than an otherwise similar economy in which households specialize and sell products to one another. During the 1950s, more than 80 percent of American mothers with small children remained at home caring for the family, but all this care added not one cent to GDP. Today most mothers with small children are in the workforce, where their labor gets counted in GDP. Meals, child care, and the like are now often purchased in markets and thus get reflected in GDP. In less developed economies, more economic activity is do-it-yourself.

GDP also ignores off-the-books production. The term **underground economy** describes market activity that goes unreported because either it's illegal or because people want to evade taxes on otherwise legal activity. Although there is no official measure of the underground economy, most economists agree that it is substantial. A federal study suggests the equivalent of 10 percent of U.S. GDP is underground production; this would have amounted to about $1.5 trillion in 2011.

For some economic activity, income must be *imputed*, or assigned a value, because market exchange does not occur. For example, included in GDP is an *imputed rental income* from home ownership, even though no rent is actually paid or received. Also included in GDP is an imputed dollar amount for (1) wages paid *in kind*, such as employers' payments for employees' medical insurance, and (2) food produced by farm families for their own consumption. *GDP therefore includes some economic production that does not involve market exchange.*

underground economy
Market transactions that go unreported either because they are illegal or because people involved want to evade taxes

Leisure, Quality, and Variety

The average U.S. workweek is much shorter now than it was a century ago, so people work less to produce today's output. People also retire earlier and live longer after retirement. As a result of a shorter work week and earlier retirement, more leisure is available. But leisure is not reflected in GDP because it is not directly bought and sold in a market. The quality and variety of products available have also improved on average over the years because of technological advances and greater competition. For example, the magazine *Consumer Reports* finds a consistent improvement in the quality of the automobile over time. Yet most of these improvements are not reflected in GDP. Recording systems, computers, tires, running shoes, cell phones, and hundreds of other products have gotten better over the years. Also, new products are being introduced all the time, such as smartphones, e-readers, and energy drinks. *The gross domestic product fails to capture changes in the availability of leisure time and often fails to reflect changes in the quality of products or in the availability of new products.*

What's Gross About Gross Domestic Product?

In the course of producing GDP, some capital wears out, such as the delivery truck that finally dies, and some capital becomes obsolete, such as an aging computer that can't run the latest software. A new truck that logs 100,000 miles its first year has been subject to wear and tear, and therefore has a diminished value as a resource. A truer picture of the *net* production that actually occurs during a year is found by subtracting this capital

depreciation

The value of capital stock used up to produce GDP or that becomes obsolete during the year

net domestic product

Gross domestic product minus depreciation

depreciation from GDP. **Depreciation** measures the value of the capital stock that is used up or becomes obsolete in the production process. Gross domestic product is called "gross" because it fails to take into account this depreciation. **Net domestic product** equals gross domestic product minus depreciation, the capital stock used up in the production process.

We now have two measures of investment. *Gross investment* is the value of all investment during a year and is used in computing GDP. *Net investment* equals gross investment minus depreciation. The economy's production possibilities depend on what happens to net investment. If net investment is positive—that is, if gross investment exceeds depreciation—the economy's capital stock increases, so its contribution to output increases as well. If net investment is zero, the capital stock remains constant, as does its contribution to output. And if net investment is negative, the capital stock declines, as does its contribution to output.

As the names imply, *gross* domestic product reflects gross investment and *net* domestic product reflects net investment. But estimating depreciation involves some guesswork. For example, what is the appropriate measure of depreciation for the roller coasters at Six Flags, the metal display shelves at Wal-Mart, or the parking lots at the Mall of America in Minnesota?

GDP Does Not Reflect All Costs

Some production and consumption degrades the quality of our environment. Trucks and automobiles pump pollution into the atmosphere, which may contribute to climate change. Housing developments displace scenic open space and forests. Paper mills foul the lungs and burn the eyes. Oil spills foul the coastline. These negative externalities—costs that fall on those not directly involved in the transactions—are mostly ignored in GDP calculations, even though they diminish the quality of life now and in the future. To the extent that growth in GDP generates negative externalities, a rising GDP may not be as attractive as it would first appear.

Although the national income accounts reflect the depreciation of buildings, machinery, vehicles, and other manufactured capital, this accounting ignores the depletion of natural resources, such as standing timber, oil reserves, fish stocks, and soil fertility. So national income accounts reflect depreciation of the physical capital stock but not the natural capital stock. For example, intensive farming may raise productivity and boost GDP temporarily, but this depletes soil fertility. Worse still, some production may speed the extinction of certain plants and animals. The U.S. Commerce Department is now in the process of developing so-called *green accounting*, or *green GDP*, trying to register the impact of production on air pollution, water pollution, soil depletion, and the loss of other natural resources.

GDP and Economic Welfare

In computing GDP, the market price of output is the measure of its value. Therefore, each dollar spent on handguns or cigarettes is counted in GDP the same as each dollar spent on baby formula or fitness programs. Positive economic analysis tries to avoid making value judgments about *how* people spend their money. Because GDP, as a number, provides no information about its composition, some economists question whether GDP is the best measure of the nation's economic welfare. One challenge to the dominance of GDP as a measure of national progress may come not from another single measure but from hundreds of measures compiled by a nonprofit group called The State of the USA. This is discussed in the following case study.

PUBLIC POLICY

GDP and The State of the USA   GDP estimates have been refined for decades and are arguably the most complex data aggregation effort in the world. But they have their limits, as discussed already, and they have their critics. One criticism is that GDP leaves out much of what's going on in the nation—with health care, the environment, the family, energy use, and so on. One challenge to GDP as the primary indicator of national progress is coming from a nonprofit group that has developed a Web site to bring together hundreds of indicators. The idea is to help Americans assess the progress of the United States by using quality data selected by experts.

First, a little background. In 2003, a team at the U.S. Government Accountability Office, the investigative arm of Congress, was looking for alternatives to GDP to assess national progress. The team became an independent nonprofit agency in 2007 and took the name "The State of the USA." With startup funding from the Gates, Hewlett, MacArthur, and Rockefeller foundations, the group set out to identify data that would amount to a report card on how the country is doing in specific areas—such as health care, education, the environment, safety, energy, transportation, the economy, the family, and so forth. The goal is to help citizens and leaders assess what progress has been made and where we need to improve.

The effort got a big boost from a small provision in the massive 2010 health care bill that requires Congress to help finance and oversee a "key national indicator system." State of the USA will become that system, overseen by the National Academy of Sciences, a group of preeminent scholars established by Abraham Lincoln in 1863 to "investigate, examine, experiment, and report upon any subject of science or art" whenever called upon to do so by any department of the government (half the 20 economists in the National Academy are Nobel laureates). Along with the federal authorization came federal funding totaling $70 million between 2010 and 2018.

The objective is not so much to replace GDP as the primary measure of economic performance, but to broaden the conversation and the debate by including many more data series. Instead of just having one gauge on the dashboard, GDP, there would be many gauges. The State of the USA Web site went live in 2010, and is accessible for free. Eventually, The State of the USA plans to offer about 300 indicators. Rather than develop original data, the site compiles and displays data gathered by others. Despite the number of data series, the group says the site will be selective, not encyclopedic. For example, in health care alone the government collects about 1,000 different measures. The State of the USA offers what they claim are the 20 most crucial health care measures. The group says its objective is not to interpret the data but to disseminate it in a strictly nonpartisan manner.

The idea is to offer data in a form that can be easily shared to promote as wide a distribution as possible. Data will be available on the national level, state level, and as far down the jurisdictional chain as possible. For example, one of the 20 health care measures reports smoking rates by state (West Virginia is the highest and Utah is the lowest). The State of the USA will also offer a variety of interactive features to encourage exploration, such as motion charts with audio tutorials focusing on health costs and outcomes for the developed world. Check out the site and see what you think.

Sources: Jon Gertner, "The Rise and Fall of the G.D.P." *New York Times*, 10 May 2010; and The State of the USA site at http://www.stateoftheusa.org/.

e activity
The Bureau of Economic Analysis is charged with estimating GDP and its components. You can find selected National Income and Product Account tables at http://www.bea.gov/national/nipaweb/index.asp. Choose "list of Selected NIPA Tables." Table 1.1.1 tells you by how much each component has grown. Table 1.1.2 shows the contribution of each component to GDP growth. Can you explain the difference between these two types of statistics? The BEA also produces the monthly report, *Survey of Current Business*, with articles describing and interpreting national income data. The current issue and back issues are accessible through http://www.bea.gov/scb/index.htm. Compare what you find at the BEA site to what you find at The State of the USA.

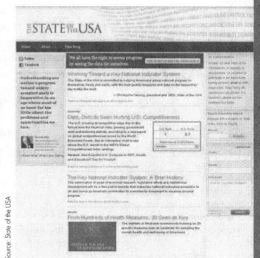

Source: State of the USA

Despite the limitations of official GDP estimates, GDP offers a useful snapshot of the U.S. economy at a point in time. Inflation, however, clouds comparability over time. In the next section, we discuss how to adjust GDP for changes in the economy's price level.

Accounting for Price Changes

As noted earlier, the national income accounts are based on the market values of final goods and services produced in a particular year. Initially, gross domestic product measures the value of output in *nominal dollars*—that is, in the dollar values at the time production occurs. When GDP is based on nominal dollars, the national income accounts measure the *nominal value* of national output. Thus, **nominal GDP** is based on the prices prevailing when production takes place. National income accounts based on nominal dollars allow for comparisons among income or expenditure components in a particular year. Because the economy's average price level changes over time, however, nominal-dollar comparisons across years can be misleading. For example, between 1979 and 1980, nominal GDP increased by about 9 percent. That sounds impressive, but the economy's average price level rose more than 9 percent. So the growth in nominal GDP came entirely from inflation. Real GDP, or GDP measured in terms of the goods and services produced, in fact declined. If nominal GDP increases in a given year, part of this increase may simply reflect inflation—pure hot air. To make meaningful comparisons of GDP across years, we must take out the hot air, or *deflate* nominal GDP. We focus on *real* changes in production by eliminating changes due solely to inflation.

nominal GDP
GDP based on prices prevailing at the time of production

Price Indexes

To compare the price level over time, let's first establish a point of reference, a base year to which prices in other years can be compared. An *index number* compares the value of some variable in a particular year to its value in a base year, or reference year. Think about the simplest of index numbers. Suppose bread is the only good produced in an economy. As a reference point, let's look at its price in some specific year. The year selected is called the **base year**; prices in other years are expressed relative to the base-year price.

base year
The year with which other years are compared when constructing an index; the index equals 100 in the base year

price index
A number that shows the average price of products; changes in a price index over time show changes in the economy's average price level

Suppose the base year is 2009, when a loaf of bread in our simple economy sold for $1.25. Let's say the price of bread increased to $1.30 in 2010 and to $1.40 in 2011. We construct a **price index** by dividing each year's price by the price in the base year and then multiplying by 100, as shown in Exhibit 3. For 2009, the base year, we divide the base price of bread by itself, $1.25/$1.25, or 1, so the price index in 2009 equals 1 × 100 = 100. *The price index in the base period is always 100.* The price index in 2010 is $1.30/$1.25, or 1.04, which when multiplied by 100 equals 104. In 2011, the index is $1.40/$1.25, or 1.12, which when multiplied by 100 equals 112. Thus, the index is 4 percent higher in 2010 than in the base year and 12 percent higher in 2011 than in the base year. The price index permits comparisons across years. For example, what if you were provided the indexes for 2010 and 2011 and asked what happened to the price level between the two years? By dividing the 2011 price index by the 2010 price index, 112/104, you find that the price level rose 7.7 percent.

This section has shown how to develop a price index assuming we already know the price level each year. Determining the price level is a bit more involved, as we'll now see.

EXHIBIT 3 Hypothetical Example of a Price Index (base year = 2009)

Year	(1) Price of Bread in Current Year	(2) Price of Bread in Base Year	(3) Price Index (3) = [(1)/(2)] × 100
2009	$1.25	$1.25	100
2010	1.30	1.25	104
2011	1.40	1.25	112

The price index equals the price in the current year divided by the price in the base year, all multiplied by 100.

Consumer Price Index

The price index most familiar to you is the **consumer price index, or CPI,** which measures changes over time in the cost of buying a "market basket" of goods and services purchased by a typical family. For simplicity, suppose a typical family's market basket for the year includes 365 packages of Twinkies, 500 gallons of heating oil, and 12 months of cable TV. Prices in the base year are listed in column (2) of Exhibit 4. The total cost of each product in the base year is found by multiplying price by quantity, as shown in column (3). The cost of the market basket in the base year is shown at the bottom of column (3) to be $1,184.85.

Prices in the current year are listed in column (4). Notice that not all prices changed by the same percentage since the base year. The price of fuel oil increased by 50 percent, but the price of Twinkies declined. The cost of that same basket in the current year is $1,398.35, shown as the sum of column (5). To compute the consumer price index for the current year, we simply divide the cost in the current year by the cost of that same basket in the base year, $1,398.35/$1,184.85, and then multiply by 100. This yields a price index of 118. We could say that between the base period and the current year, the "cost of living" increased by 18 percent, although not all prices increased by the same percentage.

The federal government uses the 36 months of 1982, 1983, and 1984 as the base period for calculating the CPI for a market basket consisting of hundreds of goods and services. The CPI is reported monthly based on prices collected from about 23,000 sellers across the country in 87 metropolitan areas. In reality, each household consumes a unique market basket, so we could theoretically develop about 115 million CPIs—one for each household.

consumer price index, or CPI
A measure of inflation based on the cost of a fixed market basket of goods and services

net bookmark

Use the Inflation Calculator to see how inflation as measured by the CPI has changed prices over the years. Enter a dollar amount in the top box, such as current tuition or wages. Choose the current year for the second box and some year in the past for the third box. Select Calculate to see the inflation-adjusted amount in the past. You can also start with an amount for the past (for example, what your grandparents paid for movie tickets) and calculate a value in the present. Find the calculator at http://data.bls.gov/cgi-bin/cpicalc.pl.

EXHIBIT 4 Hypothetical Market Basket Used to Develop the Consumer Price Index

Product	(1) Quantity in Market Basket	(2) Prices in Base Year	(3) Cost of Basket in Base Year (3) = (1) × (2)	(4) Prices in Current Year	(5) Cost of Basket in Current Year (5) = (1) × (4)
Twinkies	365 packages	$ 0.89/package	$324.85	$ 0.79	$288.35
Fuel Oil	500 gallons	1.00/gallon	500.00	1.50	750.00
Cable TV	12 months	30.00/month	360.00	30.00	360.00
			$1,184.85		$1,398.35

The cost of a market basket in the current year, shown at the bottom of column (5), sums the quantities of each item in the basket, shown in column (1), times the price of each item in the current year, shown in column (4).

Problems With the CPI

There is no perfect way to measure changes in the price level. As we have already seen, the quality and variety of some products are improving all the time, so some price increases may be as much a reflection of improved quality as of inflation. Thus, there is a *quality bias* in the CPI, because it assumes that the quality of the market basket remains relatively constant over time. *To the extent that the CPI ignores quality improvements, it overstates the true extent of inflation.* Those who come up with the CPI each month try to make some quality adjustments, as discussed in the following case study.

e activity

At http://www.bls.gov/cpi/
cpiqa.htm, the Bureau of Labor
Statistics addresses common
misconceptions about the
Consumer Price Index. Find
out how food, energy, and
housing are incorporated into
the index. You can also read
about substitution effects and
hedonic quality adjustments.

PUBLIC POLICY

Price Check on Aisle 2   The U.S. economy is one of the most dynamic in the world, marked by rapid technological change. The Bureau of Labor Statistics (BLS), the government agency that calculates the CPI each month, employs dozens of economists to analyze the impact of any quality changes to products in the CPI market basket. Each month 400 data collectors visit stores to record about 85,000 prices for 211 item categories in the CPI basket. About a week before the CPI is released, the BLS office is locked down with bright red "restricted area" signs on all the doors. A total of 90 people, including product specialists and the other economists working on the CPI, compute the basic indexes in each category. Results are released at 8:30 A.M., Eastern Time, about two weeks after the end of the month in question. This release is a big deal.

Most price adjustments are straightforward. For example, if a candy bar shrinks but its price doesn't, the CPI shows this as a price increase. But sometimes a product changed in a more complicated way. Each economist at BLS specializes in particular products, such as televisions, automobiles, kitchen appliances, and so on. One of their greatest challenges is to identify substitutes for products that are no longer available. For example, data collectors find the model of TV they priced the previous month is missing about one-fifth of the time. When a particular product is missing, a four-page checklist of features such as screen size and the type of remote control guides the data collector to the nearest comparable model. That price is reported and the product specialist in Washington must then decide whether it's an acceptable substitute.

For example, the TV specialist decided that the newer version of the 27-inch model had some important improvements, including a flat screen. A complex computer model estimated that the improvements alone would be valued by consumers as worth $135 more. After factoring improvements into the price of the $330 set, the analyst determined that the price of the TV had actually declined 29 percent [= 135/(330 + 135)]. In another example, the price of a 57-inch TV dropped from $2,239 to $1,910, for an apparent decline of 15 percent. But on closer inspection, the analyst found that the new model lacked an HDTV tuner that had been included in the model it replaced. This tuner would be valued by consumers at $514. So, instead of declining 15 percent, the price of the 57-inch TV actually rose 11 percent [= 1,910/(2,239 − 514)].

The TV analyst is applying the *hedonic method*, which breaks down the item under consideration into its characteristics, and then estimates the dollar value of each characteristic. This is a way of capturing the impact of a change in product quality on any price change. Otherwise, price changes would

Digital Vision/Getty Images

not reflect the fact that consumers are getting more or less for their money as product features change over time.

Sources: Jon Hilsenrath, "A Deeper Look at the Fed's Inflation Debate," *Wall Street Journal*, 5 April 2010; Javier Hernandez, "Prices of Consumer Goods Hold Steady, Indicating That Inflation Is at Bay," *New York Times*, 18 March 2010; and Mary Kokoski, Keith Waehrer, and Patricia Rosaklis, "Using Hedonic Methods for Quality Adjustment in the CPI," U.S. Bureau of Labor Statistics Working Paper (2000) found at http://www.bls.gov/cpi/cpiaudio.htm.

But the CPI tends to overstate inflation for another reason. Recall that the CPI holds constant over time the kind and amount of goods and services in the typical market basket. Because not all items in the market basket experience the same rate of price change, relative prices change over time. A rational household would respond to changes in relative prices by buying less of the more expensive products and more of the cheaper products. The CPI allows for some substitution within narrow categories (for example shoppers in Chicago can switch among choices of ground beef based on price), but consumers can't easily switch across categories because the point of the CPI is to look at price changes over time for a given market basket. Because the CPI holds the market basket constant for long periods, the CPI is slow to incorporate consumer responses to changes in relative prices. *The CPI calculations, by not allowing households to shift away from goods that have become more costly, overestimates the true extent of inflation experienced by the typical household.*

The CPI has also failed to keep up with the consumer shift toward discount stores such as Wal-Mart, Target, and Home Depot. Government statisticians consider goods sold by discounters as different from goods sold by regular retailers. Hence, the discounter's lower price does not necessarily translate into a reduction in the cost of living, but simply as a different consumer purchase decision.

Finally, the CPI overstates inflation because it includes an item in the market basket only after the product becomes widely used. By that time, the major price drops have already taken place. For example, the first portable video recorder and camera, the Ampex VR-3000 Backpack, weighed over 40 pounds and sold for $65,000. Now for less than $200 you can buy a high definition video camera that fits in your pocket. The CPI captured little of the major price drops. The same is true for all kinds of new products, such as the cell phone, which began as big as a brick and priced north of $1,000. Only after the price of cell phones fell far enough for wide adoption, did they make the CPI basket.

Experts conclude the CPI has overestimated inflation by about 1 percent per year. This problem is of more than academic concern because changes in the CPI determine changes in tax brackets and in an array of payments, including wage agreements that include a cost-of-living adjustment, Social Security benefits totaling more than $500 billion annually, welfare benefits, even alimony. In fact, about 30 percent of federal outlays are tied to changes in the CPI. A 1 percent correction in the upward bias of the CPI would save the federal budget nearly $200 billion annually by 2015.

Overstating the CPI also distorts other measures, such as wages, that use the CPI to adjust for inflation. For example, based on the official CPI, the average real wage in the U.S. economy fell by a total of about 2 percent in the last two decades. But if the CPI overstated inflation by 1 percent per year, as researchers now believe, then the average real wage, instead of dropping by 2 percent, actually increased by about 20 percent. The Bureau of Labor Statistics, the group that estimates the CPI, is now working on these problems and has introduced an experimental version of the CPI that would reduce measured inflation. One experiment uses scanner data at supermarkets to find out how consumers respond, for example, to a rise in the price of romaine lettuce relative to iceberg lettuce, two products assumed to be reasonable substitutes.

The GDP Price Index

GDP price index

A comprehensive inflation measure of all goods and services included in the gross domestic product

A price index is a weighted sum of various prices. Whereas the CPI focuses on just a sample of consumer purchases, a more complex and more comprehensive price index, the **GDP price index,** measures the average price of all goods and services produced in the economy. To calculate the GDP price index, we use the formula

$$\text{GDP price index} = \frac{\text{Nominal GDP} \times 100}{\text{Real GDP}}$$

where nominal GDP is the dollar value of GDP in a particular year measured in prices of that same year, and real GDP is the dollar value of GDP in a particular year measured in base-year prices. The challenge is finding real GDP in a particular year. Any measure of real GDP is constructed as the weighted sum of thousands of different goods and services produced in the economy. The question is what weights, or prices, to use. Prior to 1995, the Bureau of Economic Analysis (BEA) used prices for a particular base year (most recently 1987) to estimate real GDP. In this case, the quantity of each output in a particular year was valued by using the 1987 price of each output. So real GDP in, say, 1994 was the sum of 1994 output valued at 1987 prices.

Moving From Fixed Weights to Chain Weights

chain-weighted system

An inflation measure that adjusts the weights from year to year in calculating a price index, thereby reducing the bias caused by a fixed-price weighting system

Estimating real GDP by using prices from a base year yields an accurate measure of real GDP as long as the year in question is close to the base year. But BEA used prices that prevailed in 1987 to value production from 1929 to 1995. In early 1996, BEA switched from a fixed-price weighting system to a **chain-weighted system,** using a complicated process that changes price weights from year to year. All you need to know is that the chain-weighted real GDP adjusts the weights more or less continuously from year to year, reducing the bias caused by a fixed-price weighting system.

Even though the chain-type index adjusts the weights from year to year, any index, by definition, must still use some year as an anchor, or reference point—that is, any index must answer the question, "Compared to what?" To provide such a reference point, BEA measures U.S. real GDP and its components in *chained (2005) dollars.* Exhibit 5 presents nominal-dollar estimates of GDP as well as chained (2005) dollar estimates of real GDP. The blue line indicates nominal-dollar GDP since 1959. The red line indicates real GDP since 1959, or GDP measured in chained (2005) dollars. The two lines intersect in 2005, because that's when real GDP equaled nominal GDP. Nominal GDP is below real GDP in years prior to 2005 because real GDP is based on chained (2005) prices, which on average are higher than prices prior to 2005. Nominal GDP reflects growth in real GDP and in the price level. Chained-dollar GDP reflects growth only in real GDP. So nominal-dollar GDP grows faster than chained-dollar GDP.

Conclusion

This chapter discussed how GDP is measured and how it's adjusted for changes in the price level over time. The national income accounts have limitations, but they offer a reasonably accurate picture of the economy at a point in time as well as year-to-year movements in the economy. Subsequent chapters will refer to the distinction between real and nominal values.

The national income accounts are published in much greater detail than this chapter indicates. The appendix provides some flavor of the additional detail available.

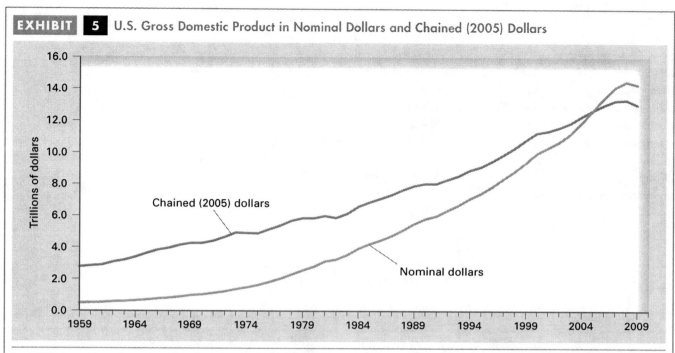

EXHIBIT 5 U.S. Gross Domestic Product in Nominal Dollars and Chained (2005) Dollars

Real GDP, the red line, shows the value of output measured in chained (2005) dollars. The blue line measures GDP in nominal dollars of each year shown. The two lines intersect in 2005, when real GDP equaled nominal GDP. Year-to-year changes in nominal-dollar GDP reflect changes in both real GDP and in the price level. Year-to-year changes in chained-dollar GDP reflect changes in real GDP only. Nominal-dollar GDP grows faster than chained-dollar GDP. Prior to 2005, nominal-dollar prices are less than chained-dollar prices, so nominal-dollar GDP is less than chained-dollar GDP.

Source: Based on annual estimates from the Bureau of Economic Analysis, U.S. Department of Commerce. For the latest data, go to http://bea.gov/national/index.htm#gdp.

Summary

1. Gross domestic product, or GDP, measures the market value of all final goods and services produced during the year by resources located in the United States, regardless of who owns those resources.

2. The expenditure approach to GDP adds up the market value of all final goods and services produced in the economy during the year. The income approach to GDP adds up all the income generated as a result of that production.

3. The circular-flow model summarizes the flow of income and spending through the economy. The aggregate income from producing GDP equals the aggregate expenditure from purchasing that GDP. Thus, aggregate income equals aggregate expenditure. Saving, net taxes, and imports leak from the circular flow. These leakages equal the injections into the circular flow from investment, government purchases, and exports. Thus, leakages from the circular flow equal injections into the circular flow.

4. GDP reflects market production in a given period, usually a year. Most household production and the underground economy are not captured by GDP. Improvements in the quality and variety of products also are not fully reflected in GDP. Nor are changes in leisure captured in GDP. In other ways GDP may overstate the value of production. GDP fails to subtract for the depreciation of the capital stock or for the depletion of natural resources and fails to account for most negative externalities arising from production.

5. Nominal GDP in a particular year values output based on market prices when the output was produced. To determine real GDP, nominal GDP must be adjusted for price changes. The consumer price index, or CPI, tracks prices for a basket of goods and services over time. The GDP price index tracks price changes for all output. No adjustment for price changes is perfect, but current approaches offer a reasonably good estimate of real GDP both at a point in time and over time.

Key Concepts

Expenditure approach to GDP   121

Income approach to GDP   121

Final goods and services   121

Intermediate goods and services   121

Double counting   121

Consumption   121

Investment   122

Physical capital   122

Residential construction   122

Inventories   122

Government purchases   122

Net exports   122

Aggregate expenditure   122

Aggregate income   122

Value added   123

Disposable income (DI)   125

Net taxes (NT)   125

Financial markets   125

Injection   126

Leakage   126

Underground economy   127

Depreciation   128

Net domestic product   128

Nominal GDP   130

Base year   130

Price index   130

Consumer price index, or CPI   131

GDP price index   134

Chain-weighted system   134

Questions for Review

1. NATIONAL INCOME ACCOUNTING   Identify the component of aggregate expenditure to which each of the following belongs:

   a. A U.S. resident's purchase of a new automobile manufactured in Japan
   b. A household's purchase of one hour of legal advice
   c. Construction of a new house
   d. An increase in semiconductor inventories over last year's level
   e. A city government's acquisition of 10 new police cars

2. NATIONAL INCOME ACCOUNTING   Define gross domestic product. Determine which of the following would be included in the 2011 U.S. gross domestic product:

   a. Profits earned by Ford Motor Company in 2011 on automobile production in Ireland
   b. Automobile parts manufactured in the United States in 2011 but not used until 2012
   c. Social Security benefits paid by the U.S. government in 2011
   d. Ground beef purchased and used by McDonald's in 2011
   e. Ground beef purchased and consumed by a private U.S. household in 2011
   f. Goods and services purchased in the United States in 2011 by a Canadian tourist

3. NATIONAL INCOME ACCOUNTING   Explain why intermediate goods and services usually are not included directly in GDP. Are there any circumstances under which they would be included directly?

4. LEAKAGES AND INJECTIONS   What are the leakages from and injections into the circular flow? How are leakages and injections related in the circular flow?

5. INVESTMENT   In national income accounting, one component of investment is net changes in inventories. Last year's inventories are subtracted from this year's inventories to obtain a net change. Explain why net inventory increases are counted as part of GDP. Also, discuss why it is not sufficient to measure the level of inventories only for the current year. (Remember the difference between stocks and flows.)

6. LIMITATIONS OF NATIONAL INCOME ACCOUNTING   Explain why each of the following should be taken into account when GDP data are used to compare the "level of well-being" in different countries:

   a. Population levels
   b. The distribution of income
   c. The amount of production that takes place outside of markets
   d. The length of the average work week
   e. The level of environmental pollution

7. NOMINAL GDP   Which of the following is a necessary condition—something that must occur—for nominal GDP to rise? Explain your answers.

   a. Actual production must increase.
   b. The price level must increase.
   c. Real GDP must increase.
   d. Both the price level and actual production must increase.
   e. Either the price level or real GDP must increase.

8. PRICE INDEXES   E-readers and HDTVs have not been part of the U.S. economy for very long. Both goods have been decreasing in price and improving in quality. What problems does this pose for people responsible for calculating a price index?

9. GDP AND DEPRECIATION   What is gross about gross domestic product? Could an economy enjoy a constant—or growing—GDP while not replacing worn-out capital?

10. CONSUMER PRICE INDEX   One form of the CPI that has been advocated by lobbying groups is a "CPI for the elderly." The Bureau of Labor Statistics currently produces only indexes for "all urban households" and "urban wage earners and clerical workers." Should the BLS produce such an index for the elderly?

11. GDP PRICE INDEX   The health expenditure component of the GDP price index has been rising steadily. How might this index be biased by quality and substitution effects? Are there any substitutes for health care?

12. Case Study: GDP and The State of the USA   Is The State of the USA designed to replace GDP as the primary measure of economic performance?

13. Case Study: Price Check on Aisle 2   What is the hedonic method and why is it sometimes used to track changes in the consumer price index?

Problems and Exercises

14. **INCOME APPROACH TO GDP**   How does the income approach to measuring GDP differ from the expenditure approach? Explain the meaning of *value added* and its importance in the income approach. Consider the following data for the selling price at each stage in the production of a 5-pound bag of flour sold by your local grocer. Use the value-added approach to calculate the final market value of the flour.

Stage of Production	Sale Price
Farmer	$0.30
Miller	0.50
Wholesaler	1.00
Grocer	1.50

15. **EXPENDITURE APPROACH TO GDP**   Given the following annual information about a hypothetical country, answer questions a through d.

	Billions of Dollars
Personal consumption expenditures	$200
Personal taxes	50
Exports	30
Depreciation	10
Government purchases	50
Gross private domestic investment	40
Imports	40
Government transfer payments	20

a. What is the value of GDP?
b. What is the value of net domestic product?
c. What is the value of net investment?
d. What is the value of net exports?

16. **INVESTMENT**   Given the following data, answer questions a through c.

	Billions of Dollars
New residential construction	$500
Purchases of existing homes	250
Sales value of newly issued stocks and bonds	600
New physical capital	800
Depreciation	200
Household purchases of new furniture	50
Net change in firms' inventories	100
Production of new intermediate goods	700

a. What is the value of gross private domestic investment?
b. What is the value of net investment?
c. Are any intermediate goods counted in gross investment?

17. **CONSUMER PRICE INDEX**   Calculate a new consumer price index for the data in Exhibit 4 in this chapter. Assume that current-year prices of Twinkies, fuel oil, and cable TV are $0.95/package, $1.25/gallon, and $15.00/month, respectively. Calculate the current year's cost of the market basket and the value of the current year's price index. What is this year's percentage change in the price level compared to the base year?

18. **CONSUMER PRICE INDEX**   Given the following data, what was the value of the consumer price index in the base year? Calculate the annual rate of consumer price inflation in 2012 in each of the following situations:

a. The CPI equals 200 in 2011 and 240 in 2012.
b. The CPI equals 150 in 2011 and 175 in 2012.
c. The CPI equals 325 in 2011 and 340 in 2012.
d. The CPI equals 325 in 2011 and 315 in 2012.

Global Economic Watch Exercises

Login to www.cengagebrain.com and access the Global Economic Watch to do these exercises.

19. **GLOBAL ECONOMIC WATCH**   Go to the Global Economic Crisis Resource Center. Select Global Issues in Context. In the Basic Search box at the top of the page, enter the phrase "G.D.P. R.I.P." On the Results page, go to the Global Viewpoints Section. Click on the link for the August 10, 2009,

article "G.D.P. R.I.P." What does the author mean by "gross domestic transactions"?

20. **GLOBAL ECONOMIC WATCH**   Go to the Global Economic Crisis Resource Center. Select Global Issues in Context. In the Basic Search box at the top of the page, enter the phrase "price index." Write a summary of an article about a price index in a foreign country.

Appendix
National Income Accounts

This chapter has focused on gross domestic product, or GDP, the measure of output of most interest in subsequent chapters. Other economic aggregates also convey useful information and get media attention. One of these, *net domestic product*, has already been introduced. Exhibit 6 shows that net domestic product equals gross domestic product minus depreciation. In this appendix we examine other aggregate measures.

National Income

So far, we have been talking about the value of production from resources located in the United States, regardless of who owns them. Sometimes we want to know how much American resource suppliers earn for their labor, capital, natural resources, and entrepreneurial ability. **National income** captures all income earned by American-owned resources, whether located in the United States or abroad. To get the net value of production from American-owned resources, we add income earned by American resources abroad and subtract income earned by resources in the United States owned by those outside the country. We also account for any statistical discrepancy created by noise in the accounting system.

National income therefore equals net domestic product plus net earnings from American resources abroad minus the statistical discrepancy. Exhibit 6 shows how to go from net domestic product to national income. We have now moved from gross domestic product to net domestic product to national income. Next we peel back another layer from the onion to arrive at personal income, the income people actually receive.

Personal and Disposable Income

Some of the income received this year was not earned this year and some of the income earned this year was not received this year by those who earned it. By adding to national income the income received but not earned and subtracting the income earned but not received, we move from national income to the income *received* by individuals, which is called **personal income**, a widely reported measure of economic welfare. The federal government estimates and reports personal income monthly.

The adjustment from national income to personal income is shown in Exhibit 7. Income *earned but not received* in the current period includes the employer's share of Social Security taxes, taxes on production (e.g., sales and property taxes) net of subsidies, corporate income taxes, and undistributed corporate profits, which are profits the firm retains rather than pays out as dividends. Income *received but not earned* in the current

EXHIBIT 6	Deriving Net Domestic Product and National Income in 2009 (trillions)
Gross domestic product (GDP)	$ 14.26
Minus depreciation	−1.86
Net domestic product	12.40
Plus net earnings of American resources abroad	+0.11
Statistical discrepancy	−0.23
National income	$ 12.28

Source: Figures are nominal estimates for 2009 from the Bureau of Economic Analysis, U.S. Department of Commerce. For the latest figures, go to http://bea.gov/national/index.htm.

EXHIBIT 7	Deriving Personal Income and Disposable Income in 2009 (trillions)
National income	$ 12.28
Income received but not earned minus income earned but not received	−0.26
Personal income	12.02
Minus personal taxes and nontax charges	−1.10
Disposable income	$ 10.92

Source: Figures are nominal estimates for 2009 from the Bureau of Economic Analysis, U.S. Department of Commerce. For the latest figures, go to http://bea.gov/national/index.htm.

period includes government transfer payments, receipts from private pension plans, and interest paid by government and by consumers.

Although business taxes have been considered so far, we have not yet discussed personal taxes, which consist mainly of federal, state, and local personal income taxes and the employee's share of the Social Security tax. Subtracting personal taxes and other government charges from personal income yields *disposable income,* which is the amount available to spend or save—the amount that can be "disposed of" by the household. Think of disposable income as take-home pay. Exhibit 7 shows that personal income minus personal taxes and other government charges yields disposable income.

Summary of National Income Accounts

Let's summarize the income side of national income accounts. We begin with *gross domestic product,* or *GDP,* the market value of all final goods and services produced during the year by resources located in the United States. We subtract depreciation from GDP to yield the *net domestic product.* To net domestic product we add net earnings from American resources abroad and allow for any statistical discrepancy to yield *national income.* We obtain *personal income* by subtracting from national income all income earned this year but not received this year (for example, undistributed corporate profits) and by adding all income received this year but not earned this year (for example, transfer payments). By subtracting personal taxes and other government charges from personal income, we arrive at the bottom line: *disposable income,* the amount people can either spend or save.

Summary Income Statement of the Economy

Exhibit 8 presents an annual income statement for the entire economy. The upper portion lists aggregate expenditure, which consists of consumption, gross investment, government purchases, and net exports. Because imports exceeded exports, net exports are negative. The aggregate income from this expenditure is allocated as shown in the lower portion of Exhibit 8. Some spending goes to cover depreciation, net taxes on production, and the statistical discrepancy; and so it's not received as income by anyone. What remains are five income sources: employee

EXHIBIT 8	Expenditure and Income Statement for the U.S. Economy in 2009 (trillions)
Aggregate Expenditure	
Consumption (C)	$ 10.09
Gross investment (I)	1.63
Government purchases (G)	2.93
Net exports (X − M)	−0.39
GDP	$ 14.26
Aggregate Income	
Depreciation	$1.86
Net taxes on production	1.10
Statistical discrepancy	0.23
Compensation of employees	7.77
Proprietors' income	1.04
Corporate profits	1.31
Net interest	0.68
Rental income of persons	0.27
GDP	$ 14.26

Source: Figures are nominal estimates for 2009 from the Bureau of Economic Analysis, U.S. Department of Commerce. For the latest figures, go to http://bea.gov/national/index.htm.

compensation, proprietors' income, corporate profits, net interest, and rental income of persons. *Employee compensation,* by far the largest income source, includes both money wages and employer contributions to cover Social Security taxes, medical insurance, and other fringe benefits. *Proprietors' income* includes the earnings of unincorporated businesses. *Corporate profits* are the net revenues received by incorporated businesses but before subtracting corporate income taxes. *Net interest* is the interest received by individuals, excluding interest paid by consumers to businesses and interest paid by government.

Each family that owns a home is viewed as a tiny firm that rents that home to itself. Because homeowners do not, in fact, rent homes to themselves, an imputed rental value is based on an estimate of market rent. *Rental income of persons* consists primarily of the imputed rental value of owner-occupied housing minus the cost of owning that property (such as property taxes, insurance, depreciation, and interest paid on the mortgage). From the totals in Exhibit 8, you can see that aggregate spending in the economy equals the income generated by that spending, thus satisfying the accounting identity.

Appendix Questions

1. **NATIONAL INCOME ACCOUNTING** Use the following data to answer the questions below:

	Billions of Dollars ($)
Net investment	110
Depreciation	30
Exports	50
Imports	30
Government purchases	150
Consumption	400
Production taxes (net of subsidies)	35
Income earned but not received	60
Income received but not earned	70
Personal income taxes	50
Employee compensation	455
Corporate profits	60
Rental income	20
Net interest	30
Proprietor's income	40
Net earnings of U.S. resources abroad	40

a. Calculate GDP using the income and the expenditure methods.

b. Calculate gross investment.

c. Calculate net domestic product, national income, personal income, and disposable income.

2. **NATIONAL INCOME ACCOUNTING** According to Exhibit 8 in this chapter, GDP can be calculated either by adding expenditures on final goods or by adding the allocations of these expenditures to the resources used to produce these goods. Why do you suppose the portion of final goods expenditures that goes to pay for intermediate goods or raw materials is excluded from the income method of calculation?

7

Unemployment and Inflation

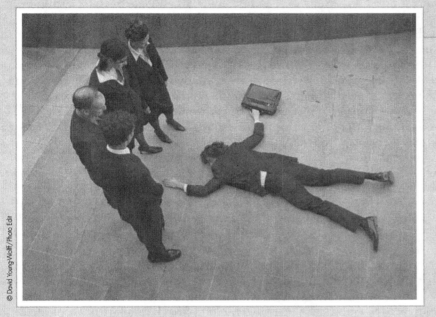

○ Who among the following would be counted as unemployed: a college student who is not working, a bank teller displaced by an automatic teller machine, Kristen Stewart between movies, or baseball slugger Alex Rodriquez in the off-season?

○ What type of unemployment might be healthy for the economy?

○ What's so bad about inflation?

○ Why is anticipated inflation less of a problem than unanticipated inflation?

These and other questions are answered in this chapter, where we explore two macroeconomic problems: unemployment and inflation.

To be sure, unemployment and inflation are not the only problems an economy could face. Sluggish growth and widespread poverty are others. But low unemployment and low inflation go a long way toward reducing other economic problems. Although unemployment and inflation are often related, each is introduced separately. The causes of each and the relationship between the two will become clearer as you learn more about how the economy works.

This chapter shows that not all unemployment or all inflation harms the economy. Even in a healthy economy, a certain amount of unemployment reflects the voluntary choices of workers and employers seeking their best options. And low inflation that is fully anticipated creates fewer distortions than does unanticipated inflation.

Topics discussed include:

- Measuring unemployment
- Frictional, structural, seasonal, and cyclical unemployment
- Full employment
- Sources and consequences of inflation
- Relative price changes
- Nominal and real interest rates

Unemployment

"They scampered about looking for work. . . . They swarmed on the highways. The movement changed them; the highways, the camps along the road, the fear of hunger and the hunger itself, changed them. The children without dinner changed them, the endless moving changed them."[1] There is no question, as John Steinbeck writes in *The Grapes of Wrath*, a novel set in the Great Depression, that a long stretch of unemployment profoundly affects the jobless and their families. The most obvious loss is a steady paycheck, but the unemployed often lose self-esteem and part of their identity as well. Losing a job often means losing the social connections to coworkers. According to psychologists, in terms of stressful events, the loss of a good job ranks only slightly below a divorce or the death of a loved one. Moreover, unemployment appears to be linked to a greater incidence of crime and to a variety of afflictions, including heart disease, suicide, and clinical depression.[2] No matter how often people complain about their jobs, they rely on those same jobs not only for their livelihood but for part of their personal identity. When strangers meet, one of the first questions asked is "what do you do for a living?" Alfred Marshall wrote that your job is often the main object of your thoughts and intellectual development.

In addition to the personal costs, unemployment imposes a cost on the economy as a whole because fewer goods and services are produced. When those who are willing and able to work can't find jobs, their labor is lost forever. *This lost output coupled with the economic and psychological cost of unemployment on the individual and the family are the true costs of unemployment.* As we begin our analysis, keep in mind that the national unemployment rate reflects millions of individuals with their own stories. As President Harry Truman once remarked, "It's a recession when your neighbor loses his job; it's a depression when you lose your own." For some lucky people, unemployment is a brief vacation between jobs. For some others, a long stretch can have a lasting effect on family stability, economic welfare, self-esteem, and personal identity.

Measuring Unemployment

The unemployment rate is the most widely reported measure of the nation's economic health. What does the unemployment rate measure? What are the sources of unemployment? How has unemployment changed over time? These are some of the questions explored in this section. Let's first see how to measure unemployment.

We begin with the U.S. *civilian noninstitutional adult population*, which consists of all civilians 16 years of age and older, except those in prison, in mental facilities, or in homes for the aged. The adjective *civilian* means the definition excludes those in the military. From here on, references to the *adult population* mean the civilian noninstitutional adult population. The **labor force** consists of the people in the adult population who are either working or looking for work. *Those who want a job but can't find one are unemployed.* The Bureau of Labor Statistics interviews 60,000 households monthly (which translates into about 110,000 individuals) and counts people as unemployed if they have no job but want one and have looked for work at least once during the preceding four weeks. Thus, the college student, the displaced bank teller, Kristen Stewart,

labor force
Those 16 years of age and older who are either working or looking for work

---

1. John Steinbeck, *The Grapes of Wrath* (Viking, 1939): 293.
2. For a study linking a higher incidence of suicides to recessions, see Christopher Ruhm, "Are Recessions Good for Your Health," *Quarterly Journal of Economics*, 115 (May 2000): 617–650. Clinical depression is also higher among the unemployed, as demonstrated in Frederick Zimmerman and Wayne Katon, "Socioeconomic Status, Depression Disparities, and Financial Strain: What Lies Behind the Income-Depression Relationship," *Health Economics*, 14 (December 2004): 1197–1215.

and Alex Rodriguez would all be counted as unemployed if they want a job and looked for work in the previous month. The **unemployment rate** measures the percentage of those in the labor force who are unemployed. Hence, the unemployment rate, which is reported monthly, equals the number unemployed—that is, people without jobs who are looking for work—divided by the number in the labor force.

Only a fraction of adults who are not working are considered unemployed. The others may have retired, are students, are caring for children at home, or simply don't want to work. Others may be unable to work because of long-term illness or disability. Some may have become so discouraged by a long, unfruitful job search that they have given up in frustration. These **discouraged workers** have, in effect, dropped out of the labor force, so they are not counted as unemployed. Finally, about one-third of those working part time would prefer to work full time, yet all part-timers are counted as employed. Because the official unemployment rate does not include discouraged workers and counts all part-time workers as employed, it may underestimate the true extent of unemployment in the economy. Later we consider some reasons why the unemployment rate may exaggerate the true extent of unemployment.

These definitions are illustrated in Exhibit 1, where circles represent the various groups, and the number (in millions) of individuals in each category and subcategory is shown in parentheses. The circle on the left depicts the entire U.S. labor force in April 2010, including both employed and unemployed people. The circle on the right represents those in the adult population who, for whatever reason, are not working. These two circles combined show the adult population. The overlapping area identifies the

unemployment rate
The number unemployed as a percentage of the labor force

discouraged workers
Those who drop out of the labor force in frustration because they can't find work

---

EXHIBIT 1 The Adult Population Sums the Employed, the Unemployed, and Those Not in the Labor Force: April 2010 (in millions)

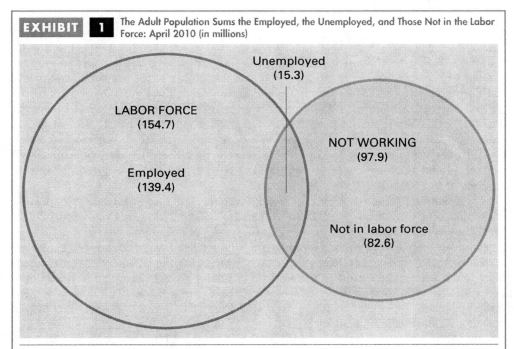

The labor force, depicted by the left circle, consists of those employed plus those unemployed. Those not working, depicted by the right circle, consists of those not in the labor force and those unemployed. The adult population sums the employed, the unemployed, and those not in the labor force.

Source: Figures are for April 2010 from the U.S. Bureau of Labor Statistics. For the latest data, go to http://www.bls.gov/news.release/empsit.toc.htm.

number of *unemployed* workers—that is, people in the labor force who are not working. The unemployment rate is found by dividing the number unemployed by the number in the labor force. In April 2010, 15.3 million people were unemployed in a labor force of 154.7 million, yielding an unemployment rate of 9.9 percent.

Labor Force Participation Rate

The productive capability of any economy depends in part on the proportion of adults in the labor force, measured as the *labor force participation rate*. In Exhibit 1, the U.S. adult population equals those in the labor force (154.7 million) plus those not in the labor force (82.6 million)—a total of 237.3 million people. The **labor force participation rate** therefore equals the number in the labor force divided by the adult population, or 65 percent (= 154.7 million/237.3 million). So, on average, about two out of three adults are in the labor force. The labor force participation rate increased from 60 percent in 1970 to 67 percent in 1990, and has remained relatively steady since then.

One striking development since World War II has been the convergence in the labor force participation rates of men and women. In 1950, only 34 percent of adult women were in the labor force. Today 59 percent are, with the greatest increase among younger women. The labor force participation rate among men has declined from 86 percent in 1950 to 72 percent today, primarily because of earlier retirement. The participation rate is higher among white males than black males but higher among black females than white females. Finally, the participation rate climbs with education—from 43 percent for those without a high school diploma to 76 percent among those with a college degree.

Unemployment Over Time

Exhibit 2 shows the U.S. unemployment rate since 1900, with shaded bars to indicate periods of recession or depression. As you can see, rates rise during contractions and fall during expansions. Most striking is the jump during the Great Depression of the 1930s, when the rate topped 25 percent. Note that the rate trended upward from the end of World War II in the mid-1940s until the early 1980s; then it backed down, from a high of 10 percent in 1982 to a low of 4 percent in 2000. With the recession of 2001, the rate gradually increased to 6 percent by 2003, then declined into 2007. But the global financial crisis of 2008 and sharp U.S. recession boosted the rate to 10 percent by the end of 2009.

Let's examine some of the broad trends over the last three decades. Why did the unemployment rate trend down from 10 percent in 1982 to only 4 percent in 2000? First, the overall economy was on a roll during that period, interrupted by only a brief recession in the early 1990s triggered by the first war in Iraq. The number employed increased by 37 million between 1982 and 2000, making the U.S. economy an incredible job machine and the envy of the world. The unemployment rate also trended down because there were fewer teenagers in the workforce. Teenagers have an unemployment rate about three times that of adults, so the declining share of teenage workers helped cut the overall unemployment rate.

But job growth between 2000 and 2010 was hobbled by a recession in 2001 and a much sharper one in 2007–2009. Employment during the decade increased by only about 4 million, not nearly enough to absorb the 13 million people joining the labor force. As a result, the number unemployed swelled from 6 million in 2000 to 15 million in 2010, and the unemployment rate climbed from only 4 percent to 10 percent. This was the worst decade of employment growth since the Great Depression.

EXHIBIT 2 The U.S. Unemployment Rate Since 1900

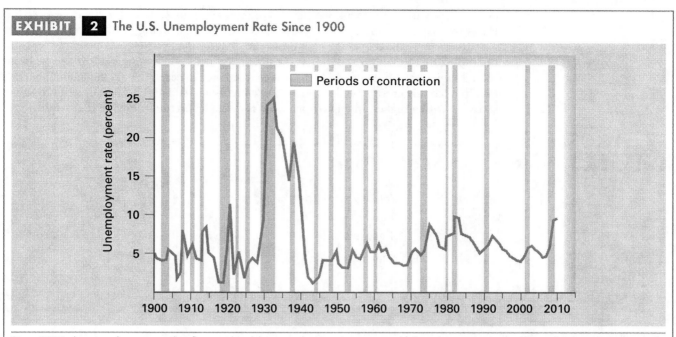

Since 1900, the unemployment rate has fluctuated widely, rising during contractions and falling during expansions. During the Great Depression of the 1930s, the rate spiked to 25 percent.

Sources: U.S. Census Bureau, *Historical Statistics of the United States: Colonial Times to 1970* (Washington, D.C. U.S. Government Printing Office, 1975); *Economic Report of the President*, February 2010; and U.S. Bureau of Labor Statistics. Figure for 2010 is estimated based on figures through June 2010, seasonally adjusted. For the latest unemployment rate, go to http://www.bls.gov/news.release/empsit.toc.htm.

Unemployment Among Various Groups

The unemployment rate says nothing about who is unemployed or for how long. The overall rate masks wide differences in the labor force based on education, race, gender, and age. For example, when the U.S. unemployment rate in April 2010 was 9.9 percent, the rate among workers 25 years of age or older who were high school dropouts was 14.7 percent; this was triple the rate among workers 25 or older who were college graduates. So education provides some insurance against unemployment. Unemployment also differs based on race and ethnicity; the rate was 9.0 percent among white workers, 16.5 percent among African Americans, 12.5 percent among those of Hispanic ethnicity, and 6.8 percent among Asian workers. Finally, the unemployment rate was 10.1 percent among males 20 and older, 8.2 percent among females 20 and older, and 25.4 percent among workers 16 to 19 years of age. Why is the unemployment rate among teenage workers so much higher than other workers? Teenagers enter the labor force with little education or job experience, so they take unskilled jobs and are first laid off if the economy slows down (last hired, first fired). Teenagers also move in and out of the labor force more frequently as they juggle school demands. Even those who have left school often shop around more than workers 20 and older, quitting one job in search of a better one.

Unemployment rates for different groups appear in Exhibit 3. Each panel shows the rate by race and by gender since 1972. Panel (a) shows the rates for workers 20 and older, and panel (b) the rates for 16- to 19-year-old workers. Periods of recession are shaded pink. As you can see, rates are higher among black workers than among white workers, and rates are higher among teenage workers than among those 20 and older. During recessions, rates climbed for all groups. Rates peaked during the recession of 1982 and then trended down. After the recession of the early 1990s, unemployment rates continued downward, with the rate among black workers falling in 2000 to the lowest on record. Rates rose again beginning with the recession of 2001, peaking at 6.0 percent in 2003. The rate then declined over the next four years, but jumped because of the sharp recession of 2007–2009. Exhibit 3 shows that the unemployment rate among black men was more than double that among white men. Notice that since the early 1990s the unemployment rate trended higher for a while even after each recession ended. This paradox of economic recovery with a higher unemployment rate is discussed in the following case study.

EXHIBIT   **3**   Unemployment Rates for Various Groups

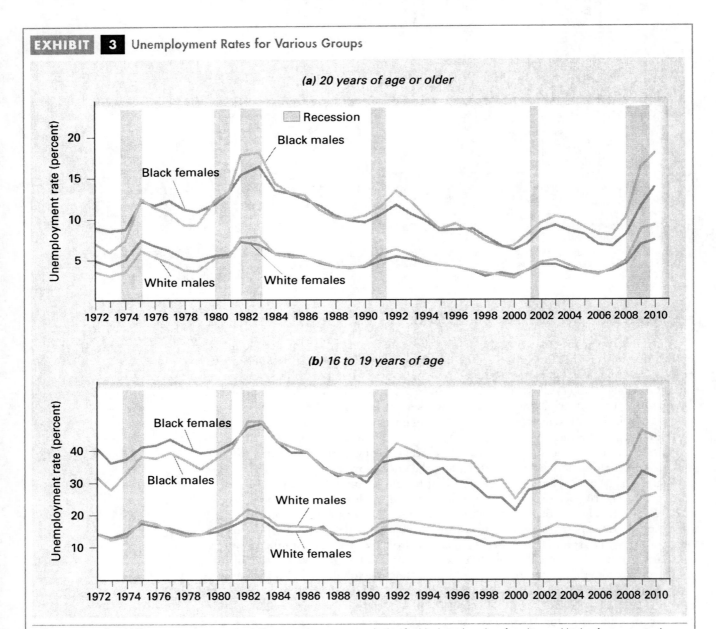

(a) 20 years of age or older

(b) 16 to 19 years of age

Different groups face different unemployment rates. The unemployment rate is higher for black workers than for white and higher for teenagers than for those 20 and older.

Source: *Economic Report of the President*, February 2010, Table B-43; and U.S. Bureau of Labor Statistics. Figures for 2010 are estimated based on figures through May 2010, seasonally adjusted. For the latest data, go to http://www.bls.gov/news.release/empsit.toc.htm.

PUBLIC POLICY

"Hiring Picks Up, But Jobless Rate Rises"   So reads the headline describing the April 2010 jobs report. In a burst of hiring, the U.S. economy added 290,000 jobs, for what was then the biggest monthly gain in four years. That sure sounds like good news—until you learn that the U.S. unemployment rate climbed too, from 9.7 percent to 9.9 percent. How could that rate rise when the economy was adding so many jobs?

Because of a severe recession, the number of unemployed increased by over 8 million between early 2008 and early 2010. But even that total understates the number who wanted jobs. Recall that to be counted as unemployed, those wanting work must have looked for a job in the prior four weeks. With 8 million people looking for work, and with firms more likely to be firing than hiring, the chances of finding a job diminished. In frustration, some gave up their search, and these people are called discouraged workers, a term already introduced. But the U.S. Labor Department identifies a second group of people who wanted a job but did not look for work in the prior four weeks. This group faced transportation problems, family problems, or some other snag that kept them from looking. It wasn't that they were frustrated with their search, they just got side-tracked with some personal issues. Discouraged workers and this group that got sidetracked are considered *marginally attached to the labor force*.

At the beginning of 2010, an estimated 2.4 million people were marginally attached to the labor force. This was 1.1 million more than before the recession began. Thus, when the economy started showing signs of life, as it did in early 2010, some people who had been sidelined for one reason or another took notice and decided to look for work, thus joining or rejoining the labor force. In April 2010 the labor force increased by about 800,000 people from the month earlier. Most of those people didn't find jobs right away, so they swelled the ranks of the unemployed. Even though the economy created 290,000 jobs during the month, that was not enough to offset the spike in the labor force. Thus, we get the seeming paradox of healthy job growth but a rising unemployment rate.

The same happened during the recession of 2001; the unemployment rate did not start to decline until two years after the recession ended. That's why the unemployment rate is often considered a lagging indicator of economic activity. Even after the economy starts to recover from a recession, the unemployment rate continues to increase for reasons that are not all bad. Those who want a job are encouraged enough by the uptick in jobs to look for one.

Sources: Jeannine Aversa, "Hiring Picks Up, But Jobless Rate Rises," *Arizona Republic*, 8 May 2010; Sara Murray and Joe Light, "Job Gains Speed Up and More Seek Work," *Wall Street Journal*, 8 May 2008; "Ranks of Discouraged Workers and Others Marginally Attached to the Labor Force Rise During Recession," *Issues in Labor Statistics*, (April 2009); and figures from the U.S. Bureau of Labor Statistics at http://www.bls.gov/.

e activity

Data on workers marginally attached to the labor force are available at http://data.bls.gov/cgi-bin/surveymost?ln. Page down to check the box for Marginally Attached to Labor Force - LNU05026642. Click the Retrieve data button. Choose the years you want to examine and check the box to "include graphs." Select the GO button.

Unemployment Varies Across Occupations and Regions

The unemployment rate varies by occupation. Professional and technical workers experience lower unemployment rates than blue-collar workers. Construction workers at times face high rates because that occupation is both seasonal and subject to wide swings over the business cycle.

Partly because certain occupations dominate labor markets in certain regions, unemployment rates also vary by region. For example, because of pressure on blue-collar jobs in smokestack industries such as autos and steel, in April 2010 unemployment rates in Illinois, Michigan, and Ohio were nearly triple those in the upper Midwest farm states of Nebraska, North Dakota, and South Dakota. Even within a state, unemployment can vary widely. For example, the California city of El Centro had nearly triple the unemployment rate of Santa Barbara.

Exhibit 4 shows unemployment rates for 27 major metropolitan areas in April 2010. As you can see, Detroit had the highest unemployment rate, at 14.8 percent. This was nearly triple the rate for the city with the lowest rate, Honolulu, at 5.2 percent. The point is that *the national unemployment rate masks differences across the country and even across an individual state*. Still, most cities in Exhibit 4 had rates between 8.0 percent and 11.0 percent.

Sources of Unemployment

Pick up any metropolitan newspaper and thumb through the classifieds. The help-wanted section may include thousands of jobs, from accountants to X-ray technicians. Online job sites such as Monster.com list hundreds of thousands of openings. Why,

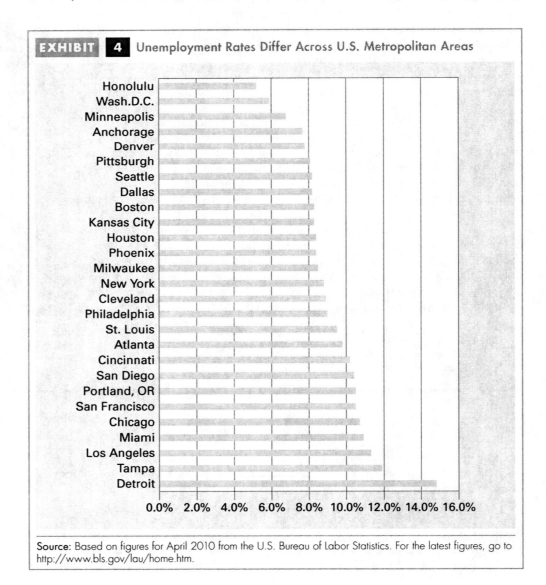

EXHIBIT 4 Unemployment Rates Differ Across U.S. Metropolitan Areas

Source: Based on figures for April 2010 from the U.S. Bureau of Labor Statistics. For the latest figures, go to http://www.bls.gov/lau/home.htm.

when millions are unemployed, are so many jobs available? To understand this, we must think about all the reasons why people are unemployed. They may be looking for a first job, or they may be reentering the labor force after an absence. They may have quit or been fired from their last job. Sixty-one percent of those unemployed in April 2010 lost their previous job, 6 percent quit, 8 percent entered the labor market for the first time, and 25 percent reentered the labor market. *Thus, 39 percent were unemployed either because they quit jobs or because they were just joining or rejoining the labor force.*

More generally, there are four sources of unemployment: frictional, seasonal, structural, and cyclical.

Frictional Unemployment

Just as employers do not always hire the first applicant who comes through the door, job seekers do not always accept the first offer. Both employers and job seekers need time to explore the job market. Employers need time to learn about the talent available, and job seekers need time to learn about employment opportunities. The time required to bring together employers and job seekers is the source of **frictional unemployment**. Although unemployment often creates economic and psychological hardships, not all unemployment is necessarily bad. Frictional unemployment does not usually last long and it results in a better match between workers and jobs, so the entire economy works more efficiently. Policy makers and economists are not that concerned about frictional unemployment.

frictional unemployment
Unemployment that occurs because job seekers and employers need time to find each other

Seasonal Unemployment

Unemployment caused by seasonal changes in labor demand during the year is called **seasonal unemployment**. During cold winter months, demand for farm hands, lifeguards, landscapers, and construction workers shrinks, as it does for dozens of other seasonal occupations. Likewise, tourism in winter destinations such as Miami and Phoenix melts in the heat of summer. The Christmas season increases the demand for sales clerks, postal workers, and Santa Clauses. Those in seasonal jobs realize their jobs disappear in the off-season. Some even choose seasonal occupations to complement their lifestyles or academic schedules. To eliminate seasonal unemployment, we would have to outlaw winter and abolish Christmas. Monthly employment data are *seasonally adjusted* to smooth out the unemployment bulges that result from seasonal factors. Policy makers and economists are not that concerned about seasonal unemployment.

seasonal unemployment
Unemployment caused by seasonal changes in the demand for certain kinds of labor

Structural Unemployment

A third reason why job vacancies and unemployment coexist is that unemployed workers often do not have the skills in demand or do not live where their skills are demanded. For example, the Lincoln Electric Company in Ohio took a long time filling 200 openings because few among the thousands who applied could operate computer-controlled machines. Unemployment arising from a mismatch of skills or geographic location is called **structural unemployment**. *Structural unemployment occurs because changes in tastes, technology, taxes, and competition reduce the demand for certain skills and increase the demand for other skills.* In our dynamic economy, some workers, such as coal miners in West Virginia, are stuck with skills no longer demanded. Likewise, golf carts replaced caddies, ATMs replaced bank tellers, and office technology is replacing clerical staff. For example, because of e-mail, voice mail, PCs, PDAs, BlackBerries, smart phones, and other wireless devices, the number of secretaries, typists, and administrative assistants in the United States has fallen by more than half over the past two decades. Structural unemployment may also arise from a change in tastes and preferences. For example, because

structural unemployment
Unemployment because (1) the skills demanded by employers do not match those of the unemployed, or (2) the unemployed do not live where the jobs are

Americans smoke less, some tobacco farmers had to look for other work. And because Americans buy fewer newspapers, employment in that industry has declined.

Whereas most frictional unemployment is short term and voluntary, structural unemployment poses more of a problem because workers must either develop the skills demanded in the local job market or look elsewhere. Moving is not easy. Most people prefer to remain near friends and relatives. Those laid off from good jobs hang around in hopes of getting rehired. Married couples with one spouse still employed may not want to give up that job to look for two jobs elsewhere. Finally, available jobs may be in regions where the living cost is much higher. So those structurally unemployed often stay put. Some federal retraining programs aim to reduce structural unemployment.

Cyclical Unemployment

cyclical unemployment
Unemployment that fluctuates with the business cycle, increasing during contractions and decreasing during expansions

As output declines during recessions, firms reduce their demand for nearly all resources, including labor. **Cyclical unemployment** increases during recessions and decreases during expansions. Between 1932 and 1934, when unemployment averaged about 24 percent, there was clearly much cyclical unemployment. Between 1942 and 1945, when unemployment averaged less than 2 percent, there was no cyclical unemployment. Cyclical unemployment means the economy is operating inside its production possibilities frontier. Government policies that stimulate aggregate demand aim to reduce cyclical unemployment.

Duration of Unemployment

A given unemployment rate tells us little about how long people have been unemployed. In April 2010, with the unemployment rate at 9.9 percent, the average duration of unemployment was 33 weeks, the longest since the Great Depression. Some people were unemployed longer than others: 18 percent were unemployed less than 5 weeks; 20 percent 5–14 weeks; 16 percent 15–26 weeks, and 46 percent 27 weeks or longer. Those out 27 weeks or longer are called the **long-term unemployed,** and are of special concern to policy makers. Thus, nearly half of those out of work in April 2010 were long-term unemployed.

long-term unemployed
Those out of work for 27 weeks or longer

The Meaning of Full Employment

In a dynamic economy such as ours, changes in product demand and in technology continually alter the supply and demand for particular types of labor. Thus, even in a healthy economy, there is some frictional, structural, and seasonal unemployment. The economy is viewed as operating at *full employment* if there is no cyclical unemployment. When economists talk about "full employment," they do not mean zero unemployment but low unemployment, with estimates ranging from 4 to 6 percent. Even when the economy is at **full employment,** there is some frictional, structural, and seasonal unemployment. Even after the recession of 2007–2009, 39 percent of those unemployed in April 2010 had quit their previous job or were new entrants or reentrants into the labor force. We can't expect people to find jobs overnight. Many in this group would be considered frictionally unemployed.

full employment
Employment level when there is no cyclical unemployment

Unemployment Compensation

As noted at the outset, unemployment often involves an economic and psychological hardship. For a variety of reasons, however, the burden of unemployment on the individual and the family may not be as severe today as it was during the Great Depression.

Today, many households have two or more workers in the labor force, so if one loses a job, another may still have one—a job that could provide health insurance and other benefits for the family. *Having more than one family member in the labor force cushions the shock of unemployment.*

Moreover, unlike the experience during the Great Depression, most who lose their jobs now collect unemployment benefits. In response to the Great Depression, Congress passed the Social Security Act of 1935, which provided unemployment insurance financed by a tax on employers. Unemployed workers who meet certain qualifications can receive **unemployment benefits** for up to six months, provided they actively look for work. During recessions, benefits usually extend beyond six months in states with especially high unemployment. During and following the recession of 2007–2009, the extension of benefits was nationwide, and many states offered benefits for up to two years. Benefits go primarily to people who have lost jobs. Those just entering or reentering the labor force are not covered, nor are those who quit their last job or those fired for just cause, such as excessive absenteeism or theft. Because of these restrictions, about two-thirds of those unemployed in April 2010 received benefits.

Unemployment benefits replace on average about half of a person's take-home pay, with a higher percentage for those whose jobs paid less. Benefits averaged about $310 per week in 2010. Because these benefits reduce the opportunity cost of remaining unemployed, they may reduce the incentives to find work. For example, if faced with a choice of washing dishes for $350 per week or collecting $250 per week in unemployment benefits, which would you choose? Evidence suggests that those collecting unemployment benefits remain out of work weeks longer than those without benefits. Many leave the labor force once their benefits are exhausted.[3] So although unemployment insurance provides a safety net, it may reduce the urgency of finding work, thereby increasing unemployment. On the plus side, because beneficiaries need not take the first job that comes along, unemployment insurance allows for a higher quality job search. As a result of a higher quality search, there is a better match between job skills and job requirements, and this promotes economic efficiency.

International Comparisons of Unemployment

How do U.S. unemployment rates compare with those around the world? Exhibit 5 shows rates since 1980 for the United States, Japan, and the average of four major European economies (France, Germany, Italy, and the United Kingdom). Over the last two decades and prior to the recent recession, unemployment trended down in the United States, trended up in Japan, and remained high in Europe. At the beginning of the period, the United States had the highest rate among the three economies. After trending lower between the early 1980s and late 2007, the U.S. rate spiked above that of Western Europe because of the 2007–2009 recession. The rate in Japan remained relatively low.

The unemployment rate in Europe averaged 8.3 percent over the last three decades versus a U.S. average of 6.2 percent. Why have rates averaged higher in Europe? The ratio of unemployment benefits to average pay is higher in Europe than in the United States, and unemployment benefits last longer there, sometimes years. So those collecting unemployment benefits have less incentive to find work. What's more, government regulations have made European employers more reluctant to hire new workers because firing them is difficult.

What's the relevance of the following statement from the *Wall Street Journal*: "The economic package approved by the Italian Parliament includes measures to encourage firms operating in the underground economy to come out in the open."

unemployment benefits
Cash transfers to those who lose their jobs and actively seek employment

---

3. See David Card, Raj Chetty, and Andrea Weber, "Cash-On-Hand and Competing Models of Intertemporal Behavior: New Evidence from the Labor Markets," *Quarterly Journal of Economics*, 122 (November 2007): 1511–1560.

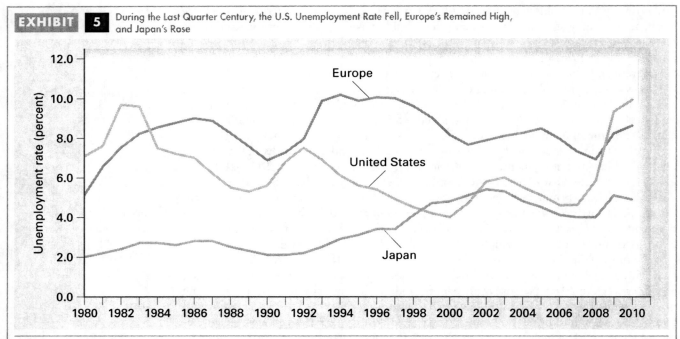

EXHIBIT   5   During the Last Quarter Century, the U.S. Unemployment Rate Fell, Europe's Remained High, and Japan's Rose

Source: Based on standardized rates in *OECD Economic Outlook* 87 (May 2010) and *Economic Report of the President,* February 2010. Figures for Europe are the averages for France, Germany, Italy, and the United Kingdom. Figures for 2010 are projections based on reported rates through the first third of the year. For the latest international data, go to http://www.bls.gov/fls/home.htm.

Historically, unemployment has been low in Japan because many firms there offered job security for life. Thus, some employees who do little or no work are still carried on company payrolls. Both labor laws and social norms limit layoffs in Japan. Unemployment has increased there since the early 1990s because more firms went bankrupt.

Problems With Official Unemployment Figures

Official unemployment statistics are not problem free. Not counting discouraged workers and others marginally attached to the labor force as unemployed understates unemployment. Official employment data also ignore the problem of **underemployment,** which arises because people are counted as employed even if they can find only part-time work or are vastly overqualified for their jobs, as when someone with a Ph.D. in literature can find only a clerk's position. Counting overqualified and part-time workers as employed tends to understate the actual amount of unemployment.

On the other hand, because unemployment insurance benefits and most welfare programs require recipients to seek work, some people may go through the motions of looking for a job just to qualify for these benefits. If they do not in fact want a job, counting them as unemployed overstates actual unemployment. Likewise, some people who would prefer to work part time can find only full-time jobs, and some forced to work overtime and weekends would prefer to work less. To the extent that people must work more than they would prefer, the official unemployment rate overstates the actual rate. Finally, people in the underground economy may not admit they have jobs because

underemployment

Workers are overqualified for their jobs or work fewer hours than they would prefer

they are breaking the law. For example, someone working off the books or someone selling illegal drugs would not admit to being employed.

On net, however, because discouraged workers and others marginally attached to the labor force aren't counted as unemployed and because underemployed workers are counted as employed, most experts agree that official U.S. unemployment figures tend to underestimate unemployment. Still, the size of this underestimation may not be huge, even in the wake of a recession. For example, counting discouraged workers as unemployed would have raised the unemployment rate in April 2010 from 9.9 percent to 10.6 percent. Adding in others who were marginally attached to the labor force would have raised the rate to 11.3 percent. There are no estimates of what the unemployment rate would be if we subtracted those looking for work only to qualify for government benefits.

Despite these qualifications and limitations, the U.S. unemployment rate is a useful measure of trends across demographic groups, across regions, and over time.

We turn next to inflation.

Inflation

As noted already, *inflation* is a sustained increase in the economy's average price level. Let's begin with a case study that underscores the problem of high inflation.

BRINGING THEORY TO LIFE

Hyperinflation in Zimbabwe   In the troubled nation of Zimbabwe in southern Africa, the Zimbabwean dollar was once worth about 1.59 U.S. dollars. But the collapse of the economy in the early 2000s severely devalued the Zimbabwean dollar. The government tried paying its bills by printing huge amounts of money, and the result was inflation on an epic scale—hyperinflation. Consider this: The price level at the end of 2008 was *150 million times* higher than at the beginning of that year. To put that in perspective, with such inflation in the United States, a gallon of gasoline that sold for $2.75 at the beginning of the year would cost $412.5 million by year-end. Jeans that sold for $25 would cost $3.8 billion at year-end. With the value of the Zimbabwean dollar cheapening by the hour, nobody wanted to hold any for long. Those fortunate enough to have jobs in this wreck of an economy wanted to get paid at least daily; they then immediately spent their pay before prices climbed more.

With such wild inflation, everyone, including merchants, had trouble keeping up with prices. Different price increases among sellers of the same product encouraged buyers to shop around more. Even though the government was printing money at an astounding rate, the huge spike in prices meant that it took mountains of cash to buy anything, an amount both difficult to round up and onerous to carry. For months, the maximum amount people could withdraw daily from their bank had the purchasing power of one U.S. dollar. Because carrying enough money for even small purchases became physically impossible, currency in Zimbabwe was issued in ever higher denominations, with the highest being a $100 trillion dollar note; that's $100,000,000,000,000. In addition to issuing these higher denominations, three times the central bank issued an entirely new series of notes, each a huge multiple of the previous one, while doing away with the old series. For example, the new Zimbabwean dollar issued in February 2009 exchanged for 1,000,000,000,000 of the dollars it replaced. Larger denominations and new series of notes facilitated transactions but fed inflation, which raged all the more.

CASE STUDY

e activity
You can find economic information about many countries at The World Factbook published by the Central Intelligence Agency (https://www.cia.gov/library/publications/the-world-factbook/index.html). Above the map of the world, click the arrow for the drop-down list and scroll to Zimbabwe. In the menu below the map of the country, click on the plus sign to expand information about the economy. Can you find the latest inflation rate?

Many merchants would accept only stable currencies such as the U.S. dollar or the South African rand, and would rather barter than accept Zimbabwean currency. No question, the country had all kinds of other problems, but hyperinflation made everything worse. For example, Zimbabwe's GDP plunged 75 percent between 2006 and 2009, and the unemployment rate reached 90 percent.

As a way out of the mess, by mid-2009 the government allowed all transactions to be conducted in foreign currencies, something that was already happening. The local currency, already worthless (a $100 trillion note was worth only U.S. pennies), mostly disappeared. Thus, Zimbabwe is now under what it calls a "multiple currency system" and the country plans to operate that way until at least through 2012. Price inflation grew only five percent in 2009 under the multiple currency system. Although Zimbabwe ended its inflation nightmare, hyperinflation is usually flaring up somewhere in the world, as yet another country looks to print money as a "free lunch" solution to budget problems. For example, inflation in Venezuela reached 30 percent in 2010.

Sources: "Zimbabwe: Reaching Rock Bottom," *The Economist*, 8 December 2008; Douglas Rogers, "Zimbabwe's Accidental Triumph," *New York Times*, 14 April 2010; and Zimbabwe's Federal Reserve Bank at http://www.rbz.co.zw/. This case study also drew on the author's visit to Zimbabwe in September 2008.

We have already discussed inflation in different contexts. If the price level bounces around—moving up one month, falling back the next month—any particular increase in the price level would not necessarily be called inflation in a meaningful sense. We typically measure inflation on an annual basis. The annual *inflation rate* is the percentage increase in the average price level from one year to the next. For example, between April 2009 and April 2010, the U.S. *consumer price index* increased 2.2 percent. Extremely high inflation, as in Zimbabwe, is called **hyperinflation.** A sustained *decrease* in the average price level is called **deflation,** as occurred in the United States during the Great Depression and in 2009. Japan, Hong Kong, and Taiwan have also experienced deflation in recent years. And a reduction in the rate of inflation is called **disinflation,** as occurred in the United States from 1981 to 1986, 1991 to 1994, and 2000 to 2002.

In this section, we first consider two sources of inflation. Then, we examine the extent and consequences of inflation in the United States and around the world.

hyperinflation
A very high rate of inflation

deflation
A sustained decrease in the price level

disinflation
A reduction in the rate of inflation

Two Sources of Inflation

Inflation is a sustained increase in the economy's price level; it results from an increase in aggregate demand, a decrease in aggregate supply, or both. Panel (a) of Exhibit 6 shows that an increase in aggregate demand raises the economy's price level from P to P'. In such cases, a shift to the right of the aggregate demand curve *pulls up* the price level. Inflation resulting from increases in aggregate demand is called **demand-pull inflation.** To generate continuous demand-pull inflation, the aggregate demand curve would have to keep shifting out along a given aggregate supply curve. Rising U.S. inflation during the late 1960s came from demand-pull inflation, when federal spending for the Vietnam War and expanded social programs boosted aggregate demand.

Alternatively, inflation can arise from reductions in aggregate supply, as shown in panel (b) of Exhibit 6, where a leftward shift of the aggregate supply curve raises the price level. For example, crop failures and OPEC price hikes reduced aggregate supply

demand-pull inflation
A sustained rise in the price level caused by a rightward shift of the aggregate demand curve

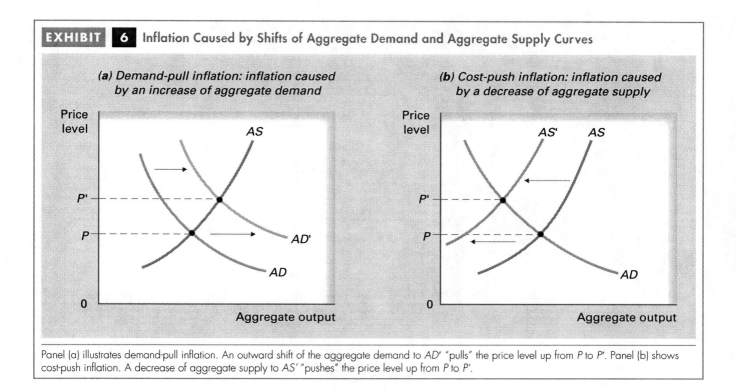

EXHIBIT 6 Inflation Caused by Shifts of Aggregate Demand and Aggregate Supply Curves

(a) Demand-pull inflation: inflation caused by an increase of aggregate demand

(b) Cost-push inflation: inflation caused by a decrease of aggregate supply

Panel (a) illustrates demand-pull inflation. An outward shift of the aggregate demand to AD' "pulls" the price level up from P to P'. Panel (b) shows cost-push inflation. A decrease of aggregate supply to AS' "pushes" the price level up from P to P'.

during 1974 and 1975, thereby raising the price level in the economy. Inflation stemming from decreases in aggregate supply is called **cost-push inflation,** suggesting that increases in the cost of production *push up* the price level. Prices increase and real GDP decreases, a combination identified earlier as *stagflation*. Again, to generate sustained and continuous cost-push inflation, the aggregate supply curve would have to keep shifting left along a given aggregate demand curve.

cost-push inflation
A sustained rise in the price level caused by a leftward shift of the aggregate supply curve

A Historical Look at Inflation and the Price Level

The consumer price index is the inflation measure you most often encounter, so it gets the most attention here. As you learned in the previous chapter, the *consumer price index*, or *CPI*, measures the cost of a market basket of consumer goods and services over time. Exhibit 7 shows prices in the United States since 1913, using the consumer price index. Panel (a) shows the price *level*, measured by an index relative to the base period of 1982 to 1984. As you can see, the price level was lower in 1940 than in 1920. Since 1940, however, it has risen steadily, especially during the 1970s.

People are concerned less about the price level and more about year-to-year changes in that level. The lower panel shows the annual *rate of change* in the CPI, or the annual rate of *inflation* or *deflation*. The 1970s was not the only period of high inflation. Inflation exceeded 10 percent from 1916 to 1919 and in 1947—periods associated with world wars. Prior to the 1950s, high inflation was war related and was usually followed by deflation. Such an inflation-deflation cycle stretches back over the last two centuries. In fact, between the Revolutionary War and World War II, the price level fell in about as many years as it rose. At the end of World War II, the price level was about where it stood at the end of the Civil War.

So fluctuations in the price level are nothing new. But prior to World War II, years of inflation and deflation balanced out over the long run. Therefore, people had good

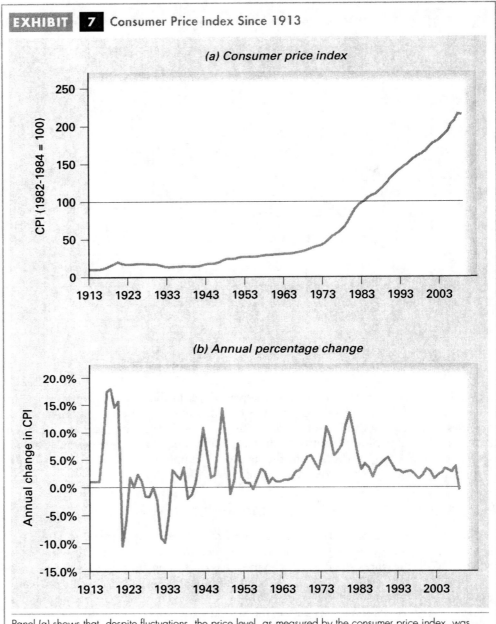

EXHIBIT   7 Consumer Price Index Since 1913

(a) Consumer price index

(b) Annual percentage change

Panel (a) shows that, despite fluctuations, the price level, as measured by the consumer price index, was lower in 1940 than in 1920. The price level began rising in the 1940s. Panel (b) shows the annual rate of change in the price level.

Source: The CPI home page of the U.S. Bureau of Labor Statistics is at http://www.bls.gov/cpi/home.htm. Go there for the latest figures.

reason to believe the dollar would retain its purchasing power over the long term. Since the end of World War II, however, the CPI has increased by an average of 3.7 percent per year. That may not sound like much, but it translates into nearly a tenfold increase in the consumer price index since 1947. *Inflation erodes confidence in the value of the dollar over the long term.*

Anticipated Versus Unanticipated Inflation

What is the effect of inflation on the economy? *Unanticipated inflation* creates more problems than *anticipated inflation*. To the extent that inflation is higher or lower than anticipated, it arbitrarily creates winners and losers. For example, suppose inflation is expected to be 3 percent next year, and you and your employer agree to a 4 percent increase in your nominal, or money, wage. You both expect your *real* wage—that is, your wage measured in dollars of constant purchasing power—to increase by 1 percent. If inflation turns out to be 3 percent, as expected, you and your employer are both satisfied. If inflation turns out to be 5 percent, your real wage will fall by 1 percent, so you are a loser and your employer a winner. If inflation turns out to be only 1 percent, your real wage increased by 3 percent, so you are a winner and your employer a loser.

More generally, if inflation is higher than expected, the losers are those who agreed to sell at a price that anticipated lower inflation and the winners are those who agreed to pay that price. If inflation is lower than expected, the situation is reversed: The losers are those who agreed to pay a price that anticipated higher inflation, and the winners are those who agreed to sell at that price. *The arbitrary gains and losses arising from unanticipated inflation is one reason inflation is so unpopular.* Inflation just doesn't seem fair.

The Transaction Costs of Variable Inflation

During long periods of price stability, people correctly believe they can predict future prices and can therefore plan accordingly. If inflation changes unexpectedly, however, the future is cloudier, so planning gets harder. Uncertainty about inflation undermines money's ability to link the present with the future. U.S. firms dealing with the rest of the world face an added burden. They must not only anticipate U.S. inflation, they must also guess how the value of the dollar will change relative to foreign currencies. Inflation uncertainty and the resulting exchange-rate uncertainty complicate international transactions. In this more uncertain environment, managers must shift attention from production decisions to anticipating the effects of inflation and exchange-rate changes on the firm's finances. Market transactions, particularly long-term contracts, become more complicated as inflation becomes more unpredictable. Some economists believe that the high and variable U.S. inflation during the 1970s and early 1980s cut economic growth during those periods.

Inflation Obscures Relative Price Changes

Even with no inflation, some prices would increase and some would decrease, reflecting normal activity in particular markets. For example, since the mid-1980s the U.S. price level has doubled, yet the prices of flat screen TVs, computers, long-distance phone service, and many other products have declined sharply. Because the prices of various goods change by different amounts, *relative prices* change. Consider price changes over a longer period. In the last hundred years, consumer prices overall increased about 2,000 percent, but the price of a hotel room in New York City jumped 7,500 percent, while the price of a three-minute phone call from New York to Chicago dropped 99 percent. Whereas the economy's price level describes the exchange rate between a market basket and *money*, relative prices describe the exchange rate among goods—that is, how much one good costs compared to another.

Inflation does not necessarily cause a change in relative prices, but it can obscure that change. During periods of volatile inflation, there is greater uncertainty about the price of one good relative to another—that is, about relative prices. But relative price changes are important signals for allocating the economy's resources efficiently. If all prices moved together, suppliers could link the selling prices of their goods to the overall inflation rate. Because prices usually do not move in unison, however, tying a particular product's price to the overall inflation rate may result in a price that is too high or too low based on market conditions. The same is true of agreements to link wages with inflation. If the price of an employer's product grows more slowly than the rate of inflation in the economy, the employer may be hard-pressed to increase wages by the rate of inflation. Consider the problem confronting oil refiners who signed labor contracts agreeing to pay their workers cost-of-living wage increases. In some years, those employers had to increase wages at a time when the price of oil was falling like a rock.

Inflation Across Metropolitan Areas

Inflation rates differ across regions mostly because of differences in housing prices, which rise or fall faster in some places than in others. But most prices, such as for automobiles, refrigerators, or jeans, do not differ that much across regions. The federal government tracks separate CPIs for each of 27 U.S. metropolitan areas. Based on these CPIs from 2005 to 2009, the average annual inflation rate is presented in Exhibit 8. Annual inflation between 2005 and 2009 averaged from a low of 1.9 percent in Detroit to a high of 3.8 percent in Honolulu. Most cities averaged between 2.0 percent and 3.0 percent. Again, the metropolitan inflation rate is heavily influenced by what's happening in the local housing market. We can conclude that the housing market in Honolulu was hotter than in Detroit.

International Comparisons of Inflation

Exhibit 9 shows annual inflation based on the CPI for the past three decades in the United States, Japan, and Europe, represented here as the average of four major nations (France, Germany, Italy, and the United Kingdom). All three economies show a similar trend, with declining inflation, or disinflation, during the first half of the 1980s, rising inflation during the second half of the 1980s to a peak in the early 1990s, and then another trend lower. The overall trend since 1980 has been toward lower inflation. Inflation rates in Europe were similar to those in the United States. Rates in Japan were consistently lower, even dipping into deflation in recent years. In the United States and Japan, the price level declined in 2009 due to slack demand from the global recession. Inflation since 1980 averaged 3.8 percent in Europe, 3.4 percent in the United States, and 0.9 percent in Japan.

The quantity and quality of data going into the price index varies across countries. Governments in less-developed countries sample fewer products and measure prices only in the capital city. Whereas hundreds of items are sampled to determine the U.S. consumer price index, as few as 30 might be sampled in some developing countries.

Inflation and Interest Rates

interest
The dollar amount paid by borrowers to lenders

interest rate
Interest per year as a percentage of the amount loaned

No discussion of inflation would be complete without some mention of the interest rate. **Interest** is the dollar amount paid by borrowers to lenders. Lenders must be rewarded for forgoing present consumption, and borrowers are willing to pay a premium to spend now. The **interest rate** is the amount paid per year as a percentage of the amount borrowed. For example, an interest rate of five percent means $5 per year on a $100 loan.

EXHIBIT **8** Average Annual Inflation from 2005 to 2009 Differed Across U.S. Metropolitan Areas

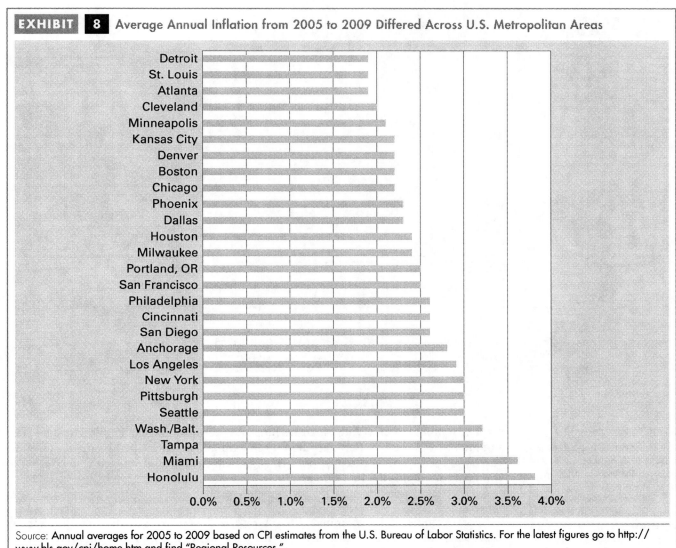

Source: Annual averages for 2005 to 2009 based on CPI estimates from the U.S. Bureau of Labor Statistics. For the latest figures go to http://www.bls.gov/cpi/home.htm and find "Regional Resources."

The greater the interest rate, other things constant, the greater the reward for lending money. The amount of money people are willing to lend, called *loanable funds*, increases as the interest rate rises, other things constant. The supply curve for loanable funds therefore slopes upward, as indicated by curve S in Exhibit 10.

These funds are demanded by households, firms, and governments to finance homes, buildings, machinery, college, and other major purchases. The lower the interest rate, other things constant, the cheaper the cost of borrowing. So the quantity of loanable funds demanded increases as the interest rate decreases, other things constant. That is, the interest rate and the quantity of loanable funds demanded are inversely related. The demand curve therefore slopes downward, as indicated by curve D in Exhibit 10. The downward-sloping demand curve and the upward-sloping supply curve intersect to yield the equilibrium nominal rate of interest, *i*.

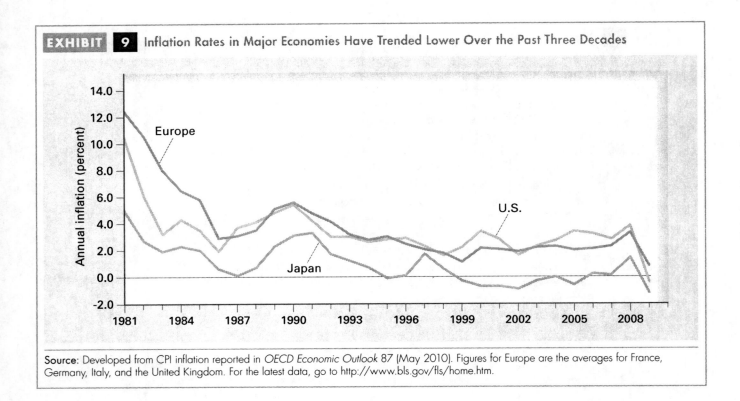

EXHIBIT 9 Inflation Rates in Major Economies Have Trended Lower Over the Past Three Decades

Source: Developed from CPI inflation reported in *OECD Economic Outlook* 87 (May 2010). Figures for Europe are the averages for France, Germany, Italy, and the United Kingdom. For the latest data, go to http://www.bls.gov/fls/home.htm.

nominal interest rate

The interest rate expressed in dollars of current value (that is, not adjusted for inflation) as a percentage of the amount loaned; the interest rate specified on the loan agreement

real interest rate

The interest rate expressed in dollars of constant purchasing power as a percentage of the amount loaned; the nominal interest rate minus the inflation rate

The **nominal interest rate** measures interest in terms of the current dollars paid. The nominal rate is the one that appears on the loan agreement; it is the rate discussed in the news media and is often of political significance. The **real interest rate** equals the nominal rate minus the inflation rate:

Real interest rate = Nominal interest rate − Inflation rate

For example, if the nominal interest rate is 5 percent and the inflation rate is 3 percent, the real interest rate is 2 percent. With no inflation, the nominal rate and the real rate would be identical. But with inflation, the nominal rate exceeds the real rate. If inflation is unexpectedly high—higher, for example, than the nominal rate—then the real interest rate would be negative. In this case, the nominal interest earned for lending money would not even cover the loss of spending power caused by inflation. Lenders would lose purchasing power. This is why lenders and borrowers are concerned more about the real rate than the nominal rate. The real interest rate, however, is known only after the fact—that is, only after inflation actually occurs.

Because the future is uncertain, lenders and borrowers must form expectations about inflation, and they base their willingness to lend and borrow on these expectations. The higher the *expected* inflation, the higher the nominal rate of interest that lenders require and that borrowers are willing to pay. Lenders and borrowers base their decisions on the *expected* real interest rate, which equals the nominal rate minus the expected inflation rate.

Although the discussion has implied that there is only one market rate of interest, there are many rates. Rates differ depending on such factors as the duration of the loan, tax treatment of interest, and the risk the loan will not be repaid.

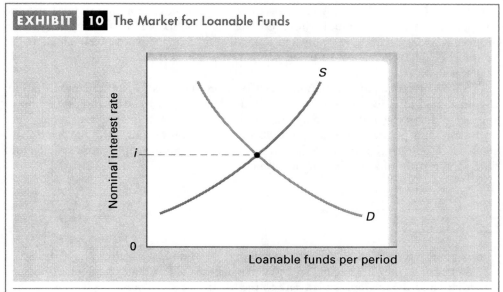

EXHIBIT 10 The Market for Loanable Funds

The upward-sloping supply curve, S, shows that more loanable funds are supplied at higher interest rates. The downward-sloping demand curve, D, shows that the quantity of loanable funds demanded is greater at lower interest rates. The two curves intersect to determine the market interest rate, i.

Why Is Inflation Unpopular?

Whenever the price level increases, spending must increase just to buy the same amount of goods and services. If you think of inflation only in terms of spending, you consider only the problem of paying those higher prices. But if you think of inflation in terms of the higher money income that results, you see that higher prices mean higher receipts for resource suppliers, including higher wages for workers. When viewed from the income side, inflation is not so bad.

If every higher price is received by some resource supplier, why are people so troubled by inflation? People view their higher incomes as well-deserved rewards for their labor, but they see inflation as a penalty that unjustly robs them of purchasing power. Most people do not stop to realize that unless they are producing more with each hour of labor, higher wages *must* result in higher prices. Prices and wages are simply two sides of the same coin. To the extent that nominal wages on average keep up with inflation, workers retain their purchasing power.

Presidents Ford and Carter could not control inflation and were turned out of office. Inflation slowed significantly during President Reagan's first term, and he won reelection easily, even though the unemployment rate was higher during his first term than during President Carter's tenure. During the 1988 election, George H. W. Bush won in part by reminding voters what inflation was in 1980, the last time a Democrat was president. But he lost his bid at reelection in part because inflation spiked to 6.0 percent in 1990, the highest in nearly a decade. Inflation remained under 3.0 percent during President Clinton's first term, and he was reelected easily. In the elections of 2000, 2004, and 2008, inflation was low enough as not to be an issue in those presidential elections.

Although inflation affects everyone to some extent, it hits hardest those whose incomes are fixed in nominal terms. For example, pensions are often fixed amounts and are eroded by inflation. And retirees who rely on fixed nominal interest income also see their incomes shrunk by inflation. But the benefits paid by the largest pension program, Social Security, are adjusted annually for changes in the CPI. Thus, Social Security recipients get a cost-of-living adjustment, or a **COLA**.

COLA
Cost-of-living adjustment; an increase in a transfer payment or wage that is tied to the increase in the price level

To Review: anticipated inflation is less of a problem than unanticipated inflation. Unanticipated inflation arbitrarily redistributes income and wealth from one group to another, reduces the ability to make long-term plans, and forces people to focus more on money and prices. The more unpredictable inflation becomes the harder it is to negotiate long-term contracts. Productivity suffers because people must spend more time coping with inflation, leaving less time for production.

Conclusion

This chapter has focused on unemployment and inflation. Although we have discussed them separately, they are related in ways that will unfold in later chapters. Politicians sometimes add the unemployment rate to the inflation rate to come up with what they refer to as the "misery index." In 1980, for example, an unemployment rate of 7.1 percent combined with a CPI increase of 13.5 percent to yield a misery index of 20.6—a number that helps explain why President Carter was not reelected. By 1984 the misery index dropped to 11.8, and by 1988 to 9.6; Republicans retained the White House in both elections. In 1992, the index climbed slightly to 10.4 percent, spelling trouble for President George H. W. Bush. And in 1996, the index fell back to 8.4 percent, helping President Clinton's reelection. During the election of 2000, the misery index was down to 7.7, which should have helped Al Gore, the candidate of the incumbent party. But during the campaign, Gore distanced himself from President Clinton and thus was not able to capitalize on the strong economy. In the 2004 election, the misery index remained about the same as in 2000, which helps explain why challenger John Kerry had difficulty making much of an issue of the economy. And a misery index of 10.4 the month before the 2008 election helped defeat the incumbent party and put Barack Obama in office.

Summary

1. The unemployment rate is the number of people looking for work divided by the number in the labor force. The unemployment rate masks differences among particular groups and across regions. The rate is lowest among white adults and highest among black teenagers.

2. There are four sources of unemployment. Frictional unemployment arises because employers and qualified job seekers need time to find one another. Seasonal unemployment stems from the effects of weather and the seasons on certain industries, such as construction and agriculture. Structural unemployment arises because changes in tastes, technology, taxes, and competition reduce the demand for certain skills and increase the demand for other skills. And cyclical unemployment results from fluctuations in economic activity caused by the business cycle.

Policy makers and economists are less concerned with frictional and seasonal unemployment. Full employment occurs when cyclical unemployment is zero.

3. Unemployment often creates both an economic and a psychological hardship. For some, this burden is reduced by an employed spouse and by unemployment insurance. Unemployment insurance provides a safety net for some and that's good, but it may also reduce incentives to find work, as is the case in Europe, and that's an unintended consequence.

4. Inflation is a sustained rise in the average price level. An increase in aggregate demand can cause demand-pull inflation. A decrease in aggregate supply can cause cost-push inflation. Prior to World War II, both inflation and deflation were

common, but since then the price level has increased nearly every year.

5. Anticipated inflation causes fewer distortions in the economy than unanticipated inflation. Unanticipated inflation arbitrarily creates winners and losers, and forces people to spend more time and energy coping with the effects of inflation. The negative effects of high and variable inflation on productivity can be observed in countries that have experienced hyperinflation, such as Zimbabwe.

6. Because not all prices change by the same amount during inflationary periods, people have trouble keeping track of the changes in relative prices. Unexpected inflation makes long-term planning more difficult and more risky.

7. The intersection of the demand and supply curves for loanable funds yields the market interest rate. The real interest rate is the nominal interest rate minus the inflation rate. Borrowers and lenders base decisions on the expected real interest rate.

Key Concepts

Labor force   142

Unemployment rate   143

Discouraged workers   143

Labor force participation rate   144

Frictional unemployment   149

Seasonal unemployment   149

Structural unemployment   149

Cyclical unemployment   150

Long-term unemployed   150

Full employment   150

Unemployment benefits   151

Underemployment   152

Hyperinflation   154

Deflation   154

Disinflation   154

Demand-pull inflation   154

Cost-push inflation   155

Interest   158

Interest rate   158

Nominal interest rate   160

Real interest rate   160

COLA   162

Questions for Review

1. LABOR FORCE   Refer to Exhibit 1 in the chapter to determine whether each of the following statements is true or false.

   a. Some people who are officially unemployed are not in the labor force.
   b. Some people in the labor force are not working.
   c. Everyone who is not unemployed is in the labor force.
   d. Some people who are not working are not unemployed.

2. UNEMPLOYMENT IN VARIOUS GROUPS   Does the overall unemployment rate provide an accurate picture of the impact of unemployment on all U.S. population groups?

3. Case Study: Hiring Picks Up, But Jobless Rate Rises   Imagine that during an expansion the U.S. economy adds 300,000 jobs. In addition, because of the improving economic conditions, the labor force increases by 200,000. Would the unemployment rate go up or down?

4. THE MEANING OF FULL EMPLOYMENT   When the economy is at full employment, is the unemployment rate at zero percent? Why or why not? How would a more generous unemployment insurance system affect the full employment figure?

5. INTERNATIONAL COMPARISONS OF UNEMPLOYMENT   How has the U.S. unemployment rate compared with rates in other major economies? Can you offer any reasons why rates on average have differed across major economies during the last three decades?

6. OFFICIAL UNEMPLOYMENT FIGURES   Explain why most experts believe that official U.S. data underestimate the actual rate of unemployment. What factors could make the official rate overstate the actual unemployment rate?

7. Case Study: Hyperinflation in Zimbabwe   In countries such as Zimbabwe, which had problems with high inflation, the increased use of another country's currency (such as the U.S. dollar or South African rand) became common. Why do you suppose this occurred?

8. SOURCES OF INFLATION   What are the two sources of inflation? How would you illustrate them graphically?

9. ANTICIPATED VERSUS UNANTICIPATED INFLATION   If actual inflation exceeds anticipated inflation, who will lose purchasing power and who will gain?

10. INFLATION AND RELATIVE PRICE CHANGES   What does the consumer price index measure? Does the index measure changes in relative prices? Why, or why not?

11. INFLATION AND INTEREST RATES   Explain as carefully as you can why borrowers would be willing to pay a higher interest rate if they expected the inflation rate to increase in the future.

12. INFLATION   Why is a relatively constant and predictable inflation rate less harmful to an economy than a rate that fluctuates unpredictably?

13. INFLATION   Why do people dislike inflation?

Problems and Exercises

14. MEASURING UNEMPLOYMENT Determine the impact on each of the following if 2 million formerly unemployed workers decide to return to school full time and stop looking for work:

    a. The labor force participation rate
    b. The size of the labor force
    c. The unemployment rate

15. MEASURING UNEMPLOYMENT Suppose that the U.S. noninstitutional adult population is 230 million and the labor force participation rate is 67 percent.

    a. What would be the size of the U.S. labor force?
    b. If 85 million adults are not working, what is the unemployment rate?

16. TYPES OF UNEMPLOYMENT Determine whether each of the following would be considered frictional, structural, seasonal, or cyclical unemployment:

    a. A UPS employee who was hired for the Christmas season is laid off after Christmas.
    b. A worker is laid off due to reduced aggregate demand in the economy.
    c. A worker in a DVD rental store becomes unemployed as video-on-demand cable service becomes more popular.
    d. A new college graduate is looking for employment.

17. INFLATION Here are some recent data on the U.S. consumer price index:

Year	CPI	Year	CPI	Year	CPI
1992	140.3	1998	163.0	2004	188.9
1993	144.5	1999	166.6	2005	195.3
1994	148.2	2000	172.2	2006	201.6
1995	152.4	2001	177.1	2007	207.3
1996	156.9	2002	179.9	2008	215.3
1997	160.5	2003	184.0	2009	214.5

Compute the inflation rate for each year 1993–2009 and determine which years were years of inflation. In which years did deflation occur? In which years did disinflation occur? Was there hyperinflation in any year?

18. SOURCES OF INFLATION Using the concepts of aggregate supply and aggregate demand, explain why inflation usually increases during wartime.

19. INFLATION AND INTEREST RATES Using a demand-supply diagram for loanable funds (like Exhibit 10), show what happens to the nominal interest rate and the equilibrium quantity of loans when both borrowers and lenders increase their estimates of the expected inflation rate from 5 percent to 10 percent.

Global Economic Watch Exercises

Login to www.cengagebrain.com and access the Global Economic Watch to do these exercises.

20. GLOBAL ECONOMIC WATCH and Case Study: Hyperinflation in Zimbabwe Go to the Global Economic Crisis Resource Center. Select Global Issues in Context. In the Basic Search box at the top of the page, enter the word "hyperinflation." On the Results page, go to the Magazines Section. Click on the link for the February 2, 2009, article "What Currency Crisis?" At the time of publication of the article, what was the price in Zimbabwean dollars of a loaf of bread?

21. GLOBAL ECONOMIC WATCH Go to the Global Economic Crisis Resource Center. Select Global Issues in Context. Go to the menu at the top of the page and click on the tab for Browse Issues and Topics. Choose Business and Economy. Click on the link for Unemployment and Joblessness. Find an article from the past three years about unemployment in a foreign country. What is the trend? Is there any information about the causes of and solutions to unemployment in that country?

Productivity and Growth

8

○ Why is the standard of living so much higher in some countries than in others?

○ How does an economy increase its living standard?

○ Why is the long-term growth rate more important than short-term fluctuations in economic activity?

○ What's labor productivity, why did it slow for a while, and why did it pick up again?

○ What's been the impact of computers and the Internet on labor productivity?

Answers to these and other questions are addressed in this chapter, which focuses on arguably the most important criteria for judging an economy's performance—productivity and growth.

The single most important determinant of a nation's standard of living in the long run is the productivity of its resources. Even seemingly low growth in productivity, if sustained for years, can have a substantial effect on the average living standard—that is, on the average availability of goods and services per capita. Growing productivity is therefore critical to a rising standard of living and has kept the U.S. economy a world leader.

Economic growth is a complicated process, one that even experts do not yet fully understand. Since before Adam Smith inquired into the sources of the *Wealth of Nations*, economists have puzzled over what makes some economies prosper while others founder. Because a market economy is not the product of conscious design, it does not reveal its secrets readily, nor can it be easily manipulated in pursuit of growth. We can't simply push here and pull there to achieve the desired result. Changing the economy is not like remodeling a home by knocking out a wall to expand the kitchen. Because we have no clear blueprint of the economy, we cannot make changes to specifications.

Still, there is much economists do know. In this chapter, we first develop a few simple models to examine productivity and growth. Then, we use these models to help explain why some nations are rich and some poor. U.S. performance gets special attention, particularly compared with other major economies around the world. We close with some controversies of technology and growth.

Topics include:

- Labor productivity
- The production function
- U.S. productivity and growth
- Technological change and unemployment

- Research and development
- Industrial Policy
- Convergence
- Income and Happiness

Theory of Productivity and Growth

Two centuries ago, 90 percent of the American workforce was in agriculture, where the hours were long and rewards unpredictable. Other workers had it no better, toiling from sunrise to sunset for a wage that bought just the bare necessities. People had little intellectual stimulation and little contact with the outside world. A skilled worker's home in 1800 was described as follows: "Sand sprinkled on the floor did duty as a carpet. . . . What a stove was he did not know. Coal he had never seen. Matches he had never heard of. . . . He rarely tasted fresh meat. . . . If the food of a [skilled worker] would now be thought coarse, his clothes would be thought abominable."[1]

Over the last two centuries, there has been an incredible increase in the U.S. *standard of living* as measured by the amount of goods and services available on average per person. An economy's standard of living grows over the long run because of (1) increases in the amount and quality of resources, especially labor and capital, (2) better technology, and (3) improvements in the *rules of the game* that facilitate production and exchange, such as tax laws, property rights, patent laws, the legal system, and the manners, customs, and conventions of the market. Perhaps the easiest way to introduce economic growth is by beginning with something you have already read about, the production possibilities frontier.

Growth and the Production Possibilities Frontier

The *production possibilities frontier*, or *PPF*, first introduced in Chapter 2, shows what the economy can produce if available resources are used efficiently. Let's briefly review the assumptions made in developing the frontier shown in Exhibit 1. During the period under consideration, usually a year, the quantity of resources in the economy

1. E. L. Bogart, *The Economic History of the United States* (Longmans Green, 1912), pp. 157–158.

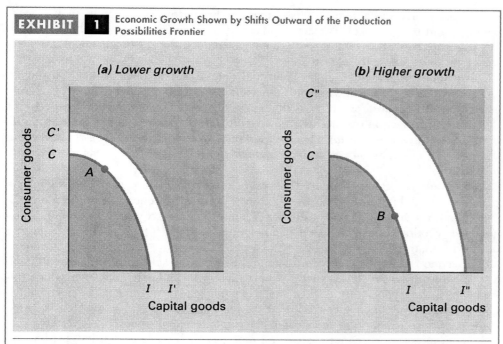

EXHIBIT 1 Economic Growth Shown by Shifts Outward of the Production Possibilities Frontier

An economy that produces more capital goods will grow more, as reflected by a shift outward of the production possibilities frontier. More capital goods are produced in panel (b) than in panel (a), so the PPF shifts out more in panel (b).

and the level of technology are assumed to be fixed. Also assumed fixed during the period are the rules of the game that facilitate production and exchange. We classify all production into two broad categories—in this case, consumer goods and capital goods. Capital goods are used to produce other goods. For example, the economy can bake pizzas and make pizza ovens. Pizzas are consumer goods, and ovens are capital goods.

When resources are employed efficiently, the production possibilities frontier *CI* in each panel of Exhibit 1 shows the possible combinations of consumer goods and capital goods that can be produced in a given year. Point *C* depicts the quantity of consumer goods produced if all the economy's resources are employed efficiently to produce them. Point *I* depicts the same for capital goods. Points inside the frontier are inefficient combinations, and points outside the frontier are unattainable combinations, given the resources, technology, and rules of the game. The production possibilities frontier is bowed out because resources are not perfectly adaptable to the production of both goods; some resources are specialized.

Economic growth is shown by an outward shift of the production possibilities frontier, as reflected in each panel of Exhibit 1. What can cause growth? An increase in resources, such as a growth in the labor supply or in the capital stock, shifts the frontier outward. Labor supply can increase either because of population growth or because the existing population works more. The capital stock increases if the economy produces more capital this year. The more capital produced this year, the more the economy grows, as reflected by an outward shift of the production frontier.

Breakthroughs in technology also shift out the frontier by making more efficient use of resources. Technological change often improves the quality of capital, but it can enhance the productivity of any resource. And technological change can free up resources for other uses. For example, the development of synthetic dyes in the 19th century freed up millions of acres of agricultural land that had been growing dye crops such as madder (red) and indigo (blue). The development of fiber-optic cable and cellular technology freed up the world's largest stock of copper in the form of existing telephone wires strung on poles across the nation.

Finally, any improvement in the rules of the game that nurtures production and exchange promotes growth and expands the frontier. For example, the economy can grow as a result of improved patent laws that encourage more inventions[2] or legal reforms that reduce transaction costs. Thus, *the economy grows because of a greater availability of resources, an improvement in the quality of resources, technological change that makes better use of resources, or improvements in the rules of the game that enhance production.*

The amount of capital produced this year shapes the PPF next year. For example, in panel (a) of Exhibit 1, the economy has chosen point A from possible points along CI. The capital produced this year shifts the PPF out to C'I' next year. But if more capital goods are produced this year, as reflected by point B in panel (b), the PPF shifts farther out next year, to C"I".

An economy that produces more capital this year is said to *invest* more in capital. As you can see, to invest more, people must give up some consumer goods this year. Thus, the opportunity cost of more capital goods this year is fewer consumer goods. More generally, we can say that people must *save* more now—that is, forgo some current consumption—to invest in capital. *Investment cannot occur without saving.* Economies that save more can invest more, as we'll see later. But let's get back to production.

What Is Productivity?

Production *is a process that transforms resources into goods and services.* Resources coupled with technology produce output. Productivity measures how efficiently resources are employed. In simplest terms, the greater the productivity, the more can be produced from a given amount of resources, and the farther out the production possibilities frontier. Economies that use resources more efficiently create a higher standard of living, meaning that more goods and services are produced per capita.

Productivity is defined as the ratio of total output to a specific measure of input. Productivity usually reflects an average, expressing total output divided by the amount of a particular kind of resource employed to produce that output. For example, **labor productivity** is the output per unit of labor and measures total output divided by the hours of labor employed to produce that output.

We can talk about the productivity of any resource, such as labor, capital, or natural resources. When agriculture accounted for most output in the economy, land productivity, such as bushels of grain per acre, was a key measure of economic welfare. Where soil was rocky and barren, people were poorer than where soil was fertile and fruitful. Even today, soil productivity determines the standard of living in some economies. Industrialization and trade, however, have liberated many from dependence on soil fertility. Today, some of the world's most productive economies have little land or have land of poor fertility. For example, Japan has a high living standard even though its population, which is 40 percent that of the United States, lives on a land area only 4 percent the size of the United States.

productivity
The ratio of a specific measure of output, such as real GDP, to a specific measure of input, such as labor; in this case productivity measures real GDP per hour of labor

labor productivity
Output per unit of labor; measured as real GDP divided by the hours of labor employed to produce that output

2. For evidence how the greater protection of intellectual property stimulates technological change, see Sunil Kanwar and Robert Evenson, "Does Intellectual Property Protection Spur Technological Change?" *Oxford Economic Papers*, 55 (April 2003): 235–264.

Labor Productivity

Labor is the resource most commonly used to measure productivity. Why labor? First, labor accounts for most production cost—about 70 percent on average. Second, labor is more easily measured than other inputs, whether we speak of hours per week or full-time workers per year. Statistics about employment and hours worked are more readily available and more reliable than those about other resources.

But the resource most responsible for increasing labor productivity is capital. As introduced in Chapter 1, the two broad categories are human capital and physical capital. *Human capital* is the accumulated knowledge, skill, and experience of the labor force. As workers acquire more human capital, their productivity and their incomes grow. That's why surgeons earn more than butchers and accountants earn more than file clerks. You are reading this book right now to enhance your human capital. *Physical capital* includes the machines, buildings, roads, airports, communication networks, and other human creations used to produce goods and services. Think about digging a ditch with bare hands versus using a shovel. Now switch the shovel for a backhoe. More physical capital obviously makes diggers more productive. Or consider picking oranges with bare hands versus using a picking machine that combs the trees with steel bristles. In less than 15 minutes the machine can pick 18 tons of oranges from 100 trees, catch the fruit, and drop it into storage carts. Without the machine, that would take four workers all day.[3] The operator of the picking machine is at least 128 times more productive than an orange picker using hands only.

In poorer countries labor is cheap and capital dear, so producers substitute labor for capital. For example, in India a beverage truck makes its rounds festooned with workers so as to minimize the time the truck, the valuable resource, spends at each stop. In the United States, where labor is more costly (compared with capital), the truck makes its rounds with just the driver. As another example, in Haiti, the poorest country in the Western Hemisphere, a ferry service could not afford to build a dock, so it hired workers to carry passengers through the water to and from the ferry on their shoulders.[4]

As an economy accumulates more capital per worker, labor productivity increases and the standard of living grows. The most productive combination of all is human capital combined with physical capital. For example, one certified public accountant with a computer and specialized software can sort out a company's finances more quickly and more accurately than could a thousand high-school-educated file clerks using just pencils and paper.

Per-Worker Production Function

We can express the relationship between the amount of capital per worker and the output per worker as an economy's **per-worker production function**. Exhibit 2 shows the amount of capital per worker, measured along the horizontal axis, and average output per worker, or labor productivity, measured along the vertical axis, other things constant—including the amount of labor, the level of technology, and rules of the game. Any point on the production function, *PF*, shows the average output per worker on the vertical axis for each level of capital per worker on the horizontal axis. For example, with *k* units of capital per worker, the average output per worker in the economy is *y*. The curve slopes

per-worker production function

The relationship between the amount of capital per worker in the economy and average output per worker

---

3. Eduardo Porter, "In Florida Groves, Cheap Labor Means Machines," *New York Times*, 22 March 2004.
4. This example was noted by Tyler Cowen, "The Ricardo Effect in Haiti," 23 February 2004, http://www .marginalrevolution.com.

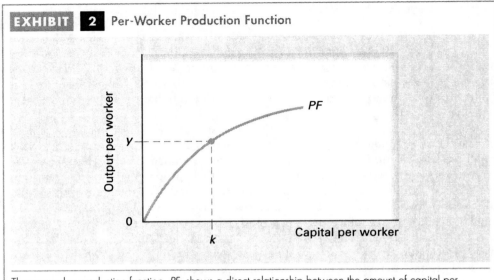

EXHIBIT 2 Per-Worker Production Function

The per-worker production function, *PF*, shows a direct relationship between the amount of capital per worker, *k*, and the output per worker, *y*. The bowed shape of *PF* reflects the law of diminishing marginal returns from capital, which holds that as more capital is added to a given number of workers, output per worker increases but at a diminishing rate and eventually could turn negative.

upward from left to right because an increase in capital per worker helps each worker produce more output. For example, bigger trucks make truck drivers more productive.

An increase in the amount of capital per worker is called **capital deepening** and is one source of rising productivity. *Capital deepening contributes to labor productivity and economic growth.* As the quantity of capital per worker increases, output per worker increases but at a diminishing rate, as reflected by the shape of the per-worker production function. The diminishing slope of this curve reflects the *law of diminishing marginal returns from capital*, which says that beyond some level of capital per worker, increases in capital add less and less to output per worker. For example, increasing the size of trucks beyond some point has diminishing returns as trucks become too large to negotiate some public roads. Thus, given the amount of labor, the level of technology, and the rules of the game, additional gains from more capital per worker eventually diminish and could turn negative.

capital deepening
An increase in the amount of capital per worker; one source of rising labor productivity

Technological Change

Held constant along a per-worker production function is the level of technology in the economy. Technological change usually improves the *quality* of capital and represents another source of increased productivity. For example, a tractor is more productive than a horse-drawn plow, a word processor more productive than a typewriter, and an Excel spreadsheet more productive than pencil and paper. Better technology is reflected in Exhibit 3 by an upward rotation in the per-worker production function from *PF* to *PF'*. As a result of a technological breakthrough, more is produced at each level of capital per worker. For example, if there are *k* units of capital per worker, a major breakthrough in technology increases the output per worker in the economy from *y* to *y'*.

Simon Kuznets, who won a Nobel Prize in part for his analysis of economic growth, claimed that technological change and the ability to apply such breakthroughs to all aspects of production are the driving forces behind economic growth in market economies. Kuznets argued that changes in the *quantities* of labor and capital account for only one-tenth of the increase in economic growth. Nine-tenths came from improvements in the *quality* of these inputs. As technological breakthroughs become *embodied* in new capital, resources are combined more efficiently, increasing total output. *From the wheel to the assembly-line robot, capital embodies the fruits of discovery and drives economic growth.*

Thus, two kinds of changes in capital improve worker productivity: (1) an increase in the *quantity* of capital per worker, as reflected by a movement along the per-worker production function, and (2) an improvement in the *quality* of capital per worker, as reflected by technological change that rotates the curve upward. More capital per worker and better capital per worker result in more output per worker, which, over time, translates into more output per capita, meaning a higher standard of living.

Rules of the Game

Perhaps the most elusive ingredients for productivity and growth are the **rules of the game,** the formal and informal institutions that promote economic activity: the laws, customs, manners, conventions, and other institutional elements that encourage people to undertake productive activity. A stable political environment and system of well-defined property rights are important. Less investment occurs if potential investors believe their capital could be seized by the government, stolen by thieves, destroyed by civil unrest, or blown up by terrorists. For example, countries whose colonizers established strong property rights hundreds of years ago have, on average, much higher incomes today than countries whose colonizers did not.[5] Improvements in the rules of the game could result in more output for each level of capital per worker, thus reflected by a rotation up in the per-worker production function as shown in Exhibit 3.

rules of the game
The formal and informal institutions that promote economic activity; the laws, customs, manners, conventions, and other institutional elements that determine transaction costs and thereby affect people's incentive to undertake production and exchange

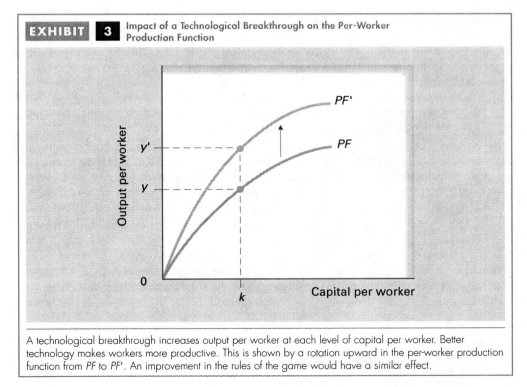

EXHIBIT 3 Impact of a Technological Breakthrough on the Per-Worker Production Function

A technological breakthrough increases output per worker at each level of capital per worker. Better technology makes workers more productive. This is shown by a rotation upward in the per-worker production function from *PF* to *PF'*. An improvement in the rules of the game would have a similar effect.

5. Daron Acemoglu, Simon Johnson, and James A. Robinson, "The Colonial Origins of Comparative Development," *American Economic Review*, 91(December 2001): 1369–1401.

We tend to think that laws are the backbone of market exchange, but we should not underestimate the role of manners, customs, and conventions. According to the 18th century British philosopher Edmund Burke, "Manners are of more importance than law. . . . The law touches us but here and there and now and then. Manners are what vex or soothe, corrupt or purify, exalt or debase, barbarize or refine us, by a constant, steady, uniform and insensible operation like that of the air we breathe in."[6] The Russian proverb, "Custom is stronger than law," makes a similar point.

Simply put, a more stable political climate could benefit productivity just like a technological improvement. Conversely, events that foster instability can harm an economy's productivity and rotate the per-worker production function downward. The terrorist attack on the World Trade Center and Pentagon was such a destabilizing event. According to Albert Abadie, a Harvard economist, the attack affected "the spinal cord of any favorable business environment"—the ability of business and workers "to meet and communicate effectively without incurring risks."[7] The 9/11 attacks increased the vacancy rates of tall buildings even in cities besides New York, such as Chicago's Sears Tower, making that capital less productive.[8] As other examples, a greater threat to airport security adds to the time and cost of flying. Shops in countries plagued by suicide bombers must hire security guards to deter such horror, and this increases the cost of doing business. And the mortgage meltdown of 2007–2009 reduced the trust that one bank had in another, thereby freezing up credit markets and increasing the cost of borrowing.

Now that you have some idea about the theory of productivity and growth, let's look at them in practice, beginning with the vast difference in performance among economies around the world. Then we turn to the United States.

Productivity and Growth in Practice

Differences in the standard of living among countries are vast. To give you some idea, per capita output in the United States, a world leader among major economies, is about 155 times that of the world's poorest countries. Poor countries are poor because they experience low labor productivity. We can sort the world's economies into two broad groups. **Industrial market countries,** or *developed countries,* make up about 16 percent of the world's population. They consist of the economically advanced capitalist countries of Western Europe, North America, Australia, New Zealand, and Japan, plus the newly industrialized Asian countries of Taiwan, South Korea, Hong Kong, and Singapore. Industrial market countries were usually the first to experience long-term economic growth during the 19th century, and today have the world's highest standard of living based on abundant human and physical capital. Industrial market countries produce nearly three-quarters of the world's output. The rest of the world, the remaining 84 percent of the world's population, consists of **developing countries,** which have a lower standard of living because they have less human and physical capital. Many workers in developing countries are farmers. Because farming methods there are primitive, labor productivity is low and most people barely subsist, much like Americans two centuries ago.

industrial market countries
Economically advanced capitalist countries of Western Europe, North America, Australia, New Zealand, and Japan, plus the newly industrialized Asian economies of Taiwan, South Korea, Hong Kong, and Singapore

developing countries
Countries with a low living standard because of less human and physical capital per worker

6.   Edmund Burke, *Letters to Parliament,* 2nd ed. (London, 1796): 105.
7.   As quoted in Greg Ip and John McKinnon, "Economy Likely Won't See Gain from War Against Terrorism," *Wall Street Journal,* 25 September 2001.
8.   Alberto Abadie and Sofia Dermisi, "Is Terrorism Eroding Agglomeration Economies in Central Business Districts? Lessons from the Office Real Estate Market in Downtown Chicago," *Journal of Urban Economics,* 64 (September 2008): 451–463.

Education and Economic Development

Another important source of productivity is human capital—the skill, experience, and education of workers. If knowledge is lacking, other resources may not be used efficiently. *Education makes workers aware of the latest production techniques and more receptive to new approaches and methods.* Exhibit 4 shows the percentage of the population ages 25 to 64 who have at least a degree beyond high school. Figures are presented for the United States and six other industrial market economies, together called the *Group of Seven*, or *G-7* (sometimes Russia is added to form the G-8, but Russia is not yet an industrial market economy and has a per capita income less than half of any G-7 country). In 1998, 35 percent of the U.S. adult population had at least a degree beyond high school, ranking second behind Canada. The U.S. percentage grew to 40 by 2007, though America slipped to third behind Canada and Japan.

But a focus on younger adults, those ages 25 to 34, indicates that more countries are passing the United States. Whereas 40 percent of Americans ages 25 to 34 had at least a degree beyond high school in 2007, 54 percent of Canadians did, as well as 54 percent of the Japanese, and 41 percent of the French. And outside of the largest economies, a half dozen other industrial economies exceeded the U.S. percentage.

Not shown in Exhibit 4 are developing countries, which have far lower education levels. For example, while the literacy rate exceeds 95 percent in industrial market economies, more than half the adults in the world's poorest countries can't read or write.

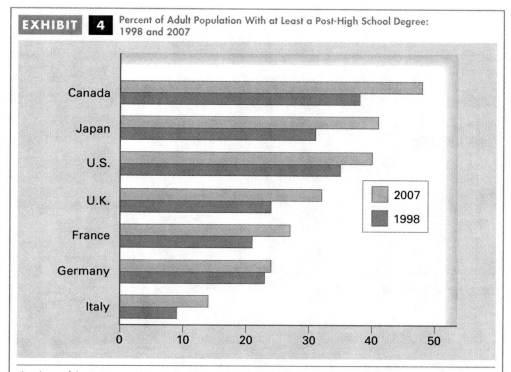

EXHIBIT 4 Percent of Adult Population With at Least a Post-High School Degree: 1998 and 2007

The share of the U.S. population ages 25 to 64 with at least a degree beyond high school increased from 35 percent in 1998 to 40 percent in 2007. The United States slipped from second among major industrial market economies in 1998 to third in 2007.

Source: Based on figures in *Education at a Glance: 2009,* OECD at http://www.oecd.org.

U.S. Labor Productivity

What has been the record of labor productivity in the United States? Exhibit 5 offers a long-run perspective, showing growth in real output per work hour for the last 140 years. Annual productivity growth is averaged by decade. The huge dip during the Great Depression and the strong rebound during World War II are unmistakable. Growth slowed during the 1970s and 1980s but recovered since 1990. Labor productivity has grown an average of 2.1 percent per year since 1870. This may not impress you, but because of the power of compounding, output per hour has jumped 1,735 percent during the period. To put this in perspective, if a roofer in 1870 could shingle one roof in a day, today's roofer could shingle more than 18 roofs in a day.

Over long periods, small differences in productivity can make huge differences in the economy's ability to produce and therefore in the standard of living. For example, if productivity grew only 1.0 percent per year instead of 2.1 percent, output per work hour since 1870 would have increased by only 303 percent, not 1,735 percent. On the

EXHIBIT **5** Long-Term Trend in U.S. Labor Productivity Growth: Annual Average by Decade

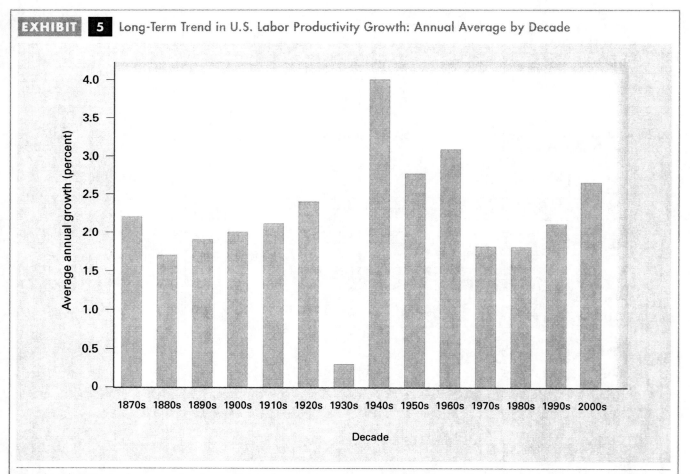

Annual productivity growth, measured as the growth in real output per work hour, is averaged by decade. For the entire period since 1870, labor productivity grew an average of 2.1 percent per year. Note the big dip during the Great Depression of the 1930s and the big bounce back during World War II. Productivity growth slowed during the 1970s and 1980s but recovered during the 1990s and 2000s.

Sources: Angus Maddison, *Phases of Capitalist Development* (New York: Oxford University Press, 1982) and U.S. Bureau of Labor Statistics. Average for the "2000s" decade goes through first half of 2010. For the latest data, go to http://www.bls.gov/lpc/.

other hand, if productivity grew 2.6 percent per year (the average since 1996), output per work hour since 1870 would have jumped 3,536 percent! The wheels of progress seem to grind slowly but they grind very fine, and the cumulative effect is powerful.

So far, we have averaged productivity growth for all workers. Productivity has grown more in some industries than in others. In ocean shipping, for example, cargo carried per worker hour is about 100 times greater now than in 1900, for an average annual growth of 4.3 percent. On the other hand, those making wooden office furniture are only about three times more productive today than in 1900, for an average annual growth in productivity of only 1.3 percent. Consider productivity gains in TV journalism. Not long ago, a TV reporter covering a story would need a camera operator, a sound technician, and a broadcast editor. Now, because of technological advances in the size, quality, and ease of equipment, TV reporters set up their own cameras on the scene, shoot their own footage, and do their own editing. One person can do what used to take four to accomplish.

Slowdown and Rebound in Productivity Growth

You can see in Exhibit 5 that productivity growth slowed to 1.8 percent per year during the 1970s and 1980s, and has recovered since 1990. By breaking the data down into intervals other than decades, we can get a better feel for years since World War II. Exhibit 6 offers average annual growth for four periods. Labor productivity growth averaged 2.9 percent per year between 1948 and 1973; these could be called the golden

EXHIBIT 6 U.S. Labor Productivity Growth Slowed During 1974 to 1982 and Then Rebounded

The growth in labor productivity declined from an average of 2.9 percent per year between 1948 and 1973 to only 1.0 percent between 1974 and 1982. A jump in the price of oil contributed to three recessions during that stretch, and new environmental and workplace regulations, though necessary and beneficial, slowed down productivity growth temporarily. The information revolution powered by the computer chip and the Internet has boosted productivity in recent years.

Source: Averages based on annual estimates from the U.S. Bureau of Labor Statistics. For the latest data go to http://www.bls.gov/lpc/home.htm. Average for 1996–2010 is through the first half of 2010.

years of productivity growth. But, between 1974 and 1982, productivity growth slowed to only a third of that, averaging just 1.0 percent. Why the slowdown? First, oil prices jumped from 1973 to 1974 and again from 1979 to 1980 as a result of OPEC actions, boosting inflation and contributing to stagflation and three recessions. Second, legislation in the early 1970s necessary to protect the environment and improve workplace safety slowed the growth of labor productivity.

Fortunately, productivity rebounded off the 1974–1982 low, averaging 1.8 percent from 1983 to 1995 and 2.7 percent from 1996 to 2010. Why the rebound? The information revolution powered by the computer chip started paying off, as discussed in the following case study.

CASE STUDY

THE INFORMATION ECONOMY

Computers, the Internet, and Productivity Growth   The first microprocessor, the Intel 4004, could perform about 400 computations per second when it hit the market in 1971. IBM's first personal computer, introduced a decade later, executed 330,000 computations per second. Today a $500 PC can handle over 6 billion computations per second, or *15 million* times what the 1971 Intel 4004 could do. Such advances in computing power have fueled a boom in computer use and made the United States a world leader. U.S. companies and universities are well ahead of other countries in high technology applications, ranging from software to biotechnology.

Computers help people work together. For example, design engineers in California can use the Web to test new ideas with marketers in New York, cutting development time in half. Sales representatives on the road can use laptops or other wireless devices to log orders and serve customers. U.S. insurance companies can coordinate data entry done as far away as India to handle claims more efficiently. An owner of multiple restaurants can use the Internet to track sales up to the minute, check the temperatures of freezers, refrigerators, and fryers, and observe each restaurant through a live video feed. New generations of machines monitor themselves and send messages detailing any problems as they arise. For example, General Electric uses the Internet to keep tabs on factory equipment thousands of miles away. Some home appliances, such as refrigerators and TVs, are also Internet compatible. Computers not only improve the quality and safety in many industries, including automobiles and airlines, but they increase the versatility of machines, which can be reprogrammed for different tasks.

Computers boost productivity through two channels: (1) efficiency gains in the production of computers and semiconductors and (2) greater computer use by industry. These two channels account for much of the gain in productivity growth since 1996. Although computer hardware manufacturers make up only a tiny fraction of the U.S. economy, their pace of innovation quickened enough since 1996 to boost overall U.S. productivity growth. For example, Intel's 3.1-gigahertz Pentium 4 processor sold for under $100, much less than the $990 for the 1.1-gigahertz Pentium 3 it ultimately replaced. What's more, efficiency in semiconductor production and price declines since 1996 advanced IT use by business more generally, which also enhanced labor productivity. America invested more and earlier in IT than did other major economies, so productivity benefits showed up here first. The jump in labor productivity that began in the 1990s resulted from greater investment in information and communication technology.

Finding the best way to use new technology takes time. There are usually lags between when a new technology is introduced and when the benefits show up—for example, cash registers tied to the inventory system in warehouses (think Wal-Mart)

e **activity**

While the application of computing technologies by U.S. firms has grown drastically, cost and technical issues have made warehouse management systems unapproachable for many small companies. But hosted warehouse systems are beginning to change this; do a search on Google at http://www.google.com for "warehouse management systems" and learn how they work. You can also visit http://www.upslogisticstech.com/pages/realstories/ for real world stories of UPS Logistics Technologies transportation management software being used to increase productivity in online grocery shopping, beverage delivery, medical supplies, and more.

and communications systems connected to offices in different buildings and even different countries (think General Electric). What really set the productivity gains in motion was the big drop in semiconductor prices during the late 1990s. Going digital became a no-brainer for business. Computers per worker increased, which boosted labor productivity throughout the entire economy but especially in the service sector.

The question is how long can the productivity pop from computers and the Internet last? Northwestern University's Robert Gordon argues that the economy enjoyed a one-time boost from computers and the Internet. Other economists are more upbeat, but they acknowledge that it takes a steady stream of innovations to keep U.S. productivity growing.

Sources: Dale Jorgenson, Mun Ho, and Kevin Stiroh, "A Retrospective Look at the U.S. Productivity Growth Resurgence," *Journal of Economic Perspectives*, 22 (Winter 2008): 3–24; "Something Is Not Working," *The Economist*, 29 April 2010; and "U.S. Productivity Growth in Quarter Tops Forecast," *New York Times*, 6 May 2010. The federal government's labor productivity home page is http://www.bls.gov/lpc/home.htm.

Higher labor productivity growth can easily make up for output lost from most recessions. For example, if over the next 10 years the U.S. labor productivity grows an average of 2.7 percent per year (the average from 1996 to 2010) instead of 1.8 percent (the average from 1983 to 1995), that higher growth would add $1.5 trillion to GDP in the 10th year—more than enough to make up for the output lost during the worst recession since the Great Depression. *This cumulative power of productivity growth is why economists pay so much attention to long-term growth.*

Output per Capita

As noted earlier, the best measure of an economy's standard of living is output per capita. *Output per capita*, or GDP divided by the population, indicates how much an economy produces on average per resident. Exhibit 7 presents real GDP per capita for the United States since 1959. Notice the general upward trend, interrupted by eight recessions, indicated by the pink bars. Real GDP per capita nearly tripled for an average annual growth rate of 2.0 percent.

International Comparisons

How does U.S. output per capita compare with that of other industrial countries? Exhibit 8 compares GDP per capita in 2009 for the United States and the six other leading industrial nations. Local currencies have been converted to U.S. dollars of 2009 purchasing power. With nominal GDP per capita of $46,400 in 2009, the United States stood alone at the top, with a per capita income 21 percent above second-ranked Canada and at least 32 percent above the rest. Thus, the United States produced more per capita than any other major economy.

Exhibit 8 looks at the *level* of output per capita. What about the *growth* in output per capita? Exhibit 9 shows growth in real GDP per capita from 1979 to 2009. With an average growth of 1.8 percent per year, the United States ranked third among the seven

net bookmark

Productivity data are available in the *Statistical Abstract of the United States.* Go to http://www.census.gov/compendia/statab/. On the menu on the left, mouse over Labor Force, Employment, and Earnings. Choose Productivity to see the available tables of statistics.

EXHIBIT **7** U.S. Real GDP per Capita has Nearly Tripled Since 1959

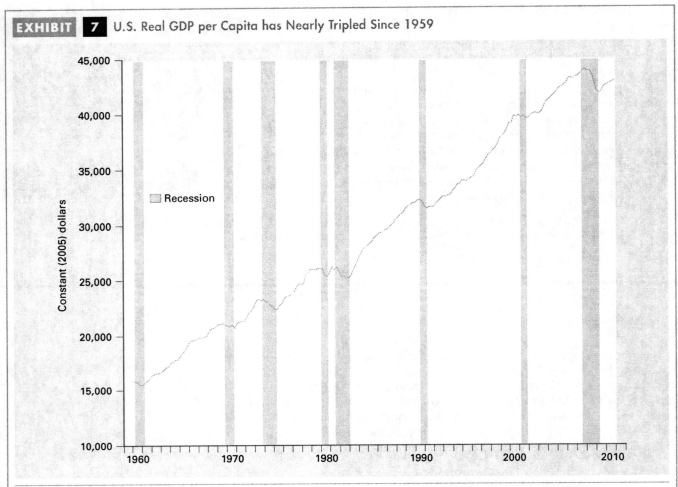

Despite eight recessions since 1959, real GDP per capita has nearly tripled. Periods of recession are indicated by the pink shaded bars.

Source: *Survey of Current Business*, 90 (May 2010), Chart D. For the latest data, go to http://www.bea.gov/scb/index.htm. Select the most recent month, go to the "National Data" section toward the end of the page, and then select "Charts."

major economies. The United Kingdom ranked first, thanks in part to Prime Minister Margaret Thatcher, who converted some crusty government enterprises into dynamic for-profit firms. Industries she *privatized* during the 1980s include coal, iron and steel, gas, electricity, railways, trucking, airlines, telecommunications, and the water supply. She also cut income tax rates.

To Review: U.S. labor productivity growth has averaged 2.1 percent per year since 1870. Productivity growth slowed between 1974 and 1982, because of spikes in energy prices and implementation of necessary but costly new environmental and workplace regulations. Since 1982 labor productivity growth has picked up, especially since 1996, due primarily to breakthroughs in information technology. Among the seven major economies, the United States experienced the third fastest growth in real GDP per capita income between 1979 and 2009, and in 2009 boasted the highest GDP per capita among major economies.

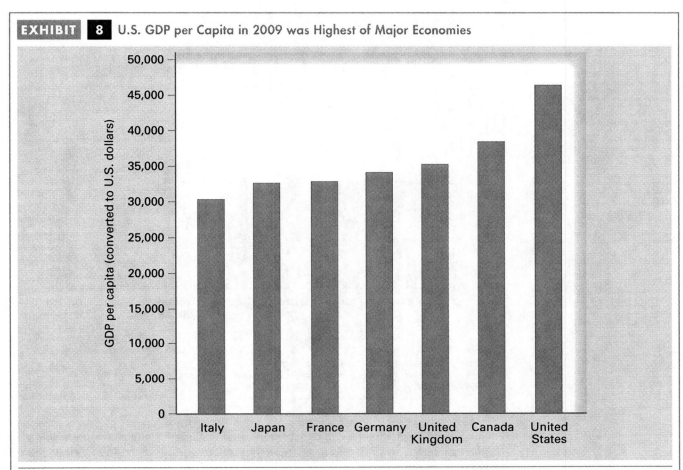

EXHIBIT   **8**   U.S. GDP per Capita in 2009 was Highest of Major Economies

Source: Based on 2009 dollar estimates from the OECD at http://www.oecd.org/home/ and *The World Factbook:* at https://www.cia.gov/library/publications/the-world-factbook/index.html. Estimates have been adjusted across countries using the purchasing power of the local currency in 2009.

Other Issues of Technology and Growth

In this section we consider some other issues of technology and growth, beginning with the question whether technological change creates unemployment.

Does Technological Change Lead to Unemployment?

Because technological change usually reduces the labor needed to produce a given amount of output, some observers fear technological change increases unemployment. True, technological change can create dislocations as displaced workers try to find jobs elsewhere. But technological change can also create new products and job opportunities and make existing products more affordable. For example, the assembly line cut the cost of automobiles, making them more affordable for the average household. This increased the quantity of automobiles demanded, boosting production and employment. Even in industries where machines displace some workers, those who keep their jobs

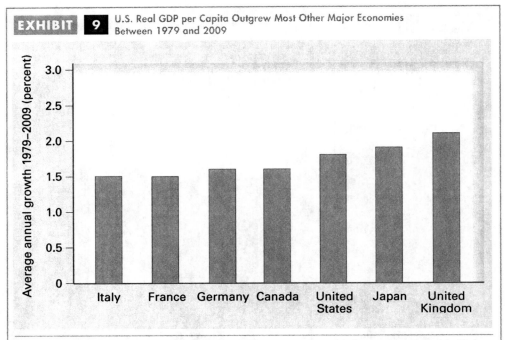

EXHIBIT 9   U.S. Real GDP per Capita Outgrew Most Other Major Economies Between 1979 and 2009

Source: Based on annual figures from 1979 to 2009 from the U.S. Bureau of Labor Statistics at ftp://ftp .bls.gov/pub/special.requests/ForeignLabor/flsgdp.txt. Figures were converted into U.S. dollars based on the purchasing power of local currency. The German growth rate prior to 1991, is for West Germany. For the latest data, go to http://www.stats.bls.gov/fls/.

become more productive, so they earn more. And *because human wants are unlimited, displaced workers usually find jobs producing other goods and services demanded in a growing economy.*

Although job data from the 19th century are sketchy, there is no evidence that the unemployment rate is any higher today than it was in 1870. Since then, worker productivity has increased over 1,700 percent, and the length of the average workweek has been cut nearly in half. Although technological change may displace some workers in the short run, long-run benefits include higher real incomes and more leisure—in short, a higher standard of living.

If technological change causes unemployment, then the recent spurt in productivity growth should have increased unemployment compared to the slow-growth years from 1974 to 1982. But the unemployment rate, the percentage of the workforce looking for jobs, averaged 7.2 percent during 1974 to 1982, compared to only 5.6 percent from 1996 to 2010. And if technological change causes unemployment, then unemployment rates should be lower in economies where the latest technology has not yet been adopted, such as in developing countries. But unemployment is much worse there, and those fortunate enough to find work earn little because they are not very productive.

Again, there is no question that technological change sometimes creates job dislocations and hardships in the short run, as workers scramble to adjust to a changing world. Some workers with specialized skills made obsolete by technology may be unable to find jobs that pay as well as the ones they lost. These dislocations are one price of progress. Over time, however, most displaced workers find other jobs, often in new industries created by technological change. In a typical year of expansion, the U.S. economy eliminates about 10 million jobs but creates nearly 12 million new ones. Out with the old, in with the new.

Research and Development

As noted several times already, a prime contributor to labor productivity growth has been an improvement in the quality of human and physical capital. Human capital has benefited from better education and more job training. Better technology embodied in physical capital has also helped labor productivity. For example, because of extensive investments in cellular transmission, new satellites, and fiber-optic technology, labor productivity in the telecommunications industry has increased by an average of 5.5 percent per year during the past three decades.

Improvements in technology arise from scientific discovery, which is the fruit of research. We can distinguish between basic research and applied research. **Basic research,** the search for knowledge without regard to how that knowledge will be used, is a first step toward technological advancement. In terms of economic growth, however, scientific discoveries are meaningless until they are implemented, which requires applied research. **Applied research** seeks to answer particular questions or to apply scientific discoveries to the development of specific products. Because technological breakthroughs may or may not have commercial possibilities, the payoff is less immediate with basic research than with applied research. *Yet basic research yields a higher return to society as a whole than does applied research.*

Because technological change is the fruit of research and development (R&D), investment in R&D improves productivity through technological discovery. One way to track R&D spending is to measure it relative to gross domestic product, or GDP. Exhibit 10 shows R&D spending as a share of GDP for the United States and the six other major economies for the 1980s, 1990s, and 2007. Overall R&D spending in the United States during the last quarter century has remained constant, averaging 2.7 percent of GDP in the 1980s, in the 1990s, and in 2007. During the 1990s and in 2007, the United States ranked second among the major economies, behind Japan.

Bar segments in the chart distinguish between R&D by businesses (shown as green segments) and R&D by governments and nonprofit institutions (shown as orange segments). Business R&D is more likely to target applied research and innovations. R&D spending by governments and nonprofits, such as universities, may generate basic knowledge that has applications in the long run (for example, the Internet sprang from R&D spending on national defense). R&D by U.S. businesses averaged about 1.9 percent of GDP in all three periods. Again, only Japan had higher business R&D than the United States in the 1990s and in 2007. In short, the United States devotes more resources to R&D than most other advanced economies, and this helps America maintain a higher standard of living.

Industrial Policy

Policy makers have debated whether government should become more involved in shaping an economy's technological future. One concern is that technologies of the future will require huge sums to develop, sums that an individual firm cannot easily raise and put at risk. Another concern is that some technological breakthroughs spill over to other firms and other industries, but the firm that develops the breakthrough may not be in a position to reap benefits from these spillover effects, so individual firms may underinvest in such research. One possible solution is more government involvement in economic planning.

Industrial policy is the idea that government, using taxes, subsidies, regulations, and coordination of the private sector, could help nurture the industries and technologies of the future to give domestic industries an advantage over foreign competitors. The idea is to secure a leading role for domestic industry in the world economy. One example of

---

basic research
The search for knowledge without regard to how that knowledge will be used

applied research
Research that seeks answers to particular questions or to apply scientific discoveries to develop specific products

industrial policy
The view that government—using taxes, subsidies, and regulations—should nurture the industries and technologies of the future, thereby giving these domestic industries an advantage over foreign competition

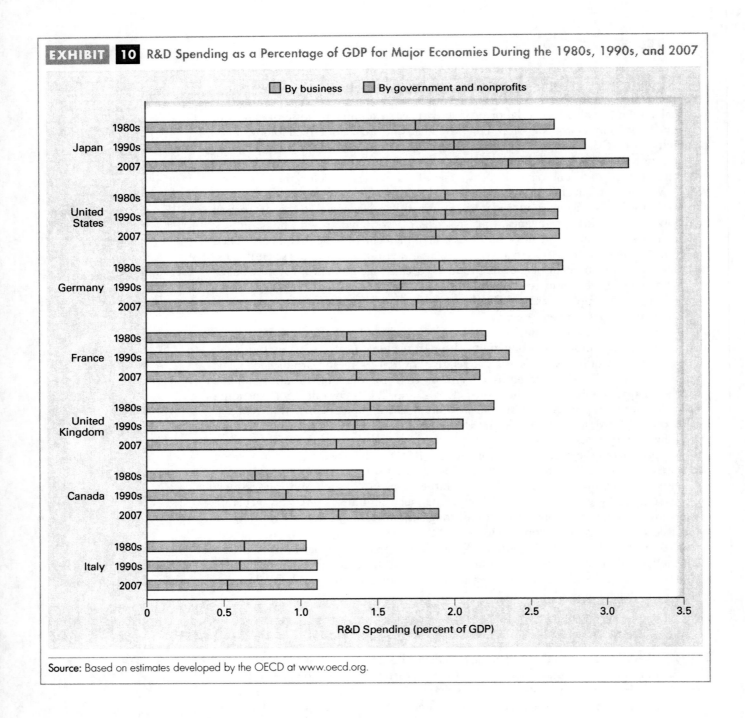

EXHIBIT 10   R&D Spending as a Percentage of GDP for Major Economies During the 1980s, 1990s, and 2007

By business   By government and nonprofits

R&D Spending (percent of GDP)

Source: Based on estimates developed by the OECD at www.oecd.org.

European industrial policy is Airbus Industrie, a four-nation aircraft consortium. With an estimated $20 billion in government aid, the aircraft maker has become Boeing's main rival. When Airbus seeks aircraft orders around the world, it can draw on government backing to promise favorable terms, such as landing rights at key European airports and an easing of regulatory constraints. U.S. producers get less government backing.

For decades, U.S. industrial policy was aimed at creating the world's most advanced military production capacity. With the demise of the Soviet Union, however, defense technologies became less important, but wars in Iraq and Afghanistan have shifted some attention back to military applications. Some argue that U.S. industrial policy should shift from a military to a civilian focus. Many state governments are also trying to identify what industries to support. Economists have long recognized that firms in some industries gain a performance advantage by *clustering*—that is, by locating in a region already thick with firms in the same industry or in related industries. Clusters such as Hollywood studios, Wall Street brokers, Broadway theaters, Las Vegas casinos, Boston colleges, Orlando theme parks, and Silicon Valley software makers facilitate communication and promote healthy competition among cluster members. The flow of information and cooperation between firms, as well as the competition among firms in close proximity, stimulates regional innovation and propels growth. By locating in a region already settled with similar firms, a firm can also tap into established local markets for specialized labor and for other inputs.

But skeptics wonder whether the government should be trusted to identify emerging technologies and to pick the industry clusters that will lead the way. Critics of industrial policy believe that markets allocate scarce resources better than governments do. For example, European governments' costly attempt to develop the supersonic transport Concorde never became cost efficient. Airbus has also run into financial difficulties, and sponsoring governments have tried to distance themselves from the company. As a U.S. example, in the early 1980s, the U.S. government spent $1 billion to help military contractors develop a high-speed computer circuit. But Intel, a company getting no federal aid, was the first to develop the circuit.

There is also concern that an industrial policy would evolve into a government giveaway program. Rather than going to the most promising technologies, the money and the competitive advantages would go to the politically connected. Critics also wonder how wise it is to sponsor corporate research when beneficiaries may share their expertise with foreign companies or even build factories abroad. Most economists would prefer to let Microsoft, General Electric, Google, or some start-up bet their own money on the important technologies of the future.

Do Economies Converge?

If given enough time, will poor countries eventually catch up with rich ones? The **convergence** theory argues that developing countries can grow faster than advanced ones and should eventually close the gap. Here's why: It is easier to copy existing technology than to develop new ones. Countries that are technologically backward can grow faster by adopting existing technology. But economies already using the latest technology must come up with a steady stream of breakthroughs to grow faster.

Leading countries, such as the United States, find growth limited by the rate of creation of new knowledge and better technology. But follower countries can grow more quickly by, for example, adding computers where they previously had none. Until 1995, the United States, which makes up just five percent of the world's population, accounted for most of the world's computer purchases by households. But by 2000, most computers were bought by non-U.S. households.

What's the evidence on convergence? Some poor countries have begun to catch up with richer ones. For example, the newly industrialized Asian economies of Hong Kong, Singapore, South Korea, and Taiwan, by adopting the latest technology and investing in human resources, are closing the gap with the world leaders. Real output per capita in South Korea has grown three times faster than the average for the seven major economies. These *Asian Tigers* have graduated from developing economies to industrial

convergence
A theory predicting that the standard of living in economies around the world will grow more similar over time, with poorer countries eventually catching up with richer ones

market economies. But these are the exceptions. According to research by the World Bank, among the nations that comprise the poorest third of the world's population, consumption per capita has grown only about 1.0 percent per year over the past two decades compared with a 2.5 percent growth in the rest of the world, so the standard of living in the poorest third of the world has grown somewhat in absolute terms but has fallen further behind in relative terms. Worse yet, a billion people seem trapped in poor economies that are going nowhere.

One reason per capita consumption has grown so slowly in the poorest economies is that birthrates there are double those in richer countries, so poor economies must produce still more just to keep up with a growing population. Another reason why convergence has not begun, particularly for the poorest third of the world, is the vast difference in the quality of human capital across countries. Whereas technology is indeed portable, the knowledge, skill, and training needed to take advantage of that technology are not. Countries with a high level of human capital can make up for other shortcomings. For example, much of the capital stock in Japan and Germany was destroyed during World War II. But the two countries retained enough of their well-educated and highly skilled labor force to rejoin elite industrial market economies in little more than a generation. But some countries, such as those in Africa, simply lack the human capital needed to identify and absorb new technology. As noted already, such poor economies tend to have low education levels and low literacy rates. What's more, some countries lack the stable macroeconomic environment and the established institutions needed to nurture economic growth. Many developing countries have serious deficiencies in their infrastructures, lacking, for example, the reliable source of electricity to power new technologies. For example, in Northern Nigeria, near the Sahara, 90 percent of the villages have no electricity. Some of the poorest nations have been ravaged by civil war for years. And simply communicating can be challenging in some developing countries. In Nigeria, for example, more than 400 languages are spoken by 250 distinct ethnic groups. (To learn more about the challenges facing the poorest nations, read the final chapter of this book, entitled "Economic Development.")

Some argue that the focus should be less on a nation's production and income and more on the happiness of the population. The link between income and happiness is discussed in this closing case study.

CASE STUDY

e activity

Gross National Happiness (GNH) is the goal proclaimed by the King of Bhutan. Learn more about GNH at http://www.grossnationalhappiness.com/. Click on Questionnaire to learn how GNH is tabulated.

PUBLIC POLICY

Income and Happiness The Declaration of Independence in 1776 identified "certain unalienable Rights, that among these are Life, Liberty, and the Pursuit of Happiness." This did not guarantee happiness but did establish the pursuit of happiness as an "unalienable" right, meaning that right cannot be taken away, given away, or sold. Eighteenth-century philosopher and social reformer Jeremy Bentham argued that government policy should promote the greatest happiness for the greatest number of people.

Many people today apparently agree. In recent polls, 77 percent of Australians and 81 percent of Brits believed that a government's prime objective should be promoting the greatest happiness rather than the greatest wealth. The United Nations sponsored an international conference on "Happiness and Public Policy." Thailand now compiles a monthly Gross Domestic Happiness Index. Even China has joined in the fun, reporting a happiness index based on polling results about living conditions, income, the environment, social welfare, and employment. Australia, Canada, Germany and the United Kingdom are also developing indexes of happiness or well being. For example, the Canadian Index of Well Being will contain a measure of social connectedness, among other things.

Economists have long shied away from asking people how they feel, preferring instead to observe their behavior. But more now see some value in asking questions. In the most extensive of polls, the Gallup organization asked people in 130 countries: "How satisfied are you with your life, on a scale of zero to ten?" The results, are not surprising. Most people in the high income areas, such as the United States, Europe, and Japan, said they are happy. Most people in the poor areas, especially in Africa, said they are not. Also, within a given country, income and happiness are positively related. After evaluating all the results of the Gallup world poll, Angus Deaton of Princeton concluded: "The very strong global relationship between per capita GDP and life satisfaction suggests that on average people have a good idea of how income, or the lack of it, affects their lives."[9]

So these results are no surprise. What does puzzle economists is that other surveys suggest that Americans on average do not seem any happier over time even though each generation became richer than the last. The proportion of Americans who say they are happy has stayed about the same despite 60 years of economic growth.

The United States is unusual in that regard. Surveys in Europe and Japan do find an increase in happiness with increases in income over time. Here's a possible explanation. Americans begin taking for granted those luxuries they most desired. For example, two generations ago color TVs, automobiles, and major appliances were luxuries, but now they are must-have items for most households. Computers and flat screen HDTVs will soon move from luxuries to necessities. As each generation attains a higher standard of living, people become less sensitive to the benefits, they take them for granted, and thus they say they are no happier.

Sources: Jon Gertner, "The Rise and Fall of the GDP," *New York Times*, 10 May 2010; Daniel Gilbert, *Stumbling On Happiness* (New York: Knopf, 2006); Guglielmo Caporale et al. "Income and Happiness Across Europe: Do Reference Values Matter?" *Journal of Economic Psychology*, 30 (February 2009): 42–51; Angus Deaton, "Income, Health, and Well-Being Around the World: Evidence from the Gallup World Poll," *Journal of Economic Perspectives*, 22 (Spring 2008): 53–72; and Betsey Stevenson and Justin Wolfers, "The Paradox of Declining Female Happiness," *American Economic Journal: Economic Policy*, 1 (August 2009): 190–225.

Conclusion

Productivity and growth depend on the supply and quality of resources, the level of technology, and the rules of the game that nurture production and exchange. These elements tend to be correlated with one another. An economy with an unskilled and poorly educated workforce usually is deficient in physical capital, in technology, and in the institutional support that promotes production and exchange. Similarly, an economy with a high-quality workforce likely excels in the other sources of productivity and growth.

We should distinguish between an economy's standard of living, as measured by output per capita, and improvements in that standard of living, as measured by the growth in output per capita. Growth in output per capita can occur when labor productivity

---

9. Angus Deaton, "Income, Health, and Well-Being Around the World: Evidence from the Gallup World Poll," *Journal of Economic Perspectives*, 22 (Spring 2008): 69.

increases or when the number of workers in the economy grows faster than the population. *In the long run, productivity growth and the growth in workers relative to the growth in population will determine whether or not the United States continues to enjoy one of the world's highest standard of living.*

Summary

1. If the population is continually increasing, an economy must produce more goods and services simply to maintain its standard of living, as measured by output per capita. If output grows faster than the population, the standard of living rises.

2. An economy's standard of living grows over the long run because of (a) increases in the amount and quality of resources, especially labor and capital, (b) better technology, and (c) improvements in the rules of the game that facilitate production and exchange, such as tax laws, property rights, patent laws, the legal system, and customs of the market.

3. The per-worker production function shows the relationship between the amount of capital per worker in the economy and the output per worker. As capital per worker increases, so does output per worker but at a decreasing rate. Technological change and improvements in the rules of the game shift the per-worker production function upward, so more is produced for each ratio of capital per worker.

4. Since 1870, U.S. labor productivity growth has averaged 2.1 percent per year. The *quality* of labor and capital is much more important than the *quantity* of these resources. Labor productivity growth slowed between 1974 and 1982, in part because of spikes in energy prices and implementation of costly but necessary environmental and workplace regulations. Since

1983 productivity growth has picked up, especially since 1996, due primarily to information technology.

5. Among the seven major industrial market economies, the United States has experienced the third highest growth rate in real GDP per capita over the last quarter of a century and most recently produced the highest real GDP per capita.

6. Technological change sometimes costs jobs and imposes hardships in the short run, as workers scramble to adapt to a changing world. Over time, however, most displaced workers find other jobs, sometimes in new industries created by technological change. There is no evidence that, in the long run, technological change increases unemployment in the economy.

7. Some governments use industrial policy in an effort to nurture the industries and technologies of the future, giving domestic industries an advantage over foreign competitors. But critics are wary of the government's ability to pick the winning technologies.

8. Convergence is a theory predicting that the standard of living around the world will grow more alike, as poorer countries catch up with richer ones. Some Asian countries that had been poor are catching up with the leaders, but many poor countries around the world have failed to close the gap.

Key Concepts

Productivity   168
Labor productivity   168
Per-worker production function   169
Capital deepening   170

Rules of the game   171
Industrial market countries   172
Developing countries   172
Basic research   181

Applied research   181
Industrial policy   181
Convergence   183

Questions for Review

1. PRODUCTIVITY   As discussed in the text, per capita GDP in many developing countries depends on the fertility of land there. However, many richer economies have little land or land of poor quality. How can a country with little land or unproductive land become rich?

2. LABOR PRODUCTIVITY   What two kinds of changes in the capital stock can improve labor productivity? How can each type be illustrated with a per-worker production function? What determines the slope of the per-worker production function?

3. SLOWDOWN IN LABOR PRODUCTIVITY GROWTH   What slowed the rate of growth in labor productivity during the 1974–1982 period?

4. OUTPUT PER CAPITA   Explain how output per capita can grow faster than labor productivity. Is it possible for labor productivity to grow faster than output per capita?

5. TECHNOLOGY AND PRODUCTIVITY   What measures can government take to promote the development of practical technologies?

6. BASIC AND APPLIED RESEARCH   What is the difference between basic research and applied research? Relate this to the human genome project—research aimed at developing a complete map of human chromosomes, showing the location of every gene.

7. RULES OF THE GAME   How do "rules of the game" affect productivity and growth? What types of "rules" should a government set to encourage growth?

8. Case Study: Computers and Productivity Growth   How has the increased use of computers affected U.S. productivity in recent years? Is the contribution of computers expected to increase or decrease in the near future? Explain.

9. INTERNATIONAL PRODUCTIVITY COMPARISONS   How does output per capita in the United States compare with output per capita in other major industrial economies? How has this comparison changed over time?

10. INDUSTRIAL POLICY   Define industrial policy. What are some arguments in favor of industrial policy?

11. TECHNOLOGICAL CHANGE AND UNEMPLOYMENT   Explain how technological change can lead to unemployment in certain industries. How can it increase employment?

12. CONVERGENCE   Explain the convergence theory. Under what circumstances is convergence unlikely to occur?

13. PRODUCTIVITY   What factors might contribute to a low *level* of productivity in an economy? Regardless of the level of labor productivity, what impact does slow *growth* in labor productivity have on the economy's standard of living?

14. Case Study: The Pursuit of Happiness   How would you explain the finding that people in high-income economies seem happier than people in low-income economies, but, over generations, Americans do not seem to become happier even though the nation grows richer?

Problems and Exercises

15. GROWTH AND THE PPF   Use the production possibilities frontier (PPF) to demonstrate economic growth.

    a. With consumption goods on one axis and capital goods on the other, show how the combination of goods selected this period affects the PPF in the next period.
    b. Extend this comparison by choosing a different point on this period's PPF and determining whether that combination leads to more or less growth over the next period.

16. LONG-TERM PRODUCTIVITY GROWTH   Suppose that two nations start out in 2011 with identical levels of output per work hour—say, $100 per hour. In the first nation, labor productivity grows by one percent per year. In the second, it grows by two percent per year. Use a calculator or a spreadsheet to determine how much output per hour each nation will be producing 20 years later, assuming that labor productivity growth rates do not change. Then, determine how much each will be producing per hour 100 years later. What do your results tell you about the effects of small differences in productivity growth rates?

17. TECHNOLOGICAL CHANGE AND UNEMPLOYMENT   What are some examples, other than those given in the chapter, of technological change that has caused unemployment? And what are some examples of new technologies that have created jobs? How do you think you might measure the net impact of technological change on overall employment and GDP in the United States?

18. SHIFTS IN THE PPF   Terrorist attacks foster instability and may affect productivity over the short and long term. Do you think the September 11, 2001, terrorist attacks on the World Trade Center and the Pentagon affected short- or long-term productivity in the United States? Explain your response and show any movements in the PPF.

Global Economic Watch Exercises

Login to www.cengagebrain.com and access the Global Economic Watch to do these exercises.

19. GLOBAL ECONOMIC WATCH   Go to the Global Economic Crisis Resource Center. Select Global Issues in Context. In the Basic Search box at the top of the page, enter the word "productivity." On the Results page, go to the Global Viewpoints Section. Click on the link for the May 15, 2009, article "Will Productivity Pull Us Out?" Traditionally, why do Canada and Europe experience slower productivity growth after a recession than does the U.S.?

20. GLOBAL ECONOMIC WATCH   Go to the Global Economic Crisis Resource Center. Select Global Issues in Context. In the Basic Search box at the top of the page, enter the phrase "economic convergence." Choose one article. Does it support the concept of economic convergence or not? Explain why.

The International Economy and Globalization

In today's world, no nation exists in economic isolation. All aspects of a nation's economy—its industries, service sectors, levels of income and employment, and living standard—are linked to the economies of its trading partners. This linkage takes the form of international movements of goods and services, labor, business enterprise, investment funds, and technology. Indeed, national economic policies cannot be formulated without evaluating their probable impacts on the economies of other countries.

The high degree of **economic interdependence** among today's economies reflects the historical evolution of the world's economic and political order. At the end of World War II, the United States was economically and politically the most powerful nation in the world, a situation expressed in the saying, "When the United States sneezes, the economies of other nations catch a cold." But with the passage of time, the U.S. economy has become increasingly integrated into the economic activities of foreign countries. The formation in the 1950s of the European Community (now known as the European Union), the rising importance in the 1960s of multinational corporations, the market power in the 1970s enjoyed by the Organization of Petroleum Exporting Countries (OPEC), and the creation of the euro at the turn of the twenty-first century have all resulted in the evolution of the world community into a complicated system based on a growing interdependence among nations.

Recognizing that world economic interdependence is complex and its effects uneven, the economic community has taken steps toward international cooperation. Conferences devoted to global economic issues have explored the avenues through which cooperation could be fostered between industrial and developing nations. The efforts of developing nations to reap larger gains from international trade and to participate more fully in international institutions have been hastened by the impact of the global recession, industrial inflation, and the burdens of high-priced energy.

Over the past 50 years, the world's market economies have become increasingly interdependent. Exports and imports as a share of national output have risen for most industrial nations, while foreign investment and international lending have expanded. This closer linkage of economies can be mutually advantageous for trading nations. It permits producers in each nation to take advantage of the specialization and efficiencies of large scale production. A nation can consume a wider variety of products at a cost less than that which could be achieved in the absence of trade. Despite these advantages, demands have grown for protection against imports. Protectionist pressures have been strongest during periods of rising unemployment caused by economic recession. Moreover, developing nations often maintain that the so-called liberalized trading system called for by industrial nations serves to keep the developing nations in poverty.

Economic interdependence also has direct consequences for a student taking an introductory course in international economics. As consumers, we can be affected by changes in the international values of currencies. Should the Japanese yen or British pound appreciate against the U.S. dollar, it would cost us more to purchase Japanese television sets or British automobiles. As investors, we might prefer to purchase Swiss securities if Swiss interest rates rise above U.S. levels. As members of the labor force, we might want to know whether the president plans to protect U.S. steelworkers and autoworkers from foreign competition.

In short, economic interdependence has become a complex issue in recent times, often resulting in strong and uneven impacts among nations and among sectors within a given nation. Business, labor, investors, and consumers all feel the repercussions of changing economic conditions and trade policies in other nations. Today's global economy requires cooperation on an international level to cope with the myriad issues and problems.

Globalization of Economic Activity

When listening to the news, we often hear about globalization. What does this term mean? **Globalization** is the process of greater interdependence among countries and their citizens. It consists of the increased interaction of product and resource markets across nations via trade, immigration, and foreign investment—that is, via international flows of goods and services, of people, and of investments in equipment, factories, stocks, and bonds. It also includes non-economic elements such as culture and the environment. Simply put, globalization is political, technological, and cultural, as well as economic.

In terms of people's daily lives, globalization means that the residents of one country are more likely now than they were 50 years ago to consume the products of another country, to invest in another country, to earn income from other countries, to talk by telephone to people in other countries, to visit other countries, to know that they are being affected by economic developments in other countries, and to know about developments in other countries.

What forces are driving globalization?[1] The first and perhaps most profound influence is technological change. Since the industrial revolution of the late 1700s, technical innovations have led to an explosion in productivity and slashed transportation costs. The steam engine preceded the arrival of railways and the mechanization of a growing number of activities hitherto reliant on muscle power. Later discoveries

---

[1]World Trade Organization, *Annual Report*, 1998, pp. 33–36.

and inventions such as electricity, the telephone, the automobile, container ships, and pipelines altered production, communication, and transportation in ways unimagined by earlier generations. More recently, rapid developments in computer information and communications technology have further shrunk the influence of time and geography on the capacity of individuals and enterprises to interact and transact around the world. For services, the rise of the Internet has been a major factor in falling communication costs and increased trade. As technical progress has extended the scope of what can be produced and where it can be produced, and advances in transport technology have continued to bring people and enterprises closer together, the boundary of tradable goods and services has been greatly extended.

Also, continuing liberalization of trade and investment has resulted from multilateral trade negotiations. For example, tariffs in industrial countries have come down from high double digits in the 1940s to about five percent in the early 2000s. At the same time, most quotas on trade, except for those imposed for health, safety, or other public policy reasons, have been removed. Globalization has also been promoted through the widespread liberalization of investment transactions and the development of international financial markets. These factors have facilitated international trade through the greater availability and affordability of financing.

Lower trade barriers and financial liberalization have allowed more and more companies to globalize production structures through investment abroad, which in turn has provided a further stimulus to trade. On the technology side, increased information flows and the greater tradability of goods and services have profoundly influenced production location decisions. Businesses are increasingly able to locate different components of their production processes in various countries and regions and still maintain a single corporate identity. As firms subcontract part of their production processes to their affiliates or other enterprises abroad, they transfer jobs, technologies, capital, and skills around the globe.

How significant is production sharing in world trade? Researchers have estimated production sharing levels by calculating the share of components and parts in world trade. They have concluded that global production sharing accounts for about 30 percent of the world trade in manufactured goods. Moreover, the trade in components and parts is growing significantly faster than the trade in finished products, highlighting the increasing interdependence of countries through production and trade.[2]

Waves of Globalization

In the past two decades, there has been pronounced global economic interdependence. Economic interdependence occurs through trade, labor migration, and capital (investment) flows such as corporation stocks and government securities. Let us consider the major waves of globalization that have occurred in recent history.[3]

---

[2] A. Yeats, *Just How Big Is Global Production Sharing?* World Bank, Policy Research Working Paper No. 1871, 1998, Washington, DC.

[3] This section draws from World Bank, *Globalization, Growth and Poverty: Building an Inclusive World Economy*, 2001.

First Wave of Globalization: 1870–1914

The first wave of global interdependence occurred from 1870 to 1914. It was sparked by decreases in tariff barriers and new technologies that resulted in declining transportation costs, such as the shift from sail to steamships and the advent of railways. The main agent that drove the process of globalization was how much muscle, horsepower, wind power, or later on, steam power a country had and how creatively it could deploy that power. This wave of globalization was largely driven by European and American businesses and individuals. Therefore, exports as a share of world income nearly doubled to about eight percent while per capita incomes, which had risen by 0.5 percent per year in the previous 50 years, rose by an annual average of 1.3 percent. The countries that actively participated in globalization, such as the United States, became the richest countries in the world.

However, the first wave of globalization was brought to an end by World War I. Also, during the Great Depression of the 1930s, governments responded by practicing protectionism: a futile attempt to enact tariffs on imports to shift demand into their domestic markets, thus promoting sales for domestic companies and jobs for domestic workers. For the world economy, increasing protectionism caused exports as a share of national income to fall to about five percent, thereby undoing 80 years of technological progress in transportation.

Second Wave of Globalization: 1945–1980

The horrors of the retreat into nationalism provided renewed incentive for internationalism following World War II. The result was a second wave of globalization that took place from 1945 to 1980. Falling transportation costs continued to foster increased trade. Also, nations persuaded governments to cooperate to decrease previously established trade barriers.

However, trade liberalization discriminated both in terms of which countries participated and which products were included. By 1980, trade between developed countries in manufactured goods had been largely freed of barriers. However, barriers facing developing countries had been eliminated for only those agricultural products that did not compete with agriculture in developed countries. For manufactured goods, developing countries faced sizable barriers. However, for developed countries, the slashing of trade barriers between them greatly increased the exchange of manufactured goods, thus helping to raise the incomes of developed countries relative to the rest.

The second wave of globalization introduced a new kind of trade: rich country specialization in manufacturing niches that gained productivity through **agglomeration economies**. Increasingly, firms clustered together, some clusters produced the same product, and others were connected by vertical linkages. Japanese auto companies, for example, became famous for insisting that their parts manufacturers locate within a short distance of the main assembly plant. For companies such as Toyota and Honda, this decision decreased the costs of transport, coordination, monitoring, and contracting. Although agglomeration economies benefit those in the clusters, they are bad news for those who are left out. A region can be uncompetitive simply because not enough firms have chosen to locate there. Thus, a divided world can emerge, in which a network of manufacturing firms is clustered in some high-wage region, while wages in the remaining regions stay low. Firms will not shift to a new location until the discrepancy in production costs becomes sufficiently large to compensate for the loss of agglomeration economies.

During the second wave of globalization, most developing countries did not participate in the growth of global trade in manufacturing and services. The combination of continuing trade barriers in developed countries, and unfavorable investment climates and antitrade policies in developing countries, confined them to dependence on agricultural and natural-resource products.

Although the second globalization wave succeeded in increasing per capita incomes within the developed countries, developing countries as a group were being left behind. World inequality fueled the developing countries' distrust of the existing international trading system, which seemed to favor developed countries. Therefore, developing countries became increasingly vocal in their desire to be granted better access to developed-country markets for manufactured goods and services, thus fostering additional jobs and rising incomes for their people.

Latest Wave of Globalization

The latest wave of globalization, which began in about 1980, is distinctive. First, a large number of developing countries, such as China, India, and Brazil, broke into the world markets for manufacturers. Second, other developing countries became increasingly marginalized in the world economy and realized decreasing incomes and increasing poverty. Third, international capital movements, which were modest during the second wave of globalization, again became significant.

Of major significance for this wave of globalization is that some developing countries succeeded for the first time in harnessing their labor abundance to provide them with a competitive advantage in labor-intensive manufacturing. Examples of developing countries that have shifted into manufacturing trade include Bangladesh, Malaysia, Turkey, Mexico, Hungary, Indonesia, Sri Lanka, Thailand, and the Philippines. This shift is partly due to tariff cuts that developed countries have made on imports of manufactured goods. Also, many developing countries liberalized barriers to foreign investment, which encouraged firms such as Ford Motor Company to locate assembly plants within their borders. Moreover, technological progress in transportation and communications permitted developing countries to participate in international production networks. However, the dramatic increase in manufactured exports from developing countries has contributed to protectionist policies in developed countries. With so many developing countries emerging as important trading countries, reaching further agreements on multilateral trade liberalization has become more complicated.

Although the world has become more globalized in terms of international trade and capital flows compared to 100 years ago, there is less globalization in the world when it comes to labor flows. The United States, for example, had a very liberal immigration policy in the late 1800s and early 1900s, and large numbers of people flowed into the country, primarily from Europe. As a large country with abundant room to absorb newcomers, the United States also attracted foreign investment throughout much of this period, which meant that high levels of migration went hand in hand with high and rising wages. However, since World War I, immigration has been a disputed topic in the United States, and restrictions on immigration have tightened. In contrast to the largely European immigration in the 1870–1914 globalization wave, contemporary immigration into the United States comes largely from Asia and Latin America.

TABLE 1.1

Manufacturing an HP Pavilion, ZD8000 Laptop Computer

Component	Major Manufacturing Country
Hard-disk drives	Singapore, China, Japan, United States
Power supplies	China
Magnesium casings	China
Memory chips	Germany, Taiwan, South Korea, Taiwan, United States
Liquid-crystal display	Japan, Taiwan, South Korea, China
Microprocessors	United States
Graphics processors	Designed in United States and Canada; produced in Taiwan

Source: From "The Laptop Trail," *The Wall Street Journal*, June 9, 2005, pp. B1 and B8.

Another aspect of the most recent wave of globalization is foreign outsourcing, in which certain aspects of a product's manufacture are performed in more than one country. As travel and communication became easier in the 1970s and 1980s, manufacturing increasingly moved to wherever costs were the lowest. For example, U.S. companies shifted the assembly of autos and the production of shoes, electronics, and toys to low-wage developing countries. This shift resulted in job losses for blue-collar workers producing these goods and cries for the passage of laws to restrict outsourcing.

When an American customer places an order online for a Hewlett-Packard (HP) laptop, the order is transmitted to Quanta Computer Inc. in Taiwan. To reduce labor costs, the company farms out production to workers in Shanghai, China. They combine parts from all over the world to assemble the laptop which is flown as freight to the United States, and then sent to the customer. About 95 percent of the HP laptop is outsourced to other countries. The outsourcing ratio is close to 100 percent for other U.S. computer producers including Dell, Apple, and Gateway. Table 1.1 shows how the HP laptop is put together by workers in many different countries.

By the 2000s, the Information Age resulted in the foreign outsourcing of white-collar work. Today, many companies' locations hardly matter. Work is connected through digitization, the Internet, and high-speed data networks around the world. Companies can now send office work anywhere, and that means places like India, Ireland, and the Philippines, where for a $1.50 to $2 per hour companies can hire college graduates to do the jobs that go for $12 to $18 per hour in the United States. Simply put, a new round of globalization is sending upscale jobs offshore, including accounting, chip design, engineering, basic research, and financial analysis, as seen in Table 1.2. Analysts estimate that foreign outsourcing can allow companies to reduce costs of a given service from 30 to 50 percent.

For example, Boeing uses aeronautics specialists in Russia to design luggage bins and wing parts for its jetliners. Having a master's degree or doctorate in math or aeronautics, these specialists are paid $650 per month in contrast to a monthly salary of $6,000 for an American counterpart. Similarly, engineers in China and India, earning $1,000 a month, develop chips for Texas Instruments and Intel; their American counterparts are paid $7,000 a month. However, companies are likely to keep crucial research and development and the bulk of office operations close to home. Many jobs cannot go anywhere because they require face-to-face contact with customers. Economists note that the vast majority of jobs in the United States consist of services such as retail, restaurants and hotels, personal care services, and the like. These services are necessarily produced and consumed locally, and thus cannot be sent off-shore.

Besides saving money, foreign outsourcing can enable companies to do things they simply couldn't do before. For example, a consumer products company in the United States found it impractical to chase down tardy customers buying less than

TABLE 1.2

GLOBALIZATION GOES WHITE COLLAR

U.S.Company	Country	Type of Work Moving
Accenture	Philippines	Accounting, software, office work
Conseco	India	Insurance claim processing
Delta Air Lines	India, Philippines	Airline reservations, customer service
Fluor	Philippines	Architectural blueprints
General Electric	India	Finance, information technology
Intel	India	Chip design, tech support
Microsoft	China, India	Software design
Philips	China	Consumer electronics, R&D
Procter & Gamble	Philippines, China	Accounting, tech support

Source: From "Is Your Job Next?" *Business Week*, February 3, 2003, pp. 50–60.

$1,000 worth of goods. When this service was run in India, however, the cost dropped so much the company could profitably follow up on bills as low as $100.

Although the Internet makes it easier for U.S. companies to remain competitive in an increasingly brutal global marketplace, is foreign outsourcing good for white-collar workers? A case can be made that Americans benefit from this process. In the 1990s, U.S. companies had to import hundreds of thousands of immigrants to ease engineering shortages. Now, by sending routine service and engineering tasks to nations with a surplus of educated workers, U.S. labor and capital can be shifted to higher-value industries and cutting-edge research and development.

However, a question remains: What happens if displaced white-collar workers cannot find greener pastures? The truth is that the rise of the global knowledge industry is so recent that most economists have not begun to figure out the implications. But people in developing nations like India see foreign outsourcing as a bonus because it helps spread wealth from rich nations to poor nations. Among its many other virtues, the Internet might turn out to be a great equalizer. Outsourcing will be further discussed at the end of Chapter 2.

The United States as an Open Economy

It is generally agreed that the U.S. economy has become increasingly integrated into the world economy (become an open economy) in recent decades. Such integration involves a number of dimensions that include the trade of goods and services, financial markets, the labor force, ownership of production facilities, and the dependence on imported materials.

Trade Patterns

To appreciate the globalization of the U.S. economy, go to a local supermarket. Almost any supermarket doubles as an international food bazaar. Alongside potatoes from Idaho and beef from Texas, stores display melons from Mexico, olive oil from Italy, coffee from Colombia, cinnamon from Sri Lanka, wine and cheese from France,

---

TABLE 1.3

THE FRUITS OF FREE TRADE: A GLOBAL FRUIT BASKET

On a trip to the grocery store, consumers can find goods from all over the globe.

Apples	New Zealand	Limes	El Salvador
Apricots	China	Oranges	Australia
Bananas	Ecuador	Pears	South Korea
Blackberries	Canada	Pineapples	Costa Rica
Blueberries	Chile	Plums	Guatemala
Coconuts	Philippines	Raspberries	Mexico
Grapefruit	Bahamas	Strawberries	Poland
Grapes	Peru	Tangerines	South Africa
Kiwifruit	Italy	Watermelons	Honduras
Lemons	Argentina		

Source: From "The Fruits of Free Trade," *Annual Report*, Federal Reserve Bank of Dallas, 2002, p. 3.

and bananas from Costa Rica. Table 1.3 shows a global fruit basket that is available for American consumers.

The grocery store isn't the only place Americans indulge their taste for foreign-made products. We buy cameras and cars from Japan, shirts from Bangladesh, DVD players from South Korea, paper products from Canada, and fresh flowers from Ecuador. We get oil from Kuwait, steel from China, computer programs from India, and semiconductors from Taiwan. Most Americans are well aware of our desire to import, but they may not realize that the United States ranks as the world's greatest exporter by selling personal computers, bulldozers, jetliners, financial services, movies, and thousands of other products to just about all parts of the globe. Simply put, international trade and investment are facts of everyday life.

As a rough measure of the importance of international trade in a nation's economy, we can look at the nation's exports and imports as a percentage of its gross domestic product (GDP). This ratio is known as **openness**.

$$Openness = \frac{(Exports + Imports)}{GDP}$$

Table 1.4 shows measures of openness for selected nations as of 2007. In that year, the United States exported 11 percent of its GDP while imports were 16 percent of GDP; the openness of the U.S. economy to trade thus equaled 27 percent. Although the U.S. economy is significantly tied to international trade, this tendency is even more striking for many smaller nations, as seen in the table. Simply put, large countries tend to be less reliant on international trade because many of their companies can attain an optimal production size without having to export to foreign nations. Therefore, small countries tend to have higher measures of openness than do large ones.

Figure 1.1 shows the openness of the U.S. economy from 1890 to 2007. One significant trend is that the United States became less open to international trade between 1890 and 1950. Openness was relatively high in the late 1800s due to the rise in world trade resulting from technological improvements in transportation (steamships) and communications (trans-Atlantic telegraph cable). However, two

TABLE 1.4

EXPORTS AND IMPORTS OF GOODS AND SERVICES AS A PERCENTAGE OF GROSS DOMESTIC PRODUCT GDP), 2007

Country	Exports as a Percentage of GDP	Imports as a Percentage of GDP	Exports Plus Imports as a Percentage of GDP
Netherlands	74	66	140
South Korea	46	45	91
Germany	45	40	85
Norway	46	29	75
Canada	38	34	72
United Kingdom	29	33	62
France	27	28	55
United States	11	16	27
Japan	14	13	27

Source: From The World Bank Group, *Data and Statistics: Country Profiles, 2008* available at **http://www.worldbank.org/data.**

world wars and the Great Depression of the 1930s caused the United States to reduce its dependence on trade, partly for national security reasons and partly to protect its home industries from import competition. Following World War II, the United States and other countries negotiated reductions in trade barriers, which contributed to rising world trade. Technological improvements in shipping and communications also bolstered trade and the increasing openness of the U.S. economy.

The relative importance of international trade for the United States has increased by about 50 percent during the past century, as seen in Figure 1.1. But a significant fact is hidden by these data. In 1890, most U.S. trade was in raw materials and

FIGURE 1.1

OPENNESS OF THE U.S. ECONOMY, 1890–2007

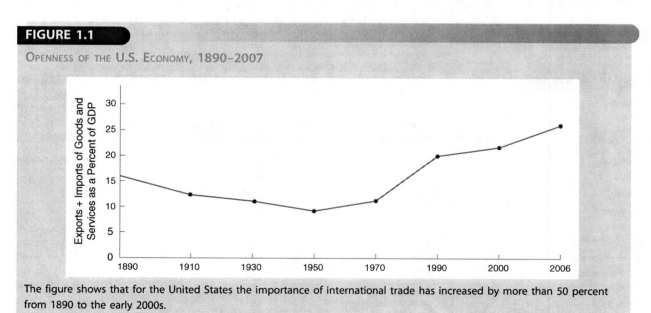

The figure shows that for the United States the importance of international trade has increased by more than 50 percent from 1890 to the early 2000s.

Source: Data from U.S. Census Bureau, Foreign Trade Division, *U.S. Trade in Goods and Services,* at **http://www.census.gov/foreign-trade/statistics.**

agricultural products, today, manufactured goods and services dominate U.S. trade flows. Therefore, American producers of manufactured products are more affected by foreign competition than they were a hundred years ago.

The significance of international trade for the U.S. economy is even more noticeable when specific products are considered. For example, we would have fewer personal computers without imported components, no aluminum if we did not import bauxite, no tin cans without imported tin, and no chrome bumpers if we did not import chromium. Students taking a 9 a.m. course in international economics might sleep through the class (do you really believe this?) if we did not import coffee or tea. Moreover, many of the products we buy from foreigners would be much more costly if we were dependent on our domestic production.

With which nations does the United States conduct trade? Canada, China, Mexico, and Japan head the list, as seen in Table 1.5.

Labor and Capital

Besides the trade of goods and services, movements in factors of production are a measure of economic interdependence. As nations become more interdependent, labor and capital should move more freely across nations.

However, during the past 100 years, labor mobility has not risen for the United States. In 1900, about 14 percent of the U.S. population was foreign born. But from the 1920s to the 1960s, the United States sharply curtailed immigration. This curtailment resulted in the foreign-born U.S. population declining to 6 percent of the total population. During the 1960s, the United States liberalized restrictions and the flow of immigrants increased. By 2009, about 12 percent of the U.S. population was foreign born while foreigners made up about 14 percent of the labor force. People from Latin America accounted for about half of this figure while Asians accounted for another quarter. These immigrants contributed to economic growth in the United States by taking jobs in labor-scarce regions and filling the types of jobs native workers often shun.

TABLE 1.5

LEADING TRADE PARTNERS OF THE UNITED STATES, 2008

Country	Value of U.S. Exports of Goods (in billions of dollars)	Value of U.S. Imports of Goods (in billions of dollars)	Total Value of Trade (in billions of dollars)
Canada	260.9	335.6	596.5
China	71.5	337.8	409.3
Mexico	151.5	215.9	367.4
Japan	66.6	139.2	205.8
Germany	54.7	97.6	152.3
United Kingdom	53.8	58.6	112.4
South Korea	34.8	48.1	82.9
France	29.2	44.0	73.2
Taiwan	25.3	36.3	61.6
Malaysia	13.0	30.7	43.7

Source: From U.S. Census Bureau, "Foreign Trade Statistics," at **http://www.census.gov/foreign-trade/statistics**. See also U.S. Department of Commerce, Bureau of Economic Analysis, *U.S. Transactions by Area*, available at **http://www.bea.gov/**.

Although labor mobility has not risen for the United States in recent decades, the country has become increasingly tied to the rest of the world through capital (investment) flows. Foreign ownership of U.S. financial assets has risen since the 1960s. During the 1970s, OPEC recycled many of their oil dollars by making investments in U.S. financial markets. The 1980s also witnessed major flows of investment funds to the United States as Japan and other nations, with dollars accumulated from trade surpluses with the United States, acquired U.S. financial assets, businesses, and real estate. By the late 1980s, the United States was consuming more than it produced, and became a net borrower from the rest of the world to pay for the difference. Increasing concerns were raised about the interest cost of this debt to the U.S. economy and about the impact of this debt burden on the living standards of future U.S. generations. As a major lender to the United States, China openly criticized the United States in 2009 for being irresponsible in its financial affairs.

Globalization has also increased in international banking. The average daily turnover in today's foreign-exchange market (where currencies are bought and sold) is estimated at almost $2 trillion, compared to $205 billion in 1986. The global trading day begins in Tokyo and Sydney and, in a virtually unbroken 24-hour cycle, moves around the world through Singapore and Hong Kong to Europe and finally across the United States before being picked up again in Japan and Australia. London remains the largest center for foreign-exchange trading, followed by the United States; significant volumes of currencies are also traded in Asia, Germany, France, Scandinavia, Canada, and elsewhere.

In commercial banking, U.S. banks developed worldwide branch networks in the 1960s and 1970s for loans, payments, and foreign-exchange trading. Foreign banks also increased their presence in the United States throughout the 1980s and 1990s, reflecting the multinational population base of the United States, the size and importance of U.S. markets, and the role of the U.S. dollar as an international medium of exchange and reserve currency. Today, more than 250 foreign banks operate in the United States; in particular, Japanese banks have been the dominant group of foreign banks operating in the United States. Like commercial banks, securities firms have also globalized their operations.

By the 1980s, U.S. government securities were traded on virtually a 24-hour basis. Foreign investors purchased U.S. treasury bills, notes, and bonds, and many desired to trade during their own working hours rather than those of the United States. Primary dealers of U.S. government securities opened offices in such locations as Tokyo and London. Stock markets became increasingly internationalized, with companies listing their stocks on different exchanges throughout the world. Financial futures markets also spread throughout the world.

Why Is Globalization Important?

Because of trade, individuals, firms, regions, and nations can specialize in the production of things they do well and use the earnings from these activities to purchase from others those items for which they are high-cost producers. Therefore, trading partners can produce a larger joint output and achieve a higher standard of living than would otherwise be possible. Economists refer to this as the law of comparative advantage, which will be further discussed in Chapter 2.

THE GLOBAL RECESSION OF 2007–2009

Although globalization has provided benefits to many countries, when economic problems arise in a country such as the United States, they can easily be transmitted abroad. Let us consider the global economic crisis of 2007–2009.

In 2007, the global financial system resembled a patient in intensive care. The body was attempting to fight off a disease that was spreading, and as it did so, the body convulsed, stabilized for a time, and then convulsed again. The doctors in charge resorted to ever-more invasive treatment and experimented with remedies that have never been tried before. How did the global economy suffer its worst crisis since the 1930s?

The immediate cause of the global economic crisis was the collapse of the U.S. housing market and the resulting surge in mortgage loan defaults. Hundreds of billions of dollars in losses on these mortgages undermined the financial institutions that originated and invested in them. The implications for creditors and bond investors were clear: RUN from all financial institutions that might fail! Therefore, creditors and uninsured depositors pulled their funds and cashed out of securities issued by risky institutions and invested in U.S. Treasury securities that were considered to have no risk of default. Many institutions failed, such as Washington Mutual and Wachovia, and others struggled to survive. Banks were fearful about making loans to one another, let alone to businesses and households. As the credit spigot closed, the global economy withered. Global stock investors dumped their holdings in expectations of declining corporate earnings. The result was a self-reinforcing adverse economic downturn.

ROOTS OF THE PROBLEM

The roots of the problem stemmed from a lack of fear in the booming housing market of 2006. Traditionally, banks accepted deposits and made loans, eking out profits under the burden of heavy bank regulations designed to protect depositors. The banks took all the risk, but that created an incentive to know the borrower and lend money only to people who could actually pay it back. However, beginning in the 1970s, government-sponsored credit agencies like Fannie Mae and Freddie Mac began purchasing huge amounts of mortgage loans from banks and packaging them into mortgage-backed securities (MBS) which were sold to investors. Banks were thus replenished with funds that could then be used for additional mortgage loans. The MBS removed the risk of default from banks and shifted it to investors and the federal government, which implicitly guaranteed the investments. This system greatly reduced the fear of bankers in making mortgage loans. Also, bankers had no fear of making mortgage loans in a booming market because the expected appreciation of house prices would increase the value of the collateral if borrowers could not or would not pay. Moreover, households had little fear of purchasing a house with little or no down payment, because they were confident that housing prices would only go up.

Government also contributed to the financial crisis by pressuring banks to serve poor borrowers and poor regions of the country. Beginning in 1992, Congress pushed Fannie Mae and Freddie Mac to increase their purchases of mortgages going to low-income borrowers. The Community Reinvestment Act did the same thing with traditional banks. This approach resulted in mortgages being made to many households who were unable to repay their loans. Also, poorly designed capital requirements resulted in banks not having sufficient safety cushions during periods of economic downturn.

According to the **law of comparative advantage**, the citizens of each nation can gain by spending more of their time and resources doing those things in which they have a relative advantage. If a good or service can be obtained more economically through trade, it makes sense to trade for it instead of producing it domestically. It is a mistake to focus on whether a good is going to be produced domestically or abroad. The central issue is how the available resources can be used to obtain each

History shows that asset bubbles tend to occur when money is plentiful and inexpensive: Cheap money encourages leverage that boosts asset prices and encourages additional leverage. And money was very abundant and cheap in the United States in the early 2000s. That was partly due to low inflation and economic stability that decreased investors' perceptions of risk, and thus interest rates. Also, a flood of capital swept into U.S. financial instruments from high-saving emerging countries such as China. This flood was reinforced by the easy money policy of the Federal Reserve.

THE CRISIS GOES GLOBAL

The financial crisis that started in the United States soon spread to Europe. European banks were drawn into the financial crisis in part due to their exposure to defaulted mortgages in the United States. As these banks had to write off losses, fear and uncertainty spread regarding which banks had bad loans and whether they had enough capital to pay off their debt obligations. As banks became reluctant to lend money to each other, the interest rates on interbank loans increased. A number of European banks failed and stock market indexes declined worldwide. Investors transferred vast capital resources into stronger currencies such as the U.S. dollar, the yen, and the Swiss franc, leading many emerging nations to seek aid from the International Monetary Fund.

The financial crisis also spread to emerging economies that generally lacked the resources to restore confidence in their financial systems. Highly leveraged countries, such as Iceland, were vulnerable to the flight of capital. Countries that got rich during the commodities boom, such as oil-abundant Russia, were vulnerable to the global recession. Extremely poor countries suffered from decreases in foreign aid by wealthy countries. Even China experienced a substantial slowdown in growth as the global recession depressed its export markets.

Simply put, the global economic crisis of 2008–2009 was essentially a crisis of confidence. It started with bad real estate loans and highly leveraged bets on those loans. Then it froze credit markets in which banks would not lend to each other and businesses and households could not get the short-term loans needed to finance day-to-day operations.

One way to combat a crisis in confidence is to bolster the balance sheet of institutions that appear to be at risk, making it clear to creditors that they can once again safely lend to those institutions. This method should restore confidence and lessen the impact on the real economy. After some delay and confusion, the governments of the United States and Europe announced plans to pump liquidity into troubled financial institutions and to provide increased or unlimited deposit insurance to prevent runs on banks. Also, central banks in these countries engineered coordinated interest-rate reductions and purchased commercial paper and other money market instruments directly from corporate issuers and money market funds. Moreover, governments initiated large fiscal stimulus packages in the form of tax cuts and increased government spending. Finally, the International Monetary Fund provided financial aid to Iceland, Ukraine, Hungary, and other emerging countries. At the writing of this book in December 2009, it appeared that the recession was ending in the United States. Other aspects of the global economic downturn will be discussed in subsequent chapters of this book.

good at the lowest possible cost. When trading partners use more of their time and resources producing things they do best, they are able to produce a larger joint output, which provides the source for mutual gain.

International trade also results in gains from the competitive process. Competition is essential to both innovation and efficient production. International competition helps keep domestic producers on their toes and provides them with a strong incentive to improve the quality of their products. Also, international trade usually weakens monopolies. As countries open their markets, their monopoly producers face competition from foreign firms.

With globalization and import competition, U.S. prices have decreased for many products, like TV sets, toys, dishes, clothing, and so on. However, prices increased for many products untouched by globalization, such as cable TV, hospital services, sports tickets, rent, car repair, and others. From 1987 to 2003, faster growing import competition wrung inflationary pressures from domestic producer prices in a large range of industries, as seen in Figure 1.2. The gains from global markets are not restricted to goods traded internationally. They extend to such non-traded goods as houses, which contain carpeting, wiring, and other inputs now facing greater international competition.

FIGURE 1.2

GLOBAL COMPETITION LOWERS INFLATION

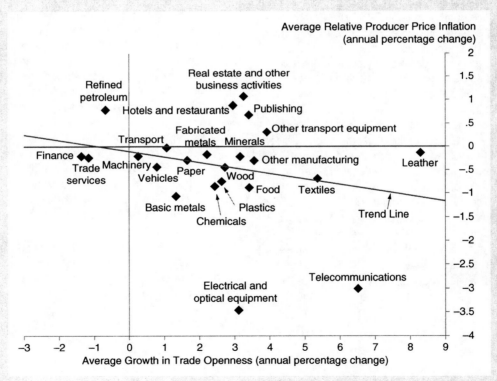

World imports relative to U.S. consumption have doubled over the past four decades, making more of what consumers purchase subject to increased competition inherent in international trade. This added competition tends to hold down the cost of goods and services as seen for the period 1987 to 2003.

Source: Drawn from "The Best of All Worlds: Globalizing the Knowledge Economy," *2006 Annual Report*, Federal Reserve Bank of Dallas, p. 12.

For example, during the 1950s General Motors (GM) was responsible for about 60 percent of all passenger cars produced in the United States. Although GM officials praised the firm's immense size for providing economies of scale in individual plant operations, skeptics were concerned about the monopoly power resulting from GM's dominance of the auto market. Some argued that GM should be broken up into several independent companies to inject more competition into the market. Today, however, stiff foreign competition has resulted in GM's current share of the market to stand at less than 24 percent.

Not only do open economies have more competition, but they also have more firm turnover. Being exposed to competition around the globe can result in high-cost domestic producers exiting the market. If these firms are less productive than the remaining firms, then their exit represents productivity improvements for the industry. The increase in exits is only part of the adjustment. The other part is new firms entering the market, unless there are significant barriers. With these new firms comes more labor market churning as workers formerly employed by obsolete firms must now find jobs in emerging ones. However, inadequate education and training can make some workers unemployable for emerging firms creating new jobs that we often cannot yet imagine. This is probably the key reason why workers find globalization to be controversial. Simply put, the higher turnover of firms is an important source of the dynamic benefits of globalization. In general, dying firms have falling productivity, and new firms tend to increase their productivity over time.

FIGURE 1.3

TARIFF BARRIERS VERSUS ECONOMIC GROWTH

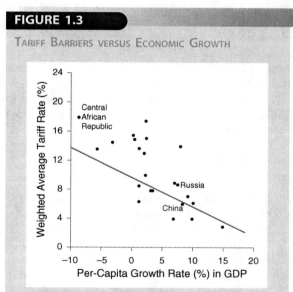

The figure shows the weighted average tariff rate and per-capita growth rate in GDP for 23 nations in 2002. According to the figure, there is evidence of an inverse relationship between the level of tariff barriers and the economic growth of nations.

Source: Data taken from The World Bank Group, *2005 World Development Indicators*, available at **http://www.worldbank.org/data/**.

Also, economists have generally found that economic growth rates have a close relation to openness to trade, education, and communications infrastructure. For example, countries that open their economies to international trade tend to benefit from new technologies and other sources of economic growth. As Figure 1.3 shows, there appears to be some evidence of an inverse relation between the level of trade barriers and the economic growth of nations. That is, nations that maintain high barriers to trade tend to realize a low level of economic growth.

International trade can also provide stability for producers, as seen in the case of Invacare Corporation, an Ohio-based manufacturer of wheelchairs and other health care equipment. For the wheelchairs it sells in Germany, the electronic controllers come from the firm's New Zealand factories; the design is largely American; and the final assembly is done in Germany, with parts shipped from the United States, France, and the United Kingdom. By purchasing parts and components worldwide, Invacare can resist suppliers' efforts to increase prices for aluminum, steel, rubber, and other materials. By selling its products in 80 nations, Invacare can maintain a more stable workforce in Ohio than if it was completely dependent on the U.S. market. If sales decline anytime in the United States, Invacare has an ace up its sleeve—exports.

On the other hand, rapid growth in countries like China and India has helped to increase the demand for commodities like crude oil, copper, and steel. Thus, American consumers and companies pay higher prices for items like gasoline. Rising gasoline prices, in turn, have spurred governmental and private-sector initiatives to increase the supply of gasoline substitutes like biodiesel or ethanol. Increased demand for these alternative forms of energy has helped to increase the price of soybeans, and corn, which are key inputs in the production of chicken, pork, beef, and other foodstuffs.

Moreover, globalization can make the domestic economy vulnerable to disturbances initiated overseas, as seen in the case of India. In response to India's agricultural crisis, some 1,200 Indian cotton farmers committed suicide during 2005–2007 to escape debts to money lenders. The farmers borrowed money at exorbitant rates, so they could sink wells and purchase expensive biotech cotton seeds. But the seeds proved inadequate for small plots, resulting in crop failures. Moreover, farmers suffered from the low world price of their cotton crop, which fell by more than a third from 1994–2007. Prices were low partly because cotton was heavily subsidized by wealthy countries, mainly the United States. According to the World Bank, cotton prices would have risen about 13 percent if the subsidies had been eliminated.

Although India's government could impose a tariff on imported cotton to offset the foreign subsidy, its textile manufacturers, who desired to keep production costs low, welcomed cheap fibers. Thus, India's cotton tariff was only 10 percent, much lower than its tariffs on most other commodities.

The simple solution to the problem of India's farmers would be to move them from growing cotton to weaving it in factories. But India's restrictive labor laws discourage industrial employment, and the lack of a safety net resulted in farmers clinging to their marginal plots of land.

There is great irony in the plight of India's cotton farmers. The British developed India's long-fiber cotton in the 1800s to supply British cotton mills. As their inexpensive cloth drove India's weavers out of business, the weavers were forced to work the soil. By the early 2000s, India's textile-makers were enjoying a revival, but its farmers could not leave the soil to work in factories.[4]

Globalization: Increased Competition From Abroad

Although economists recognize that globalization and free trade can provide benefits to many firms, workers, and consumers they can inflict burdens on others. Consider the cases of the Schwinn Bicycle Company and the Dell Computer Corporation.

Bicycle Imports Force Schwinn to Downshift

The Schwinn Bicycle Company illustrates the notion of globalization and how producers react to foreign competitive pressure. Founded in Chicago in 1895, Schwinn grew to produce bicycles that became the standard of the industry. Although the Great Depression drove most bicycle companies out of business, Schwinn survived by producing durable and stylish bikes; sold by dealerships that were run by people who understood bicycles and were anxious to promote the brand. Schwinn emphasized continuous innovation that resulted in features such as built-in kickstands, bal-

---

[4]"Cotton Suicides: The Great Unraveling," *The Economist*, January 20, 2007, p. 34.

loon tires, chrome fenders, head and taillights, and more. By the 1960s, the Schwinn Sting-Ray became the bicycle that virtually every child wanted. Celebrities such as Captain Kangaroo and Ronald Reagan pitched ads claiming that "Schwinn bikes are the best."

Although Schwinn dominated the U.S. bicycle industry, the nature of the bicycle market was changing. Cyclists wanted features other than heavy, durable bicycles that had been the mainstay of Schwinn for decades. Competitors emerged such as Trek, which built mountain bikes, and Mongoose, which produced bikes for BMX racing.

Moreover, falling tariffs on imported bicycles encouraged Americans to import from companies in Japan, South Korea, Taiwan, and eventually China. These companies supplied Americans with everything ranging from parts and entire bicycles under U.S. brand names, or their own brands. Using production techniques initially developed by Schwinn, foreign companies hired low-wage workers to manufacture competitive bicycles at a fraction of Schwinn's cost.

As foreign competition intensified, Schwinn moved production to a plant in Greenville, Mississippi in 1981. The location was strategic. Like other U.S. manufacturers, Schwinn relocated production to the South in order to hire nonunion workers at lower wages. Schwinn also obtained parts produced by low-wage workers in foreign countries. However, the Greenville plant suffered from uneven quality and low efficiency, and it produced bicycles no better than the ones imported from the Far East. As losses mounted for Schwinn, the firm declared bankruptcy in 1993.

Eventually Schwinn was purchased by the Pacific Cycle Company which farmed the production of Schwinn bicycles out to low-wage workers in China. Most Schwinn bicycles today are built in Chinese factories and are sold by Wal-Mart and other discount merchants. And cyclists do pay less for a new Schwinn under Pacific's ownership. It may not be the industry standard that was the old Schwinn, but it sells at Wal-Mart for approximately $180, about a third of the original price in today's dollars. Although cyclists lament that a Schwinn is no longer the bike it used to be, Pacific Cycle officials note that it is not as expensive as in the past either.[5]

Dell Sells Factories in Effort to Slash Costs

The personal computer (PC) business is full of rags-to-riches stories. But perhaps none is more dramatic than the rise (and fall) of Dell Computer Corporation.

In 1984, as a nineteen year old student at the University of Texas, Michael Dell started a computer company from a dorm room with a $1,000 in capital and built it into an industry powerhouse with a market capitalization of more than $100 billion. Initially, Dell Computer produced PCs in its own factories for a market that was dominated by business customers purchasing large quantities of desktop PCs. The firm pioneered an innovative strategy of selling computers directly to customers, only manufacturing them after they were ordered. After a customer placed an order over the phone or through the Web, the firm's factories assembled the needed components, installed PCs with software, and shipped them in a matter of hours.

[5]Judith Crown and Glenn Coleman, *No Hands: The Rise and Fall of the Schwinn Bicycle Company, an American Institution.* (New York, Henry Holt and Co., 1996) and Jay Pridmore, *Schwinn Bicycles.* (Osceola, WI, Motorbooks International, 2002). See also Griff Wittee, "A Rough Ride for Schwinn Bicycle," *The Washington Post*, December 3, 2004.

This system slashed idle inventory and allowed the firm to avoid marketing expenses associated with selling through retail channels. By 1999, Dell overtook Compaq to become the largest seller of PCs in the United States.

Although Dell has been highly efficient in producing desktop PCs, the firm has not been a low-cost manufacturer of laptops. Years ago, competitors such as Hewlett-Packard (HP) and Apple realized cost savings by entering into agreements with other firms to produce their laptops; many of these manufacturers are in low-wage countries such as Malaysia and China. Moreover, by the early 2000s, growth had switched to laptops sold to consumers at retail stores such as Best Buy and Office Max. However, Dell continued to lag behind its competitors in developing an efficient system to manufacture laptops. This lack of development resulted in a fall in Dell's sales and earnings and the replacement of the firm by HP as the world's biggest PC maker.

These adversities have forced Dell to sell many of its factories in an attempt to cut costs. Rather than producing PCs itself, the firm has increasingly contracted with foreign companies to manufacture them. In 2008, analysts estimated that Dell had reduced production costs for each computer by 15 to 20 percent by shifting manufacturing from the United States to China. It remains to be seen if Dell can chop its production costs further so as to regain its market leadership.

These two examples highlight how international trade is dynamic in nature as producers gain and lose competitiveness in response to changing market conditions.[6]

Common Fallacies of International Trade

Despite the gains derived from international trade, fallacies abound.[7] One fallacy is that trade is a zero-sum activity—if one trading party gains, the other must lose. In fact, just the opposite occurs—both partners gain from trade. Consider the case of trade between Brazil and the United States. These countries are able to produce a larger joint output when Brazilians supply coffee and Americans supply wheat. The larger production makes it possible for Brazilians to gain by using revenues from their coffee sales to purchase American wheat. At the same time, Americans gain by doing the opposite, by using revenues from their wheat sales to purchase Brazilian coffee. In turn, the larger joint output provides the basis for the mutual gains achieved by both. By definition, if countries specialize in what they are comparatively best at producing, they must import goods and services that other countries produce best. The notion that imports are "bad" but exports are "good"—popular among politicians and the media—is incorrect.

Another fallacy is that imports reduce employment and act as a drag on the economy, while exports promote growth and employment. This fallacy stems from a failure to consider the link between imports and exports. For example, American imports of German machinery provide Germans with the purchasing power to buy our computer software. If Germans are unable to sell as much to Americans, then they will have fewer dollars with which to buy from Americans. Thus, when the vol-

---

[6]Michael Dell, *Direct From Dell: Strategies that Revolutionized an Industry*, 2006, New York, Harper-Collins Publishers, Steven Holzner, *How Dell Does It*, 2006, McGraw Hill and Justin Scheck, "Dell Plans to Sell Factories in Effort to Cut Costs," *The Wall Street Journal*, September 5, 2008.

[7]*Twelve Myths of International Trade*, U.S. Senate, Joint Economic Committee, June 1999, pp. 2–4.

ume of U.S. imports decreases, the automatic secondary effect is that Germans have fewer dollars with which to purchase American goods. Therefore, sales, production, and employment will decrease in the U.S. export industries.

Also, people often feel that tariffs, quotas, and other import restrictions will save jobs and promote a higher level of employment. Like the previous fallacy, this one also stems from the failure to recognize that a reduction in imports does not occur in isolation. When we restrict foreigners from selling to us, we are also restricting their ability to obtain the dollars needed to buy from us. Thus, trade restrictions that reduce the volume of imports will also reduce exports. As a result, jobs saved by the restrictions tend to be offset by jobs lost due to a reduction in exports.

Why don't we use tariffs and quotas to restrict trade among the 50 states? After all, think of all the jobs that are lost when, for example, Michigan "imports" oranges from Florida, apples from Washington, wheat from Kansas, and cotton from Georgia. All of these products could be produced in Michigan. However, the residents of Michigan generally find it cheaper to "import" these commodities. Michigan gains by using its resources to produce and "export" automobiles, and other goods it can produce economically. Indeed, most people recognize that free trade among the 50 states is a major source of prosperity for each of the states. Similarly, most recognize that "imports" from other states do not destroy jobs—at least not for long.

The implications are identical for trade among nations. Free trade among the 50 states promotes prosperity; so, too, does free trade among nations. Of course, the sudden removal of trade barriers might harm producers and workers in protected industries. It can be costly to quickly transfer the protected resources to other, more productive activities. Gradual removal of the barriers would minimize this shock effect and the accompanying cost of relocation.

Does Free Trade Apply to Cigarettes?

When President George W. Bush pressured South Korea in 2001 to stop imposing a 40 percent tariff on foreign cigarettes, administration officials said the case had nothing to do with public health. Instead, it was a case against protecting the domestic industry from foreign competition. However, critics maintained that nothing is that simple with tobacco. They recognized that free trade, as a rule, increases competition, lowers prices, and makes better products available to consumers, leading to higher consumption. Usually, that's a good thing. However, with cigarettes, the result can be more smoking, disease, and death.

Globally, about 4 million people die each year from lung cancer, emphysema, and other smoking-related diseases, making cigarettes the largest single cause of preventable death. By 2030, the annual number of fatalities could hit 10 million, according to the World Health Organization. That has antismoking activists and even some economists arguing that cigarettes are not normal goods but are, in fact, "bads" that require their own set of regulations. They contend that the benefits of free trade do not apply to cigarettes and that they should be treated as an exception to trade rules.

This view is finding favor with some governments, as well. In recent talks of the World Health Organization, dealing with a global tobacco-control treaty, a range of nations expressed support for provisions to emphasize antismoking measures over free-trade rules. However, the United States opposed such measures. In fact, the

United States, which at home has sued tobacco companies for falsifying cigarettes' health risks, has promoted freer trade in cigarettes. For example, President Bill Clinton demanded a sharp reduction in Chinese tariffs, including those on tobacco, in return for U.S. support of China's entry into the World Trade Organization. Those moves, combined with free-trade pacts that have decreased tariffs and other barriers to trade, have helped stimulate the international sales of cigarettes.

The United States, first under President Clinton and then President Bush, has only challenged rules imposed to aid local cigarette makers, not nondiscriminatory measures to protect public health. The United States opposed South Korea's decision to impose a 40-percent tariff on imported cigarettes because it was discriminatory and aimed at protecting domestic producers and not at protecting the health and safety of the Korean people, according to U.S. trade officials. However, antismoking activists maintain that this is a false distinction and that anything that makes cigarettes more widely available at a lower price is harmful to public health. However, cigarette makers oppose limiting trade in tobacco. They maintain that there is no basis for creating new regulations that weaken the principle of open trade protected by the World Trade Organization.

Current trade rules permit countries to enact measures to protect the health and safety of their citizens, as long as all goods are treated equally, tobacco companies argue. For example, a trade-dispute panel notified Thailand that, although it could not prohibit foreign cigarettes, it could ban advertisements for both domestic and foreign-made smokes. But tobacco-control activists worry that the rules could be used to stop governments from imposing antismoking measures. They contend that special products need special rules, pointing to hazardous chemicals and weapons as goods already exempt from regular trade policies. Cigarettes kill more people every year than AIDS. Anti-tobacco activists think it's time for health concerns to be of primary importance in the case of smoking, too.

Is International Trade an Opportunity or a Threat to Workers?

- Tom lives in Chippewa Falls, Wisconsin. His former job as a bookkeeper for a shoe company, which employed him for many years, was insecure. Although he earns $100 a day, promises of promotion never panned out, and the company eventually went bankrupt as cheap imports from Mexico forced shoe prices down. Tom then went to a local university, earned a degree in management information systems, and was hired by a new machine-tool firm that exports to Mexico. He now enjoys a more comfortable living even after making the monthly payments on his government-subsidized student loan.

- Rosa and her family recently moved from a farm in southern Mexico to the country's northern border, where she works for a U.S.-owned electronics firm that exports to the United States. Her husband, Jose, operates a janitorial service and sometimes crosses the border to work illegally in California. Rosa, Jose, and their daughter have improved their standard of living since moving out of subsistence agriculture. However, Rosa's wage has not increased in the past year; she still earns about $2.25 per hour with no future gains in sight.

Workers around the globe are living increasingly intertwined lives. Most of the world's population now lives in countries that either are integrated into world markets for goods and finance or are rapidly becoming so. Are workers better off as a result of these globalizing trends? Stories about losers from international trade are often featured in newspapers: how Tom lost his job because of competition from poor Mexicans. But Tom currently has a better job, and the U.S. economy benefits from his company's exports to Mexico. Producing goods for export has led to an improvement in Rosa's living standard, and her daughter can hope for a better future. Jose is looking forward to the day when he will no longer have to travel illegally to California.

International trade benefits many workers. It enables them to shop for the cheapest consumption goods and permits employers to purchase the technologies and equipment that best complement their workers' skills. Trade also allows workers to become more productive as the goods they produce increase in value. Moreover, producing goods for export generates jobs and income for domestic workers. Workers in exporting industries appreciate the benefits of an open trading system.

But not all workers gain from international trade. The world trading system, for example, has come under attack by some in industrial countries in which rising unemployment and wage inequality have made people feel apprehensive about the future. Cheap exports produced by lower-cost, foreign workers threatens to eliminate jobs for some workers in industrial countries. Others worry that firms are relocating abroad in search of low wages and lax environmental standards or fear that masses of poor immigrants will be at their company's door, offering to work for lower wages. Trade with low-wage developing countries is particularly threatening to unskilled workers in the import-competing sectors of industrial countries.

As an economy opens up to international trade, domestic prices become more aligned with international prices; wages tend to increase for workers whose skills are more scarce internationally than at home and to decrease for workers who face increased competition from foreign workers. As the economies of foreign nations open up to trade, the relative scarcity of various skills in the world marketplace changes still further, harming those countries with an abundance of workers who have the skills that are becoming less scarce. Increased competition also suggests that unless countries match the productivity gains of their competitors, the wages of their workers will deteriorate. It is no wonder that workers in import-competing industries often lobby for restrictions on the importation of goods so as to neutralize the threat of foreign competition. Slogans such as "Buy American" and "American goods create American jobs" have become rallying cries among many U.S. workers.

However, keep in mind that what is true for the part is not necessarily true for the whole. It is certainly true that imports of steel or automobiles can eliminate American jobs. But it is not true that imports decrease the total number of jobs in a nation. A large increase in U.S. imports will inevitably lead to a rise in U.S. exports or foreign investment in the United States. In other words, if Americans suddenly wanted more European autos, eventually American exports would have to increase to pay for these products. The jobs lost in one industry are replaced by jobs gained in another industry. The long-run effect of trade barriers is thus not to increase total domestic employment, but at best to reallocate workers away from export industries and toward less efficient, import-competing industries. This reallocation leads to a less efficient utilization of resources.

Simply put, international trade is just another kind of technology. Think of it as a machine that adds value to its inputs. In the United States, trade is the machine that turns computer software, which the United States makes very well, into CD players, baseballs, and other things that it also wants, but does not make quite so well. International trade does this at a net gain to the economy as a whole. If somebody invented a device that could do this, it would be considered a miracle. Fortunately, international trade has been developed.

If international trade is squeezing the wages of the less skilled, so are other kinds of advancing technology, only more so. Yes, you might say, but to tax technological progress or put restrictions on labor-saving investment would be idiotic: that would only make everybody worse off. Indeed it would, and exactly the same goes for international trade—whether this superior technology is taxed (through tariffs) or over-regulated (in the form of international efforts to harmonize labor standards).

This is not an easy thing to explain to American textile workers who compete with low-wage workers in China, Malaysia, etc. However, free-trade agreements will be more easily reached if those who might lose by new trade are helped by all of the rest of us who gain.

Backlash Against Globalization

Proponents of free trade and globalization note how it has helped the United States and other countries prosper. Open borders permit new ideas and technology to flow freely around the world, fueling productivity growth and increasing living standards. Moreover, increased trade helps restrain consumer prices, so inflation becomes less likely to disrupt economic growth. Estimates of the net benefits that flow from free trade are substantial: International trade has increased the real income of U.S. households by between $7,000 and $13,000 since the end of World War II. It also has increased the variety of goods and services available to American consumers by a factor of four between 1972 and 2001.[8] Without trade, coffee drinkers in the United States would pay much higher prices because the nation's supply would depend solely on Hawaiian or Puerto Rican sources.

In spite of the advantages of globalization, critics maintain that U.S. policies primarily benefit large corporations rather than average citizens—of the United States or any other country. Environmentalists argue that elitist trade organizations, such as the World Trade Organization, make undemocratic decisions that undermine national sovereignty on environmental regulation. Also, unions maintain that unfettered trade permits unfair competition from countries that lack labor standards. Moreover, human rights activists contend that the World Bank and International Monetary Fund support governments that allow sweatshops and pursue policies that bail out governmental officials at the expense of local economies. Put simply, a gnawing sense of unfairness and frustration has emerged about trade policies that ignore the concerns of the environment, American workers, and international labor standards.

The noneconomic aspects of globalization are at least as important in shaping the international debate as are the economic aspects. Many of those who object to globalization resent the political and military dominance of the United States, and they also resent the influence of foreign (mainly American) culture, as they see it, at the expense of national and local cultures.

---

[8]Scott Bradford, Paul Grieco, and Gary Hufbauer, "The Payoff to America from Globalization," *The World Economy*, July 2006, pp. 893–916.

The World Trade Organization's summit meeting in Seattle, Washington, in 1999 attests to a globalization backlash in opposition to continued liberalization of trade, foreign investment, and foreign immigration. About 100,000 anti-globalization demonstrators swamped Seattle to vocalize their opposition. The meeting was characterized by shattered storefront windows, looting, tear gas, pepper spray, rubber bullets, shock grenades, and a midnight-to-dawn curfew. Police in riot gear and the National Guard were called in to help restore order.

Such backlash reflects concerns about globalization, and these appear to be closely related to the labor-market pressures that globalization might be imparting to American workers. Public opinion surveys note that many Americans are aware of both the benefits and costs of interdependence with the world economy, but they consider the costs to be more than the benefits. In particular, less-skilled workers are much more likely to oppose freer trade and immigration than their more-skilled counterparts who have more job mobility. While concerns about the effect of globalization on the environment, human rights, and other issues are an important part of the politics of globalization, it is the tie between policy liberalization and worker interests that forms the foundation for the backlash against liberalization in the United States.[9] Table 1.6 summarizes some of the pros and cons of globalization.

The way to ease the fear of globalization is to help people to move to different jobs as comparative advantage shifts rapidly from one activity to the next. This process implies a more flexible labor market and a regulatory system that fosters investment. It implies an education system that provides people with the skills that make them mobile. It also implies removing health care and pensions from employment,

---

TABLE 1.6

ADVANTAGES AND DISADVANTAGES OF GLOBALIZATION

Advantages	Disadvantages
Productivity increases faster when countries produce goods and services in which they have a comparative advantage. Living standards can increase more rapidly.	Millions of Americans have lost jobs because of imports or shifts in production abroad. Most find new jobs that pay less.
Global competition and cheap imports keep a constraint on prices, so inflation is less likely to disrupt economic growth.	Millions of other Americans fear getting laid off, especially at those firms operating in import-competing industries.
An open economy promotes technological development and innovation, with fresh ideas from abroad.	Workers face demands of wage concessions from their employers, which often threaten to export jobs abroad if wage concessions are not accepted.
Jobs in export industries tend to pay about 15 percent more than jobs in import-competing industries.	Besides blue-collar jobs, service and white-collar jobs are increasingly vulnerable to operations being sent overseas.
Unfettered capital movements provide the United States access to foreign investment and maintain low interest rates.	American employees can lose their competitiveness when companies build state-of-the-art factories in low-wage countries, making them as productive as those in the United States.

Source: "Backlash Behind the Anxiety over Globalization," *Business Week*, April 24, 2000, p. 41.

---

[9]Kevin Kliesen, "Trading Barbs: A Primer on the Globalization Debate," *The Regional Economist*, Federal Reserve Bank of St. Louis, October 2007, pp. 5–9.

so that when you move to a new job, you are not risking an awful lot besides. And for those who lose their jobs, it implies strengthening training policies to help them find work. Indeed, these activities are expensive, and they may take years to work. But an economy that finds its national income increasing because of globalization can more easily find the money to pay for it.

Terrorism Jolts the Global Economy

Some critics point to the terrorist attack on the United States on September 11, 2001, as what can occur when globalization ignores the poor people of the world. The terrorist attack resulted in the tragic loss of life for thousands of innocent Americans. It also jolted America's golden age of prosperity, and the promise it held for global growth, that existed throughout the 1990s. Because of the threat of terrorism, Americans have become increasingly concerned about their safety and their livelihoods.

As the United States retaliated against Osama bin Laden and his band of terrorists, analysts were concerned that this conflict might undo a decades-long global progression toward tighter economic, political, and social interdependence—the process known as globalization. Fueled by trade, globalization has advanced the ambitions, and boosted the profits, of some of the world's largest corporations, many of them based in the United States, Europe, and Japan. Indeed, companies such as General Electric, Ford Motor Company, Toyota, Honda, and Coca-Cola have been major beneficiaries of globalization. Also, globalization has provided developing countries a chance to be included in the growing global economy and share in the wealth. In many developing countries, it has succeeded: life expectancies and per capita income have increased, and local economies have flourished.

But the path to globalization has been rocky. Critics argue that it has excluded many of the world's poor, and that the move toward prosperity has often come at the expense of human rights and the quality of the environment. For many Islamic fundamentalists, globalization represents an intolerable secularization of society, and must be prevented. This view contrasts with much of the Western criticism, which calls for the reform of globalization, not its undoing.

Globalization certainly isn't going to disintegrate—the world's markets are too interdependent to roll back now. But globalization could well become slower and more costly. With continuing terrorism, companies will likely have to pay more to insure and provide security for overseas staff and property. Heightened border inspections could slow shipments of cargo, forcing companies to stock more inventory. Tighter immigration policies could reduce the liberal inflows of skilled and blue-collar laborers that have permitted companies to expand while keeping wages in check. Moreover, a greater preoccupation with political risk has companies greatly narrowing their horizons when making new investments. Put simply, the rapid expansion in trade and capital flows in the past has been driven by the idea that the world is becoming a seamless, frictionless place. Continuing terrorism imperils all of these and puts sand in the gears of globalization.

Many economists view international trade to be a weapon in the war against terrorism in the long-run. They maintain that expanded trade wraps the world more tightly in a web of commerce, lifting living standards in impoverished regions and eliminating an important cause of war and terror. For example, following the 2001 terrorist attack against the United States, the U.S. government negotiated

COMPETITION IN THE WORLD STEEL INDUSTRY

TRADE CONFLICTS

During the 1960s and 1970s, the relatively low production costs of foreign steelmakers encouraged their participation in the U.S. market. In 1982, the average cost per ton of steel for integrated U.S. producers was $685 per ton— 52 percent higher than for Japanese producers, the highest of the Pacific Rim steelmakers. This cost differential was largely due to a strong U.S. dollar and higher domestic costs of labor and raw materials, which accounted for 25 and 45 percent, respectively, of total cost. Moreover, domestic operating rates were relatively low, resulting in high fixed costs of production for each ton of steel.

This cost disadvantage encouraged U.S. steelmakers to initiate measures to reduce production costs and regain competitiveness. Many steel companies closed obsolete and costly steel mills, coking facilities, and ore mines. They also negotiated long-term contracts permitting materials, electricity, and natural gas to be obtained at lower prices. Labor contracts were also renegotiated, with a 20 to 40 percent improvement in labor productivity. However, U.S. steel companies were burdened with large unfunded pension obligations and healthcare costs for hundreds of thousands of retirees, while their employee base was shrinking.

By the turn of the century, the U.S. steel industry had substantially reduced its cost of producing a ton of steel. The productivity of the U.S. steelworker was estimated to be higher than that of most foreign competitors, a factor that enhanced U.S. competitiveness. But

semi-industrialized nations, such as South Korea, Brazil, and China, had labor-cost advantages because of lower wages and other employee costs. Overall, the cost disadvantage of U.S. steel companies narrowed considerably from the 1980s to the early in the first decade of the 2000s. Table 1.7 shows the average costs of producing a ton of steel for selected nations in 2009. At that time, Russia's average cost was the lowest at $424 per ton.

TABLE 1.7

WORLD STEEL COST COMPARISONS: COST PER TON OF STEEL, 2009

Country	Average Cost Per Ton
Japan	$634
United States	
Integrated mills	613
Mini mills	466
Western Europe	602
China	579
Eastern Europe	557
India	500
Brazil	480
Russia	424
Global average	563

Source: From Peter F. Marcus and Karlis M. Kirsis, World Steel Dynamics, *Steel Strategist #35*, September 2009.

trade deals with Jordan, Vietnam, Chili, and various Central American countries. Put simply, trade cannot make peace, but trade can help. If you look at history, strong trading relations have rarely led to conflict. Of course, trade needs to be accompanied by other factors, such as strong commitments to universal education and well-run governments, to promote world peace.

However, these economists note that a trade-based strategy to unite the world would require a far greater investment of money and political capital than the United States and Europe have demonstrated. Moreover, they argue that the United States and Europe must push for massive debt relief for impoverished nations. They also recommend that industrial countries slash tariffs and quotas for the steel, textiles, clothing, and crops produced by poor nations, even though increased imports could harm U.S. and European producers. Indeed, these recommendations invite much debate concerning the political and economic stability of the world.

The Plan of this Text

This text is an examination of the functioning of the international economy. Although the emphasis is on the theoretical principles that govern international trade, there also is considerable coverage of the empirical evidence of world trade patterns and trade policies of the industrial and developing nations. The book is divided into two major parts. Part One deals with international trade and commercial policy; Part Two stresses the balance of payments and the adjustment in the balance of payments.

Chapters 2 and 3 deal with the theory of comparative advantage, as well as theoretical extensions and empirical tests of this model. This topic is followed by a treatment of tariffs, nontariff trade barriers, and contemporary trade policies of the United States in Chapters 4 through 6. Discussions of trade policies for the developing nations, regional trading arrangements, and international factor movements in Chapters 7 through 9 complete the first part of the text.

The treatment of international financial relations begins with an overview of the balance of payments, the foreign-exchange market, and the exchange-rate determination in Chapters 10 through 12. The balance-of-payments adjustment under alternate exchange rate regimes is discussed in Chapters 13 through 15. Chapter 16 considers macroeconomic policy in an open economy, and Chapter 17 analyzes the international banking system.

Summary

1. Throughout the post-World War II era, the world's economies have become increasingly interdependent in terms of the movement of goods and services, business enterprise, capital, and technology.
2. The United States has seen growing interdependence with the rest of the world in its trade sector, financial markets, ownership of production facilities, and labor force.
3. Largely owing to the vastness and wide diversity of its economy, the United States remains among the countries for which exports constitute a small fraction of national output.
4. Proponents of an open trading system contend that international trade results in higher levels of consumption and investment, lower prices of commodities, and a wider range of product choices for consumers. Arguments against free trade tend to be voiced during periods of excess production capacity and high unemployment.
5. International competitiveness can be analyzed in terms of a firm, an industry, and a nation. Key to the concept of competitiveness is productivity, or output per worker hour.
6. Researchers have shown that exposure to competition with the world leader in an industry improves a firm's performance in that industry. Global competitiveness is a bit like sports: You get better by playing against folks who are better than you.
7. Although international trade helps workers in export industries, workers in import-competing industries feel the threat of foreign competition. They often see their jobs and wage levels undermined by cheap foreign labor.
8. Among the challenges that the international trading system faces are dealing with fair labor standards and concerns about the environment.

Key Concepts & Terms

- Agglomeration economies (p. 4)
- Economic interdependence (p. 1)
- Globalization (p. 2)
- Law of comparative advantage (p. 12)
- Openness (p. 8)

Study Questions

1. What factors explain why the world's trading nations have become increasingly interdependent, from an economic and political viewpoint, during the post-World War II era?
2. What are some of the major arguments for and against an open trading system?
3. What significance does growing economic interdependence have for a country like the United States?
4. What factors influence the rate of growth in the volume of world trade?
5. Identify the major fallacies of international trade.
6. What is meant by international competitiveness? How does this concept apply to a firm, an industry, and a nation?
7. What do researchers have to say about the relation between a firm's productivity and exposure to global competition?
8. When is international trade an opportunity for workers? When is it a threat to workers?
9. Identify some of the major challenges confronting the international trading system.
10. What problems does terrorism pose for globalization?

CHAPTER 6

Importing, Exporting, and Trade Relations

PhotoDisc/Getty Images

The Scoop on Ice Cream Exports

What's your favorite ice cream flavor? Popular flavors in Japan include octopus, seaweed, corn, and sweet potato. In Venezuela, people eat tuna and carrot ice cream. While these are not the most common flavors in these countries, local preferences need to be considered when exporting ice cream.

In addition to figuring out what flavors to offer, U.S. producers of ice cream face other concerns as they seek new international customers. Refrigeration, or rather the lack of it, can greatly influence market potential. In many areas of China, for example, few homes have freezers. As a result, most Chinese prefer their ice cream in the form of small snacks and consume at the point of purchase.

During the late 1980s, annual exports of U.S. ice cream to Japan were only $200,000. This was due to a Japanese import quota for ice cream and frozen yogurt. With the elimination of that trade barrier, Japanese customers bought more ice cream from U.S. companies. After ice cream sales in Asian countries dropped in the late 1990s due to poor economic conditions, demand started to increase when the economy improved.

In Costa Rica and other Central American countries, there was little or no market for ice cream in the mid 1990s. The market improved when Costa Rica honored its commitment to the World Trade Organization by reducing a 44 percent tariff and increasing the 500-ton import quota.

Another strong growth area for ice cream exports is the Caribbean market. The hot climate attracts many tourists to the region where they create a strong demand for frozen snacks and desserts.

Think Critically

1. What factors have increased the demand for U.S. ice cream in other countries?
2. What obstacles might an ice cream exporter encounter when doing business in other countries?
3. Go to the web site of the Foreign Agricultural Service of the U.S. Department of Agriculture to obtain current information about ice cream exports.

6-1 Importing Procedures

GOALS

- Explain the importance of importing.
- Identify the four steps for importing.

PhotoDisc/Getty Images

The Importance of Importing

Imagine how life in the United States would be without international business. Most television sets, athletic shoes, and coffee bought in the United States come from other countries. And these products are only a few of the imported products in use each day. Importing provides a wide variety of products and services for U.S. consumers. Exporting creates jobs and expands business opportunities. Importing and exporting are primary international business activities.

Imports are services or products bought by a company or government from businesses in other countries. Businesses can get involved in international trade by importing goods and services and selling them in their own country. The importing business can create new sales or expand sales with existing customers. Companies get involved in importing for one of three reasons: (1) consumer demand for products unique to foreign countries, (2) lower costs of foreign-made products, or (3) sources of parts needed for domestic manufacturing.

Product Demand Customers who want a unique item or a certain quality may purchase a foreign-made product. Some goods and services may be available only from other countries. Almost all bananas, cocoa, and coffee consumed in the United States are imported.

Lower Costs The prices of goods and services are constantly changing. An item from one country may be less expensive than the same item from another country. Electronic products manufactured in Asian countries are frequently less expensive than similar items produced elsewhere.

Production Inputs Companies regularly purchase raw materials and components for processing or assembly from other countries. These production inputs may not be easily available in the company's home country. For example, the radios, engines, transmissions, and windshield washer systems for many cars assembled in the United States come from companies in Canada, Mexico, Brazil, Japan, Korea, and other countries.

✓ CheckPoint

What are the three main reasons companies import?

Work as a Team

Work with your team to identify 20 items that you own or use regularly that were imported. Examine labels and other marks on clothing and other items to determine the country of origin.

Importing Activities

What does a company have to do to become an importer? Importing usually involves four main activities or steps, as shown in Figure 6-1 on the next page.

STEP 1 DETERMINE DEMAND

The first activity is to determine potential consumer demand for imports. Companies must conduct market research to find out if people will buy certain imported products. As with any business venture, there are risks. Sometimes companies import goods, only to have these items remain in a warehouse because no one wants them due to differences in buying habits.

STEP 2 CONTACT SUPPLIERS

The second importing activity is to contact foreign suppliers. It takes time and energy to locate foreign companies that are able to provide what you want when you want. By using information sources, such as government agencies and foreign business contacts, importers can identify the companies that will best serve their needs.

STEP 3 FINALIZE PURCHASE

The third importing activity is to finalize the *purchase agreement.* The importing company must come to an agreement with the supplier on specific terms for the purchase. The agreement must include the price the importer will pay for the goods, but there are other things that need to be agreed upon. Who will pay for shipping? When will items be delivered? How will payment

Importing Activities

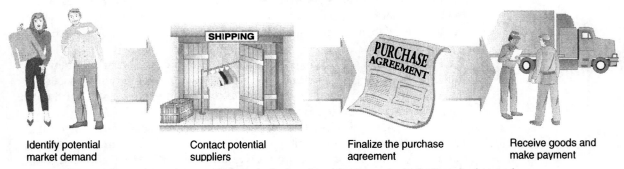

| Identify potential market demand | Contact potential suppliers | Finalize the purchase agreement | Receive goods and make payment |

Figure 6-1 Importers go through several steps to find and purchase products that are in demand.

GLOBAL BUSINESS SPOTLIGHT

AN IMPORTING ERROR

Clear and complete communication for foreign suppliers is vital. Misunderstandings or lack of oversight can result in costly mistakes as demonstrated by the following example.

A U.S. retailer contracted with a foreign company to manufacture cashmere sweaters. The contract stated that the sweaters must be made of 100 percent cashmere. The manufacturer provided shirt labels to that effect. The manufacturer produced sweaters that were 20 percent cashmere and 80 percent wool.

Without verifying the material content, the U.S. company accepted the shirts and sold them with the incorrect information on the label. The Federal Trade Commission fined the company for deceptive labeling.

Think Critically

How might this situation have been avoided?

be made? Will payment be made in advance, during shipping, or after the receipt of the goods? These are just some of the details that need to be described in the purchase agreement.

STEP 4 RECEIVE GOODS

The fourth activity is to receive the goods and make payment. This includes checking the order for accuracy and damage, paying for the order, and paying any import duties. This tax can be based on either the value of goods or other factors, such as quantity or weight.

Import duties are paid to customs officials. A customs official is a government employee authorized to collect the duties levied on imports. The term *customs* also refers to the procedures involved in the collection of duties. You may have heard a person traveling to another country say "I have to go through customs." This means travelers must report to customs officials the value of anything bought in the country they are leaving or anything they plan to sell in the country they are entering.

IMPORT ASSISTANCE

U.S. government agencies are available to assist companies and individuals interested in importing. For example, Customs and Border Protection (CBP), part of the Department of Homeland Security, provides current information on import regulations. The Food and Drug Administration (FDA) and the Department of Agriculture (USDA) are resources for companies importing agriculture products, food, drugs, cosmetics and medical devices.

✓ **Check**Point

What are the four steps involved in importing?

IMPORT-EXPORT OPPORTUNITIES

"Will the shipment arrive by the 23rd of the month?" "Do we have the proper paperwork to clear customs in Cambodia?" "Are the shirts properly labeled for sale in this country?"

People who work in import and export careers face these kinds of concerns each day. Businesses involved in importing and exporting offer a wide variety of career opportunities. Some positions that deal with regulations, transportation, and finance are unique to international business.

Businesses involved in importing or exporting need professionals who understand the rules and regulations related to cross-border transactions. For example, an export document control specialist creates and maintains databases of required licenses and agreements. These documents are required for both sides of the transactions. They allow products to be shipped out of the exporting country and they permit products to enter the receiving nation. In addition to knowing and understanding import and export regulations, this position requires strong communication skills for interacting with colleagues, suppliers, and customers around the world. Adaptability to change and willingness to learn are required because import-export regulations change frequently.

Working for a freight forwarder as a logistics coordinator is an example of a career in the transportation aspect of importing and exporting. A freight clerk plans travel routes and prepares necessary shipping documents. In some cases, a freight clerk may also be involved in negotiating cargo space and pricing. This position requires strong math and computer skills, along with a working knowledge of geography. Time management skills and the ability to work under pressure are important.

With over 300,000 U.S. import companies bringing goods worth more than $600 billion into the country each year, financing activities create other career opportunities. The Export-Import Bank, for example, employs loan specialists, accountants, financial analysts, and economists. Preparation for these careers usually requires a college degree in business. Some positions require graduate degrees.

In addition to the skills required for a specific position, interpersonal skills and the ability to work well with people from different cultural backgrounds are critical in the international business environment. The ability to speak more than one language is an asset for any career related to importing and exporting.

Think Critically

1. What skills required for import-export careers are you interested in developing?
2. Conduct an Internet search to obtain additional information about career opportunities in importing and exporting.

stask/iStockphoto.com

6-1 Assessment

REVIEW GLOBAL BUSINESS TERMS

Define the following term.

1. customs official

REVIEW GLOBAL BUSINESS CONCEPTS

2. What are the main reasons companies import goods?

3. What is the purpose of the customs department of a country's government?

SOLVE GLOBAL BUSINESS PROBLEMS

For each of the following situations, predict whether the imports will be successful in your country. Explain your reasons.

4. Imported ice skates that are more expensive than those already on the market but that have the reputation of being the best in the world.

5. Ten thousand cases of shampoo in bottles with foreign-language labels that can be sold for a price matching the lowest-price shampoo on the market.

6. An imported soy-based dessert called *Zenzip*.

7. Imported clothing sized in an inconsistent manner compared with other brands.

8. An imported packaged dinner entrée that contains blue pasta.

THINK CRITICALLY

9. What types of imports should not be allowed to enter the United States?

10. Do imports threaten the jobs of people in the importing country?

MAKE ACADEMIC CONNECTIONS

11. STATISTICS If South Korea has exports of $419 billion, Singapore $235 billion, and Taiwan $255 billion, what is the average value of exports for the three countries?

12. TECHNOLOGY Find a web site for one of the larger countries in the Asia-Pacific Rim Country Regional Profile. List the country and its five largest imports.

13. VISUAL ARTS Prepare a flow chart or other visual representation of the importing process.

14. CULTURAL STUDIES Collect examples of unusual food products imported from other countries.

6-2 Exporting Procedures

GOALS

- Identify the steps of the exporting process.
- Describe the exporting of services.

PhotoDisc/Getty Images

The Exporting Process

Companies commonly export goods or services to companies in other countries. *Indirect exporting* occurs when a company sells its products in a foreign market without actively seeking out those opportunities. More often, however, a business will conduct *direct exporting* by actively seeking export opportunities.

Exporting activities are the other side of the importing transaction. As exporters, however, businesses face different decisions. The process of exporting involves five steps, as shown in Figure 6-2.

The Exporting Process

STEP 1	STEP 2	STEP 3	STEP 4	STEP 5
Find Potential Customers	Meet the Needs of Customers	Agree on Sales Terms	Deliver Products or Services	Complete the Transaction

Figure 6-2 Successful exporting can help a nation expand its economic activities and create additional jobs.

GLOBAL TECHNOLOGY TRENDS

Online Retailing and Lower Barriers to Entry

Buying books, music, videos, software, clothing, and even groceries without leaving home is nothing new. People have been able to do this for years with mail-order buying and television shopping channels. Today this buying process is even easier.

The Internet has reduced some barriers to entry for new companies. In the past, an entrepreneur had to rent a store, hire employees, obtain inventory, and advertise when starting a business. Now a person can begin operations with a computer. Contacting suppliers, promoting the company, and filling orders are all done online.

This ease of start-up for an online retailer (sometimes called an *e-tailer*) has resulted in lower barriers to entry and increased competition. No longer must a

company have a store, an office, or a factory. Instead, a book or clothing seller can serve customers with an online transaction, with the shipping company representative being the only one who has to leave home.

Think Critically

1. What types of enterprises are best suited for doing business online?
2. How will expanded online buying affect job opportunities and economic development in local communities?
3. Locate a web site that offers customers a variety of products online. How does the company attempt to attract customers?

STEP 1 FIND POTENTIAL CUSTOMERS

Before you sell anything, you have to find buyers. Who are the people who want to buy your goods and services? Where are these people located? Are the potential customers willing and able to purchase your products?

Answers to these questions may be found through an Internet search and library research. Businesses use many sources to find out about the buying habits of people in different countries. Also, businesspeople familiar with foreign markets have experience helping companies that want to sell in other countries.

The U.S. Department of Commerce and other agencies and organizations provide *trade leads* listing export opportunities for companies planning to do business overseas. For example, a recent listing identified an opportunity to sell cosmetics manufacturing machinery in Chennai, India. The U.S. Commercial Service, the Foreign Agricultural Service, and the Federation of International Trade Associations are sources for information on potential customers in other countries.

STEP 2 MEET THE NEEDS OF CUSTOMERS

Next, determine if people in other countries can use your product or service. Sending company representatives to possible markets around the world is one way to make sure your product can be sold there. If visits are not possible, companies can obtain reliable information from other sources.

Will your product be accepted by foreign customers exactly as it is, or will it be necessary to adapt it? Product adaptation may need to be in the form of smaller packages, different ingredients, or revised label information to meet geographic, social, cultural, and legal requirements.

Some products are *standardized* or sold the same around the world. Popular soft drinks, some clothing, and many technical products (such as cameras, computers, and home entertainment systems) are frequently sold in various geographic areas with only minor changes. However, food products, personal care items, and laundry detergent usually need to be *adapted* to the tastes, customs, and culture of a society.

STEP 3 AGREE ON SALES TERMS

Every business transaction involves shipping and payment terms. These terms require businesses to answer a number of important questions. What is the price of the items? How will the products be shipped? Who will pay for shipping costs, the buyer or the seller? In what currency will the payment be made? What foreign exchange rate will be used? When is the payment due?

Shipping costs vary for different types of transportation. Airfreight is more costly than water transportation. However, it is much quicker. Items in high demand or perishable products might require the quickest available method of delivery.

Transportation costs can be a major portion of the cost of exporting. It is important to consider which party will pay transportation costs. Sometimes the seller pays for shipping. In other situations, the buyer pays. Certain terms are used to describe the shipping and payment methods. Free on board (FOB) means the selling price of the product includes the cost of loading the exported goods onto transport vessels at the specified place. Cost, insurance, and freight (CIF) means that the cost of the goods, insurance, and freight are included in the price quoted. Cost and freight (C&F) indicates that the price includes the cost of the goods and freight, but the buyer must pay for insurance separately.

Banks and other financial institutions are likely to be involved in the payment phase of export transactions. A company may have to borrow funds to finance the cost of manufacturing and shipping a product for which payment will not be received until a later date. Besides loans, international financial institutions may also offer other exporting services.

choicegraphx/iStockphoto.com

STEP 4 DELIVER PRODUCTS OR SERVICES

After agreement is reached on selling terms, the products or services must be delivered. This means raw materials, parts, or finished goods are shipped. If the exchange involves a service, the company must now perform the required tasks for its foreign customers.

Some exporters make arrangements for shipping their own products, but others prefer to rely on experts for help with shipping. A freight forwarder is a company that arranges to ship goods to customers. Like a travel agent for cargo, these companies take care of the reservations needed to get an exporter's merchandise to the required destination.

GLOBAL BUSINESS SPOTLIGHT

EXPORTING CULTURE

The demand for U.S. clothing, soft drinks, fast food, candy, movies, music, television programs, and other entertainment is very strong in many parts of the world. Jeans, T-shirts, sports team hats, and athletic shoes are top sellers around the globe. People in some nations will wait in line for hours to pay for Coca-Cola or for a McDonald's hamburger.

Television programs such as *The Simpsons, Grey's Anatomy, Survivor, and Lost* are seen by hundreds of millions of television viewers each day. CNN, ESPN, and MTV have created international channels for worldwide viewing. Movie characters such as Batman, Spiderman, Indiana Jones, Lara Croft, James Bond, and Harry Potter earn film studios millions of dollars in profits outside the United States. The music of Miley Cyrus, Beyonce, Usher, and the Jonas Brothers is played on radio stations, in stores, and in homes in more than 150 countries.

While soccer (called football in most countries) remains the world's most popular sport, others are attempting to gain ground. National Basketball Association (NBA) teams have held games in 10 countries outside of North America. In recent years, the World Baseball Classic has included teams representing 16 nations. And, the National Football League (NFL) has a European league, while NFL games have been played in England, Japan, Germany, and Mexico.

Think Critically

1. What effect could exporting of U.S. culture have on the cultural environment of other countries?
2. What are the benefits associated with exporting culture?
3. Locate a web site with information about country's cultural exports. What are the country's largest cultural exports? How does the volume of cultural exports compare with other exported goods and services?

Photodisc/Getty Images

Often a freight forwarder will accumulate several small export shipments and combine them into one large shipment to get lower freight rates. Because these companies are actively involved in international trade, freight forwarders are excellent sources of information about export regulations, shipping costs, and foreign import regulations.

Companies must prepare export documents for shipping merchandise to other countries. Customers, insurers, government agencies and others involved in the process have specific documentation requirements. Two common shipping documents are a bill of lading and a certificate of origin. A bill of lading is a document stating the agreement between the exporter and the transportation company. This document serves as a receipt for the exported items. A certificate of origin is a document that states the name of the country in which the shipped goods were produced. This document may be used to determine the amount of any import tax.

STEP 5 COMPLETE THE TRANSACTION

If payment has not already been received, it would be due when the products are received by the purchaser. Often, payment involves exchanging one country's currency for another's. Financial institutions convert currency and are usually involved in the payment step. Electronic payments are common.

✓ **Check**Point

What are the five steps of the exporting process?

Other Exporting Issues

In addition to the five steps of exporting described above, companies face a variety of obstacles. Also, the exporting of services must be addressed in a slightly different manner than the global selling of a tangible product.

OBSTACLES TO EXPORTING

The United States Department of Commerce estimates that thousands of small and medium-sized businesses could easily get involved in international business, but they don't. There are several reasons companies may not export.

- No company representatives in foreign countries
- Products not appropriate for foreign consumers
- Insufficient production facilities to manufacture enough goods for exporting
- High costs of doing business in other countries
- Difficulty understanding foreign business procedures
- Difficulty obtaining payment from foreign customers

Many of these obstacles could be overcome if companies obtained assistance from agencies

Photodisc/Getty Images

such as the U.S. Department of Commerce, the U.S. Small Business Administration, and the USA Trade Center.

EXPORTING SERVICES

Most people can relate to selling, packing, and shipping a tangible item. However, a major portion of U.S. exports involves the sale of *intangible* items—services. Service industries account for about 70 percent of GDP in the United States. International trade by service industries is significant. Services provided by U.S. companies are more than 20 percent of the world's total cross-border sales of services.

Companies export services with some of the same techniques they use to export products. These techniques include international consulting, direct exporting, licensing, franchising, and joint venture.

The most commonly exported services include hospitality (hotels and food service), entertainment (movies, music, television production, and amusement parks), and financial services (insurance and real estate). Other areas of expanding service exports involve health care, information processing, distribution services, and education and training services. Exporting of services, such as health care, occurs when a company provides on-site training, technical assistance, or medical treatment services in another country.

✓ **CheckPoint**
What services are most commonly exported by U.S. companies?

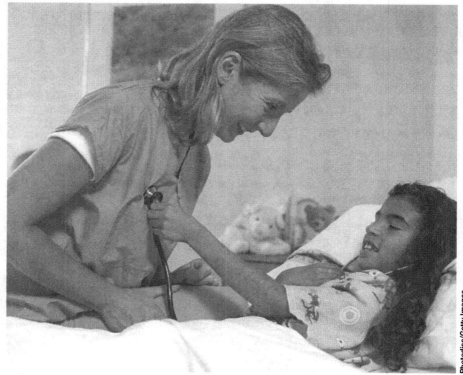

Photodisc/Getty Images

REVIEW GLOBAL BUSINESS TERMS
Define each of the following terms.

1. free on board (FOB)

2. cost, insurance, and freight (CIF)

3. cost and freight (C&F)

4. freight forwarder

5. bill of lading

6. certificate of origin

REVIEW GLOBAL BUSINESS CONCEPTS

7. How can exporting companies determine if their products can be sold in other countries?

8. Why are banks often involved in export transactions?

9. What determines whether an exporter ships by air or water?

SOLVE GLOBAL BUSINESS PROBLEMS

For each of the following exporting situations, decide whether the company should sell the same product (standardize) as in other countries or adapt the product (customize) to local tastes, customs, and culture. Explain your reasons.

10. Exporting World Cup championship shirts and hats.

11. Exporting digital cameras for sale in major cities across Europe and North America.

12. Exporting electrical appliances to a country with a different voltage system.

13. Exporting plain, unflavored yogurt to a country in which the people do not usually eat yogurt.

14. Exporting forklift trucks for use in warehouses in Asia.

THINK CRITICALLY

15. How does the exporting of services differ from exporting goods?

16. Why are governments frequently interested in encouraging exports?

MAKE ACADEMIC CONNECTIONS

17. TECHNOLOGY Visit the web site of the Bureau of Industry and Security to learn more about exporting regulations faced by U.S. companies.

18. SCIENCE Describe recent scientific developments that have improved the speed and efficiency of exporting.

19. HISTORY Research the effect of various inventions on the major exports of a country.

20. TECHNOLOGY Use the Internet to research local rules and regulations for exporting from various countries around the world.

6-3 Importance of Trade Relations

GOALS

• Identify the economic effects of foreign trade.

• Describe the types of trade agreements between countries.

Photodisc/Getty Images

The Economic Effect of Foreign Trade

Every importing and exporting transaction has economic effects. The difference between a country's exports and imports is called its *balance of trade*. Some countries continually buy more foreign goods than they sell. The result is a trade deficit, which is the result of importing more goods and services than the country is exporting. In contrast, a trade surplus occurs when a country exports more than it imports.

The United States, despite being the largest exporter in the world, has had a trade deficit for many years. This situation can result in a country borrowing from other countries. Borrowing means the country must pay back money in the future, reducing the amount available for other spending. Balance of trade does not include all international business transactions, just imports and exports. Another economic measure is needed to summarize the total economic effect of foreign trade. Balance of payments, illustrated in Figure 6-3, measures the total flow of money coming into a country minus the total flow going out. Included in this economic measurement are exports, imports, investments, tourist spending, and financial assistance. For example, tourism can help a country's balance of payments as a result of an increase in the flow of money entering the nation.

A country's balance of payments can be either positive or negative. A *positive*, or *favorable*, balance of payments occurs when a nation receives more money in a year than it pays out. A *negative* balance of payments is *unfavorable*. It is the result when a country sends more money out than it brings in.

Balance of Payments

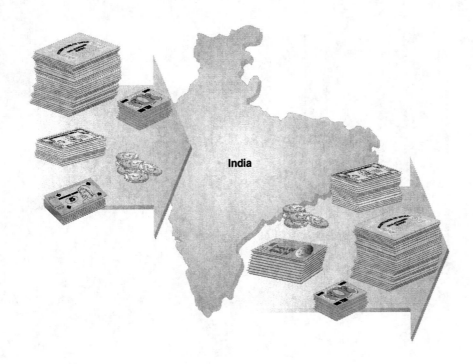

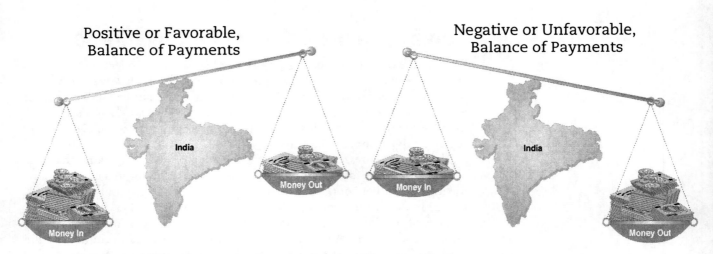

Positive or Favorable, Balance of Payments

Negative or Unfavorable, Balance of Payments

Figure 6-3 Balance of payments is the total flow of money coming into a country minus the total flow of money going out of a country. A country may have a favorable balance of payments some years, as shown on the left. In other years the balance of payments may be unfavorable, as shown on the right.

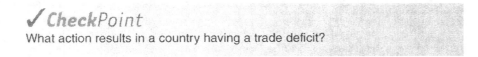

✓ **Check**Point
What action results in a country having a trade deficit?

Trade Agreements

How can a country improve its international trade situation? One answer is by negotiating trade agreements. Trade agreements between countries promote economic development on a worldwide basis or in a geographic region. In some cases individual nations and companies enter agreements that encourage international business activities.

THE WORLD TRADE ORGANIZATION

After World War II, world leaders who wanted to promote peaceful international trade developed a set of ground rules to guide the conduct of international trade. The General Agreement on Tariffs and Trade (GATT) was negotiated in 1947 and began operating in January 1948 when 23 countries signed the treaty agreement.

This multicountry agreement intended to reduce trade barriers and to promote trade. The goals of GATT were to promote world trade through negotiation and to make world trade secure. Working toward these goals helped increase global economic growth and development.

In 1995, GATT was replaced by a new organization—the World Trade Organization (WTO). With over 150 member countries, WTO has many of the same goals as GATT. But in addition, WTO has the power to settle trade disputes and enforce the free-trade agreements between its members.

Based in Geneva, Switzerland, the WTO deals with the rules of trade between nations. Its goal is to help producers of goods and services, exporters, and importers conduct their business. The WTO encourages international trade in several ways.

- Lowering tariffs that discourage free trade
- Eliminating import quotas, subsidies, and unfair technical standards that reduce competition in the world market
- Recognizing protection for patents, copyrights, trademarks, and other intellectual properties, such as software
- Reducing barriers for banks, insurance companies, and other financial services
- Assisting poor countries with trade policies and economic growth

Work as a Team

Prepare a list of benefits and concerns associated with economic communities and countertrade.

NETBookmark

The World Trade Organization (WTO) is a major international organization that helps assure that trade flows smoothly and freely. WTO focuses on the global rules of trade between nations. To learn more about the history and functions of this organization, access the web site shown below and click on the link for Chapter 6. After navigating this web site and reading the information, discuss one benefit of and one misunderstanding about the WTO trading system.

www.cengage.com/school/genbus/intlbiz

REGIONAL COOPERATION

An economic community is an organization of countries that work together to allow a free flow of products. The group acts as a single country for business activities with other regions of the world. An economic community is also called a *common market*. Membership in an economic community has several main benefits.

- Expanded trade with other regions of the world
- Reduced tariffs for the member countries
- Lower prices for consumers within the group
- Expanded employment and investment opportunities

EUROPEAN UNION

The European Union (EU) is an economic and political organization with member nations across Europe. This relationship allows over 500 million consumers to purchase products from any of the countries without paying import or export taxes.

The European Union is headquartered in Brussels, Belgium. The EU Commission has 20 commissioners who are responsible for areas such as labor, health, the environment, education, transportation, and trade. The policy-setting body is the Council of the European Union consisting of the heads of state or government from the member countries. Voters in each member country elect the European Parliament. The parliament, with more than 700 representatives, is in Strasbourg, France.

This economic community works toward several goals.

- Eliminating tariffs and other trade barriers
- Creating a uniform tariff schedule
- Forming a common market for free movement of labor, capital, and business enterprises
- Establishing common agricultural and food safety policies
- Channeling capital from more advanced to less developed regions

In 1999, the EU introduced a common currency—the *euro*. During the transition to full use of this new monetary unit, prices in the stores of EU countries were stated in both euros and the previous national currencies such as the franc, lira, and deutsche mark.

After starting with six countries, today the EU has 27 members. Bulgaria and Romania are the most recent additions.

Think Critically

1. What are some concerns with a highly integrated economic community such as the European Union?
2. Go to the web site of the European Union to obtain current information about the activities of this economic community. Which countries, if any, are currently members of the EU? Which countries, if any, are seeking to gain membership to the EU?

Examples of this type of regional economic cooperation among countries include the European Union (EU), Latin American Free Trade Association (LAFTA), the Association of Southeast Asian Nations (ASEAN), the Economic Community of West African States (ECOWAS), and the North American Free Trade Agreement (NAFTA).

BARTER AGREEMENTS

Most people have traded one item for another at some time. The exchange of goods and services between two parties with no money involved is direct barter. A company may use this method for international business transactions.

Because trading items of equal value is difficult, a different barter method is used. Countertrade is the exchange of products or services between companies in different countries with the possibility of some currency exchange. For example, when PepsiCo owned Pizza Hut, it sold soft drinks in China in exchange for mushrooms used on pizzas. Countertrade can involve companies in several countries, as shown in Figure 6-4 on the next page.

Because countertrades are quite complex, they usually involve large companies. Smaller companies, however, can get involved in countertrade by working with large trading agents who bring together many buyers and sellers.

Companies use countertrade to avoid the risk of receiving payment in a monetary unit with limited value. Currencies from some nations are not in demand due to the weakness of those countries' economies. Countertrade

Countertrade in Action

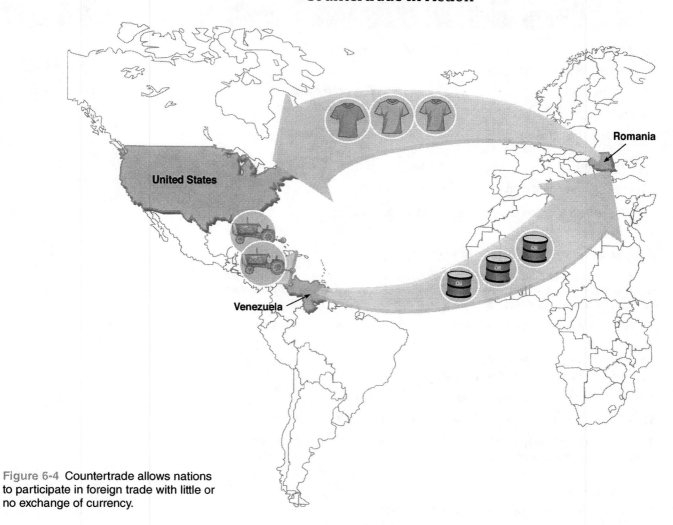

Figure 6-4 Countertrade allows nations to participate in foreign trade with little or no exchange of currency.

also occurs when the government of an importing country requires the selling company to purchase products in return. This helps the importing country to avoid a trade deficit while stimulating economic growth.

FREE-TRADE ZONES

A *free-trade zone* is an area designated by a government for duty-free entry of nonprohibited goods. Free-trade zones are commonly located at a point of entry into a nation, such as a harbor or an airport. Merchandise may be stored, displayed, or used without duties being paid. Duties (import taxes) are imposed on the goods only when the items pass from the free-trade zone into an area of the country subject to customs.

✓ **Check**Point

What are examples of trade agreements among countries?

REVIEW GLOBAL BUSINESS TERMS

Define each of the following terms.

1. trade deficit
2. trade surplus
3. balance of payments
4. economic community
5. direct barter
6. countertrade

REVIEW GLOBAL BUSINESS CONCEPTS

6. How can a trade deficit affect a country's economy?

7. Why is countertrade used in international business?

SOLVE GLOBAL BUSINESS PROBLEMS

For the company or country mentioned in each of the following situations, decide whether the balance of payments or the trade balance is affected and whether the effect would be favorable or unfavorable.

8. A country in Europe receives foreign aid from the government of another country.

9. A six-month long World's Fair is held in the United States and attracts over a million tourists from other countries.

10. An Asian country imports oil that it will pay for later.

11. A multinational company in England pays cash for a factory in India.

12. A new advance in genetic testing is made in Argentina, and the technology is exported all over the world.

THINK CRITICALLY

13. What can a government do to improve a trade deficit?

14. What are some possible concerns of labor unions, environmental groups, and public interest organizations regarding actions of the World Trade Organization?

MAKE ACADEMIC CONNECTIONS

15. MATHEMATICS If a country has inflows of $376 billion and outflows of $402 billion, what is the amount of the favorable (or unfavorable) balance of payments?

16. HISTORY Research the start of the European Economic Community in the 1950s. What factors influenced the start of this common market?

17. COMMUNICATIONS Without using words, demonstrate a barter transaction between people from different cultures.

6-4 The Nature of Competition

GOALS

- List factors that affect international business competition.
- Explain the types of competitive market situations.

Photodisc/Getty Images

International Business Competition

Most likely you have participated in a sport or an activity in which you attempted to do better than others or better than you had done previously. While winning may not always be the main goal, competition is an on-going activity for people, companies, and nations. In an effort to improve a country's economic situation, a strong competitive effort may be beneficial.

Companies compete in both domestic and international markets. The *domestic market* is made up of all the companies that sell similar products within the same country. In contrast, the *international market* is made up of companies that compete against companies in several countries. For example, major soft drink companies have competition in other countries with Crazy Cola in Russia and Thums Up Cola in India.

For companies or countries to gain a competitive advantage they need to do something better, faster, or cheaper than others do. While many people believe the best product is always successful, sometimes a company can also succeed through an effective delivery system. For example, candy products from Nestlé are available around the world. This distribution program creates a *competitive advantage* and makes it difficult for other candy manufacturers to gain sales.

Companies can also compete by successfully doing one thing and doing it well. For example, the demand for airplanes made in Japan is not as high as the demand for planes made in the United States. Japanese companies, however, have specialized in producing components used by U.S. aircraft manufacturers, such as fuselage parts, landing-gear doors, and on-board computers. In addition to direct exporting, the airline parts companies are involved in hundreds of joint ventures and licensing agreements. These efforts have resulted in a significant increase in Japanese aerospace exports.

FACTORS AFFECTING COMPETITION

Three major factors affect the degree of competition among businesses. These factors are the number of companies, business costs, and product differences.

Number of Companies When many companies are selling the same product, there may appear to be a high degree of competition. However, if just a few large firms control the major portion of sales, then competition is limited.

Business Costs The cost of doing business often affects competition. Expensive equipment or having to compete against well-known brands might prevent new companies from starting. Conditions that make it extremely difficult to enter a business are called *barriers to entry*. For example, if a business needs large amounts of capital and equipment to start operations, only a few companies are likely to enter the market. Or, if an existing company has an established brand name, it will be very costly for new companies to make their name known.

Product Differences The third factor that creates competition is product differences. Companies use advertising, brand names, packages, and ingredients to convince consumers that their products are different and better. The addition of flavoring to toothpaste and packaging that can be reused for other purposes are examples of attempts by companies to gain a competitive advantage. Companies use advertising messages to inform consumers about the benefits of their products and to persuade them to buy.

COMMUNICATION ACROSS BORDERS

UNDERSTANDING ASIAN NAMES

When communicating with Asians about trading opportunities, it is important to realize that their naming practices may be different from yours.

A surname, also known as a family name, is the name that links family members. Many surnames have their origins in occupations and locations. In the United States, a surname often is called a last name.

In many Asian countries, the family name comes first, followed by the given name. In Korea, Kim Yun is Mr. Kim, not Mr. Yun.

In the People's Republic of China, more than 100 million people, about 10 percent of the population, have the same surname—Zhang. Fewer than 20 surnames account for more than 60 percent of the population. In Korea, four surnames account for more than 50 percent of the population. Thus, the surnames in some Asian countries are not as distinctive an identifier as they are in the United States. Therefore, it is necessary to learn full names, titles, and divisions within a business in order to communicate with the desired Asian business associates.

Think Critically

1. What kind of an impression will you create if you reverse the order of the names of a potential Asian business partner?
2. What question should you ask to find out about the naming customs in another country?

BENEFITS AND CONCERNS OF COMPETITION

Competition can improve the economic situation and living conditions of a nation. Individual and company efforts to create better goods and services in less time have been a benefit for many nations. Some business competition, however, can result in major concerns. If a company becomes so large that it controls a geographic area or a portion of an economy, many people may suffer. Consumers will have to pay whatever the business charges. Workers will have to work for the amount the company wants to pay because other jobs may not be available. For these reasons, most countries have laws that limit the power of companies.

✓ CheckPoint

What are common barriers to entry for new competitors in an industry?

Types of Competitive Situations

Have you ever wondered why there are so many breakfast cereals or why only a few stores sell a certain brand of shoes? These questions can be answered with an understanding of the competitive situations in an industry. An *industry* refers to companies in the same type of business. For example, Kellogg, General Mills, Kraft General Foods, and Quaker are the major companies in the breakfast cereal industry. Nike, Reebok, and Adidas are in the athletic shoe industry. The competitive situation among companies is also called the *market structure* of an industry. Four main competitive situations may be present in a country's economy, as shown in Figure 6-5.

©Osa, 2009/ Used under license from Shutterstock.com

PURE COMPETITION

Pure competition is a market situation with many sellers, each offering the same product. For example, when farmers sell their wheat or corn, there is little difference from one bushel to another. Supply and demand determines the price. Rivalry among businesses is most free when many companies offer identical or very similar products to buyers. Various factors in our economy and society, however, limit pure competition.

Competitive Market Situations

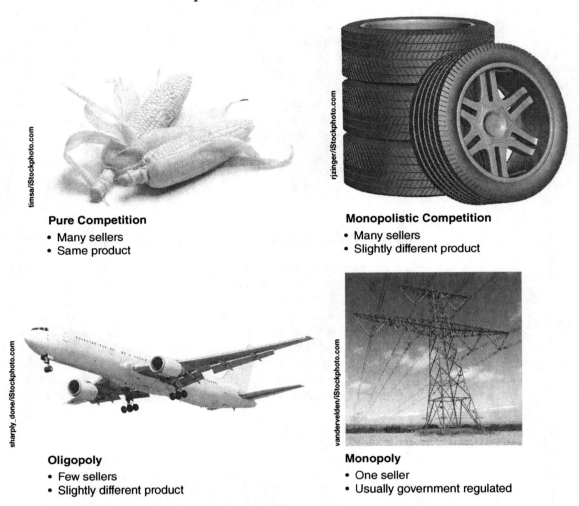

Pure Competition
- Many sellers
- Same product

Monopolistic Competition
- Many sellers
- Slightly different product

Oligopoly
- Few sellers
- Slightly different product

Monopoly
- One seller
- Usually government regulated

Figure 6-5 The number of businesses and differences in products affect the amount of competition in a market.

MONOPOLISTIC COMPETITION

In order for companies to attract customers, they make their products slightly different. One fast-food hamburger restaurant offers a special sauce, another adds bacon and cheese, while another gives away a game or toy with the sandwich. Monopolistic competition refers to a market situation with many sellers, each with a slightly different product. The difference in products can be actual (such as ingredients) or implied (such as different advertisements, a brand name, or a package design).

OLIGOPOLY

When a few large companies control an industry, an oligopoly exists. In this market situation, the few sellers usually offer products that are slightly different. However, competition is mainly the result of large companies being able to advertise and sell their goods in many geographic areas. For example,

Photodisc/Getty Images

only a few large companies make automobile tires. Therefore, these large manufacturers are able to control the market. Another example is that with only a few countries having oil as a natural resource, companies in these nations can influence the availability and price of oil.

MONOPOLY

When one company controls the total supply of a product or service, there is no competition. A monopoly is a situation in which one seller controls the entire market for a product or service. It is very unusual for this to happen without actions by government or other businesses. Like pure competition, few examples of true monopolies exist. Situations that are near monopolies include South Africa's diamond mines and a small village or town served by only one store. Monopolies that exist in the United States, such as cable television, local water service, and first-class mail delivery service, are government regulated.

✓ **Check**Point

What are the four types of competitive situations?

REVIEW GLOBAL BUSINESS TERMS

Define each of the following terms.

1. industry
2. pure competition
3. monopolistic competition
4. oligopoly
5. monopoly

REVIEW GLOBAL BUSINESS CONCEPTS

6. What are the main factors that affect the amount of business competition?

7. What are the advantages of competition?

8. What is the difference between actual and implied differences in monopolistic competition?

SOLVE GLOBAL BUSINESS PROBLEMS

For each of the follow situations, decide which competitive situation is present: pure competition, monopolistic competition, oligopoly, or monopoly.

9. A country in Asia allows only one company to manufacture a product.

10. In a European country, four companies control over 85 percent of sales in the supermarket industry.

11. In a region of western Africa, minerals are mined and sold by many extracting companies.

12. In an area of the Middle East, many small shops offer a variety of clothing styles.

THINK CRITICALLY

13. What types of actions could consumers and government take to promote competition?

14. What kind of competition exists in the microcomputer operating systems market today?

MAKE ACADEMIC CONNECTIONS

15. CULTURAL STUDIES Select a product that you use frequently. Determine what appeals to you about the product, including how it is advertised. Consider whether the elements you have determined would appeal to people in other countries. Write a summary of your findings.

16. LAW Research the start of antitrust legislation in the United States. What applications of those laws are in the news today?

CHAPTER SUMMARY

6-1 IMPORTING PROCEDURES

A Importing is important to business for meeting consumer demand, lowering operating costs, and obtaining production inputs.

B The four steps of importing are (1) determine demand, (2) contact suppliers, (3) finalize purchases, and (4) receive goods.

6-2 EXPORTING PROCEDURES

A The five steps of the exporting process are (1) find potential customers, (2) meet the needs of customers, (3) agree on sales terms, (4) provide products or services, and (5) complete the transaction.

B The exporting of services can be a significant percentage of a country's export activities.

6-3 IMPORTANCE OF TRADE RELATIONS

A A country's balance of payments measures the total flow of money coming into a country minus the total flow going out and may be positive or negative. A trade deficit is the total amount a country owes to other countries as a result of importing more goods and services than are exported.

B The main types of trade agreements are the World Trade Organization, economic communities, barter agreements, and free-trade zones.

6-4 THE NATURE OF COMPETITION

A The competitive situation in a country is affected by (1) the number of companies, (2) business costs, and (3) product differences.

B The four main types of competitive markets are pure competition, monopolistic competition, oligopoly, and monopoly.

GLOBAL **REFOCUS**

Read the Global Focus at the beginning of this chapter, and answer the following questions.

1. What actions might an ice cream company take to expand export activities?

2. How could foreign companies become more competitive in the global ice cream industry?

REVIEW GLOBAL BUSINESS TERMS

Match the terms listed with the definitions. Some terms may not be used.

1. Government employee who is authorized to collect the dutites levied on imports.
2. A company that arranges to ship goods to customers.
3. The exchange of products or services between companies in different countries with the possibility of some currency exchange.
4. Control of an industry by a few large companies.
5. A document that states the agreement between the exporter and the transportation company.
6. The total flow of money coming into a country minus the total flow going out.
7. A market situation with many sellers, each with a slightly different product.
8. An organization of countries that bond together to allow a free flow of products.
9. Terms of sale that mean the selling price of the product includes the cost of loading the exported goods onto transport vessels at the specified place.
10. A situation in which one seller controls the entire market for a product or service.

a. balance of payments
b. bill of lading
c. certificate of origin
d. cost and freight (C&F)
e. cost, insurance, and freight (CIF)
f. countertrade
g. customs official
h. direct barter
i. economic community
j. free on board (FOB)
k. freight forwarder
l. industry
m. monopolistic competition
n. monopoly
o. oligopoly
p. pure competition
q. trade deficit
r. trade surplus

11. The cost of the goods, insurance, and freight are included in the price quoted.
12. The exchange of goods and services between two parties with no money involved.
13. A group of companies in the same type of business.
14. A document that states the name of the country in which the shipped goods were produced.
15. A market situation with many sellers, each offering the same product.
16. The result of a country importing more goods and services than the country is exporting.
17. The price includes the cost of the goods and freight, but the buyer must pay for insurance separately.

MAKE GLOBAL BUSINESS DECISIONS

18. Name some examples of imported products that the people in the United States need and want.
19. Why are taxes imposed on products imported into various countries?
20. List some resources you could use to determine the buying habits in different countries.
21. What factors would affect whether the buyer or the seller pays for the shipping costs in an international business transaction?

22. Why might a country's balance of payments be a better measurement of its international business activities than its balance of trade?

23. What problems might arise when nations create an economic community for international trade?

24. Describe some examples of countertrade involving products from different countries with which you are familiar.

MAKE ACADEMIC CONNECTIONS

25. TECHNOLOGY Go to the web site of the World Trade Organization to obtain additional information about the current activities of this global trade association.

26. LAW Investigate the duties and customs procedures of one of the following countries: Malaysia, Australia, Taiwan, China, India, South Korea, Singapore, or New Zealand.

27. GEOGRAPHY Find the location of the free-trade zone closest to your city. Draw a map that includes your state, the location of the free-trade zone, and all states in between. Then draw a line between your city and the free-trade zone. Mark the distance above the line. If the free-trade zone is in your city, draw a map of your city, and identify the location of the free-trade zone.

28. COMMUNICATIONS Talk to someone who has shipped goods to another country. Prepare a short oral report about the procedures for transporting merchandise to a foreign country.

29. CULTURAL STUDIES Collect advertisements, packages, and other information about products made in another country and sold in the United States. Ask five friends or relatives to identify the country of origin for the product.

30. SCIENCE Many products in our society compete on the basis of very minor differences. Collect information on five different brands of soap, toothpaste, breakfast cereal, or shampoo from advertisements, packages, and periodicals. Based on your analysis and comments from others, list the similarities and differences of the brands selected. *Consumer Reports* is a good source of information for this activity.

31. CAREER PLANNING Obtain information about the imports and exports of a country of your choice. What types of job opportunities would be created by these foreign business activities?

32. TECHNOLOGY Use the Internet to find examples of businesses that are involved in pure competition, monopolistic competition, oligopolies, and monopolies.

33. ECONOMICS Go to the web site of an economic community. Make a list of the members of that community and some of the activities in which it engages.

The GLOBAL *Entrepreneur*

CREATING AN INTERNATIONAL BUSINESS PLAN

Developing an Exporting Plan

Use a product or service that your chosen company is actively exporting or that you believe has potential for sales in other countries. Then select a country that would provide a market opportunity for that product or service. Use information collected for Chapters 1–5 and additional research to prepare an exporting plan. Include the following components.

1. Product description
   - Describe the product or service in detail, including specific features.
   - Describe any changes in the product or service that may be necessary before exporting.

2. Foreign business environment
   - List cultural and social factors that may affect the sale of the product.
   - Discuss the geography of the country to which you have chosen to export this product or service.
   - Describe economic conditions that may affect exporting this product.
   - Report any political or legal factors that could affect exporting activities.

3. Market potential
   - Describe the type of customer who is best suited for this product or service in the country you have chosen.
   - Identify methods that could be used to contact potential buyers in the country you have chosen.
   - Estimate sales for the product or service based on country size, market demand, and competition.

4. Export transaction details
   - Describe import taxes or other restrictions that may affect exporting costs.
   - Discuss the shipping and documentation requirements for the country you have selected.
   - Identify the amount of time the exporting plan will take to execute.

Sources of information for researching your exporting plan are listed below.

   - reference books such as encyclopedias, almanacs, and atlases
   - current news, business, and travel articles, including news stories, company profiles, and advertisements
   - web sites for exporting information
   - materials from companies, airlines, travel bureaus, government agencies, and other organizations involved in international business
   - interviews with people who have been to the country

International Trade

18

AP Photo/Reed Saxon

○ This morning you pulled on your Levi's jeans from Mexico, pulled over your Benetton sweater from Italy, and laced up your Timberland boots from Thailand. After a breakfast that included bananas from Honduras and coffee from Brazil, you climbed into your Volvo from Sweden fueled by Venezuelan oil and headed for a lecture by a visiting professor from Hungary. If the United States is such a rich and productive country, why do we import so many goods and services?

○ Why don't we produce everything ourselves?

○ How can the U.S. economy grow if we import more goods and services?

○ And why do some producers try to block imports?

Answers to these and other questions are addressed in this chapter.

The world is a giant shopping mall, and Americans are big spenders. For example, the U.S. population is less than 5 percent of the world's population, but Americans buy more than half the Rolls Royces and diamonds sold around the world. Americans also buy Japanese cars, French wine, European vacations, Chinese products galore, and thousands of other goods and services from around the globe. Foreigners buy U.S. products too—grain, aircraft, movies, software, trips to New York City, and thousands of other goods and services.

In this chapter, we examine the gains from international trade and the effects of trade restrictions on the allocation of resources. The analysis is based on the familiar tools of demand and supply.

Topics discussed include:

- Gains from trade
- Absolute and comparative advantage revisited
- Tariffs and quotas

- Cost of trade restrictions
- Arguments for trade restrictions
- Free trade agreements

The Gains From Trade

A family from Virginia that sits down for a meal of Kansas prime rib, Idaho potatoes, and California string beans, with Georgia peach cobbler for dessert, is benefiting from interstate trade. You already understand why the residents of one state trade with those of another. Back in Chapter 2, you learned about the gains arising from specialization and exchange. You may recall how you and your roommate could maximize output when you each specialized. The law of comparative advantage says that the individual with the lowest opportunity cost of producing a particular good should specialize in that good. Just as individuals benefit from specialization and exchange, so do states and, indeed, nations. To reap the gains that arise from specialization, countries engage in international trade. *Each country specializes in making goods with the lowest opportunity cost.*

A Profile of Exports and Imports

Just as some states are more involved in interstate trade than others, some nations are more involved in international trade than others. For example, exports account for about one-quarter of the gross domestic product (GDP) in Canada and the United Kingdom; about one-third of GDP in Germany, Sweden, and Switzerland; and about half of GDP in the Netherlands. Despite the perception that Japan has a huge export sector, exports make up only about one-sixth of its GDP.

U.S. Exports

U.S. exports of goods and services amounted to $1.6 trillion, or 11 percent of GDP in 2009. The left panel of Exhibit 1 shows the composition by major category. The largest category is services, which accounted for 32 percent of U.S. exports in 2009. U.S. service exports include transportation, insurance, banking, education, consulting, and tourism. Capital goods ranked second at 27 percent of exports, with aircraft the largest export industry (Boeing is the top U.S. exporter in any industry). Third most important are industrial supplies, at 19 percent of the total, with chemicals and plastics most important here. Capital goods and industrial supplies help foreign producers make stuff and together accounted for nearly half of U.S. exports. Consumer goods (except food, which appears separately) accounted for only 10 percent of exports (pharmaceuticals tops this group). Consumer goods include entertainment products, such as movies and recorded music.

U.S. Imports

U.S. imports of goods and services in 2009 totaled $1.9 trillion, or about 14 percent relative to GDP. The right panel of Exhibit 1 shows the composition of U.S. imports. The biggest category, at 25 percent, is industrial supplies, with oil-related products accounting for most of this. Whereas consumer goods accounted for only 10 percent of U.S. exports, they were 23 percent of U.S. imports, with pharmaceuticals the largest item. Ranked third in importance is capital goods, at 20 percent, with computers the largest item. Note that services, which accounted for 32 percent of U.S. exports, were only 19 percent of imports.

Trading Partners

To give you some feel for America's trading partners, here were the top 10 destinations for merchandise exports for 2009 in order of importance: Canada, Mexico, China, Japan, United Kingdom, Germany, Netherlands, South Korea, France, and Brazil. The

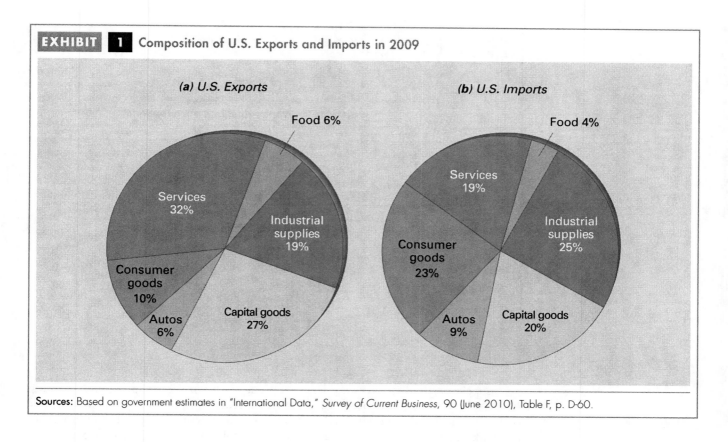

EXHIBIT   1   Composition of U.S. Exports and Imports in 2009

(a) U.S. Exports

Food 6%

Services 32%

Industrial supplies 19%

Consumer goods 10%

Autos 6%

Capital goods 27%

(b) U.S. Imports

Food 4%

Services 19%

Industrial supplies 25%

Consumer goods 23%

Autos 9%

Capital goods 20%

Sources: Based on government estimates in "International Data," *Survey of Current Business*, 90 (June 2010), Table F, p. D-60.

top 10 sources of merchandise imports in order of importance were China, Canada, Mexico, Japan, Germany, United Kingdom, South Korea, France, Taiwan, and Ireland.

Production Possibilities without Trade

The rationale behind most international trade is obvious. The United States grows little coffee because our climate is not suited to coffee. More revealing, however, are the gains from trade where the comparative advantage is not so obvious. Suppose that just two goods—food and clothing—are produced and consumed and that there are only two countries in the world—the United States, with a labor force of 100 million workers, and the mythical country of Izodia, with 200 million workers. The conclusions derived from this simple model have general relevance for international trade.

Exhibit 2 presents production possibilities tables for each country, based on the size of the labor force and the productivity of workers in each country. The exhibit assumes that each country has a given technology and that labor is efficiently employed. If no trade occurs between countries, Exhibit 2 also represents each country's *consumption possibilities* table. The production numbers imply that each worker in the United States can produce either 6 units of food or 3 units of clothing per day. If all 100 million U.S. workers produce food, they make 600 million units per day, as shown in column U_1 in panel (a). If all U.S. workers make clothing, they produce 300 million units per day, as shown in column U_6. The columns in between show some workers making food and some making clothing. Because a U.S. worker can produce either 6 units of food or 3 units of clothing, *the opportunity cost of 1 more unit of clothing is 2 units of food.*

EXHIBIT 2   Production Possibilities Schedules for the United States and Izodia

(a) United States

**Production Possibilities with
100 Million Workers (millions of units per day)**

	U_1	U_2	U_3	U_4	U_5	U_6
Food	600	480	360	240	120	0
Clothing	0	60	120	180	240	300

(b) Izodia

**Production Possibilities with
200 Million Workers (millions of units per day)**

	I_1	I_2	I_3	I_4	I_5	I_6
Food	200	160	120	80	40	0
Clothing	0	80	160	240	320	400

Suppose Izodian workers are less educated, work with less capital, and farm less fertile soil than U.S. workers, so each Izodian worker can produce only 1 unit of food or 2 units of clothing per day. If all 200 million Izodian workers specialize in food, they can make 200 million units per day, as shown in column I_1 in panel (b) of Exhibit 2. If they all make clothing, total output is 400 million units per day, as shown in column I_6. Some intermediate production possibilities are also listed in the exhibit. Because an Izodian worker can produce either 1 unit of food or 2 units of clothing, *the opportunity cost of 1 more unit of clothing is 1/2 unit of food.*

We can convert the data in Exhibit 2 to a production possibilities frontier for each country, as shown in Exhibit 3. In each diagram, the amount of food produced is measured on the vertical axis and the amount of clothing on the horizontal axis. U.S. combinations are shown in the left panel by U_1, U_2, and so on. Izodian combinations are shown in the right panel by I_1, I_2, and so on. Because we assume for simplicity that resources are perfectly adaptable to the production of each commodity, each production possibilities curve is a straight line. The slope of this line differs between countries because the opportunity cost of production differs between countries. The slope equals the opportunity cost of clothing—the amount of food a country must give up to produce another unit of clothing. The U.S. slope is −2, and the Izodian slope is −1/2. The U.S. slope is steeper because its opportunity cost of producing clothing is greater.

Exhibit 3 illustrates possible combinations of food and clothing that residents of each country can produce and consume if all resources are efficiently employed and there is no trade between the two countries. **Autarky** is the situation of national self-sufficiency, in which there is no economic interaction with foreign producers or consumers. Suppose that U.S. producers maximize profit and U.S. consumers maximize utility with the combination of 240 million units of food and 180 million units of clothing—combination U_4. This is called the *autarky equilibrium*. Suppose also that Izodians are in autarky equilibrium, identified as combination I_3, of 120 million units of food and 160 million units of clothing.

autarky

National self-sufficiency; no economic interaction with foreigners

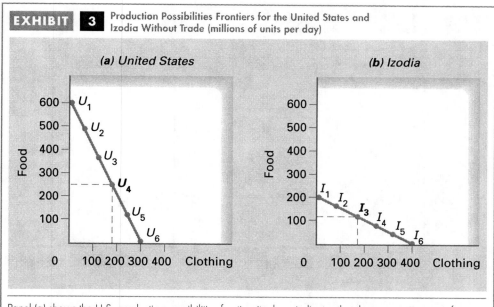

EXHIBIT   3   Production Possibilities Frontiers for the United States and Izodia Without Trade (millions of units per day)

Panel (a) shows the U.S. production possibilities frontier; its slope indicates that the opportunity cost of an additional unit of clothing is 2 units of food. Panel (b) shows production possibilities for Izodia; an additional unit of clothing costs 1/2 unit of food. Clothing has a lower opportunity cost in Izodia.

Consumption Possibilities Based on Comparative Advantage

In our example, each U.S. worker can produce more clothing and more food per day than can each Izodian worker, so Americans have an *absolute advantage* in the production of both goods. Recall from Chapter 2 that having an absolute advantage means being able to produce something using fewer resources than other producers require. Should the U.S. economy remain in autarky—that is, self-sufficient in both food and clothing productions—or could there be gains from specialization and trade?

As long as the opportunity cost of production differs between the two countries, there are gains from specialization and trade. *According to the law of comparative advantage, each country should specialize in producing the good with the lower opportunity cost.* The opportunity cost of producing 1 more unit of clothing is 2 units of food in the United States compared with 1/2 unit of food in Izodia. Because the opportunity cost of producing clothing is lower in Izodia than in the United States, both countries gain if Izodia specializes in clothing and exports some to the United States, and the United States specializes in food and exports some to Izodia.

Before countries can trade, however, they must agree on how much of one good exchanges for another—that is, they must agree on the **terms of trade**. As long as Americans can get more than ½ a unit of clothing for each unit of food produced, and as long as Izodians can get more than ½ a unit of food for each unit of clothing produced, both countries will be better off specializing. Suppose that market forces shape the terms of trade so that 1 unit of clothing exchanges for 1 unit of food. Americans thus trade 1 unit of food to Izodians for 1 unit of clothing. To produce 1 unit of clothing themselves, Americans would have to sacrifice 2 units of food. Likewise, Izodians trade 1 unit of clothing to Americans for 1 unit of food, which is only half what Izodians would sacrifice to produce 1 unit of food themselves.

Exhibit 4 shows that with 1 unit of food trading for 1 unit of clothing, Americans and Izodians can consume anywhere along their blue consumption possibilities frontiers.

terms of trade

How much of one good exchanges for a unit of another good

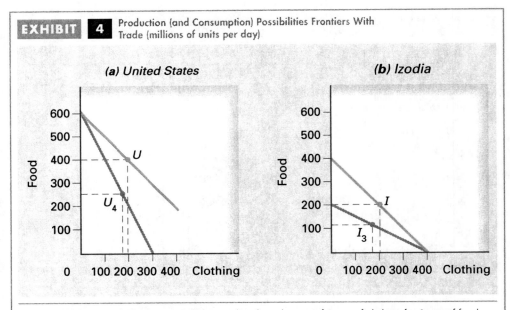

EXHIBIT 4 Production (and Consumption) Possibilities Frontiers With Trade (millions of units per day)

If Izodia and the United States can specialize and trade at the rate of 1 unit of clothing for 1 unit of food, both can benefit as shown by the blue lines. By trading with Izodia, the U.S. can produce only food and still consume combination U, which has more food and more clothing than U_4. Likewise, Izodia can attain preferred combination I by trading some clothing for U.S. food.

The consumption possibilities frontier shows a nation's possible combinations of goods available as a result of specialization and exchange. (Note that the U.S. consumption possibilities curve does not extend to the right of 400 million units of clothing, because Izodia could produce no more than that.) The amount each country actually consumes depends on the relative preferences for food and clothing. Suppose Americans select combination U in panel (a) and Izodians select point I in panel (b).

Without trade, the United States produces and consumes 240 million units of food and 180 million units of clothing. With trade, Americans specialize to produce 600 million units of food; they eat 400 million units and exchange the rest for 200 million units of Izodian clothing. This consumption combination is reflected by point U. Through exchange, Americans increase their consumption of both food and clothing.

Without trade, Izodians produce and consume 120 million units of food and 160 million units of clothing. With trade, Izodians specialize to produce 400 million units of clothing; they wear 200 million and exchange the rest for 200 million units of U.S. food. This consumption combination is shown by point I. Through trade, Izodians, like Americans, are able to increase their consumption of both goods. How is this possible?

Because Americans are more efficient in the production of food and Izodians more efficient in the production of clothing, total output increases when each specializes. Without specialization, world production was 360 million units of food and 340 million units of clothing. With specialization, food increases to 600 million units and clothing to 400 million units. Thus, both countries increase consumption with trade. *Although the United States has an absolute advantage in both goods, differences in the opportunity cost of production between the two nations ensure that specialization and exchange result in mutual gains.* Remember that comparative advantage, not absolute advantage, creates gains from specialization and trade. The only constraint on trade is that, for each good, *world production must equal world consumption.*

We simplified trade relations in our example to highlight the gains from specialization and exchange. We assumed that each country would completely specialize in producing a particular good, that resources were equally adaptable to the production of either good, that the costs of transporting goods from one country to another were inconsequential, and that there were no problems in arriving at the terms of trade. The world is not that simple. For example, we don't expect a country to produce just one good. Regardless, specialization based on the law of comparative advantage still leads to gains from trade.

Reasons for International Specialization

Countries trade with one another—or, more precisely, people and firms in one country trade with those in another—because each side expects to gain from exchange. How do we know what each country should produce and what each should trade?

Differences in Resource Endowments

Differences in resource endowments often create differences in the opportunity cost of production across countries. Some countries are blessed with an abundance of fertile land and favorable growing seasons. The United States, for example, has been called the "breadbasket of the world" because of its rich farmland ideal for growing wheat. Coffee grows best in the climate and elevation of Colombia, Brazil, and Jamaica. Honduras has the ideal climate for bananas. Thus, the United States exports wheat and imports coffee and bananas. Seasonal differences across countries also encourage trade. For example, in the winter, Americans import fruit from Chile, and Canadians travel to Florida for sun and fun. In the summer, Americans export fruit to Chile, and Americans travel to Canada for camping and hiking.

Resources are often concentrated in particular countries: crude oil in Saudi Arabia, fertile soil in the United States, copper ore in Chile, rough diamonds in South Africa. The United States grows abundant supplies of oil seeds such as soybeans and sunflowers, but does not have enough crude oil to satisfy domestic demand. Thus, the United States exports oil seeds and imports crude oil. More generally, *countries export products they can produce more cheaply in return for products that are unavailable domestically or are cheaper elsewhere.*

Exhibit 5 shows, for 12 key resources, U.S. production as a percentage of U.S. consumption. If production falls short of consumption, this means the United States imports the difference. For example, because America grows coffee only in Hawaii, U.S. production is only 1 percent of U.S. consumption, so nearly all coffee is imported. The exhibit also shows that U.S. production falls short of consumption for oil and for metals such as gold, zinc, copper, and aluminum. If production exceeds consumption, the United States exports the difference. For example, U.S.-grown cotton amounts to 417 percent of U.S. cotton consumption, so most U.S. grown cotton is exported. U.S. production also exceeds consumption for other crops, including wheat, oil seeds, and coarse grains (corn, barley, oats). In short, when it comes to basic resources, the United States is a net importer of oil and metals and a net exporter of crops.

Economies of Scale

If production is subject to *economies of scale*—that is, if the long-run average cost of production falls as a firm expands its scale of operation—countries can gain from trade if each nation specializes. Such specialization allows firms in each nation to produce

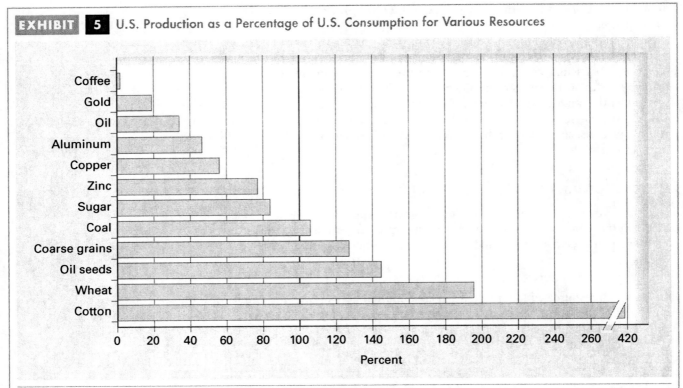

EXHIBIT   5   U.S. Production as a Percentage of U.S. Consumption for Various Resources

If U.S. production is less than 100 percent of U.S. consumption, then imports make up the difference. If U.S. production exceeds U.S. consumption, then the amount by which production exceeds 100 percent of consumption is exported.

Source: Based on annual figures selected from *The Economist Pocket World in Figures: 2010 Edition* (Profile Books, 2010).

more, which reduces average costs. The primary reason for establishing the single integrated market of the European Union was to offer producers there a large, open market of now more than 500 million consumers. Producers could thereby achieve economies of scale. Firms and countries producing at the lowest opportunity costs are most competitive in international markets. For example, 60 percent of the world's buttons come from a single Chinese city.

Differences in Tastes

Even if all countries had identical resource endowments and combined those resources with equal efficiency, each country would still gain from trade as long as tastes differed across countries. Consumption patterns differ across countries and some of this results from differences in tastes. For example, the Czechs and Irish drink three times as much beer per capita as do the Swiss and Swedes. The French drink three times as much wine as do Australians. The Danes eat twice as much pork as do Americans. Americans eat twice as much chicken as do Hungarians. Americans like chicken, but not all of it. The United States is the world's leading exporter of chicken feet, and China is the world's leading importer (Tyson Foods alone sends more than 2.8 billion chicken feet to China each year). Soft drinks are four times more popular in the United States than in Europe. The English like tea; Americans, coffee. Algeria has an ideal climate for growing grapes (vineyards there date back to Roman times). But Algeria's population is 99 percent Muslim, a religion that forbids alcohol consumption. Thus, Algeria exports wine.

Trade Restrictions and Welfare Loss

Despite the benefits of exchange, nearly all countries at one time or another erect trade barriers, which benefit some domestic producers but harm other domestic producers and all domestic consumers. In this section, we consider the effects of trade barriers and the reasons they are imposed.

Consumer Surplus and Producer Surplus From Market Exchange

Before we explore the net effects of world trade on social welfare, let's develop a framework showing the benefits that consumers and producers get from market exchange. Consider a hypothetical market for apples shown in Exhibit 6. The height of the demand curve shows what consumers are willing and able to pay for each additional pound of apples. In effect, the height of the demand curve shows the *marginal benefit* consumers expect from each pound of apples. For example, the demand curve indicates that some consumers in this market are willing to pay $3.00 or more per pound for the first few pounds of apples. But every consumer gets to buy apples at the market-clearing price,

---

EXHIBIT **6** **Consumer Surplus and Producer Surplus**

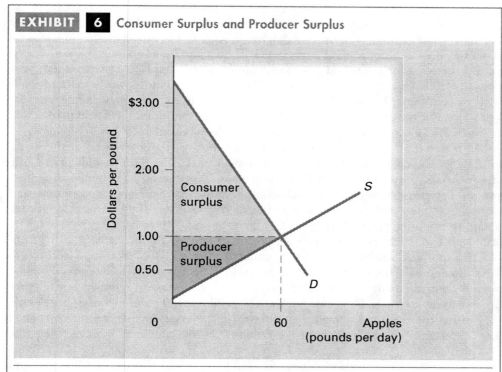

Consumer surplus, shown by the blue triangle, indicates the net benefits consumers reap from buying 60 pounds of apples at $1.00 per pound. Some consumers would have been willing to pay $3.00 or more per pound for the first few pounds. Consumer surplus measures the difference between the maximum sum of money consumers would pay for 60 pounds of apples and the actual sum they pay. Producer surplus, shown by the gold triangle, indicates the net benefits producers reap from selling 60 pounds at $1.00 per pound. Some producers would have supplied apples for $0.50 per pound or less. Producer surplus measures the difference between the actual sum of money producers receive for 60 pounds of apples and the minimum amount they would accept for this amount.

which here is $1.00 per pound. Most consumers thus get a bonus, or a surplus, from market exchange.

The blue-shaded triangle below the demand curve and above the market price reflects the *consumer surplus* in this market, which is the difference between the most that consumers would pay for 60 pounds of apples per day and the actual amount they do pay. We all enjoy a consumer surplus from most products we buy.

Producers usually derive a similar surplus. The height of the supply curve shows what producers are willing and able to accept for each additional pound of apples. That is, the height of the supply curve shows the expected *marginal cost* from producing each additional pound. For example, the supply curve indicates that some producers face a marginal cost of $0.50 or less per pound for supplying the first few pounds. But every producer gets to sell apples for the market-clearing price of $1.00 per pound. The gold-shaded triangle above the supply curve and below the market price reflects the *producer surplus*, which is the difference between the actual amount that producers receive for 60 pounds and what they would accept to supply that amount.

The point is that market exchange usually generates a surplus, or a bonus, for both consumers and producers. In the balance of this chapter, we look at the gains from international trade and how trade restrictions affect consumer and producer surplus.

Tariffs

A *tariff*, a term first introduced in Chapter 3, is a tax on imports. (Tariffs can apply to exports, too, but we will focus on import tariffs.) A tariff can be either *specific,* such as a tariff of $5 per barrel of oil, or *ad valorem,* such as 10 percent on the import price of jeans. Consider the effects of a specific tariff on a particular good. In Exhibit 7, *D* is the U.S. demand for sugar and *S* is the supply of sugar from U.S. growers (there were about 10,000 U.S. sugarcane growers in 2010). Suppose that the world price of sugar is $0.10 per pound. The **world price** is determined by the world supply and demand for a product. It is the price at which any supplier can sell output on the world market and at which any demander can purchase output on the world market.

world price
The price at which a good is traded on the world market; determined by the world demand and world supply for the good

With free trade, any U.S. consumers could buy any amount desired at the world price of $0.10 per pound, so the quantity demanded is 70 million pounds per month, of which U.S. producers supply 20 million pounds and importers supply 50 million pounds. Because U.S. buyers can purchase sugar at the world price, U.S. producers can't charge more than that. Now suppose that a specific tariff of $0.05 is imposed on each pound of imported sugar, raising the U.S. price from $0.10 to $0.15 per pound. U.S. producers can therefore raise their own price to $0.15 per pound without losing business to imports. At the higher price, the quantity supplied by U.S. producers increases to 30 million pounds, but the quantity demanded by U.S. consumers declines to 60 million pounds. Because quantity demanded has declined and quantity supplied by U.S. producers has increased, U.S. imports fall from 50 million to 30 million pounds per month.

Because the U.S. price is higher after the tariff, U.S. consumers are worse off. Their loss in consumer surplus is identified in Exhibit 7 by the combination of the blue- and pink-shaded areas. Because both the U.S. price and the quantity supplied by U.S. producers have increased, their total revenue increases by the areas *a* plus *b* plus *f*. But only area *a* represents an increase in producer surplus. Revenue represented by the areas *b* plus *f* merely offsets the higher marginal cost U.S. producers face in expanding sugar output from 20 million to 30 million pounds per month. Area *b* represents part of the net welfare loss to the domestic economy because those 10 million pounds could have been imported for $0.10 per pound rather than produced domestically at a higher marginal cost.

Government revenue from the tariff is identified by area *c,* which equals the tariff of $0.05 per pound multiplied by the 30 million pounds imported, for tariff revenue

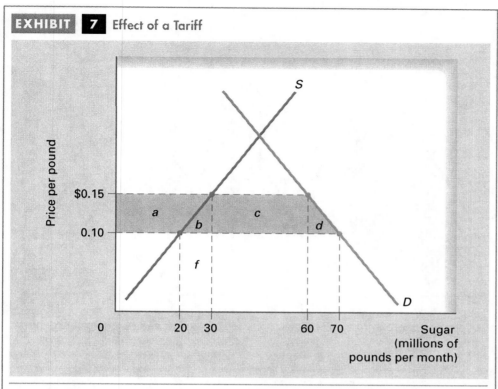

EXHIBIT   7   Effect of a Tariff

At a world price of $0.10 per pound, U.S. consumers demand 70 million pounds of sugar per month, and U.S. producers supply 20 million pounds per month; the difference is imported. After the imposition of a $0.05 per pound tariff, the U.S. price rises to $0.15 per pound. U.S. producers supply 30 million pounds, and U.S. consumers cut back to 60 million pounds. At the higher U.S. price, consumers are worse off; their loss of consumer surplus is the sum of areas *a, b, c,* and *d.* The net welfare loss to the U.S. economy consists of areas *b* and *d.*

of $1.5 million per month. Tariff revenue is a loss to consumers, but because the tariff goes to the government, it can be used to lower taxes or to increase public services, so it's not a loss to the U.S. economy. Area *d* shows a loss in consumer surplus because less sugar is consumed at the higher price. This loss is not redistributed to anyone else, so area *d* reflects part of the net welfare loss of the tariff. Therefore, areas *b* and *d* show the domestic economy's net welfare loss of the tariff; *the two triangles measure a loss in consumer surplus that is not offset by a gain to anyone in the domestic economy.*

In summary: Of the total loss in U.S. consumer surplus (areas *a, b, c,* and *d*) resulting from the tariff, area *a* goes to U.S producers, area *c* becomes government revenue, but areas *b* and *d* are net losses in domestic social welfare.

Import Quotas

An *import quota* is a legal limit on the amount of a commodity that can be imported. Quotas usually target imports from certain countries. For example, a quota may limit furniture from China or shoes from Brazil. To have an impact on the domestic market, a quota must be less than what would be imported with free trade. Consider a quota on the U.S. market for sugar. In panel (a) of Exhibit 8, *D* is the U.S. demand curve and *S* is the supply curve of U.S. sugar producers. Suppose again that the world price of sugar

EXHIBIT 8 Effect of a Quota

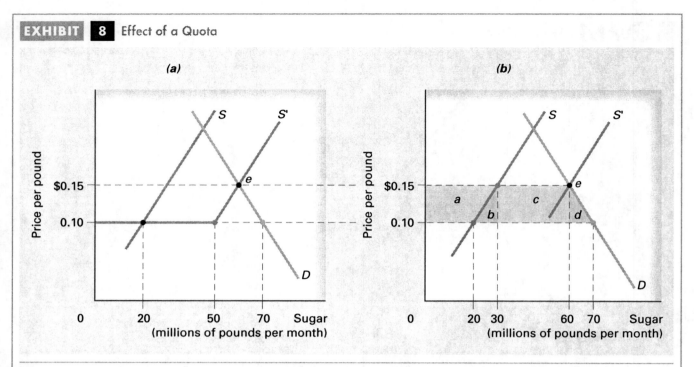

In panel (a), D is the U.S. demand curve and S is the supply curve of U.S. producers. If the government establishes a sugar quota of 30 million pounds per month, the supply curve combining U.S. production and imports becomes horizontal at the world price of $0.10 per pound and remains horizontal until the quantity supplied reaches 50 million pounds. For higher prices, the new supply curve equals the horizontal sum of the U.S. supply curve, S, plus the quota of 30 million pounds. The new U.S. price, $0.15 per pound, is determined by the intersection of the new supply curve, S', with the U.S. demand curve, D. Panel (b) shows the welfare effect of the quota. As a result of the higher U.S. price, consumer surplus is cut by the shaded area. The blue-shaded areas illustrate the loss in consumer surplus that is captured by domestic producers and those who are permitted to fulfill the quota, and the pink-shaded triangles illustrate the net welfare cost of the quota on the U.S. economy.

is $0.10 per pound. With free trade, that price would prevail in the U.S. market as well, and a total of 70 million pounds would be demanded per month. U.S. producers would supply 20 million pounds and importers, 50 million pounds. With a quota of 50 million pounds or more per month, the U.S. price would remain the same as the world price of $0.10 per pound, and the U.S. quantity would be 70 million pounds per month. In short, a quota of at least 50 million pounds would not raise the U.S. price above the world price because 50 million pounds were imported without a quota. A more stringent quota, however, would cut imports, which, as we'll see, would raise the U.S. price.

Suppose U.S. trade officials impose an import quota of 30 million pounds per month. As long as the U.S. price is at or above the world price of $0.10 per pound, foreign producers will supply 30 million pounds. So at prices at or above $0.10 per pound, the total supply of sugar to the U.S. market is found by adding 30 million pounds of imported sugar to the amount supplied by U.S. producers. U.S. and foreign producers would never sell in the U.S. market for less than $0.10 per pound because they can always get that price on the world market. Thus, the supply curve that sums domestic production and imports is horizontal at the world price of $0.10 per pound and remains so until the quantity supplied reaches 50 million pounds.

Again, for prices above $0.10 per pound, the new supply curve, S', adds horizontally the 30-million-pound quota to S, the supply curve of U.S. producers. The U.S. price is found where this new supply curve, S', intersects the domestic demand curve, which in

Exhibit 8 occurs at point *e*. *By limiting imports, the quota raises the domestic price of sugar above the world price and reduces quantity below the free trade level.* (Note that to compare more easily the effects of tariffs and quotas, this quota is designed to yield the same equilibrium price and quantity as the tariff examined earlier.)

Panel (b) of Exhibit 8 shows the distribution and efficiency effects of the quota. As a result of the quota, U.S. consumer surplus declines by the combined blue and pink areas. Area *a* becomes U.S. producer surplus and thus involves no loss of U.S. welfare. Area *c* shows the increased economic profit to those permitted by the quota to sell Americans 30 million pounds for $0.15 per pound, or $0.05 above the world price. If foreign exporters rather than U.S. importers reap this profit, area *c* reflects a net loss in U.S. welfare.

Area *b* shows a welfare loss to the U.S. economy, because sugar could have been purchased abroad for $0.10 per pound, and the U.S. resources employed to increase sugar production could instead have been used more efficiently producing other goods. Area *d* is also a welfare loss because it reflects a reduction in consumer surplus with no offsetting gain to anyone. Thus, areas *b* and *d* in panel (b) of Exhibit 8 measure the minimum U.S. welfare loss from the quota. If the profit from quota rights (area *c*) accrues to foreign producers, this increases the U.S. welfare loss.

Quotas in Practice

The United States has granted quotas to specific countries. These countries, in turn, distribute these quota rights to their exporters through a variety of means. *By rewarding domestic and foreign producers with higher prices, the quota system creates two groups intent on securing and perpetuating these quotas.* Lobbyists for foreign producers work the halls of Congress, seeking the right to export to the United States. This strong support from producers, coupled with a lack of opposition from consumers (who remain rationally ignorant for the most part), has resulted in quotas that have lasted decades. For example, sugar quotas have been around more than 50 years. For the past three decades, U.S. sugar prices have been double the world price, on average, costing U.S. consumers billions. Sugar growers, who account for only 1 percent of U.S. farm sales, have accounted for 17 percent of political contributions from agriculture since 1990.[1]

Some economists have argued that if quotas are to be used, the United States should auction them off to foreign producers, thereby capturing at least some of the difference between the world price and the U.S. price. Auctioning off quotas would not only increase federal revenue at a time when it's desperately needed, but an auction would reduce the profitability of quotas, which would reduce pressure on Washington to perpetuate them. American consumers are not the only victims of sugar quotas. Thousands of poor farmers around the world miss out on an opportunity to earn a living by growing sugar cane for export to America.

Tariffs and Quotas Compared

Consider the similarities and differences between a tariff and a quota. Because both have identical effects on the price in our example, they both lead to the same change in quantity demanded. In both cases, U.S. consumers suffer the same loss of consumer surplus, and U.S. producers reap the same gain of producer surplus. The primary difference is that the revenue from the tariff goes to the U.S. government, whereas the revenue from the quota goes to whoever secures the right to sell foreign goods in the U.S. market. *If quota rights accrue to foreigners, then the domestic economy is worse*

---

1.   Michael Schroeder, "Sugar Growers Hold Up Push for Free Trade," *Wall Street Journal*, 3 February 2004.

off with a quota than with a tariff. But even if quota rights go to domestic importers, quotas, like tariffs, still increase the domestic price, restrict quantity, and thereby reduce consumer surplus and economic welfare. Quotas and tariffs can also raise production costs. For example, U.S. candy manufacturers face higher production costs because of sugar quotas, making them less competitive on world markets. Finally, and most importantly, *quotas and tariffs encourage foreign governments to retaliate with quotas and tariffs of their own, thus shrinking U.S. export markets, so the welfare loss is greater than shown in Exhibits 7 and 8.*

Other Trade Restrictions

Besides tariffs and quotas, a variety of other measures limit free trade. A country may provide *export subsidies* to encourage exports and *low-interest loans* to foreign buyers. Some countries impose *domestic content requirements* specifying that a certain portion of a final good must be produced domestically. Other requirements masquerading as health, safety, or technical standards often discriminate against foreign goods. For example, European countries once prohibited beef from hormone-fed cattle, a measure aimed at U.S. beef. Purity laws in Germany bar many non-German beers. Until the European Community adopted uniform standards, differing technical requirements forced manufacturers to offer as many as seven different versions of the same TV for that market. Sometimes exporters will voluntarily limit exports, as when Japanese automakers agreed to cut exports to the United States. The point is that *tariffs and quotas are only two of many devices used to restrict foreign trade.*

Recent research on the cost of protectionism indicates that international trade barriers slow the introduction of new goods and better technologies. So, rather than simply raising domestic prices, trade restrictions slow economic progress.

Freer Trade by Multilateral Agreement

Mindful of how high tariffs cut world trade during the Great Depression, the United States, after World War II, invited its trading partners to negotiate lower tariffs and other trade barriers. The result was the **General Agreement on Tariffs and Trade (GATT)**, an international trade treaty adopted in 1947 by 23 countries, including the United States. Each GATT member agreed to (1) reduce tariffs through multinational negotiations, (2) reduce import quotas, and (3) treat all members equally with respect to trade.

Trade barriers have been reduced through trade negotiations among many countries, or "trade rounds," under the auspices of GATT. Trade rounds offer a package approach rather than an issue-by-issue approach to trade negotiations. Concessions that are necessary but otherwise difficult to defend in domestic political terms can be made more acceptable in the context of a larger package that also contains politically and economically attractive benefits. Most early GATT trade rounds were aimed at reducing tariffs. The Kennedy Round in the mid-1960s included new provisions against **dumping**, which is selling a commodity abroad for less than is charged in the home market or less than the cost of production. The Tokyo Round of the 1970s was a more sweeping attempt to extend and improve the system.

The most recently completed round was launched in Uruguay in September 1986 and ratified by 123 participating countries in 1994. The number of signing countries now exceeds 150. This so-called **Uruguay Round,** the most comprehensive of the eight postwar multilateral trade negotiations, included 550 pages of tariff reductions on 85 percent of world trade. The Uruguay Round also created the World Trade Organization (WTO) to succeed GATT.

General Agreement on Tariffs and Trade (GATT)
An international tariff-reduction treaty adopted in 1947 that resulted in a series of negotiated "rounds" aimed at freer trade; the Uruguay Round created GATT's successor, the World Trade Organization (WTO)

dumping
Selling a product abroad for less than charged in the home market or for less than the cost of production

Uruguay Round
The final multilateral trade negotiation under GATT; this 1994 agreement cut tariffs, formed the World Trade Organization (WTO), and will eventually eliminate quotas

The World Trade Organization

The **World Trade Organization (WTO)** now provides the legal and institutional foundation for world trade. Whereas GATT was a multilateral agreement with no institutional foundation, the WTO is a permanent institution in Geneva, Switzerland. A staff of about 500 economists and lawyers helps shape policy and resolves trade disputes between member countries. Whereas GATT involved only merchandise trade, the WTO also covers services and trade-related aspects of intellectual property, such as books, movies, and computer programs. The WTO will eventually phase out quotas, but tariffs will remain legal. As a result of the Uruguay Round, average tariffs fell from 6 percent to 4 percent of the value of imports (when GATT began in 1947, tariffs averaged 40 percent).

Whereas GATT relied on voluntary cooperation, the WTO settles disputes in a way that is faster, more automatic, and less susceptible to blockage than the GATT system was. The WTO resolved more trade disputes in its first decade than GATT did in nearly 50 years. Since 2000, developing countries have filed 60 percent of the disputes. But the WTO has also become a lightning rod for globalization tensions, as discussed in the following case study.

World Trade Organization (WTO)

The legal and institutional foundation of the multilateral trading system that succeeded GATT in 1995

BRINGING THEORY TO LIFE

CASE STUDY

Doha Round and Round   The trade-barrier reductions from the Uruguay Round were projected to boost world income by more than $500 billion when fully implemented, or about $72 per person. In poor countries around the world, any additional income from reduced trade barriers could be a lifesaver.

But when WTO members met in Seattle in November 1999 to set an agenda and timetable for the next round of trade talks (later to become known as the Doha Round), all hell broke loose, as 50,000 protesters disrupted the city. Most were peaceful, but police made more than 500 arrests over three days, and property damage reached $3 million. T-shirts sold the week before the meeting dubbed the event the "Battle in Seattle," and so it was.

Organizers used their objections to free trade as a recruiting and fund-raising tool for a variety of interest groups, including labor unions, environmentalists, and farmers. Union members feared losing jobs overseas, environmentalists feared that producers would seek out countries with lax regulations, farmers in Japan, South Korea, Europe, and the United States feared foreign competition, and other groups feared technological developments such as hormone-fed beef and genetically modified food. The Seattle protest was by far the largest demonstration against free trade in the United States.

Protestors would probably be surprised to learn that WTO members are not of one mind about trade issues. For example, the United States and Europe usually push to protect worker rights around the world, but developing countries, including Mexico, Egypt, India, and Pakistan, object strenuously to focusing on worker rights. These poorer nations are concerned that the clothing, shoes, and textiles they make have not gained access to rich nations quickly enough. Many developing countries view attempts to impose labor and environmental standards as just the latest effort to block goods coming from poor countries. For example, workers in China rioted when U.S. companies operating there proposed shortening the work week. Chinese workers wanted a longer work week, believing they could earn more.

Without international groups such as the WTO to provide a forum for discussing labor and environmental issues around the world, conditions in poor countries would likely be worse. Working conditions in many poor countries have been slowly improving, thanks in part to trade opportunities along with pressure for labor rights from

e activity

The World Trade Organization's Web site describes its role and functions and explains the value of reducing trade barriers. The basics on what the WTO is and how it operates can be found at http://www.wto.org/english/ thewto_e/whatis_e/whatis_e .htm. What policies support the goal of nondiscriminatory trade? For an example of how one industry has been affected, read the WTO disputes involving textiles at http://www.wto.org/english/ tratop_e/texti_e/texti_e .htm. For more on how Nike is responding to criticisms of its labor practices visit its Web site on the subject at http://www.nikebiz.com/ responsibility/ (click on Workers/Factories, then on Audit Tools).

Imaginechina via AP Images

Doha Round

The multilateral trade negotiation round launched in 2001, but still unsettled as of 2010; aims at lowering tariffs on a wide range of industrial and agricultural products; the first trade round under WTO

WTO and other international groups. For example, Cambodia is one of the poorest countries in the world, but the highest wages in the country are earned by those working in the export sector. Take, for example, Deth, a young mother who sewed T-shirts and shorts at the June Textile factory in Cambodia, mostly for Nike. She worked from 6:15 A.M. to 2:15 P.M. with a half hour for lunch, extra pay for overtime, and double pay for working holidays. Though her pay was low by U.S. standards, it supported her family and was more than twice what judges and doctors average in Cambodia. Factories tend to hire young women, a group otherwise offered few job opportunities. Factory jobs have provided women with status and social equality they never had. Still, protest groups in rich countries called the June Textile factory a "sweatshop" and wanted it shut down. In part because of media pressure, Nike ended its contract with the factory. Researchers have also found that freer trade with Mexico has increased job opportunities there for women.

After failing to get off the ground in Seattle, the round of talks was launched two years later in Doha, Qatar. In setting the agenda for the **Doha Round**, members agreed to improve market access around the world, phase out export subsidies, and substantially reduce distorting government subsidies in agriculture. Reaching agreement proved easier said than done. Headed by Brazil and India, a group of developing countries demanded stronger commitments to reduce agricultural subsidies in the United States, Europe, and Japan. But farmers in these industrial economies wanted to keep their subsidies and protection from imports. For example, the average farm in Japan is about four acres, so farming there is inefficient and costly (rice in Japan is triple the world price). Talks in Cancun in 2003, Hong Kong in 2005, and Geneva in 2006 and 2008 ended bitterly as the Doha Round went round and round. By late 2010 the Doha Round was still spinning its wheels.

Even in the absence of a Doha agreement, some countries continue to reduce trade barriers through *bilateral* agreements, or agreements between two countries. For example, the United States abolished tariffs on Korean flat TV screens and cars.

Sources: David Wessel, "Free-Trade Winds May Be Blowing Again," *Wall Street Journal*, 1 July 2010; Sewell Chan and Jackie Calmes, "White House to Push Free Trade Deal with South Korea," *New York Times*, 27 June 2010; Ernesto Aguayo-Tellez et al., "Did Trade Liberalization Help Women? The Case of Mexico in the 1990s," NBER Working Paper 16195, (July 2010); Gina Chon, "Dropped Stitches," *Asiaweek*, 22 December 2000; and the Web site for the World Trade Organization at http://www.wto.org.

Common Markets

Some countries looked to the success of the U.S. economy, which is essentially a free trade zone across 50 states, and have tried to develop free trade zones of their own. The largest and best known is the European Union, which began in 1958 with a half dozen countries and expanded by 2010 to 27 countries and over 500 million people. The idea was to create a barrier-free European market like the United States in which goods, services, people, and capital are free to flow to their highest-valued use. Sixteen members of the European Union have also adopted a common currency, the *euro,* which replaced national currencies in 2002.

The United States, Canada, and Mexico have developed a free trade pact called the North American Free Trade Agreement (NAFTA). Through NAFTA, Mexico hopes to attract more U.S. investment by guaranteeing companies that locate there duty-free access to U.S. markets, which is where over two-thirds of Mexico's exports go. Mexico's 115 million people represent an attractive export market for U.S. producers, and Mexico's oil reserves could ease U.S. energy problems. The United States would also like to support Mexico's efforts to become more market oriented, as is reflected, for example, by Mexico's privatization of its phone system and banks. Creating job opportunities in Mexico also reduces pressure for Mexicans to cross the U.S. border illegally to find work. After more than a decade of NAFTA, agricultural exports to Mexico have doubled, as has overall trade among the three nations, but Americans still buy much more from Mexicans and Canadians than the other way around.

Free trade areas are springing up around the world. The United States signed a free trade agreement with the Dominican Republic and five Central American countries, called DR-CAFTA. Ten Latin American countries form Mercosur. The association of Southeast Asian nations make up ASEAN. And South Africa and its four neighboring countries form the Southern African Customs Union. Regional trade agreements require an exception to WTO rules because bloc members can make special deals among themselves and thus discriminate against outsiders. Under WTO's requirements, any trade concession granted to one country must usually be granted to *all other* WTO members.

Arguments for Trade Restrictions

Trade restrictions are often little more than handouts for the domestic industries they protect. Given the loss in social welfare that results from these restrictions, it would be more efficient simply to transfer money from domestic consumers to domestic producers. But such a bald payoff would be politically unpopular. Arguments for trade restrictions avoid mention of transfers to domestic producers and instead cite loftier goals. As we shall now see, none of these goals makes a strong case for restrictions, but some make a little more sense than others.

National Defense Argument

Some industries claim they need protection from import competition because their output is vital for national defense. Products such as strategic metals and military hardware are often insulated from foreign competition by trade restrictions. Thus, national defense considerations outweigh concerns about efficiency and equity. How valid is this argument? Trade restrictions may shelter the defense industry, but other means, such as government subsidies, might be more efficient. Or the government could stockpile basic military hardware so that maintaining an ongoing productive capacity would become less critical. Still, technological change could make certain weapons obsolete. Because most industries can play some role in national defense, instituting trade restrictions on this basis can get out of hand. For example, many decades ago U.S. wool producers secured trade protection at a time when some military uniforms were still made of wool.

The national defense argument has also been used to discourage foreign ownership of U.S. companies in some industries. For example, in 2005 a Chinese state-owned company was prevented from buying Unocal Oil. And in 2010, the Congressional Steel Caucus tried to block a Chinese plan to buy a Mississippi steel plant, saying that such a deal "threatens American jobs and our national security."[2]

2. Yjun Zhang, "China Steel Group Accuses U.S. Lawmakers of Protectionism," *Wall Street Journal*, 5 July 2010.

Infant Industry Argument

The infant industry argument was formulated as a rationale for protecting emerging domestic industries from foreign competition. In industries where a firm's average cost of production falls as output expands, new firms may need protection from imports until these firms grow enough to become competitive. Trade restrictions let new firms achieve the economies of scale necessary to compete with mature foreign producers.

But how do we identify industries that merit protection, and when do they become old enough to look after themselves? Protection often fosters inefficiencies. The immediate cost of such restrictions is the net welfare loss from higher domestic prices. These costs may become permanent if the industry never realizes the expected economies of scale and thus never becomes competitive. As with the national defense argument, policy makers should be careful in adopting trade restrictions based on the infant industry argument. Here again, temporary production subsidies may be more efficient than import restrictions.

Antidumping Argument

As we have noted already, *dumping* is selling a product abroad for less than in the home market or less than the cost of production. Exporters may be able to sell the good for less overseas because of export subsidies, or firms may simply find it profitable to sell for less in foreign markets where consumers are more sensitive to prices. But why shouldn't U.S. consumers pay as little as possible? If dumping is *persistent,* the increase in consumer surplus would more than offset losses to domestic producers. *There is no good reason why consumers should not be allowed to buy imports for a persistently lower price.*

An alternative form of dumping, termed *predatory dumping,* is the *temporary* sale abroad at prices below cost to eliminate competitors in that foreign market. Once the competition is gone, so the story goes, the exporting firm can raise the price in the foreign market. The trouble with this argument is that if dumpers try to take advantage of their monopoly position by sharply increasing the price, then other firms, either domestic or foreign, could enter the market and sell for less. There are few documented cases of predatory dumping.

Sometimes dumping may be *sporadic,* as firms occasionally try to unload excess inventories. Retailers hold periodic "sales" for the same reason. Sporadic dumping can be unsettling for domestic producers, but the economic impact is not a matter of great public concern. Regardless, all dumping is prohibited in the United States by the Trade Agreements Act of 1979, which calls for the imposition of tariffs when a good is sold for less in the United States than in its home market or less than the cost of production. In addition, WTO rules allow for offsetting tariffs when products are sold for "less than fair value" and when there is "material injury" to domestic producers. For example, U.S. producers of lumber and beer frequently accuse their Canadian counterparts of dumping.

Jobs and Income Argument

One rationale for trade restrictions that is commonly heard in the United States, and is voiced by WTO protestors, is that they protect U.S. jobs and wage levels. Using trade restrictions to protect domestic jobs is a strategy that dates back centuries. One problem with such a policy is that other countries usually retaliate by restricting *their* imports to save *their* jobs, so international trade is reduced, jobs are lost in export industries, and potential gains from trade fail to materialize. That happened big time during the Great Depression, as high tariffs choked trade and jobs.

Wages in other countries, especially developing countries, are often a fraction of wages in the United States. Looking simply at differences in wages, however, narrows the focus too much. Wages represent just one component of the total production cost and may not necessarily be the most important. Employers are interested in the labor cost per unit of output, which depends on both the wage and labor productivity. Wages are high in the United States partly because U.S. labor productivity remains the highest in the world. High productivity can be traced to better education and training and to the abundant computers, machines, and other physical capital that make workers more productive. U.S. workers also benefit greatly from a relatively stable business climate.

But what about the lower wages in many developing countries? Low wages are often linked to workers' lack of education and training, to the meager physical capital available to each worker, and to a business climate that is less stable and hence less attractive for producers. But once multinational firms build plants and provide techno- logical know-how in developing countries, U.S. workers lose some of their competitive edge, and their relatively high wages could price some U.S. products out of the world market. This has already happened in the consumer electronics and toy industries. China makes 80 percent of the toys sold in the United States. Some U.S. toy sellers, such as the makers of Etch A Sketch, would no longer survive had they not outsourced manufacturing to China.

Domestic producers do not like to compete with foreign producers whose costs are lower, so they often push for trade restrictions. But if restrictions negate any cost advantage a foreign producer might have, the law of comparative advantage becomes inoperative and domestic consumers are denied access to the lower-priced goods.

Over time, as labor productivity in developing countries increases, wage differen- tials among countries will narrow, much as they narrowed between the northern and southern United States during the last century. As technology and capital spread, U.S. workers, particularly unskilled workers, cannot expect to maintain wage levels that are far above comparable workers in other countries. So far, research and development has kept U.S. producers on the cutting edge of technological developments, but staying ahead in the technological race is a constant battle.

Declining Industries Argument

Where an established domestic industry is in jeopardy of closing because of lower- priced imports, could there be a rationale for *temporary* import restrictions? After all, domestic producers employ many industry-specific resources—both specialized labor and specialized machines. This human and physical capital is worth less in its best alternative use. If the extinction of the domestic industry is forestalled through trade restrictions, specialized workers can retire voluntarily or can gradually pursue more promising careers. Specialized machines can be allowed to wear out naturally.

Thus, in the case of declining domestic industries, trade protection can help lessen shocks to the economy and can allow for an orderly transition to a new industrial mix. But the protection offered should not be so generous as to encourage continued invest- ment in the industry. Protection should be of specific duration and should be phased out over that period.

The clothing industry is an example of a declining U.S. industry. The 22,000 U.S. jobs saved as a result of one trade restriction paid an average of less than $30,000 per year. But a Congressional Budget Office study estimated that the higher domestic clothing prices resulting from trade restrictions meant that U.S. consumers paid two to three times more than apparel workers earned. Trade restrictions in the U.S. clothing and textile industry started phasing out in 2005 under the Uruguay Round of trade agreements.

Free trade may displace some U.S. jobs through imports, but it also creates U.S. jobs through exports. When Americans celebrate a ribbon-cutting ceremony for a new software company, nobody credits free trade for those jobs, but when a steel plant closes here, everyone talks about how those jobs went overseas. What's more, many foreign companies have built plants in the United States and employ U.S. workers. For example, a dozen foreign television manufacturers and all major Japanese automakers now operate plants in the United States.

The number employed in the United States has nearly doubled in the last four decades. To recognize this job growth is not to deny the problems facing workers displaced by imports. Some displaced workers, particularly those in steel and other unionized, blue-collar industries, are not likely to find jobs that pay nearly as well as the ones they lost. As with infant industries, however, the problems posed by declining industries need not require trade restrictions. To support the affected industry, the government could offer wage subsidies or special tax breaks that decline over time. The government has also funded programs to retrain affected workers for jobs that are in greater demand.

Problems With Trade Protection

Trade restrictions raise a number of problems in addition to those already mentioned. First, protecting one stage of production usually requires protecting downstream stages of production as well. Protecting the U.S. textile industry from foreign competition, for example, raised the cost of cloth to U.S. apparel makers, reducing *their* competitiveness. Thus, when the government protected domestic textile manufacturers, the domestic garment industry also needed protection. Second, the cost of protection includes not only the welfare loss from the higher domestic price but also the cost of the resources used by domestic producer groups to secure the favored protection. The cost of *rent seeking*—lobbying fees, propaganda, and legal actions—can sometimes equal or exceed the direct welfare loss from restrictions. A third problem with trade restrictions is the transaction costs of enforcing the myriad quotas, tariffs, and other trade restrictions. These often lead to smuggling and black markets. A fourth problem is that economies insulated from foreign competition become less innovative and less efficient. The final and biggest problem with imposing trade restrictions is that other countries usually retaliate, thus shrinking the gains from trade. Retaliation can set off still greater trade restrictions, leading to an outright trade war.

Consider steel tariffs discussed in the following case study.

CASE STUDY

e activity

Read news feeds about the steel industry at http://www. steelonthenet.com/feeds/. You can follow the steel industry in different regions of the world.

PUBLIC POLICY

Steel Tariffs   The U.S. steel industry has been slow to adopt the latest technology and consequently has suffered a long, painful decline for decades—a death from a thousand cuts. Between 1997 and 2001, about 30 percent of U.S. steel producers filed for bankruptcy, including Bethlehem Steel and National Steel. During that stretch, 45,000 U.S. steel jobs disappeared, leaving about 180,000 jobs remaining. Imports accounted for 30 percent of the U.S. market, with most of that steel coming from Europe.

Steel leaders turned to the White House for help, arguing that the industry needed a technological tune-up to become more competitive but needed trade protection during the process. This is a variant of the infant-industry argument. Many of the jobs lost were in "rust-belt" states, such as Ohio, West Virginia, and Pennsylvania, states also critical in presidential elections. We can only speculate what role politics played in the decision, but in March 2002, President George W. Bush imposed tariffs on steel, claiming that imports caused "material injury" to the U.S. steel industry. The tariffs, which ranged from 8 percent to 30 percent on 10 steel categories, were scheduled to last three years.

As expected, the tariffs cut imports and boosted the U.S. price of steel. By 2003, steel imports slumped to their lowest level in a decade. The higher domestic price of steel helped U.S. steel makers but made steel-using industries here less competitive on world markets. For example, the tariffs added about $300 to the average cost of a U.S. automobile. According to one estimate, the tariffs cost 15,000 to 20,000 jobs in steel-user industries.

The European Union and other steel-exporting nations filed a complaint, and in November 2003, the WTO ruled that the tariffs violated trade agreements. The European Union, with about 300,000 of its own steel jobs at stake, announced that if the tariffs were not repealed, EU countries would retaliate with tariffs on U.S. exports. Japan and South Korea also threatened retaliatory tariffs.

After the negative WTO ruling and facing threats of retaliation, the White House repealed the steel tariffs in December 2003, claiming that they had served their purpose. Approximately $650 million in higher tariffs was collected during the 21 months they were imposed. The steelworkers union called the repeal "an affront to all workers." But union members should not have been surprised in light of the WTO ruling, threatened retaliation from abroad, and the fact that several months earlier, the steelworkers union endorsed a Democrat for president.

A big threat to the steel industry has come not from foreign competition but from the financial crisis. In August 2008, U.S. steel makers were operating at 90 percent of capacity. The global financial panic of 2008 temporarily cut U.S. steel production to only 40 percent of capacity by December 2008.

The only tariff threats in recent years have been against Chinese exporters. In 2009, the Obama White House imposed a 35 percent tariff on Chinese tires. Despite minor trade skirmishes, and despite clamors in Washington to insulate U.S. jobs from Chinese goods, and despite the rocky going for the Doha Round, the trend among industrial economies is toward lower tariffs, especially on raw materials. The United States, the European Union, and Japan have eliminated nearly all tariffs on raw materials.

Sources: Steven Greenhouse, "With a Receptive White House, Labor Begins to Line-Up Battles," *New York Times,* 22 September 2009; James Areddy, "U.S. Businesses Back More Trade Action Vs. China," *Wall Street Journal,* 24 May 2010; Robert Guy Matthews, "Industry Cuts Back as Steel Prices Fall," *Wall Street Journal,* 6 July 2010; and "Steel Industry Executive Summary: May 2010," International Trade Administration, U.S. Dept. of Commerce at http://hq-web03.ita.doc .gov/License/Surge.nsf/webfiles/SteelMillDevelopments/$file/exec%20summ.pdf?openelement.

Conclusion

International trade arises from voluntary exchange among buyers and sellers pursuing their self-interest. Since 1950 world output has risen eightfold, while world trade has increased nearly twentyfold. World trade offers many advantages to the trading countries: access to markets around the world, lower costs through economies of scale, the opportunity to utilize abundant resources, better access to information about markets and technology, improved quality honed by competitive pressure, and, most importantly, lower prices for consumers. Comparative advantage, specialization, and trade allow people to use their scarce resources efficiently to satisfy their unlimited wants.

Despite the clear gains from free trade, restrictions on international trade date back centuries, and pressure on public officials to impose trade restrictions continues today. Domestic producers (and their resource suppliers) benefit from trade restrictions in their markets because they can charge domestic consumers more. Trade restrictions insulate domestic producers from the rigors of global competition, in the process stifling innovation and leaving the industry vulnerable to technological change from abroad. With trade quotas, the winners also include those who have secured the right to import goods at the world prices and sell them at the domestic prices. Consumers, who must pay higher prices for protected goods, suffer from trade restrictions, as do the domestic producers who import resources. Other losers include U.S. exporters, who face higher trade barriers as foreigners retaliate with their own trade restrictions.

Producers have a laser-like focus on trade legislation, but consumers remain largely oblivious. Consumers purchase thousands of different goods and thus have no special interest in the effects of trade policy on any particular good. Congress tends to support the group that makes the most noise, so trade restrictions often persist, despite the clear and widespread gains from freer trade.

Summary

1. Even if a country has an absolute advantage in all goods, that country should specialize in producing the goods in which it has a comparative advantage. If each country specializes and trades according to the law of comparative advantage, all countries will benefit from greater consumption possibilities.

2. Quotas benefit those with the right to buy goods at the world price and sell them at the higher domestic price. Both tariffs and quotas harm domestic consumers more than they help domestic producers, although tariffs at least yield government revenue, which can be used to fund public programs or to cut taxes.

3. Despite the gains from free trade, restrictions have been imposed for centuries. The General Agreement on Tariffs and Trade (GATT) was an international treaty ratified in 1947 to reduce trade barriers. Subsequent negotiations lowered tariffs and reduced trade restrictions. The Uruguay Round, ratified in 1994, lowered tariffs, phases out quotas, and created the World Trade Organization (WTO) as the successor to GATT. The Doha Round was launched in 2001, but failed to reach an agreement as of 2010.

4. Arguments used by producer groups to support trade restrictions include promoting national defense, nurturing infant industries, preventing foreign producers from dumping goods in domestic markets, protecting domestic jobs, and allowing declining industries time to wind down and exit the market.

5. Trade restrictions impose a variety of strains on the economy besides the higher costs to consumers. These include (1) the need to protect downstream stages of production as well, (2) expenditures made by favored domestic industries to seek trade protection, (3) costs incurred by the government to enforce trade restrictions, (4) the inefficiency and lack of innovation that result when an industry is insulated from foreign competition, and (5), most important, the trade restrictions imposed by other countries in retaliation.

Key Concepts

Autarky   396
Terms of trade   397
World price   402

General Agreement on Tariffs
    and Trade (GATT)   406
Dumping   406

Uruguay Round   406
World Trade Organization (WTO)   407
Doha Round   408

Questions for Review

1. **PROFILE OF IMPORTS AND EXPORTS**   What are the major U.S. exports and imports? How does international trade affect consumption possibilities?

2. **REASONS FOR TRADE**   What are the primary reasons for international trade?

3. **GAINS FROM TRADE**   Complete each of the following sentences:

    a. When a nation has no economic interaction with foreigners and produces everything it consumes, the nation is in a state of _____.

    b. According to the law of comparative advantage, each nation should specialize in producing the goods in which it has the lowest _____.

    c. The amount of one good that a nation can exchange for one unit of another good is known as the _____.

    d. Specializing according to comparative advantage and trading with other nations results in _____.

4. **REASONS FOR INTERNATIONAL SPECIALIZATION**   What determines which goods a country should produce and export?

5. TARIFFS   High tariffs usually lead to black markets and smuggling. How is government revenue reduced by such activity? Relate your answer to the graph in Exhibit 7 in this chapter. Does smuggling have any social benefits?

6. TRADE RESTRICTIONS   Exhibits 7 and 8 show net losses to the economy of a country that imposes tariffs or quotas on imported sugar. What kinds of gains and losses would occur in the economies of countries that export sugar?

7. THE WORLD TRADE ORGANIZATION   What is the World Trade Organization (WTO) and how does it help foster multilateral trade? (Check the WTO Web site at http://www.wto.org/.)

8. Case Study: The Doha Round and Round   What was the major sticking point holding up progress in the Doha Round?

9. ARGUMENTS FOR TRADE RESTRICTIONS   Explain the national defense, declining industries, and infant industry arguments for protecting a domestic industry from international competition.

10. ARGUMENTS FOR TRADE RESTRICTIONS   Firms hurt by cheap imports typically argue that restricting trade will save U.S. jobs. What's wrong with this argument? Are there ever any reasons to support such trade restrictions?

11. Case Study: Steel Tariffs   How did the steel tariff affect the domestic steel industry, the workers in the steel industry, workers in steel-use industries, and consumers?

Problems and Exercises

12. COMPARATIVE ADVANTAGE   Suppose that each U.S. worker can produce 8 units of food or 2 units of clothing daily. In Fredonia, which has the same number of workers, each worker can produce 7 units of food or 1 unit of clothing daily. Why does the United States have an absolute advantage in both goods? Which country enjoys a comparative advantage in food? Why?

13. COMPARATIVE ADVANTAGE   The consumption possibilities frontiers shown in Exhibit 4 assume terms of trade of 1 unit of clothing for 1 unit of food. What would the consumption possibilities frontiers look like if the terms of trade were 1 unit of clothing for 2 units of food?

14. IMPORT QUOTAS   How low must a quota be in effect to have an impact? Using a demand-and-supply diagram, illustrate and explain the net welfare loss from imposing such a quota. Under what circumstances would the net welfare loss from an import quota exceed the net welfare loss from an equivalent tariff (one that results in the same price and import level as the quota)?

15. TRADE RESTRICTIONS   Suppose that the world price for steel is below the U.S. domestic price, but the government requires that all steel used in the United States be domestically produced.

   a. Use a diagram like the one in Exhibit 7 to show the gains and losses from such a policy.

   b. How could you estimate the net welfare loss (deadweight loss) from such a diagram?

   c. What response to such a policy would you expect from industries (like automobile producers) that use U.S. steel?

   d. What government revenues are generated by this policy?

Global Economic Watch Exercises

Login to www.cengagebrain.com and access the Global Economic Watch to do these exercises.

18. GLOBAL ECONOMIC WATCH   Go to the Global Economic Crisis Resource Center. Select Global Issues in Context. In the Basic Search box at the top of the page, enter the phrase "Doha Round." On the Results page, go to the News Section. Click on the link for the October 1, 2010, article "America Embraces Trade Discrimination." In what ways does the author criticize U.S. trade policy?

19. GLOBAL ECONOMIC WATCH   Go to the Global Economic Crisis Resource Center. Select Global Issues in Context. Go to the menu at the top of the page and click on the tab for Browse Issues and Topics. Choose Business and Economy. Click on the link for Globalization. Find one article in favor of globalization and international trade and one article against. Compare and contrast the arguments in the articles.

Our attention so far has been on the international flow of goods and services. However, some of the most dramatic changes in the world economy have been due to the international flow of factors of production, comprising labor and capital. In the 1800s, European capital and labor (along with African and Asian labor) flowed to the United States and fostered its economic development. In the 1960s, the United States sent large amounts of investment capital to Canada and Western Europe; in the 1980s and 1990s, investment flowed from Japan to the United States. Today, workers from southern Europe find employment in northern European factories, while Mexican workers migrate to the United States. The tearing down of the Berlin Wall in 1990 triggered a massive exodus of workers from East Germany to West Germany.

The economic forces underlying the international movement in factors of production are virtually identical to those underlying the international flow of goods and services. Productive factors move, when they are permitted to, from nations where they are abundant (low productivity) to nations where they are scarce (high productivity). Productive factors flow in response to differences in returns (such as wages and yields on capital) as long as these are large enough to more than outweigh the cost of moving from one country to another.

This chapter considers the role of international capital flows (investment) as a substitute for trade in capital-intensive products. Special attention is given to the multinational enterprise that carries on the international reallocation of capital. The chapter also analyzes the international mobility of labor as a substitute for trade in labor-intensive products.

The Multinational Enterprise

Although the term *enterprise* can be precisely defined, there is no universal agreement on the exact definition of a **multinational enterprise (MNE)**. But a close look at some representative MNEs suggests that these businesses have a number of

TABLE 9.1

THE WORLD'S LARGEST CORPORATIONS, 2008

Firm	Headquarters	Revenues ($ billions)
Wal-Mart Stores	United States	378.8
Exxon Mobil	United States	372.8
Royal Dutch Shell	Netherlands	355.8
BP	United Kingdom	291.4
Toyota Motor	Japan	230.2
Chevron	United States	210.8
ING Group	Netherlands	201.5
Total	France	187.3
General Motors	United States	182.3
ConocoPhillips	United States	178.6

Source: From "The 2009 Global 500," *Fortune*, available at http://www.fortune.com.

identifiable features. Operating in many host countries, MNEs often conduct research and development (R&D) activities in addition to manufacturing, mining, extraction, and business-service operations. The MNE cuts across national borders and is often directed from a company planning center that is distant from the host country. Both stock ownership and company management are usually multinational in character. A typical MNE has a high ratio of foreign sales to total sales, often 25 percent or more. Regardless of the lack of agreement as to what constitutes an MNE, there is no doubt that the multinational phenomenon is massive in size. Table 9.1 provides a glimpse of some of the world's largest corporations.

Multinationals may diversify their operations along vertical, horizontal, and conglomerate lines within the host and source countries. **Vertical diversification** often occurs when the parent MNE decides to establish foreign subsidiaries to produce intermediate goods or inputs that go into the production of a finished good. For industries such as oil refining and steel, such *backward* diversification may include the extraction and processing of raw materials. Most manufacturers tend to extend operations backward only to the production of component parts. The major international oil companies represent a classic case of backward vertical diversification on a worldwide basis. Oil-production subsidiaries are located in areas such as the Middle East, whereas the refining and marketing operations occur in the industrial nations of the West. Multinationals may also practice *forward diversification* in the direction of the final consumer market. Automobile manufacturers, for example, may establish foreign subsidiaries to market the finished goods of the parent company. In practice, most vertical foreign diversification is backward. Multinationals often wish to diversify their operations vertically to benefit from economies of scale and international specialization.

Horizontal diversification occurs when a parent company producing a commodity in the source country sets up a subsidiary to produce an identical product in the host country. These subsidiaries are independent units in productive capacity and are established to produce and market the parent company's product in overseas markets. Coca-Cola and Pepsi-Cola, for example, are bottled not only in the United States but also throughout much of the world. Multinationals sometimes locate production facilities overseas to avoid stiff foreign tariff barriers, which would place their products at a competitive disadvantage. Parent companies also like to locate close to their customers because differences in national preferences may require special designs for their products.

Besides making horizontal and vertical foreign investments, MNEs may diversify into nonrelated markets, in what is known as **conglomerate diversification.** For example, in the 1980s, U.S. oil companies stepped up their nonenergy acquisitions in response to anticipated declines in future investment opportunities for oil and gas. ExxonMobil acquired a foreign copper-mining subsidiary in Chile, and Tenneco bought a French company producing automotive exhaust systems.

To carry out their worldwide operations, MNEs rely on **foreign direct investment**—acquisition of a controlling interest in an overseas company or facility. Foreign direct investment typically occurs when (1) the parent company obtains sufficient common stock in a foreign company to assume voting control (the U.S. Department of Commerce defines a company as directly foreign owned when a "foreign person" holds a ten percent interest in the company); (2) the parent company acquires or constructs new plants and equipment overseas; (3) the parent company shifts funds abroad to finance an expansion of its foreign subsidiary; or (4) earnings of the parent company's foreign subsidiary are reinvested in plant expansion.

Table 9.2 summarizes the position of the United States with respect to foreign direct investment in 2007. Data are provided concerning U.S. direct investment abroad and foreign direct investment in the United States. In recent years, the majority of U.S. foreign direct investment has flowed to Europe, Latin America, and Canada, especially in the manufacturing sector. Most foreign direct investment in the United States has come from Europe, Canada, and Asia—areas that have invested heavily in U.S. manufacturing, petroleum, and wholesale trade facilities.

Motives for Foreign Direct Investment

The case for opening markets to foreign direct investment is as compelling as it is for trade. More open economies enjoy higher rates of private investment, which is a major determinant of economic growth and job creation. Foreign direct investment is actively courted by countries, not least because it generates spillovers such as improved management and better technology. As is true with firms that trade, firms and sectors where foreign direct investment is intense tend to have higher average labor productivity and pay higher wages. Outward investment allows firms to remain

TABLE 9.2

DIRECT INVESTMENT POSITION OF THE UNITED STATES ON AN HISTORICAL COST BASIS, 2007*

Country	U.S. DIRECT INVESTMENT ABROAD		FOREIGN DIRECT INVESTMENT IN U.S	
	Amount (billions of dollars)	Percentage	Amount (billions of dollars)	Percentage
Canada	257.1	9.2	213.2	10.2
Europe	1,551.2	55.6	1,483.0	70.9
Latin America	472.0	16.9	62.9	3.0
Africa	27.8	1.0	1.1	0.0
Middle East	29.4	1.0	12.9	0.6
Asia and Pacific	453.9	16.3	319.8	15.3
	2,791.4	100.0	2,092.9	100.0

*Historical-cost valuation is based on the time the investment occurred, with no adjustment for price changes.

Source: From U.S. Department of Commerce, *U.S. Direct Investment Position Abroad and Foreign Direct Investment Position in the United States on a Historical-Cost Basis*, available at http://www.bea.doc.gov/. See also U.S. Department of Commerce, *Survey of Current Business*, Washington, DC (Government Printing Office).

competitive and thus supports employment at home. Investment abroad stimulates exports of machinery and other capital goods.

New MNEs do not pop up haphazardly in foreign nations; they develop as a result of conscious planning by corporate managers. Both economic theory and empirical studies support the idea that foreign direct investment is conducted in anticipation of *future profits*. It is generally assumed that investment flows from regions of low anticipated profit to those of high anticipated profit, after allowing for risk. Although expected profits may ultimately explain the process of foreign direct investment, corporate management may emphasize a variety of other factors when asked about their investment motives. These factors include market-demand conditions, trade restrictions, investment regulations, labor costs, and transportation costs. All these factors have a bearing on cost and revenue conditions and hence on the level of profit.

Demand Factors

The quest for profits encourages MNEs to search for new markets and sources of demand. Some MNEs set up overseas subsidiaries to tap foreign markets that cannot be maintained adequately by export products. This set up sometimes occurs in response to dissatisfaction over distribution techniques abroad. Consequently, a business may set up a foreign marketing division and, later, manufacturing facilities. This incentive may be particularly strong with the realization that local taste and design differences exist. A close familiarity with local conditions is of utmost importance to a successful marketing program.

The location of foreign manufacturing facilities may be influenced by the fact that some parent companies find their productive capacity already sufficient to meet domestic demands. If they wish to enjoy growth rates that exceed the expansion of domestic demand, they must either export or establish foreign production operations. General Motors (GM), for example, has felt that the markets of such countries as the United Kingdom, France, and Brazil are strong enough to permit the survival of GM manufacturing subsidiaries. But Boeing has centralized its manufacturing operations in the United States and exports abroad because an efficient production plant for jet planes is a large investment relative to the size of most foreign markets.

Market competition may also influence a firm's decision to set up foreign facilities. Corporate strategies may be defensive in nature if they are directed at preserving market shares from actual or potential competition. The most certain method of preventing foreign competition from becoming a strong force is to acquire foreign businesses. For the United States, the 1960s and early 1970s witnessed a tremendous surge in the acquisition of foreign businesses. Approximately half of the foreign subsidiaries operated by U.S. MNEs were originally acquired through the purchase of already existing concerns during this era. Once again, GM exemplifies this practice, purchasing and setting up auto producers around the globe. General Motors has been successful in gaining control of many larger foreign-model firms, including Monarch (GM Canada) and Opel (GM Germany). It did not acquire smaller-model firms such as Toyota, Datsun, and Volkswagen, all of which have become significant competitors for General Motors.

DO U.S. MULTINATIONALS EXPLOIT FOREIGN WORKERS?

 TRADE CONFLICTS

TABLE 9.3

AVERAGE ANNUAL WAGE PAID BY FOREIGN AFFILIATES OF U.S. MULTINATIONALS AND
AVERAGE ANNUAL DOMESTIC MANUFACTURING WAGE BY HOST-COUNTRY*

	All Countries	High-Income	Middle-Income	Low-Income
Average wage paid by affiliates/ thousands of Dollars	15.1	32.4	9.5	3.4
Average domestic manufacturing wage/thousands of dollars	9.9	22.6	5.4	1.7
Ratio	1.5	1.4	1.8	2.0

*Calculations exclude wages of the multinationals' expatriate employees

Source: From Edward Graham, *Fighting the Wrong Enemy* (Washington, DC: Institute for International Economics, 2000).

Do U.S. multinational businesses exploit workers in developing countries? According to critics, maximizing profits is the only thing that matters to multinationals: They search the globe for the cheapest labor when deciding where to locate factories. The only gain from this behavior, critics argue, accrues to the owners of the businesses who have shifted operations from low-wage factories in industrialized countries to poverty-wage factories in developing countries. Simply put, workers in developing countries are underpaid, according to critics.

Indeed, multinationals are in business for profits. But this does not seem to be troublesome for many workers in developing countries who compete to work for them. People who go to work for a foreign-owned business do so because they prefer it to the alternative, whatever that may be. In their own view, the new jobs make them better off.

Assume that the critics are right, and that these workers are being exploited. One remedy would be to admonish multinationals for operating in developing countries at all. If multinationals stopped hiring workers in developing countries, the workers would, in their own estimation, become worse off. Another course is to entice multinationals to pay workers in developing countries wages that are as high as the wages paid to workers in industrial countries. However, this would discourage direct investment in developing countries. Why? Workers in developing countries are paid less than workers in industrial countries because they are generally less productive: They often work with less advanced machinery, and the surrounding infrastructure is inadequate, which

reduces productivity. These workers are attractive to multinationals, in spite of their lower productivity, because they are cheap. If you were to wipe out that offsetting advantage, you would make them unemployable. Put simply, bucking under pressure to extend U.S. or European pay scales to developing countries could mean shutting down local factories—hurting people, not helping them.

Productivity aside, should "responsible" multinationals pay their developing-country employees more than other local workers? To hire workers, they may not have to provide a premium over local wages if they can offer other advantages, such as a modern factory in which to work rather than a sweatshop. By participating in the local labor market and adding to the total demand for labor, the multinationals would most likely be increasing wages for all workers, not just those they employ.

However, evidence suggests that multinationals do pay a wage premium, which apparently reflects their desire to recruit relatively skilled workers. Table 9.3 shows that in 1994, the wages paid by multinationals to poor-country workers were about double the local manufacturing wage; wages paid by multinationals to workers in middle-income countries were about 1.8 times the local manufacturing wage. In short, do U.S. multinationals underpay workers in developing countries? By U.S. standards, they do. But U.S. standards are irrelevant in developing countries: Very few workers are paid at U.S. levels in these countries. The key point is that, by local standards, these workers typically fare quite well.

Cost Factors

Multinationals often seek to increase profit levels through reductions in production costs. Such cost-reducing foreign direct investments may take a number of forms. The pursuit of essential raw materials may underlie a company's intent to go multinational. This is particularly true of the extractive industries and certain agricultural commodities. United Fruit, for example, has established banana-producing facilities in Honduras to take advantage of the natural trade advantages afforded by the weather and growing conditions. Similar types of natural trade advantages explain why Anaconda has set up mining operations in Bolivia and why Shell produces and refines oil in Indonesia. Natural supply advantages such as resource endowments or climatic conditions may indeed influence a company's decision to invest abroad.

Production costs include factors other than material inputs, notably labor. *Labor costs* tend to differ among national economies. Multinationals may be able to hold costs down by locating part or all of their productive facilities abroad. Many U.S. electronics firms, for instance, have had their products produced or at least assembled abroad to take advantage of cheap foreign labor. (The mere fact that the United States may pay higher wages than those prevailing abroad does not necessarily indicate higher costs. High wages may result from U.S. workers being more productive than their foreign counterparts. Only when high U.S. wages are not offset by superior U.S. labor productivity will foreign labor become relatively more attractive.)

Multinational location can also be affected by transportation costs, especially in industries where transportation costs are a high fraction of product value. When the cost of transporting raw materials used by an MNE is significantly higher than the cost of shipping its finished products to markets, the MNE will generally locate production facilities closer to its raw material sources than to its markets; lumber, basic chemicals, aluminum, and steel are among the products that fit this description. Conversely, when the cost of transporting finished products is significantly higher than the cost of transporting the raw materials that are used in their manufacture, MNEs locate production facilities close to their markets. Beverage manufacturers, such as Coca-Cola and Pepsi-Cola, transport syrup concentrate to plants all over the world, which add water to the syrup, bottle it, and sell it to consumers. When transportation costs are a minor fraction of product value, MNEs tend to locate where the availability and cost of labor and other inputs provide them the lowest manufacturing cost. Multinationals producing electronic components, garments, and shoes offer examples of such locational mobility.

Government policies may also lead to foreign direct investment. Some nations seeking to lure foreign manufacturers to set up employment-generating facilities in their countries may grant subsidies, such as preferential tax treatment or free factory buildings, to MNEs. More commonly, direct investment may be a way of circumventing import tariff barriers. The very high tariffs that Brazil levies on auto imports means that foreign auto producers wishing to sell in the Brazilian market must locate production facilities in that country. Another example is the response of U.S. business to the formation of the EU, which imposed common external tariffs against outsiders while reducing trade barriers among member nations. American companies were induced to circumvent these barriers by setting up subsidiaries in the member nations. Another example is Japanese businesses that located additional auto-assembly plants in the United States in the 1980s and 1990s to defuse mounting protectionist pressures.

Supplying Products to Foreign Buyers: Whether to Produce Domestically or Abroad

Once a firm knows that foreign demand for its goods exists, it must ascertain the lowest-cost method of supplying these goods abroad. Suppose Anheuser-Busch (A-B) of the United States wants to sell its Budweiser beer in Canada. Anheuser considers these following ways: (1) build a brewery in Wisconsin to produce Bud for sale to U.S. consumers in the Upper Midwest and also to Canadian consumers (direct exporting); (2) build a brewery in Canada to produce Bud and sell it to Canadian consumers (foreign direct investment); or (3) license the rights to a Canadian brewery to produce and market Bud in Canada. The method A-B chooses depends on the extent of economies of scale, transportation and distribution costs, and international trade barriers. These considerations are discussed in the following sections.

Direct Exporting versus Foreign Direct Investment/Licensing

Let us consider A-B's strategy of supplying Bud to Canadians via direct exporting as opposed to foreign direct investment or a licensing agreement. We will first analyze the influence of economies of scale on this strategy. One would expect economies of scale to encourage A-B to export Bud to Canada when the quantity of beer demanded in Canada is relatively small, and to encourage Canadian production, via either a licensing agreement or foreign direct investment, when a relatively large quantity of beer is demanded in Canada.

To illustrate this principle, assume that average production cost curves are identical for A-B's potential brewery in Wisconsin, A-B's potential brewery in Canada, and a Canadian brewery that could be licensed to produce Bud. These cost curves are denoted by AC in Figure 9.1. As these breweries increase output, the average costs of producing a case of beer decrease up to a point, after which average costs no longer decrease, but stabilize.

Suppose A-B estimates that U.S. consumers will demand 200 cases of Bud per year, as seen in Figure 9.1. Producing this quantity at A-B's Wisconsin brewery allows the realization of sizable economies of scale, which result in a production cost of $8 per case. Also assume that Canadians are estimated to demand a relatively small quantity of Bud, say 100 cases. Because the Wisconsin brewery already produces 200 cases for U.S. consumption, increasing output to meet the extra demand in Canada permits the brewery to slide down its average cost curve until it produces 300 cases at a cost of $6 per case.

The alternative to producing Bud in Wisconsin and exporting it to Canada is to produce it in Canada. However, because Canadian consumers are estimated to demand only 100 cases of Bud, the size of the market is too small to allow economies of scale to be fully realized. That is, A-B's potential brewery in Canada or the licensed Canadian brewer would produce Bud at a cost of $11 per case. Therefore, the production cost saving for A-B of brewing Bud in Wisconsin and exporting it to Canada is $5 per case ($11 − $6 = $5). If the cost of transporting and distributing Bud to Canadians is less than this amount, A-B would maximize profits by exporting Bud to Canada.

However, if the quantity of Bud demanded in Canada exceeds 300 cases, it might be more profitable for A-B to use a licensing agreement or foreign direct investment.

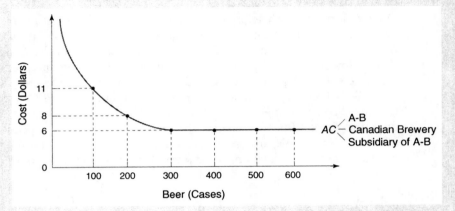

FIGURE 9.1

THE CHOICE BETWEEN DIRECT EXPORTING AND FOREIGN DIRECT INVESTMENT/LICENSING

When the Canadian market's size is large enough to permit efficient production in Canada, a U.S. firm increases profits by establishing a Canadian production subsidiary or licensing the rights to a Canadian firm to produce and market its product in Canada. The U.S. firm increases profits by exporting its product to Canada when the Canadian market is too small to permit efficient production.

To illustrate this possibility, refer to Figure 9.1. Suppose that Canadians are estimated to demand 400 cases of Bud per year whereas the quantity of Bud demanded by U.S. consumers remains at 200 cases. With economies of scale exhausted at 300 cases, the larger Canadian demand does not permit A-B to produce Bud at a cost lower than $6 per case. By producing 400 cases, the licensed Canadian brewery or the Canadian subsidiary brewery of A-B could match the efficiency of A-B's Wisconsin brewery, and each would realize a production cost of $6 per case. Given equal production costs, A-B minimizes total cost by avoiding the additional cost of transporting and distributing beer to Canadians. Thus, A-B increases profits by either licensing its beer technology to a Canadian brewer or investing in a brewing subsidiary in Canada.

Similar to transportation costs, trade restrictions can neutralize production-cost advantages. If Canada has high import tariffs, the production-cost advantage of A-B's Wisconsin brewery may be offset, so that foreign direct investment or licensing is the only feasible way of penetrating the Canadian market.

Foreign Direct Investment versus Licensing

Once a firm chooses foreign production as a method of supplying goods abroad, it must decide whether it is more efficient to establish a foreign production subsidiary or license the technology to a foreign firm to produce its goods. In the United Kingdom, there are Kentucky Fried Chicken establishments that are owned and run by local residents. The parent U.S. organization merely provides its name and operating procedures in return for royalty fees paid by the local establishments. Although licensing is widely used in practice, it presupposes that local firms are capable of adapting their operations to the production process or technology of the parent organization.

FIGURE 9.2

THE CHOICE BETWEEN FOREIGN DIRECT INVESTMENT AND LICENSING

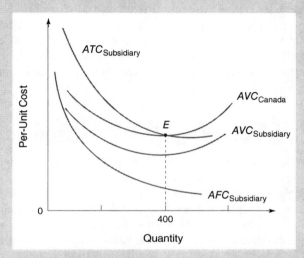

The decision to establish foreign operations through direct investment or licensing depends on (1) the extent to which capital is used in the production process, (2) the size of the foreign market, and (3) the amount of fixed cost a business must bear when establishing an overseas facility.

Figure 9.2 portrays the hypothetical cost conditions confronting A-B as it contemplates whether to license Bud production technology to a Canadian brewery or invest in a Canadian brewing subsidiary. Curve $AVC_{Subsidiary}$ represents the average variable cost (such as labor and materials) of A-B's brewing subsidiary, and AVC_{Canada} represents the average variable cost of a Canadian brewery. The establishment of a foreign brewing subsidiary also entails fixed costs denoted by curve $AFC_{Subsidiary}$. These include expenses of coordinating the subsidiary with the parent organization and the sunk costs of assessing the market potential of the foreign country. The total unit costs that A-B faces when establishing a foreign subsidiary are given by $ATC_{Subsidiary}$.

Comparing $ATC_{Subsidiary}$ with AVC_{Canada}, for a relatively small market of less than 400 cases of beer, the Canadian brewery has an absolute cost advantage. Licensing Bud production technology to a Canadian brewery in this case is more profitable for A-B. But if the Canadian market for Bud exceeds 400 cases, A-B's brewing subsidiary has an absolute cost advantage; A-B increases profits by supplying beer to Canadians via foreign direct investment.

Several factors influence the output level at which A-B's brewing subsidiary begins to realize an absolute cost advantage vis-à-vis the Canadian brewery (400 cases in Figure 9.2). To the extent that production is capital-intensive and A-B's brewing subsidiary can acquire capital at a lower cost than that paid by the Canadian brewery, the variable cost advantage of the subsidiary is greater. This advantage neutralizes the influence of a fixed-cost disadvantage for the subsidiary at a lower level of output. The amount of the brewing subsidiary's fixed costs also has a bearing on this minimum output level. Smaller fixed costs lower the subsidiary's average total costs, again resulting in a smaller output at which the subsidiary first begins to have an absolute cost advantage.

As noted, international business decisions are influenced by such factors as production costs, fixed costs of locating overseas, the relative importance of labor and capital in the production process, and the size of the foreign market. Another factor is the element of risk and uncertainty. When determining where to locate production operations, management is concerned with possibilities such as currency fluctuations and subsidiary expropriations.

Country Risk Analysis

Although investing or lending abroad can be rewarding, these activities come with accompanying risks. For example, the Russian government might expropriate the assets of foreign investors or make foreign loan repayments illegal. Thus, MNES and banks carry out a **country risk analysis** to help them decide whether to do business abroad.

Individuals holding positions of responsibility with internationally oriented firms and banks engage in country risk analysis by evaluating the risk for each country in which they are considering doing business. For example, officers at Chase Manhattan Bank may establish limits on the amount of loans that they are willing to make to clients in Turkey according to the risk of terrorism, as well as market factors. Moreover, if Toyota fears runaway inflation and escalating labor costs in Mexico, it may refrain from establishing an auto assembly plant there.

Assessing the cost and benefits of doing business abroad entails analyses of political, financial, and economic risk. *Political risk* analysis is intended to assess the political stability of a country and includes criteria such as government stability, corruption, domestic conflict, religious tensions, and ethnic tensions. *Financial risk* analysis investigates a country's ability to finance its debt obligations and includes factors such as foreign debt as a percentage of GDP, loan default, and exchange rate stability. And, *economic risk* analysis determines a country's current economic strengths and weaknesses by looking at its rate of growth in GDP, per capita GDP, inflation rate, and the like. Analysts then calculate a composite country risk rating based on these three categories of risk. This composite rating provides an overall assessment of the risk of doing business in some country.

Country risk analysis is intended for a particular user. For example, a company engaged in international tourism will be concerned about country risk as it applies to its attractiveness as a vacation destination. In this case, the composite risk rating of, say Venezuela, may not be of much use. It is possible that Venezuela might be considered high risk in its composite rating, but not present a substantial risk to travelers because its composite risk is decreased by such factors as low financial or economic risk, a miserable investment climate, or other factors that do not threaten tourists. However, Israel might be judged as moderately risky overall due to a stable government and sound economic policies, but still present significant political risk to tourists due to religious and ethnic tensions. In these cases, a better understanding of risk can be ascertained by taking into account particular components of risk, such as law and order or internal conflict, rather than the composite risk rating.

When conducting country risk analysis, MNEs and banks may obtain help from organizations that analyze risk. For example, Political Risk Services publishes a

TABLE 9.4

SELECTED COUNTRY RISKS RANKED BY COMPOSITE RATINGS, JULY 2008

Country	Composite Risk Rating (100 point maximum)	
Norway	91.8	Very Low Risk
Luxembourg	89.3	
Brunei	88.5	
Switzerland	88.5	
Germany	86.0	
Hong Kong	85.0	
United States	76.5	
Egypt	65.8	
Iraq	53.0	
Somalia	39.3	Very High Risk

Source: From Political Risk Services, *International Country Risk Guide*, 2008, available at https://www.prsgroup.com/FreeSamplePage.aspx/.

monthly report called the *International Country Risk Guide*.[1] The guide provides individual ratings on more than 130 advanced and developing countries for political, financial, and economic risk, plus a composite rating. In calculating the composite risk rating, the political risk factors are given a weighting of 50 percent, while the financial and economic risk factors each contribute 25 percent. Examples of composite ratings are provided in Table 9.4. In assessing a country's composite risk, a higher score indicates a lower risk, and a lower score indicates a higher risk. Such information can be helpful to a firm as a predictive tool for international investments and financial transactions.

After a firm determines a country's risk rating, it must decide whether that risk is tolerable. If the risk is estimated to be too high, then the firm does not need to pursue the feasibility of the proposed project any further. If the risk rating of a country is in the acceptable range, any project related to that country deserves further consideration. In terms of the *International Country Risk Guide's* ratings of country risk, the following categories are used to identify levels of risk: (1) low risk, 80–100 points; (2) moderate risk, 50–79 points; (3) high risk, 0–49 points. However, these broad categories must be tempered to fit the needs of particular MNEs and banks.

International Trade Theory and Multinational Enterprise

Perhaps the main explanation of the development of MNEs lies in the strategies of corporate management. The reasons for engaging in international business can be outlined in terms of the comparative-advantage principle. Corporate managers see advantages they can exploit in the forms of access to factor inputs, new technologies and products, and managerial know-how. Organizations establish overseas subsidiaries largely because profit prospects are best enhanced by foreign production.

From a trade-theory perspective, the multinational-enterprise analysis is fundamentally in agreement with the predictions of the comparative-advantage principle. Both approaches contend that a given commodity will be produced in a low-cost country. The major difference between the multinational-enterprise analysis and the conventional trade model is that the former stresses the international movement of factor inputs, whereas the latter is based on the movement of merchandise among nations.

International trade theory suggests that the aggregate welfare of both the source and host countries is enhanced when MNEs make foreign direct investments for their own benefit. The presumption is that if businesses can earn a higher return on overseas investments than on those at home, resources are transferred from lower to higher productive uses, and on balance the world allocation of resources

---

[1]There are other services that measure country risk, some of the more popular ones being *Euromoney*, Economist Intelligence Unit, Bank of America World Information Services, Business Environment Risk Intelligence, Institutional Investor, Standard and Poor's Rating Group, and Moody's Investor Services.

will improve. Thus, analysis of MNEs is essentially the same as conventional trade theory, which rests on the movement of products among nations.

Despite the basic agreement between conventional trade theory and the multinational-enterprise analysis, there are some notable differences. The conventional model presupposes that goods are exchanged between independent organizations on international markets at competitively determined prices. But MNEs are generally vertically diversified companies whose subsidiaries manufacture intermediate goods as well as finished goods. In an MNE, sales become *intrafirm* when goods are transferred from subsidiary to subsidiary. Although such sales are part of international trade, their value may be determined by factors other than a competitive pricing system.

Japanese Transplants in the U.S. Automobile Industry

Since the 1980s, the growth of Japanese direct investment in the U.S. auto industry has been widely publicized. Japanese automakers have invested billions of dollars in U.S.-based assembly facilities, known as **transplants**, as seen in Table 9.5. Establishing transplants in the United States provides a number of benefits to Japanese automakers, including opportunities to:

- Silence critics who insist that autos sold in the United States must be built there.
- Avoid the potential import barriers of the United States.
- Gain access to an expanding market at a time when the Japanese market is nearing saturation.
- Provide a hedge against fluctuations in the yen–dollar exchange rate.

For example, Toyota has pledged to produce in North America at least two-thirds of the vehicles it sells in the region. It regards manufacturing more vehicles in the United States as a type of political insurance. By sprinkling manufacturing jobs across many states, Toyota has built a network of state and federal government officials friendly to the company.

The growth of Japanese investment in the U.S. auto industry has led to both praise and concern over the future of U.S.-owned auto-manufacturing and parts-supplier industries. Proponents of foreign direct investment maintain that it fosters improvement in the overall competitive position of the domestic auto-assembly and parts industries. They also argue that foreign investment generates jobs and provides consumers with a wider product choice at lower prices than would otherwise be available. However, the United Auto Workers (UAW) union maintains that this foreign investment results in job losses in the auto-assembly and parts-supplier industries.

TABLE 9.5

JAPANESE AUTO PLANTS IN THE UNITED STATES

Plant Name/Parent Company	Location
Honda of America, Inc. (Honda)	Marysville, Ohio East Liberty, Ohio
Nissan Motor Manufacturing Corp. (Nissan)	Smyrna, Tennessee
New United Motor Manufacturing, Inc. (Toyota/General Motors)	Fremont, California
Toyota Motor Manufacturing, USA, Inc. (Toyota)	Georgetown, Kentucky
Mazda Motor Manufacturing, USA, Inc. (Mazda)	Flat Rock, Michigan
Ford Motor Co. (Nissan/Ford)	Avon Lake, Ohio

One factor that influences the number of workers hired is a company's *job classifications*, which stipulate the scope of work each employee performs. As the number of job classifications increases, the scope of work decreases, along with the flexibility of using available employees; this decrease can lead to falling worker productivity and rising production costs.

Japanese-affiliated auto companies have traditionally used significantly fewer job classifications than traditional U.S. auto companies. Japanese transplants use work teams, and each team member is trained to do all the operations performed by the team. A typical Japanese-affiliated assembly plant has three to four job classifications: one team leader, one production technician, and one or two maintenance technicians. Often, jobs are rotated among team members. In contrast, traditional U.S. auto plants have enacted more than 90 different job classifications, and employees generally perform only those operations specifically permitted for their classification. These trends have contributed to the superior labor productivity of Japanese transplants compared to the U.S. Big Three (GM, Ford, and Chrysler). Although powerful forces within the U.S. Big Three have resisted change, international competition has forced U.S. automakers to slowly dismantle U.S. management and production methods and remake them along Japanese lines.

For policy makers, the broader issue is whether the Japanese transplants have lived up to expectations. When the Japanese initiated investment in U.S. auto-manufacturing facilities in the 1980s, many Americans viewed them as models for a revitalized U.S. auto industry and new customers for U.S. auto-parts suppliers. Transplants were seen as a way of providing jobs for U.S. autoworkers whose jobs were dwindling as imports increased. When the transplant factories were announced, Americans anticipated that transplant production would be based primarily on American parts, material, and labor; transplant production would displace imports in the U.S. market while transferring new management techniques and technology to the United States.

Certainly, the transplant factories boosted the economies in the regions where they located. There is also no doubt that the transplants helped to transfer Japanese quality control, just-in-time delivery, and other production techniques to the United States. However, the original expectations of the transplants were only partially fulfilled. Skeptics contended that Japanese manufacturing operations were twice as likely to import parts for assembly in the United States as the average foreign company, and four times as likely to import parts as the average U.S. company. Extensive use of imported parts by Japanese transplants contributed to a U.S. automotive trade deficit with Japan and resulted in fewer jobs for U.S. autoworkers.

International Joint Ventures

Another area of multinational enterprise involvement is **international joint ventures**. A joint venture is a business organization established by two or more companies that combines their skills and assets. It may have a limited objective (research or production) and be short lived. It may also be multinational in character, involving cooperation among several domestic and foreign companies. Joint ventures differ from mergers in that they involve the creation of a *new* business firm, rather than the union of two existing companies. Table 9.6 provides examples of recent joint ventures between U.S. and foreign companies.

TABLE 9.6

JOINT VENTURES BETWEEN U.S. AND FOREIGN COMPANIES

Joint Venture	Partner	Foreign Partner	Products
CAMMI	General Motors	Suzuki (Japan)	Subcompact cars
AutoAlliance	Ford	Mazda (Japan)	Subcompact cars
New United Motor Manufacturing	General Motors	Toyota (Japan)	Subcompact cars
National Steel	National Intergroup	Nippon Kokan	Steel
Siecor	Corning Glass Works	Siemens (Germany)	Optical cable
Himont	Hercules	Montedison (Italy)	Polypropylene resin
International Aero Engines	United Technologies	Rolls-Royce (UK)	Aircraft engines
Tokyo Disneyland	Walt Disney Productions	Oriental Land Company	Entertainment

There are three types of international joint ventures. The first is a joint venture formed by two businesses that conduct business in a third country. For example, a U.S. oil firm and a UK oil firm may form a joint venture for oil exploration in the Middle East. Next is the formation of a joint venture with local private interests. Honeywell Information Systems of Japan was formed by Honeywell, Inc., of the United States and Mitsubishi Office Machinery Company of Japan to sell information system equipment to the Japanese. The third type of joint venture includes participation by local government. Bechtel of the United States, Messerschmitt-Boelkow-Blom of West Germany, and National Iranian Oil (representing the government of Iran) formed the Iran Oil Investment Company for oil extraction in Iran.

Several reasons have been advanced to justify the creation of joint ventures. Some functions, such as R&D, can involve costs too large for any one company to absorb by itself. Many of the world's largest copper deposits have been owned and mined jointly by the largest copper companies on the grounds that joint financing is required to raise enough capital. The exploitation of oil deposits is often done by a consortium of several oil companies. Exploratory drilling projects typically involve several companies united in a joint venture, and several refining companies traditionally own long-distance crude oil pipelines. Oil refineries in foreign countries may be co-owned by several large U.S. and foreign oil companies.

Another factor that encourages the formation of international joint ventures is the restrictions some governments place on the foreign ownership of local businesses. Governments in developing nations often close their borders to foreign companies unless they are willing to take on local partners. Mexico, India, and Peru require that their own national companies represent a major interest in any foreign company conducting business within their borders. The foreign investor is forced to either accept local equity participation or forgo operation in the country. Such government policies are defended on the grounds that joint ventures result in the transfer of managerial techniques and know-how to the developing nation. Joint ventures may also prevent the possibility of excessive political influence on the part of foreign investors. Also, joint ventures help minimize dividend transfers abroad and thus strengthen the developing nation's balance of payments.

International joint ventures are also viewed as a means of forestalling protectionism against imports. Apparently motivated by the fear that rising protectionism might restrict their access to U.S. markets, Japanese manufacturers (Toyota Motor Enterprise) increasingly formed joint ventures with U.S. enterprises in the 1980s. Such ventures typically resulted in U.S. workers assembling Japanese components, with the finished goods sold to U.S. consumers. Not only did this process permit Japanese production to enter the U.S. market, but it also blurred the distinction between U.S. and Japanese production. Just who is us? And who is them? The rationale for protecting domestic output and jobs from foreign competition is thus lessened.

However, there are disadvantages to forming an international joint venture. A joint venture is a cumbersome organization compared with a single organization. Control is divided, creating the problem of "two masters." Success or failure depends on how well companies can work together despite having different objectives, corporate cultures, and ways of doing things. The action of corporate chemistry is difficult to predict, but it is critical, because joint-venture agreements usually provide both partners an ongoing role in management. When joint-venture ownership is divided equally, as often occurs, deadlocks in decision making can take place. If balance is to be preserved between different economic interests, negotiation must establish a hierarchical command. Even when negotiated balance is achieved, it can be upset by changing corporate goals or personnel.

Welfare Effects

International joint ventures can yield both welfare-increasing and welfare-decreasing effects for the domestic economy. Joint ventures lead to *welfare gains* when (1) the newly established business adds to pre-existing productive capacity and fosters additional competition, (2) the newly established business is able to enter new markets that neither parent could have entered individually, or (3) the business yields cost reductions that would have been unavailable if each parent performed the same function separately. However, the formation of a joint venture may also result in *welfare losses.* For instance, it may give rise to increased market power, suggesting greater ability to influence market output and price. This is especially likely to occur when the joint venture is formed in markets in which the parents conduct business. Under such circumstances, the parents, through their representatives in the joint venture, agree on prices and output in the very market that they themselves operate. Such coordination of activities limits competition, reinforces upward pressure on prices, and lowers the level of domestic welfare.

Let's consider an example that contrasts two situations: two competing companies sell autos in the domestic market and form a joint venture that operates as a single seller (a monopoly) in the domestic market. We would expect to see a higher price and smaller quantity when the joint venture behaves as a monopoly. This result will always occur as long as the marginal cost curve for the joint venture is identical to the horizontal sum of the marginal cost curves of the individual competitors. The result of this *market-power effect* is a deadweight welfare loss for the domestic economy—a reduction in consumer surplus that is not offset by a corresponding gain to producers. If, however, the formation of the joint venture entails *productivity gains* that neither parent can realize prior to its formation, domestic welfare may increase. This is because a smaller amount of the domestic economy's resources is now required to produce any given output. Whether domestic welfare rises or falls because of the joint venture depends on the magnitudes of these two opposing forces.

FIGURE 9.3

THE WELFARE EFFECTS OF AN INTERNATIONAL JOINT VENTURE

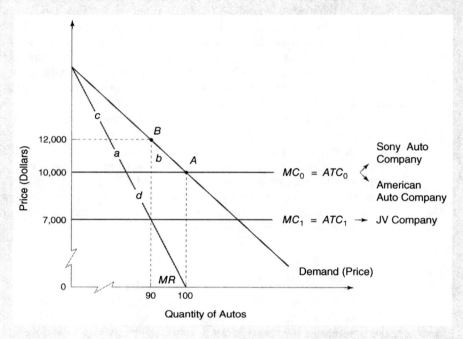

An international joint venture can yield a welfare-decreasing market-power effect and a welfare-increasing cost-reduction effect. The source of the cost-reduction effect may be lower resource prices or improvements in technology and productivity. The joint venture leads to improvements in national welfare if its cost-reduction effect is due to improvements in technology and productivity and if it more than offsets the market-power effect.

Figure 9.3 illustrates the welfare effects of two parent companies' forming a joint venture in the market in which they operate. Assume that Sony Auto Company of Japan and American Auto Company of the United States are the only two firms producing autos for sale in the U.S. market. Suppose each company realizes constant long-term costs, suggesting that the average total cost equals marginal cost at each level of output. Let the cost schedules of each company prior to the formation of the joint venture be $MC_0 = ATC_0$, which equals $10,000. Thus, $MC_0 = ATC_0$ becomes the long-term market supply schedule for autos.

Assume that the Sony Auto Company and the American Auto Company initially operate as competitors, charging a price equal to marginal cost. In Figure 9.3, market equilibrium exists at point A, where 100 autos are sold at a price of $10,000 per unit. Consumer surplus totals area $a + b + c$. Producer surplus does not exist, given the horizontal supply schedule of autos (recall that producer surplus equals the sum of the differences between the market price and each of the minimum prices indicated on the supply schedule for quantities between zero and the market output).

Now suppose that the two competitors announce the formation of a joint venture known as JV Company, which manufactures autos for sale in the United

States. The autos sold by JV replace the autos sold by the two parents in the United States.

Suppose the formation of JV Company entails new production efficiencies that result in cost reductions. Let JV's new cost schedule, $MC_1 = ATC_1$, be located at $7,000. As a monopoly, JV maximizes profit by equating marginal revenue with marginal cost. Market equilibrium exists at point B, where 90 autos are sold at a price of $12,000 per unit. The price increase leads to a reduction in consumer surplus equal to area $a + b$. Of this amount, area a is transferred to JV as producer surplus. Area b represents the loss of consumer surplus that is *not* transferred to JV and that becomes a deadweight welfare loss for the U.S. economy (the consumption effect).

Against this deadweight welfare loss lies the efficiency effect of JV Company: a decrease in unit costs from $10,000 to $7,000 per auto. JV can produce its profit-maximizing output, 90 autos, at a cost reduction equal to area d as compared with the costs that would exist if the parent companies produced the same output. Area d thus represents additional producer surplus, which is a welfare gain for the U.S. economy. Our analysis concludes that, for the United States, the formation of JV Company is desirable if area d exceeds area b.

It has been assumed that JV Company achieves cost reductions that are unavailable to either parent as a stand-alone company. Whether the cost reductions benefit the overall U.S. economy depends on their source. If they result from *productivity* improvements (for example, new work rules leading to higher output per worker), a welfare gain exists for the economy, because fewer resources are required to produce a given number of autos and the excess can be shifted to other industries. However, the cost reductions stemming from JV Company's formation may be *monetary* in nature. Being a newly formed company, JV may be able to negotiate wage concessions from domestic workers that could not be achieved by the American Auto Company. Such a cost reduction represents a transfer of dollars from domestic workers to JV profits and does not constitute an overall welfare gain for the economy.

Multinational Enterprises as a Source of Conflict

Advocates of MNEs often point out the benefits these enterprises can provide for the nations they affect, including both the source country where the parent organization is located and the host country where subsidiary firms are established. Benefits allegedly exist in the forms of additional levels of investment and capital, creation of new jobs, and the development of technologies and production processes. But critics contend that MNEs often create trade restraints, cause conflict with national economic and political objectives, and have adverse effects on a nation's balance of payments. These arguments perhaps explain why some nations frown on direct investment, while others welcome it. This section examines some of the more controversial issues involving multinationals. The frame of reference is the U.S. MNE, although the same issues apply no matter where the parent organization is based.

Employment

One of the most hotly debated issues surrounding the MNE is its effects on employment in both the host and source countries. Multinationals often contend that their foreign direct investment yields favorable benefits to the labor force of the recipient nation. Setting up a new multinational automobile manufacturing plant in Canada creates more jobs for Canadian workers. But the MNE's effect on jobs varies from business to business. One source of controversy arises when the direct investment spending of foreign-based MNEs is used to purchase already existing local businesses rather than to establish new ones. In this case, the investment spending may not result in additional production capacity and may not have noticeable effects on employment in the host country. Another problem arises when MNEs bring in foreign managers and other top executives to run the subsidiary in the host country. In U.S. oil companies located in Saudi Arabia, the Saudis are increasingly demanding that their own people be employed in high-level positions.

As for the source country, the issues of runaway jobs and cheap foreign labor are of vital concern to home workers. Because labor unions are confined to individual countries, the multinational nature of these businesses permits them to escape much of the collective-bargaining influence of domestic unions. It is also pointed out that MNEs can seek out those countries where labor has minimal market power.

The ultimate impact that MNEs have on employment in the host and source countries seems to depend in part on the time scale. In the short term, the source country will likely experience an employment decline when production is shifted overseas. But other industries in the source country may find foreign sales rising over time. This is because foreign labor consumes as well as produces and tends to purchase more as employment and income increase as a result of increased investment. Perhaps the main source of controversy stems from the fact that the MNEs are involved in rapid changes in technology and in the transmission of productive enterprises to host countries. Although such efforts may promote global welfare in the long term, the potential short-term adjustment problems facing source-country labor cannot be ignored.

Technology Transfer

Besides promoting runaway jobs, multinationals can foster the transfer of technology (knowledge and skills applied to how goods are produced) to other nations. Such a process is known as **technology transfer**.

Technology has been likened to a contagious disease: it spreads further and more quickly if there are more personal contacts. Foreign trade is viewed as a channel through which people in different nations make contacts and through which people in one nation get to know about the products of other nations. Foreign direct investment is an even more effective method of technology transfer. When foreign firms with technological advantages establish local production subsidiaries, the personal contacts between these subsidiaries and local firms are more frequent and closer than when firms are located abroad.

International trade and foreign direct investment also facilitate technology transfer via the so-called *demonstration effect*: as a firm shows how its products operate, this sends important information to other firms that such products exist and are usable. Technology transfer is also aided by the *competition effect*: When a foreign firm manufactures a superior product that is popular among consumers, other firms are threatened. To survive, they must innovate and improve the quality of their products.

Although technology transfer may increase the productivity and competitiveness of recipient nations, donor nations may react against it because it is detrimental to their economic base. Donor nations contend that the establishment of production operations abroad by multinational enterprises decreases their export potential and leads to job losses for their workers. By sharing technical knowledge with foreign nations, a donor nation may eventually lose its international competitiveness, thus causing a decrease in its rate of economic growth.

Consider the case of the U.S. technology transfer to China in the mid-1990s. After decades of mutual hostility, the United States hoped that, by the 1990s, China would open itself to the outside world and engage in free trade so that foreign nations could trade with China according to the principle of comparative advantage. Instead, China used its leverage as a large buyer of foreign products to pressure multinational enterprises to localize production and transfer technology to China to help it become competitive. With multinational enterprises willing to outbid each other to woo Chinese bureaucrats, China was in a favorable position to reap the benefits of technology transfer.

For example, Microsoft Corporation, under the threat of having its software banned, co-developed a Chinese version of Windows 95 with a local partner and agreed to aid efforts to develop a Chinese software industry. Another example was General Motors. To beat out Ford for the right to become a partner in manufacturing sedans in Shanghai, GM agreed to bring in dozens of joint ventures for auto parts and to design most of the car in China. It also agreed to establish five research institutes to teach Chinese engineers to turn technological theory in fields such as power trains and fuel-injection systems into commercial applications.

American multinationals argued that transferring technology to China was largely risk-free because a competitive challenge from China was decades away. However, the acceleration of technology transfer in the mid-1990s became increasingly unpopular with U.S. labor unions, which feared that their members were losing jobs to lower-paid Chinese workers. United States government officials also feared that the technology transfer was helping create a competitor of extreme proportions. Let us consider the case of General Electric's technology transfer to China.

General Electric's Trade-Off for Entry into the Chinese Market: Short-Term Sales for Long-Term Competition

For decades, General Electric (GE) had an effective strategy for being competitive in the Chinese market for power-generating equipment: sell the best equipment at the lowest price. However, by the first decade of the 2000s, the formula was altered. Besides offering high quality gas-fired turbines at a competitive price, GE had to agree to share with the Chinese sophisticated technology for producing the turbines. To be considered for turbine contracts worth several billion dollars, GE, Mitsubishi, Siemens, and other competitors were obligated to form joint ventures with state-owned Chinese power companies. General Electric was also required to transfer to its new partners the technology and advanced manufacturing specifications for its gas-fired turbine, which GE had spent more than $500 million to develop. Officials from GE noted that the Chinese wanted to have complete access to its technology, while GE wanted to protect the technology in which it made a large financial investment.

The vast size of China's electricity market convinced GE executives that this market was worth pursuing in spite of the technology demands. The U.S. market for gas-fired turbines was weak because of past spending sprees to increase capacity by power companies and utilities. On the other hand, China was expected to spend more than $10 billion a year constructing electricity plants in the near future. General Electric officials thus faced the trade-off of short-term sales in China for long-term competition from Chinese manufacturers. In the end, GE won an order for 13 of its gas-fired turbines, and as part of the agreement also had to share technology with its Chinese partners.

Before the gas-fired turbine venture with GE, Chinese manufacturers had mastered only the technology required for making much less efficient steam-powered turbines. That technology was obtained in part through previous joint ventures with firms such as Westinghouse Electric Co. However, the Chinese demanded the technology behind the more efficient gas-fired turbines.

General Electric officials noted that Chinese competition was not imminent in highly advanced products like gas-fired turbines. In the past, even after acquiring expertise from foreign corporations, Chinese firms lacked the skill necessary to fully exploit the technology and become competitive in world markets. Moreover, by the time Chinese companies mastered the technology they initially obtained from GE, GE had developed more advanced technologies. Nonetheless, Chinese officials looked ahead to new rounds of power-generating equipment bidding by GE and its competitors, when Chinese officials hoped to obtain even more lucrative technology-sharing deals.[2]

National Sovereignty

Another controversial issue involving the conduct of MNEs is their effect on the economic and political policies of the host and source governments. Many nations fear that the presence of MNEs in a given country results in a loss of its national sovereignty. For example, MNEs may resist government attempts to redistribute national income through taxation. By using accounting techniques that shift profits overseas, an MNE may be able to evade the taxes of a host country. An MNE could accomplish this evasion by raising prices on goods from its subsidiaries in nations with modest tax rates to reduce profits on its operations in a high-tax nation where most of its business actually takes place.

The political influence of MNEs is also questioned by many, as illustrated by the case of Chile. For years, U.S. businesses had pursued direct investments in Chile, largely in copper mining. When Salvador Allende was in the process of winning the presidency, he was opposed by U.S. businesses fearing that their Chilean operations would be expropriated by the host government. International Telephone and Telegraph tried to prevent the election of Allende and attempted to promote civil disturbances that would lead to his fall from power. Another case of MNEs' meddling in host-country affairs is that of United Brands (now Chiquita), who engaged in food-product sales. In 1974, the company paid a $1.25 million bribe to the president of Honduras in return for an export-tax reduction applied to bananas. When the payoff was revealed, the president was removed from office.

There are other areas of controversy. Suppose a Canadian subsidiary of a U.S.-based MNE conducts trade with a country subject to U.S. trade embargoes. Should U.S. policymakers outlaw such activities? The Canadian subsidiary may be pressured by the parent organization to comply with U.S. foreign policy. During

---

[2]"China's Price for Market Entry: Give Us Your Technology, Too," *The Wall Street Journal*, February 26, 2004, pp. A-1 and A-6.

international crises, MNEs may move funds rapidly from one financial center to another to avoid losses (make profits) from changes in exchange rates. This conduct makes it difficult for national governments to stabilize their economies.

In a world where national economies are interdependent and factors of production are mobile, the possible loss of national sovereignty is often viewed as a necessary cost whenever direct investment results in foreign control of production facilities. Whether the welfare gains accruing from the international division of labor and specialization outweigh the potential diminution of national independence involves value judgments by policymakers and interested citizens.

Balance of Payments

The United States offers a good example of how an MNE can affect a nation's balance of payments. In brief, the *balance of payments* is an account of the value of goods and services, capital movements (including foreign direct investment), and other items that flow into or out of a country. Items that make a positive contribution to a nation's payments position include exports of goods and services and capital inflows (foreign investment entering the home country); whereas the opposite flows weaken the payments position. At first glance, we might conclude that when U.S. MNEs make foreign direct investments, these payments represent an outflow of capital from the United States and hence a negative factor on the U.S. payments position. Although this view may be true in the short term, it ignores the positive effects on trade flows and earnings that direct investment provides in the long term.

When a U.S. MNE sets up a subsidiary overseas, it generally purchases U.S. capital equipment and materials needed to run the subsidiary. Once in operation, the subsidiary tends to purchase additional capital equipment and other material inputs from the United States. Both of these factors stimulate U.S. exports, strengthening its balance-of-payments position.

Another long-term impact that U.S. foreign direct investment has on its balance of payments is the return inflow of income generated by overseas operations. Such income includes earnings of overseas affiliates, interest and dividends, and fees and royalties. These items generate inflows of revenues for the economy and strengthen the balance-of-payments position.

Transfer Pricing

Controversy also confronts MNEs in their use of **transfer pricing**, the pricing of goods within an MNE. For example, goods from the company's production division may be sold to its foreign marketing division, or inputs obtained by a parent company can come from a foreign subsidiary. The transfer price may be a purely arbitrary figure which means that it may be unrelated to costs incurred or to operations carried out. The choice of the transfer prices affects the division of the total profit among the parts of the company and thus influences its overall tax burden.

For example, suppose that Dell Inc. produces computers in the United States and buys microchips from its own subsidiary in Malaysia. Also suppose that corporate taxes are 34 percent in the United States and 20 percent in Malaysia. Suppose that Dell tells its subsidiary to sell microchips to Dell at a grossly inflated price (the

DOES THE U.S. TAX CODE SEND AMERICAN JOBS OFFSHORE?

One of the most controversial issues involving MNEs for U.S. policymakers is the taxation of income stemming from foreign direct investment. Labor unions and other groups often contend that U.S. tax laws provide a disincentive to invest at home that results from tax concessions offered by the U.S. government on foreign direct investment. Such tax concessions result in the shipping of American jobs overseas, according to unions. These concessions include *foreign tax credits* and *tax deferrals*.

According to U.S. tax law, an MNE headquartered in the United States is permitted credits against its U.S. income-tax liabilities in an amount equal to the income taxes it pays to foreign governments. Assuming that a Canadian subsidiary earns $100,000 taxable income and that Canada's income-tax rate is 25 percent, the company would pay the Canadian government $25,000. But if that income were applied to the parent organization in the United States, the tax owed to the U.S. government would be $35,000, given an income-tax rate of 35 percent. Under the tax credit system, the parent organization would pay the U.S. government only $10,000 ($35,000 − $25,000 = $10,000). The rationale of the foreign tax credit is that MNEs headquartered in the United States should not be subject to double taxation.

United States-based MNEs also enjoy a tax-deferral advantage. Under U.S. tax laws, the parent organization has the option of deferring U.S. taxes paid on the income of its foreign subsidiary as long as that income is retained overseas rather than repatriated to the United States. This system amounts to an interest-free loan extended by the U.S. government to the parent for as long as the income is maintained abroad. Retained earnings of an overseas subsidiary can be reinvested abroad without being subject to U.S. taxes. Therefore, the tax deferral puts a U.S.-based MNE, which has a subsidiary in, say, China, on the same footing as a local company operating in China or on the same footing as, say, a French-based MNE that operates a subsidiary in China. When the income is repatriated to the United States, it is no longer being used by that subsidiary, so there is no longer any need for that tax leveling. Thus, the MNE gets taxed by the United States but with a foreign tax credit for the foreign tax which has previously been paid.

In 2009, President Barack Obama proposed to close tax loopholes on U.S.-based MNEs and crack down on overseas tax havens. His goal was to help create jobs in the United States, make the tax code fairer, and raise additional revenue for the federal government. Obama's proposal was opposed vigorously by U.S. corporate officials who noted that such a measure would place them at a competitive disadvantage in the global marketplace unless it was accompanied by a reduction in the corporate tax rate. At the writing of this text, it remains to be seen if Obama's proposal will be enacted.

transfer price). Dell thus has a large business expense to deduct when determining its taxable income on its other profitable operations in the United States. To the extent that transfer pricing allows Dell to reduce its taxable income in the United States, the firm avoids being taxed at the rate of 34 percent. Moreover, the increased income of Dell's Malaysian subsidiary, which occurs because of the inflated transfer price, is taxed at the lower rate of 20 percent. Simply put, Dell can reduce its overall tax burden by reporting most of its income in Malaysia, the low tax country, even though the income is earned in the United States, the high-tax country. But note that the tax paid to the U.S. government decreases while the tax paid to the Malaysian government increases. In other words, one government's loss is the other government's gain. So one government can be expected to want to legislate against unfair transfer pricing practices, while the other government can be expected to resist such legislation.

Both foreign governments and the U.S. government are interested in the part that transfer prices play in the realization of corporate profits. Abuses in pricing across national borders are illegal if they can be proved. According to U.S. Internal Revenue Service (IRS) regulations, enterprises dealing with their own subsidiaries are required to set prices "at arms length," just as they would for unrelated customers that are not part of the same corporate structure. This process means that prices must relate to actual costs incurred and to operations actually carried out. However, proving that the prices that one subsidiary charges another are far from market prices is very difficult.

International Labor Mobility: Migration

Historically, the United States has been a favorite target for international **migration**. Because of its vast inflow of migrants, the United States has been described as the melting pot of the world. Table 9.7 indicates the volume of immigration to the United States from the 1820s to 2008. Western Europe was a major source of immigrants during this era, with Germany, Italy, and the United Kingdom among the largest contributors. In recent years, large numbers of Mexicans have migrated to the United States, as well as people from Asia. Migrants have been motivated by better economic opportunities and by noneconomic factors such as politics, war, and religion.

Although international labor movements can enhance the world economy's efficiency, they are often restricted by government controls. The United States, like most countries, limits immigration. Following waves of immigration at the turn of the century, the Immigration Act of 1924 was enacted. Besides restricting the overall flow of immigrants to the United States, the act implemented a quota that limited the number of immigrants from each foreign country. Because the quotas were based on the number of U.S. citizens who had previously emigrated from those countries, the allocation system favored emigrants from northern Europe relative to southern Europe. In the late 1960s, the quota formula was modified, which led to increasing numbers of Asian immigrants to the United States.

TABLE 9.7

U.S. IMMIGRATION, 1820–2008

Period	Number (thousands)
1820–1840	743
1841–1860	4,311
1861–1880	5,127
1881–1900	8,934
1901–1920	14,531
1921–1940	4,636
1941–1960	3,551
1961–1980	7,815
1981–2000	16,433
2001–2008	8,328

Source: From U.S. Department of Homeland Security, Office of Immigration Statistics, *Yearbook of Immigration Statistics*, 2008 available at http://www.uscis.gov/graphics/shared/statistics/yearbook/. See also U.S. Department of Commerce, Bureau of the Census, *Statistical Abstracts of the United States*, Washington, DC: Government Printing Office, available at www.census.gov/.

The Effects of Migration

Figure 9.4 illustrates the economics of labor migration. Suppose the world consists of two countries, the United States and Mexico, which are initially in isolation. The horizontal axes denote the total quantity of labor in the United States and Mexico, and the vertical

FIGURE 9.4

THE EFFECTS OF LABOR MIGRATION FROM MEXICO TO THE UNITED STATES

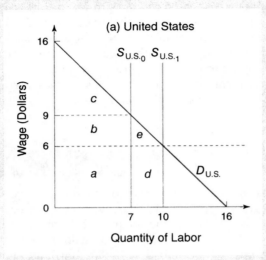
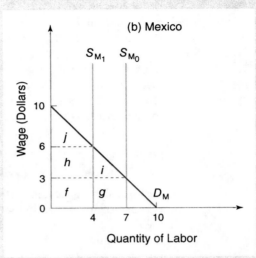

Prior to migration, the wage rate in the United States exceeds that of Mexico. Responding to the wage differential, Mexican workers immigrate to the United States; this leads to a reduction in the Mexican labor supply and an increase in the U.S. labor supply. Wage rates continue to rise in Mexico and fall in the United States until they eventually are equalized. The labor migration hurts native U.S. workers but helps U.S. owners of capital; the opposite occurs in Mexico. Because migrant workers flow from uses of lower productivity to higher productivity, world output expands.

axes depict the wages paid to labor. For each country, the demand schedule for labor is designated by the value of the marginal product (VMP) of labor.[3] Also assume a fixed labor supply of seven workers in the United States, denoted by $S_{U.S.0}$, and seven workers in Mexico, denoted by S_{M0}.

The equilibrium wage in each country is determined at the point of intersection of the supply and demand schedules for labor. In Figure 9.4(a), the U.S. equilibrium wage is $9, and total labor income is $63; this amount is represented by the area $a + b$. The remaining area under the labor demand schedule is area c, which equals $24.50; this value represents the share of the nation's income accruing to owners

---

[3]The value of the marginal product of labor (VMP) refers to the amount of money producers receive from selling the quantity that was produced by the last worker hired; in other words, VMP = product price × the marginal product of labor. The VMP curve is the labor demand schedule. This curve follows from an application of the rule that a business hiring under competitive conditions finds it most profitable to hire labor up to the point at which the price of labor (wage rate) equals its VMP. The location of the VMP curve depends on the marginal productivity of labor and the price of the product that it produces. Under pure competition, price is constant. Therefore, it is because of diminishing marginal productivity that the labor demand schedule is downward-sloping.

of capital.[4] In Figure 9.4(*b*), the equilibrium wage for Mexico is $3; labor income totals $21, represented by area *f* + *g*; capital owners enjoy incomes equaling area *h* + *i* + *j*, or $24.50.

Suppose labor can move freely between Mexico and the United States and assume that migration is costless and occurs solely in response to wage differentials. Because U.S. wage rates are relatively high, there is an incentive for Mexican workers to migrate to the United States and compete in the U.S. labor market; this process will continue until the wage differential is eliminated. Suppose three workers migrate from Mexico to the United States. In the United States, the new labor supply schedule becomes $S_{U.S.1}$; the excess supply of labor at the $9 wage rate causes the wage rate to fall to $6. In Mexico, the labor emigration results in a new labor supply schedule at S_{M1}; the excess demand for labor at wage rate $3 causes the wage rate to rise to $6. The effect of **labor mobility** is thus to equalize wage rates in the two countries.[5] Our next job is to assess how labor migration in response to wage differentials affects the world economy's efficiency. Does world output expand or contract with open migration? For the United States, migration increases the labor supply from $S_{U.S.0}$ to $S_{U.S.1}$. This increase leads to an expansion of output; the value of the additional output is denoted by area *d* + *e* ($22.50). For Mexico, the decrease in labor supply from S_{M0} to S_{M1} results in a contraction in output; the value of the lost output is represented by area *g* + *i* ($13.50). The result is a net gain of $9 in world output as a result of labor migration. This is because the *VMP* of labor in the United States exceeds that of Mexico throughout the relevant range. Workers are attracted to the United States by the higher wages paid. These higher wages signal to Mexican labor the higher value of worker productivity, thus attracting workers to those areas where they will be most efficient. As workers are used more productively, world output expands.

Migration also affects the *distribution of income*. As we will see, the gains in world income resulting from labor mobility are not distributed equally among all nations and factors of production. The United States as a whole benefits from immigration; its overall income gain is the sum of the losses by native U.S. workers, gains by Mexican immigrants now living in the United States, and gains by U.S. owners of capital. Mexico experiences overall income losses as a result of its labor emigration; however, workers remaining in Mexico gain relative to Mexican owners of capital. As previously suggested, the Mexican immigrants gain from their relocation to the United States.

For the United States, the gain in income as a result of immigration is denoted by area *d* + *e* ($22.50) in Figure 9.4(*a*). Of this amount, Mexican immigrants capture area *d* ($18), while area *e* ($4.50) is the extra income accruing to U.S. owners of

---

[4]How do we know that area *c* represents the income accruing to U.S. owners of capital? My analysis assumes two productive factors, labor and capital. The total income (value of output) that results from using a given quantity of labor with a fixed amount of capital equals the area under the *VMP* curve of labor for that particular quantity of labor. Labor's share of that area is calculated by multiplying the wage rate times the quantity of labor hired. The remaining area under the *VMP* curve is the income accruing to the owners of capital.

[5]Wage-rate equalization assumes unrestricted labor mobility in which workers are concerned only about their incomes. It also assumes that migration is costless for labor. In reality, there are economic and psychological costs of migrating to another country. Such costs may result in only a small number of persons finding the wage gains in the immigrating country high enough to compensate them for their migration costs. Thus, complete wage equalization may not occur.

capital thanks to the availability of additional labor to use with the capital. However, immigration forces wage rates down from $9 to $6. The earnings of the native U.S. workers fall by area b ($21); this amount is transferred to U.S. owners of capital.

As for Mexico, its labor emigration results in a decrease in income equal to $g + i$ ($13.50); this decrease represents a transfer from Mexico to the United States. The remaining workers in Mexico gain area h ($12) as a result of higher wages. However, Mexican capital owners lose because less labor is available for use with their capital.

Although immigration may lower wage rates for some native U.S. workers, it should also be noted that these lower wage rates benefit U.S. producers. Lower wage rates also result in lower equilibrium product prices, thereby benefiting consumers. From society's perspective, the gains from immigration to producers and consumers should be weighed against the losses to low-wage workers.

We can conclude that the effect of labor mobility is to increase overall world income and to redistribute income from labor to capital in the United States and from capital to labor in Mexico. Migration has an impact on the distribution of income similar to an increase in exports of labor-intensive goods from Mexico to the United States.

Immigration as an Issue

The preceding example makes it clear why domestic labor groups in capital-abundant nations often prefer restrictions on immigration; open immigration tends to reduce their wages. When migrant workers are unskilled, as is typically the case, the negative effect on wages mainly affects unskilled domestic workers. Conversely, domestic manufacturers will tend to favor unrestricted immigration as a source of cheap labor.

Another controversy about immigrants is whether they are a drain on government resources. Nations that provide generous welfare payments to the economically disadvantaged may fear they will induce an influx of nonproductive people who will not produce as did the immigrants of Figure 9.4, but will enjoy welfare benefits at the expense of domestic residents and working immigrants. However, fiscal relief may not be far away. The children of immigrants will soon enter the labor force and begin paying taxes, thus supporting not only their children's education, but also their parents' retirement. In a matter of two generations, most immigrant families tend to assimilate to the point that their fiscal burdens are indistinguishable from those of other natives. When it's all added up, most long-term calculations show that immigrants make a net positive contribution to public coffers.

Developing nations have sometimes feared open immigration policies because they can result in a **brain drain**—emigration of highly educated and skilled people from developing nations to industrial nations, thus limiting the growth potential of the developing nations. The brain drain has been encouraged by national immigration laws, as in the United States and other industrial nations, which permit the immigration of skilled persons while restricting that of unskilled workers.

In the previous labor-migration example, we implicitly assumed that the Mexican workers' migration decision was more or less permanent. In practice, most labor migration is temporary, especially in the European Union. That is, a country such as France will allow the immigration of foreign workers on a temporary basis when needed; these workers are known as **guest workers**. During periods of business recession, France will refuse to issue work permits when foreign workers are no longer needed. Such a practice tends to insulate the French economy from labor shortages during business expansions and labor surpluses during business recessions. However, the labor-adjustment problem is shifted to the labor-emigrating countries.

Illegal migration is also a problem. In the United States, this type of migration has become a political hot potato, with millions of illegal immigrants finding employment in the so-called underground economy, often below minimum wage. Some 3 to 15 million illegal immigrants are estimated to be in the United States, many of them from Mexico. For the United States, and especially the southwestern states, immigration of Mexican workers has provided a cheap supply of agricultural and low-skilled workers. For Mexico, it has been a major source of foreign exchange and a safety cushion against domestic unemployment. Illegal immigration also affects the distribution of income for U.S. natives because it tends to reduce the income of low-skilled U.S. workers.

On the other hand, immigrants not only diversify an economy, but they may also contribute to economic growth. It is because immigrants are often different from natives that the economy as a whole profits. In many instances, immigrants both cause prices to fall, which benefits all consumers, and enable the economy to domestically produce a wider variety of goods than natives could alone. If immigrants weren't different from natives, they would only augment the population and the scale of the economy, but not have an effect on the overall growth rate of per capita income. According to the National Research Council, the overall effect of immigration on the U.S. gross domestic product is between $1 billion and $10 billion a year.[6] Although these amounts may seem negligible in an $8 trillion economy (about one-eighth of one percent at most), they are still a gain—and not the drain many believe immigration to be.

As we learned from Figure 9.4, immigrants increase the supply of labor in the economy. This results in a lower market wage for all workers *if all workers are the same*. But all workers are not the same. Some natives will compete with immigrants for positions because they possess similar skills; others will work alongside immigrants, complementing the immigrants' skills with their own. This skill distinction means that not all native workers will receive a lower wage. Those who compete with (are substitutes for) immigrants will receive a lower wage than they would without immigration, while those who complement immigrants will receive a higher wage. Most analyses of various countries have found that a ten percent increase in the immigrant share of the population reduces native wages by one percent at most. This finding suggests that most immigrants are not substituting for native labor—skilled or unskilled—but are, instead, complementing it.[7]

Advocates of increased immigration note that children do not begin working the minute they are born. Producing an adult worker requires substantial expenditures in the form of food, clothing, shelter, education, and other child-rearing costs. These investments in human capital formation are quite substantial. Immigrant workers, unlike newborn children, are able to begin engaging in productive activities upon their arrival in the country. The cost of much of their human capital formation

[6]See National Research Council Panel on the Demographic and Economic Impacts of Immigration. *The New Americans: Economic, Demographic, and Fiscal Effects of Immigration* (Washington D.C.: National Academy Press, 1997).

[7]Friedberg, R. M. and J. Hunt, "The Impact of Immigrants on Host Country Wages, Employment and Growth," *Journal of Economic Perspectives*, Spring 1995, pp. 23–44.

DOES U.S. IMMIGRATION POLICY HARM DOMESTIC WORKERS?

The net gains from current immigration are small, so it is unlikely that these gains can play a crucial role in the policy debate. Economic research teaches a very valuable lesson: the economic impact of immigration is essentially distributional. Current immigration redistributes wealth from unskilled workers, whose wages are lowered by immigrants, to skilled workers and owners of companies that buy immigrants' services, and from taxpayers who bear the burden of paying for the social services used by immigrants to consumers who use the goods and services produced by immigrants.

George Borjas, "The New Economics of Immigration,"
The Atlantic Online, November 1996.

Highly skilled immigrants, who also create jobs for Americans, are not the only ones contributing to our economic boom. Even the less-skilled immigrants contribute to our economy and our lives by working in jobs most Americans do not want, such as cleaning offices, cooking in restaurants, and ringing up purchases in the grocery store. They, in turn, contribute by buying homes, clothes, and groceries. The wonderful cultural diversity brought to the United States by immigrants has become secondary to their willingness to work hard and become part of today's America.

Bronwyn Lance, "The Economic Impact of Immigrants,"
May 2000, available at http://www.worldandihomeschool.com/.

Most U.S. residents today are the descendants of immigrants who arrived in the United States during the past 150 years. Concerns about the effect of immigration on domestic workers, however, have resulted in the passage of several laws designed to restrict immigration. Unions, in particular, have argued for a more restrictive immigration policy on the grounds that immigration lowers the wage and employment levels for domestic residents.

No substantial restrictions were placed on immigration into the United States until the passage of the Quota Law of 1921. This law set quotas on the number of immigrants based on the country of origin. The Quota Law primarily restricted immigration from eastern and southern Europe. The Immigration and Nationality Act Amendments of 1965 eliminated the country-specific quota system and instead established a limit on the maximum number of immigrants allowed into the United States. Under this act, preferential treatment is given to those who immigrate for the purpose of family reunification. Those possessing exceptional skills are also given priority. However, no limit is placed on the number of political refugees allowed to immigrate into the United States. Not all immigrants, of course, enter the country through legal channels. Individuals often enter on student or tourist visas and begin working in violation of their visa status. Other individuals enter the country illegally without a valid U.S. visa. The Immigration Reform and Control Act of 1986 addresses the issue of illegal immigration by imposing substantial fines on employers that hire illegal immigrants.

The Illegal Immigration Reform and Immigrant Responsibility Act of 1996 provided several new restrictions to immigration. Host families can only accept immigrants if the host family receives an income that is at least 125 percent of the poverty level. This act also requires that the Immigration and Naturalization Service maintain stricter records of entry and exit by nonresident aliens.

was borne by the country from which they emigrated. Because most immigrants arrive at a stage in their life in which they are relatively productive, higher immigration rates generally result in an increase in the proportion of the population that is working. As the proportion of the population that is working rises, per capita income also rises.

Concern over the future of social security is also used to support relaxed immigration restrictions. Declining birthrates in the United States, combined with rising life spans, result in a steady increase in the ratio of retired to working individuals over the next few decades. An increase in the number of younger immigrants could help to alleviate this problem.

TABLE 9.8

LABOR MARKETS WORK: PERCENTAGE WAGE CHANGE
DUE TO 1980–2000 IMMIGRATION INFLUX (IN PERCENT)

Labor Category	PERCENTAGE WAGE CHANGE	
	Short Run	Long Run
All workers	−3.3%	0.1%
High school dropouts	−8.2	−4.8
High school graduates	−2.2	1.1
Some college	−2.6	0.8
College graduates	−3.8	−0.5

Source: George Borjas and Lawrence Katz, *The Evolution of the Mexican-Born Workforce in the United States.* National Bureau of Economic Research, Cambridge, MA, 2005.

Do Immigrants Really Hurt American Workers' Wages?

One study of the wage effect of immigration deserves attention. Researchers at the National Bureau of Economic Research have examined whether immigrants entering the U.S. labor market depress the wages of competing U.S. workers. They investigated the wage effect of immigration (mainly of Mexican origin) into the United States during 1980–2000. They found that in the short term, immigration lowered the average wage of competing U.S. workers by three percent. For competing workers that dropped out of high school, the average wage fell by eight percent. The results of the researchers' findings are summarized in Table 9.8.

However, they also noted that over the long term, wages depend on the supply of capital as well as labor. Alone, an influx of immigrants increases the supply of workers and thus decreases wages. But cheaper labor increases the potential return of employers to building new factories. In so doing, they create extra demand for workers. Once capital has fully adjusted, the final effect on overall wages should be a wash, as long as the immigrants have not changed the productivity of the workforce as a whole. It turns out that the researchers found that the wage of the average competing worker was not affected by immigration in the long term, but the wage of high school dropouts still decreased by approximately five percent. These findings confirmed the idea that in the long term, immigration had only a small negative effect on the pay of America's least skilled workers. If Congress wants to reduce wage inequality, building border walls is a very questionable way of going about it.

Summary

1. Today the world economy is characterized by the international movement of factor inputs. The multinational enterprise plays a central part in this process.
2. There is no single agreed upon definition of what constitutes an MNE. Some of the most identifiable characteristics of multinationals are the following: (a) Stock ownership and management are multinational in character; (b) company headquarters may be far removed from the country where a particular activity occurs; and (c) foreign sales represent a high proportion of total sales.
3. Multinationals have diversified their operations along vertical, horizontal, and conglomerate lines.
4. Among the major factors that influence decisions to undertake foreign direct investment are (a) market demand, (b) trade restrictions, (c) investment regulations, and (d) labor productivity and costs.
5. In planning to set up overseas operations, a business must decide whether to construct (or purchase) plants abroad or extend licenses to foreign businesses to produce its goods.
6. The theory of multinational enterprise essentially agrees with the predictions of the comparative-advantage principle. However, conventional trade theory assumes that commodities are traded between independent, competitive businesses, whereas MNEs are often vertically diversified businesses, with substantial intrafirm sales. Thus, MNEs may use transfer pricing to maximize overall company profits rather than the profits of any single subsidiary.

7. In recent years, companies have increasingly linked up with former rivals in a vast array of joint ventures. International joint ventures can yield welfare-increasing effects as well as market-power effects.

8. Some of the more controversial issues involving MNEs are (a) employment, (b) technology transfer, (c) national sovereignty, (d) balance of payments, and (e) taxation.

9. International labor migration occurs for economic and noneconomic reasons. Migration increases output and decreases wages in the country of immigration, as it decreases output and increases wages in the country of emigration. For the world as a whole, migration leads to net increases in output.

Key Concepts & Terms

- Brain drain (p. 334)
- Conglomerate diversification (p. 310)
- Country risk analysis (p. 318)
- Foreign direct investment (p. 311)
- Guest workers (p. 334)
- Horizontal diversification (p. 310)
- International joint ventures (p. 321)
- Labor mobility (p. 333)
- Migration (p. 331)
- Multinational enterprise (MNE) (p. 309)
- Technology transfer (p. 326)
- Transfer pricing (p. 329)
- Transplants (p. 320)
- Vertical diversification (p. 310)

Study Questions

1. Multinational enterprises may diversify their operations along vertical, horizontal, and conglomerate lines within the host and source countries. Distinguish among these diversification approaches.

2. What are the major foreign industries in which U.S. businesses have chosen to place direct investments? What are the major industries in the United States in which foreigners place direct investments?

3. Why is it that the rate of return on U.S. direct investments in the developing nations often exceeds the rate of return on its investments in industrial nations?

4. What are the most important motives behind an enterprise's decision to undertake foreign direct investment?

5. What is meant by the term *multinational enterprise*?

6. Under what conditions would a business wish to enter foreign markets by extending licenses or franchises to local businesses to produce its goods?

7. What are the major issues involving multinational enterprises as a source of conflict for source and host countries?

8. Is the theory of multinational enterprise essentially consistent or inconsistent with the traditional model of comparative advantage?

9. What are some examples of welfare gains and welfare losses that can result from the formation of international joint ventures among competing businesses?

10. What effects does labor migration have on the country of immigration? The country of emigration? The world as a whole?

11. Table 9.9 illustrates the revenue conditions facing ABC, Inc., and XYZ, Inc., which operate as competitors in the U.S. calculator market. Each firm realizes constant long-term costs ($MC = AC$) of $4 per unit. On graph paper, plot the enterprise demand, marginal revenue, and $MC = AC$ schedules. On the basis of this information, answer the following questions.

TABLE 9.9

PRICE AND MARGINAL REVENUE:
CALCULATORS

Quantity	Price ($)	Marginal Revenue ($)
0	9	—
1	8	8
2	7	6
3	6	4
4	5	2
5	4	0
6	3	−2
7	2	−4

a. With ABC and XYZ behaving as competitors, the equilibrium price is $ _____ and output is _____. At the equilibrium price, U.S. households attain $ _____ of consumer surplus, while company profits total $ _____.

b. Suppose the two organizations jointly form a new one, JV, Inc., whose calculators replace the output sold by the parent companies in the U.S. market. Assuming that JV operates as a monopoly and that its costs ($MC = AC$) equal $4 per unit, the company's output would be _____ at a price of $ _____, and total profit would be $ _____. Compared to the market equilibrium position achieved by ABC and XYZ as competitors, JV as a monopoly leads to a deadweight loss of consumer surplus equal to $ _____.

c. Assume now that the formation of JV yields technological advances that result in a per-unit cost of only $2; sketch the new $MC = AC$ schedule in the figure. Realizing that JV results in a deadweight loss of consumer surplus, as described in part *b*, the net effect of the formation of JV on U.S. welfare is a gain/loss of $ _____. If JV's cost reduction was due to the wage concessions of JV's U.S.

employees, the net welfare gain/ loss for the United States would equal $ _____. If JV's cost reductions resulted from changes in work rules leading to higher worker productivity, the net welfare gain/loss for the United States would equal $ _____.

12. Table 9.10 illustrates the hypothetical demand and supply schedules of labor in the United States. Assume that labor and capital are the only two factors of production. On graph paper, plot these schedules.

TABLE 9.10

DEMAND AND SUPPLY OF LABOR

Wage ($)	Quantity Demanded	Quantity Supplied$_0$	Quantity Supplied$_1$
8	0	2	4
6	2	2	4
4	4	2	4
2	6	2	4
0	8	2	4

a. Without immigration, suppose the labor force in the United States is denoted by schedule S_0. The equilibrium wage rate is $ _____; payments to native U.S. workers total $ _____, while payments to U.S. capital owners equal $ _____.

b. Suppose immigration from Hong Kong results in an overall increase in the U.S. labor force to S_1. Wages would rise/fall to $ _____, payments to native U.S. workers would total $ _____, and payments to Hong Kong immigrants would total $ _____. U.S. owners of capital would receive payments of $ _____.

c. Which U.S. factor of production would gain from expanded immigration? Which U.S. factor of production would likely resist policies permitting Hong Kong workers to freely migrate to the United States?

International Finance

19

YOSHIKAZU TSUNO/AFP/Getty Images

- ○ How can the United States export more than nearly any other country yet still have the world's highest trade deficit?
- ○ Are high trade deficits a worry?
- ○ What's the official "fudge factor" used to compute the balance of payments?
- ○ What's meant by a "strong dollar"?
- ○ Why does a nation try to influence the value of its currency?
- ○ And what's up with China?

  Answers to these and other questions are explored in this chapter, which focuses on international finance.

If Starbucks wants to buy 1,000 espresso machines from the German manufacturer, Krups, it will be quoted a price in euros. Suppose the machines cost a total of €1 million (euros). How much is that in dollars? The dollar cost will depend on the exchange rate. When trade takes place across international borders, two currencies are usually involved. Supporting the flows of goods and services are flows of currencies that fund international transactions. The exchange rate between currencies—the price of one in terms of the other—is how the price of a product in one country translates into the price facing a buyer in another country. Cross-border trade therefore depends on the exchange rate.

In this chapter we examine the market forces that affect the relative value of one currency in terms of another.

Topics discussed include:

- Balance of payments
- Trade deficits and surpluses
- Foreign exchange markets
- Purchasing power parity
- Flexible exchange rates
- Fixed exchange rates
- International monetary system
- Bretton Woods agreement
- Managed float

Balance of Payments

A country's gross domestic product, or GDP, measures the economy's income and output during a given period. To account for dealings abroad, countries must also keep track of international transactions. A country's *balance of payments,* as introduced in Chapter 3, summarizes all economic transactions during a given period between residents of that country and residents of other countries. *Residents* include people, firms, organizations, and governments.

International Economic Transactions

The balance of payments measures economic transactions between a country and the rest of the world, whether these transactions involve goods and services, real and financial assets, or transfer payments. The balance of payments measures a *flow* of transactions during a particular period, usually a year. Some transactions do not involve actual payments. For example, if *Time* magazine ships a new printing press to its Australian subsidiary, no payment is made, yet an economic transaction involving another country has occurred. Similarly, if CARE sends food to Africa or the Pentagon provides military assistance to the Middle East, these transactions must be captured in the balance of payments. So remember, although we speak of the *balance of payments,* a more descriptive phrase would be the *balance-of-economic transactions.*

Balance-of-payments accounts are maintained according to the principles of *double-entry bookkeeping.* Some entries are called *credits,* and others are called *debits.* As you will see, the balance of payments consists of several individual accounts. An individual account may not balance, but a deficit in one or more accounts must be offset by a surplus in the other accounts. Because total credits must equal total debits, there is a *balance* of payments—hence, the name. During a given period, such as a year, the inflow of receipts from the rest of the world, which are entered as credits, must equal the outflow of payments to the rest of the world, which are entered as debits.

The first of two major categories in the balance of payments is the current account. The current account records *current* flows of funds into and out of the country, including imports and exports of goods and services, net income earned by U.S. residents from foreign assets, and net transfer payments from abroad. These are discussed in turn.

The Merchandise Trade Balance

The *merchandise trade balance,* a term introduced in Chapter 3, equals the value of merchandise exports minus the value of merchandise imports. The merchandise account reflects trade in goods, or tangible products (stuff you can put in a box), like French wine or U.S. computers, and is often referred to simply as the *trade balance.* The value of U.S. merchandise exports is a credit in the U.S. balance-of-payments account because U.S. residents get *paid* for the exported goods. The value of U.S. merchandise imports is a debit in the balance-of-payments account because U.S. residents *pay* foreigners for imported goods.

If merchandise exports exceed merchandise imports, the trade balance is in *surplus.* If merchandise imports exceed merchandise exports, the trade balance is in *deficit.* The merchandise trade balance, which is reported monthly, influences foreign exchange markets, the stock market, and other financial markets. The trade balance depends on a variety of factors, including the relative strength and competitiveness of the domestic

EXHIBIT **1** U.S. Imports Have Topped Exports Since 1976, and the Trade Deficit Has Widened

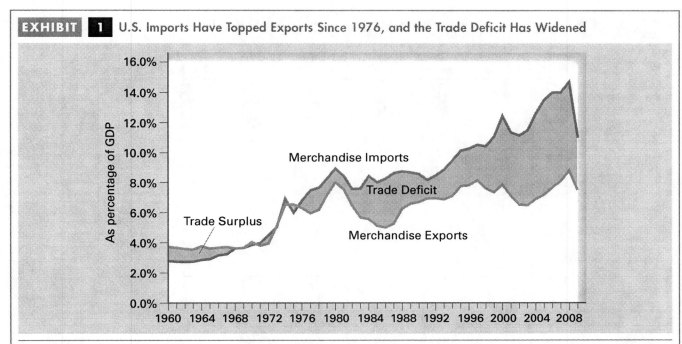

Note that since 1980, merchandise exports have remained in the range of about 5 percent to 8 percent of GDP. But merchandise imports have trended up from about 9 percent in 1980 to about 15 percent in 2008, before backing off to 11 percent in 2009, the year following the financial crisis.

Source: Developed from merchandise trade data from the *Economic Report of the President*, February 2010, and *Survey of Current Business*, 90 (June 2010), U.S. Department of Commerce. For the latest data, go to http://bea.gov.

economy compared with other economies and the relative value of the domestic currency compared with other currencies. Strong economies with growing incomes tend to buy more of everything, including imports.

U.S. merchandise trade since 1960 is depicted in Exhibit 1, where exports, the blue line, and imports, the red line, are expressed as a percentage of GDP. During the 1960s, exports exceeded imports, and the resulting trade surpluses are shaded blue. Since 1976, imports have exceeded exports, and the resulting trade deficits are shaded pink. Trade deficits as a percentage of GDP increased from 1.3 percent in 1991 to a peak of 6.3 percent in 2006. The recession of 2007–2009 slowed U.S. imports more than U.S. exports, so by 2009 the trade deficit relative to GDP fell to 3.5 percent, the lowest in more than a decade.

Because per capita income in the United States ranks among the highest in the world, the United States imports more goods from each of the world's major economies than it exports to them. Exhibit 2 shows the U.S. merchandise trade deficit with major economies or regions of the world in 2009. The $227 billion trade deficit with China was by far the largest, nearly four times that with Latin America, the European Union, or the OPEC nations. The Chinese bought $69 billion in U.S. goods in 2009, but Americans bought $296 billion in Chinese goods, or about $2,575 per U.S. household. So China sold America four times more than it bought from America. Chances are, most of the utensils in your kitchen were made in China; most toys are also Chinese made. The United States is the world's biggest importer and has a trade surplus with only a few major economies, including Australia, Brazil, and the Netherlands.

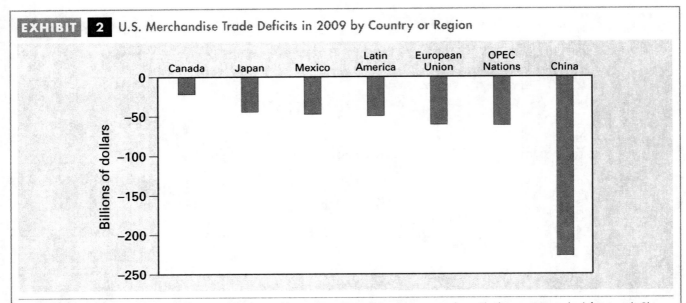

EXHIBIT **2** U.S. Merchandise Trade Deficits in 2009 by Country or Region

The United States imports more goods from each of the world's major economies than it exports to them. The largest U.S. trade deficit is with China, which exported four times more to the United States in 2009 than it imported from the United States.

Source: Developed from data in "Exports, Imports, and Trade Balance by Country and Area: 2009 Annual Totals," Exhibit 13, U.S. Bureau of Economic Analysis, 10 June 2010.

Balance on Goods and Services

The merchandise trade balance focuses on the flow of goods, but services are also traded internationally. *Services* are intangibles, such as transportation, insurance, banking, education, consulting, and tourism. Services are often called "invisibles" because they are not tangible. The value of U.S. service exports, as when an Irish tourist visits New York City, is listed as a credit in the U.S. balance-of-payments account because U.S. residents get paid for these services. The value of U.S. service imports, like computer programming outsourced to India, is listed as a debit in the balance-of-payments account because U.S. residents must pay for the imported services.

Because the United States exports more services than it imports, services have been in surplus for the last three decades. The **balance on goods and services** is the export value of goods and services minus the import value of goods and services, or *net exports*, a component of GDP.

Net Investment Income

U.S. residents earn investment income, such as interest and dividends, from assets owned abroad. This investment income flows to the United States and is a credit in the balance-of-payments account. On the other side, foreigners earn investment income on assets owned in the United States, and this payment flows out of the country. This outflow is a debit in the balance-of-payments account. **Net investment income from abroad** is U.S. investment earnings from foreign assets minus foreigners' earnings from their U.S. assets. From year to year, this figure bounces around

balance on goods and services

The portion of a country's balance-of-payments account that measures the value of a country's exports of goods and services minus the value of its imports of goods and services

net investment income from abroad

Investment earnings by U.S. residents from their foreign assets minus investment earnings by foreigners from their assets in the United States

between a positive and a negative number. In 2009, net investment income from foreign holdings was $89 billion.

Unilateral Transfers and the Current Account Balance

Unilateral transfers consist of government transfers to foreign residents, foreign aid, money workers send to families abroad, personal gifts to friends and relatives abroad, charitable donations, and the like. Money sent out of the country is a debit in the balance-of-payments account. For example, immigrants in the United States often send money to families back home. **Net unilateral transfers abroad** equal the unilateral transfers received from abroad by U.S. residents minus unilateral transfers sent to foreign residents by U.S. residents. U.S. net unilateral transfers have been negative since World War II, except for 1991, when the U.S. government received sizable transfers from foreign governments to help pay their share of the Persian Gulf War. In 2009, net unilateral transfers were a negative $130.2 billion, with private transfers accounting for most of that (government grants and transfers made up the rest). Net unilateral transfers abroad averaged about $430 per U.S. resident in 2009.

The United States places few restrictions on money sent out of the country. Other countries, particularly developing countries, strictly limit the amount that may be sent abroad. More generally, many developing countries, such as China, restrict the convertibility of their currency into other currencies.

When we add net unilateral transfers to net exports of goods and services and net income from assets owned abroad, we get the **balance on current account**, which is reported quarterly. Thus, *the current account includes all international transactions in currently produced goods and services, net income from foreign assets, and net unilateral transfers.* It can be negative, reflecting a current account deficit; positive, reflecting a current account surplus; or zero.

The Financial Account

The current account records international transactions in goods, services, asset income, and unilateral transfers. The **financial account** records international purchases of assets, including financial assets, such as stocks, bonds, and bank balances, and real assets such as land, housing, factories, and other physical assets. For example, U.S. residents purchase foreign securities to earn a higher return and to diversify their portfolios. Money flows out when Americans buy foreign assets or build factories overseas. Money flows in when foreigners buy U.S. assets or build factories here. The international purchase or sale of assets is recorded in the financial account.

Between 1917 and 1982, the United States ran a financial account deficit, meaning that U.S. residents purchased more foreign assets than foreigners purchased assets from the United States. The net income from these foreign assets improved our current account balance. But in 1983, for the first time in 65 years, foreigners bought more assets in the United States than U.S. residents purchased abroad. Since 1983, foreigners have continued to buy more U.S. assets most years than the other way around, meaning there has usually been a surplus in the financial account.

By the end of 2009, foreigners owned $21.1 trillion in U.S. assets and U.S. residents owned $18.4 trillion in foreign assets. Thus, foreigners owned $2.7 trillion more assets in the United States than U.S. residents owned abroad. This is not as bad as it sounds, because foreign purchases of assets in the United States add to America's productive capacity and promote employment and labor productivity here. But the income from these assets flows to their foreign owners, not to Americans. Remember, the investment income from these assets shows up in the current account.

Deficits and Surpluses

Nations, like households, operate under a budget constraint. Spending cannot exceed income plus cash on hand and borrowed funds. We have distinguished between *current* transactions, which include exports, imports, asset income, and unilateral transfers, and *financial* transactions, which reflect purchases of foreign real and financial assets. Any surplus or deficit in one account must be offset by deficits or surpluses in other balance-of-payments accounts.

Exhibit 3 presents the U.S. balance-of-payments statement for 2009. All transactions requiring payments from foreigners to U.S. residents are entered as credits, indicated by a plus sign (+), because they result in an inflow of funds from foreign residents to U.S. residents. All transactions requiring payments to foreigners from U.S. residents are entered as debits, indicated by a minus sign (–), because they result in an outflow of funds from U.S. residents to foreign residents. As you can see, a surplus in the financial account of $197.7 billion was more than offset by a current account deficit of $419.8 billion. A *statistical discrepancy* is required to balance the payments, and that amounts to $222.1 billion. Think of the statistical discrepancy as the official "fudge factor" that (1) measures the error in the balance-of-payments and (2) satisfies the double-entry bookkeeping requirement that total debits must equal total credits. The statistical discrepancy was especially large in 2009, because the global financial crisis created unusual gyrations in international accounts.

Foreign exchange is the currency of another country needed to carry out international transactions. A country runs a deficit in its current account when the amount of foreign exchange received from exports, from foreign assets, and from unilateral transfers falls short of the amount needed to pay for imports, pay foreign holders of U.S. assets, and make unilateral transfers. If the current account is in deficit, the necessary foreign exchange must come from a net inflow in the financial account. Such an inflow

---

EXHIBIT 3   U.S. Balance of Payments for 2009 (billions of dollars)

Current Account

1. Merchandise exports	+1,045.5
2. Merchandise imports	−1,562.5
3. Merchandise trade balance (1 + 2)	−517.0
4. Service exports	+509.2
5. Service imports	−370.8
6. Goods and services balance (3 + 4 + 5)	−378.6
7. Net investment income from abroad	+89.0
8. Net unilateral transfers	−130.2
9. Current account balance (6 + 7 + 8)	−419.8

Financial Account

10. Change in U.S. owned assets abroad	−237.5
11. Change in foreign-owned assets in United States	+435.2
12. Financial account balance (10 + 11)	+197.7
13. Statistical discrepancy	+222.1
TOTAL (9 + 12 + 13)	**0.0**

Source: Computed from estimates in "U.S. International Transactions," *Survey of Current Business,* 90 (June 2010), Table F.2., p. D-61.

in the financial account could stem from borrowing from foreigners, selling domestic stocks and bonds to foreigners, selling a steel plant in Pittsburgh or a ski lodge in Aspen to foreigners, and so forth.

If a country runs a current account surplus, the foreign exchange received from exports, from foreign assets, and from unilateral transfers from abroad exceeds the amount needed to pay for imports, to pay foreign holders of U.S. assets, and to make unilateral transfers abroad. If the current account is in surplus, this excess foreign exchange results in a net outflow in the financial account through lending abroad, buying foreign stocks and bonds, buying a shoe plant in Italy or a villa on the French Riviera, and so forth.

When all transactions are considered, accounts must balance, though specific accounts usually don't. The statistical discrepancy ensures that, in the aggregate, accounts sum to zero. A deficit in a particular account should not necessarily be viewed as a source of concern, nor should a surplus be a source of satisfaction. The deficit in the U.S. current account in recent years has usually been offset by a financial account surplus. As a result, foreigners have been acquiring more claims on U.S. assets.

Foreign Exchange Rates and Markets

Now that you have some idea about international flows, we can take a closer look at the forces that determine the underlying value of the currencies involved. Let's begin by looking at exchange rates and the market for foreign exchange.

Foreign Exchange

Foreign exchange, recall, is foreign money needed to carry out international transactions. The **exchange rate** is the price measured in one country's currency of buying one unit of another country's currency. Exchange rates are determined by the interaction of the households, firms, private financial institutions, governments, and central banks that buy and sell foreign exchange. The exchange rate fluctuates to equate the quantity of foreign exchange demanded with the quantity supplied. Typically, foreign exchange is made up of bank deposits denominated in the foreign currency. When foreign travel is involved, foreign exchange often consists of foreign paper money.

exchange rate
The price measured in one country's currency of purchasing one unit of another country's currency

The foreign exchange market incorporates all the arrangements used to buy and sell foreign exchange. This market is not so much a physical place as a network of telephones and computers connecting financial centers all over the world. Perhaps you have seen pictures of foreign exchange traders in New York, Frankfurt, London, or Tokyo in front of computer screens amid a tangle of phone lines. The foreign exchange market is like an all-night diner—it never closes. A trading center is always open somewhere in the world.

We will consider the market for the euro in terms of the dollar. But first, a little more about the euro. For decades the nations of Western Europe tried to increase their economic cooperation and trade. These countries believed they would be more productive and more competitive with the United States if they acted less like many separate economies and more like the 50 United States, with a single set of trade regulations and a single currency. Imagine the hassle involved if each of the 50 states had its own currency.

In 2002, euro notes and coins entered circulation in the 12 European countries adopting the common currency. The big advantage of a common currency is that Europeans no longer have to change money every time they cross a border or trade with another country in the group. Again, the inspiration for this is the United States, arguably the most successful economy in world history.

So the euro is the common currency of the *euro zone,* as the now 16-country region is usually called. The price, or exchange rate, of the euro in terms of the dollar is the number of dollars required to purchase one euro. An increase in the number of dollars needed to purchase a euro indicates weakening, or **depreciation,** of the dollar. A decrease in the number of dollars needed to purchase a euro indicates strengthening, or **appreciation,** of the dollar. Put another way, a decrease in the number of euros needed to purchase a dollar is a depreciation of the dollar, and an increase in the number of euros needed to purchase a dollar is an appreciation of the dollar.

Because the exchange rate is usually a market price, it is determined by demand and supply: The equilibrium price is the one that equates quantity demanded with quantity supplied. To simplify the analysis, suppose that the United States and the euro zone make up the entire world, so the demand and supply for euros in international finance is the demand and supply for foreign exchange from the U.S. perspective.

The Demand for Foreign Exchange

Whenever U.S. residents need euros, they must buy them in the foreign exchange market, which could include your local bank, paying for them with dollars. Exhibit 4 depicts a market for foreign exchange—in this case, euros. The horizontal axis shows the quantity of foreign exchange, measured here in billions of euros per day. The vertical axis shows the price per unit of foreign exchange, measured here in dollars per euro. The demand curve *D* for foreign exchange shows the inverse relationship between the dollar price of the euro and the quantity of euros demanded, other things assumed constant. Assumed constant along the demand curve are the incomes and preferences of U.S. consumers, expected inflation in the United States and in the euro zone, the

currency depreciation
With respect to the dollar, an increase in the number of dollars needed to purchase one unit of foreign exchange in a flexible rate system

currency appreciation
With respect to the dollar, a decrease in the number of dollars needed to purchase one unit of foreign exchange in a flexible rate system

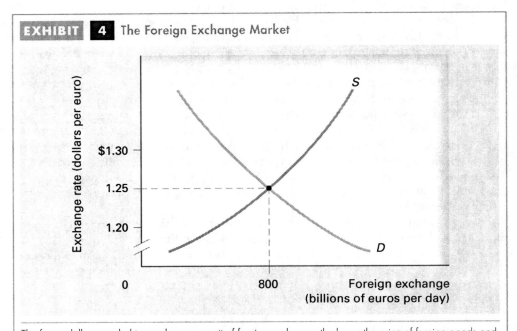

EXHIBIT **4** The Foreign Exchange Market

The fewer dollars needed to purchase one unit of foreign exchange, the lower the price of foreign goods and the greater the quantity of foreign goods demanded. Thus, the demand curve for foreign exchange slopes downward. An increase in the exchange rate makes U.S. products cheaper for foreigners. This implies an increase in the quantity of foreign exchange supplied. The supply curve of foreign exchange slopes upward.

euro price of goods in the euro zone, and interest rates in the United States and in the euro zone. U.S. residents have many reasons for demanding foreign exchange, but in the aggregate, the lower the dollar price of foreign exchange, other things constant, the greater the quantity of foreign exchange demanded.

A drop in the dollar price of foreign exchange, in this case the euro, means that fewer dollars are needed to purchase each euro, so the dollar prices of euro zone products (like German cars, Italian shoes, tickets to the Louvre, and euro zone securities), which list prices in euros, become cheaper. The cheaper it is to buy euros, the lower the dollar price of euro zone products to U.S. residents, so the greater the quantity of euros demanded by U.S. residents, other things constant. For example, a cheap enough euro might persuade you to tour Rome, climb the Austrian Alps, wander the museums of Paris, or crawl the pubs of Dublin.

The Supply of Foreign Exchange

The supply of foreign exchange is generated by the desire of foreign residents to acquire dollars—that is, to exchange euros for dollars. Euro zone residents want dollars to buy U.S. goods and services, acquire U.S. assets, make loans in dollars, or send dollars to their U.S. friends and relatives. Euros are supplied in the foreign exchange market to acquire the dollars people want. An increase in the dollar-per-euro exchange rate, other things constant, makes U.S. products cheaper for foreigners because foreign residents need fewer euros to get the same number of dollars. For example, suppose a Dell computer sells for $600. If the exchange rate is $1.20 per euro, that computer costs 500 euros; if the exchange rate is $1.25 per euro, it costs only 480 euros. The number of Dell computers demanded in the euro zone increases as the dollar-per-euro exchange rate increases, other things constant, so more euros will be supplied on the foreign exchange market to buy dollars.

The positive relationship between the dollar-per-euro exchange rate and the quantity of euros supplied on the foreign exchange market is expressed in Exhibit 4 by the upward-sloping supply curve for foreign exchange (again, euros in our example). The supply curve assumes that other things remain constant, including euro zone incomes and tastes, expectations about inflation in the euro zone and in the United States, and interest rates in the euro zone and in the United States.

Determining the Exchange Rate

Exhibit 4 brings together the demand and supply for foreign exchange to determine the exchange rate. At a rate of $1.25 per euro, the quantity of euros demanded equals the quantity supplied—in our example, 800 billion euros per day. Once achieved, this equilibrium rate will remain constant until a change occurs in one of the factors that affect supply or demand. If the exchange rate is allowed to adjust freely, or to *float,* in response to market forces, the market will clear continually, as the quantities of foreign exchange demanded and supplied are equated.

What if the initial equilibrium is upset by a change in one of the underlying forces that affect demand or supply? For example, suppose higher U.S. incomes increase American demand for all normal goods, including those from the euro zone. This shifts the U.S. demand curve for foreign exchange to the right, as Americans buy more Italian marble, Dutch chocolate, German machines, Parisian vacations, and euro zone securities.

This increased demand for euros is shown in Exhibit 5 by a rightward shift of the demand curve for foreign exchange. The demand increase from D to D' leads to an increase in the exchange rate per euro from $1.25 to $1.27. Thus, the euro increases in

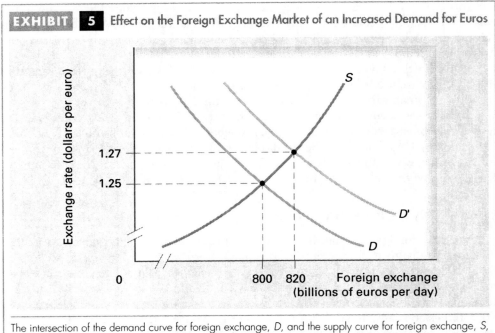

EXHIBIT 5   Effect on the Foreign Exchange Market of an Increased Demand for Euros

The intersection of the demand curve for foreign exchange, *D*, and the supply curve for foreign exchange, *S*, determines the exchange rate. At an exchange rate of $1.25 per euro, the quantity of euros demanded equals the quantity supplied. An increase in the demand for euros from *D* to *D'* increases the exchange rate from $1.25 to $1.27 per euro.

value, or appreciates, while the dollar falls in value, or depreciates. An increase in U.S. income should not affect the euro supply curve, though it does increase the *quantity of euros supplied.* The higher exchange value of the euro prompts those in the euro zone to buy more American products and assets, which are now cheaper in terms of the euro.

To Review: Any increase in the demand for foreign exchange or any decrease in its supply, other things constant, increases the number of dollars required to purchase one unit of foreign exchange, which is a depreciation of the dollar. On the other hand, any decrease in the demand for foreign exchange or any increase in its supply, other things constant, reduces the number of dollars required to purchase one unit of foreign exchange, which is an appreciation of the dollar.

Arbitrageurs and Speculators

Exchange rates between two currencies are nearly identical at any given time in markets around the world. For example, the dollar price of a euro is the same in New York, Frankfurt, Tokyo, London, Zurich, Hong Kong, Istanbul, and other financial centers. **Arbitrageurs**—dealers who take advantage of any difference in exchange rates between markets by buying low and selling high—ensure this equality. Their actions help to equalize exchange rates across markets. For example, if one euro costs $1.24 in New York but $1.25 in Frankfurt, an arbitrageur could buy, say, $1,000,000 worth of euros in New York and at the same time sell them in Frankfurt for $1,008,065, thereby earning $8,065 minus the transaction costs of the trades.

Because an arbitrageur buys and sells simultaneously, little risk is involved. In our example, the arbitrageur increased the demand for euros in New York and increased

arbitrageur
Someone who takes advantage of temporary geographic differences in the exchange rate by simultaneously purchasing a currency in one market and selling it in another market

the supply of euros in Frankfurt. These actions increased the dollar price of euros in New York and decreased it in Frankfurt, thereby squeezing down the difference in exchange rates. Exchange rates may still change because of market forces, but they tend to change in all markets simultaneously.

The demand and supply of foreign exchange arises from many sources—from importers and exporters, investors in foreign assets, central banks, tourists, arbitrageurs, and speculators. **Speculators** buy or sell foreign exchange in hopes of profiting by trading the currency at a more favorable exchange rate later. By taking risks, speculators aim to profit from market fluctuations—they try to buy low and sell high. In contrast, arbitrageurs take less risk, because they *simultaneously* buy currency in one market and sell it in another.

Finally, people in countries suffering from economic and political turmoil, such as occurred in Russia, Indonesia, the Philippines, and Zimbabwe, may buy *hard* currency as a hedge against the depreciation and instability of their own currencies. The dollar has long been accepted as an international medium of exchange. It is also the currency of choice in the world markets for oil and illegal drugs. But the euro eventually may challenge that dominance, in part because the largest euro denomination, the 500 euro note, is worth about six times the largest U.S. denomination, the $100 note. So it would be six times easier to smuggle euro notes than U.S. notes of equal value.

speculator
Someone who buys or sells foreign exchange in hopes of profiting from fluctuations in the exchange rate over time

Purchasing Power Parity

As long as trade across borders is unrestricted and as long as exchange rates are allowed to adjust freely, the **purchasing power parity (PPP) theory** predicts that the exchange rate between two currencies will adjust in the long run to reflect price differences between the two currency regions. *A given basket of internationally traded goods should therefore sell for about the same around the world (except for differences reflecting transportation costs and the like).* Suppose a basket of internationally traded goods that sells for $10,000 in the United States sells for €8,000 in the euro zone. According to the purchasing power parity theory, the equilibrium exchange rate should be $1.25 per euro. If this were not the case—if the exchange rate were, say, $1.20 per euro—then you could exchange $9,600 for €8,000, with which you buy the basket of commodities in the euro zone. You could then sell that basket of goods in the States for $10,000, yielding you a profit of $400 minus any transaction costs. Selling dollars and buying euros will also drive up the dollar price of euros.

purchasing power parity (PPP) theory
The idea that the exchange rate between two countries will adjust in the long run to equalize the cost between the countries of a basket of internationally traded goods

The purchasing power parity theory is more of a long-run predictor than a day-to-day indicator of the relationship between changes in the price level and the exchange rate. For example, a country's currency generally appreciates when inflation is low compared with other countries and depreciates when inflation is high. Likewise, a country's currency generally appreciates when its real interest rates are higher than those in the rest of the world, because foreigners are more willing to buy and hold investments denominated in that high-interest currency. As a case in point, the dollar appreciated during the first half of the 1980s, when real U.S. interest rates were relatively high, and depreciated during 2002 to 2004, when real U.S. interest rates were relatively low.

Because of trade barriers, central bank intervention in exchange markets, and the fact that many products are not traded or are not comparable across countries, the purchasing power parity theory usually does not explain exchange rates at a particular point in time that well. For example, if you went shopping in Switzerland tomorrow, you would soon notice a dollar does not buy as much there as it does in the United States. The following case study considers the purchasing power parity theory based on the price of Big Macs around the globe.

CASE STUDY

e activity

You will need a subscription
to search The Economist's
archive at http://www.
economist.com/. But you can
register for a complimentary
14-day pass and then search
for the Big Mac Index. Read
the article by Nicholas Vardy
at http://seekingalpha.com/
article/26635-burgernomics-
profiting-from-the-bigmac-
index. What weaknesses does
Vardy say the Big Mac Index
has, and why do economists
still use it? Another article
at http://www.comsec.com.
au/public/news.aspx?id=809
states The Economist should
replace the Big Mac Index with
the iPod Index. Do you agree?

BRINGING THEORY TO LIFE

The Big Mac Index   As you have already learned, the PPP theory predicts that in the long run the exchange rate between two currencies should move toward equalizing the cost in each country of an identical basket of internationally traded goods. A lighthearted test of the theory has been developed by *The Economist* magazine, which compares prices around the world for a "market basket" consisting simply of one McDonald's Big Mac—a product that, though not internationally traded, is essentially the same in more than 100 countries. *The Economist* begins with the price of a Big Mac in the local currency and then converts that price into dollars based on the exchange rate prevailing at the time. A comparison of the dollar price of Big Macs across countries offers a crude test of the PPP theory, which predicts that prices should be roughly equal in the long run.

Exhibit 6 lists the dollar price of a Big Mac in March 2010, in 22 surveyed countries plus the euro zone average. By comparing the price of a Big Mac in the United States (shown as the green bar) with prices in other countries, we can derive a crude measure of whether particular currencies, relative to the dollar, are overvalued (red bars) or undervalued (blue bars). For example, because the price of a Big Mac in Norway, at $6.87, was 92 percent higher than the U.S. price of $3.58, the Norwegian krone was the most overvalued relative to the dollar of the countries listed. But Big Macs were cheaper in most of the countries surveyed. The cheapest was in China, where $1.83 was 49 percent below the U.S. price. Hence, the Chinese yuan was the most undervalued relative to the dollar.

Thus, Big Mac prices in March 2010 ranged from 92 percent above to 49 percent below the U.S. price. The euro was 29 percent overvalued. The price range lends little

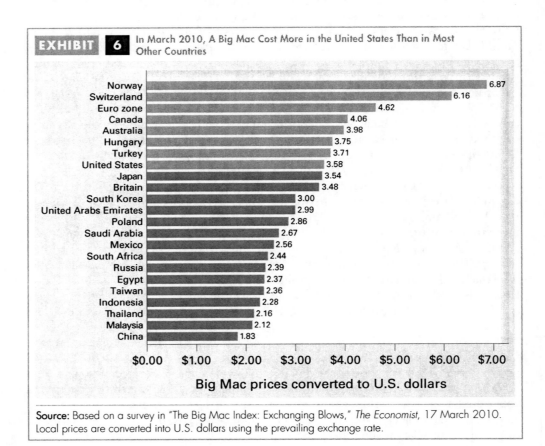

EXHIBIT 6   In March 2010, A Big Mac Cost More in the United States Than in Most Other Countries

Big Mac prices converted to U.S. dollars

Norway	6.87
Switzerland	6.16
Euro zone	4.62
Canada	4.06
Australia	3.98
Hungary	3.75
Turkey	3.71
United States	3.58
Japan	3.54
Britain	3.48
South Korea	3.00
United Arabs Emirates	2.99
Poland	2.86
Saudi Arabia	2.67
Mexico	2.56
South Africa	2.44
Russia	2.39
Egypt	2.37
Taiwan	2.36
Indonesia	2.28
Thailand	2.16
Malaysia	2.12
China	1.83

Source: Based on a survey in "The Big Mac Index: Exchanging Blows," *The Economist*, 17 March 2010. Local prices are converted into U.S. dollars using the prevailing exchange rate.

support to the PPP theory, but that theory relates only to traded goods. The Big Mac is not traded internationally. Part of the price of a Big Mac must cover rent, which can vary substantially across countries. Taxes and trade barriers, such as tariffs and quotas on beef, may also distort local prices. And wages differ across countries, with a McDonald's worker averaging about $8 an hour in the United States versus more like $1 an hour in China. So there are understandable reasons why Big Mac prices differ across countries.

Sources: "The Big Mac Index: Exchanging Blows," *The Economist*, 17 March 2010; David Parsley and Shang-Jin Wei, "In Search of a Euro Effect: Big Lessons from a Big Mac Meal?" *Journal of International Money and Finance*, 27 (March 2008): 260–276; Ali Kutan et al., "Toward Solving the PPP Puzzle: Evidence from 113 Countries," *Applied Economics*, 41 (Issue 24, 2009): 3057–3066; and the McDonald's Corporation international Web site at http://www.mcdonalds.com.

Flexible Exchange Rates

For the most part, we have been discussing a system of **flexible exchange rates**, which are determined by demand and supply. Flexible, or *floating*, exchange rates adjust continually to the myriad forces that buffet foreign exchange markets. Consider how the exchange rate is linked to the balance-of-payments accounts. Debit entries in the current or financial accounts increase the demand for foreign exchange, resulting in a depreciation of the dollar. Credit entries in these accounts increase the supply of foreign exchange, resulting in an appreciation of the dollar.

flexible exchange rate Rate determined in foreign exchange markets by the forces of demand and supply without government intervention

Fixed Exchange Rates

When exchange rates are flexible, governments usually have little direct role in foreign exchange markets. But if governments try to set exchange rates, active and ongoing central bank intervention is often necessary to establish and maintain these **fixed exchange rates**. Suppose the European Central Bank selects what it thinks is an appropriate rate of exchange between the dollar and the euro. It attempts to *fix,* or to *peg*, the exchange rate within a narrow band around the particular value selected. If the euro threatens to climb above the maximum acceptable exchange rate, monetary authorities must sell euros and buy dollars, thereby keeping the dollar price of the euro down. Conversely, if the euro threatens to drop below the minimum acceptable exchange rate, monetary authorities must sell dollars and buy euros. This increased demand for the euro will keep its value up relative to the dollar. Through such intervention in the foreign exchange market, monetary authorities try to stabilize the exchange rate, keeping it within the specified band.

fixed exchange rate Rate of exchange between currencies pegged within a narrow range and maintained by the central bank's ongoing purchases and sales of currencies

If monetary officials must keep selling foreign exchange to keep the value of their domestic currency from falling, they risk running out of foreign exchange reserves. Faced with this threat, the government has several options for eliminating the exchange rate disequilibrium. First, the pegged exchange rate can be increased, meaning that foreign currency costs more in terms of the domestic currency. This is a **devaluation** of the domestic currency. (A decrease in the pegged exchange rate is called a **revaluation**.) Second, the government can reduce the domestic demand for foreign exchange directly by imposing restrictions on imports or on financial outflows. Many developing countries do this. Third, the government can adopt policies to slow the domestic economy, increase interest rates,

currency devaluation An increase in the official pegged price of foreign exchange in terms of the domestic currency

currency revaluation A reduction in the official pegged price of foreign exchange in terms of the domestic currency

or reduce inflation relative to that of the country's trading partners, thereby indirectly decreasing the demand for foreign exchange and increasing the supply of foreign exchange. Several Asian economies, such as South Korea and Indonesia, pursued such policies to stabilize their currencies. Finally, the government can allow the disequilibrium to persist and ration the available foreign reserves through some form of foreign exchange control.

This concludes our introduction to the theories of international finance. Let's examine international finance in practice.

Development of the International Monetary System

gold standard
An arrangement whereby the currencies of most countries are convertible into gold at a fixed rate

From 1879 to 1914, the international financial system operated under a **gold standard**, whereby the major currencies were convertible into gold at a fixed rate. For example, the U.S. dollar could be redeemed at the U.S. Treasury for one-twentieth of an ounce of gold. The British pound could be redeemed at the British Exchequer, or treasury, for one-fourth of an ounce of gold. Because each British pound could buy five times as much gold as each dollar, one British pound exchanged for $5.

The gold standard provided a predictable exchange rate, one that did not vary as long as currencies could be redeemed for gold at the announced rate. But the money supply in each country was determined in part by the flow of gold between countries, so each country's monetary policy was influenced by the supply of gold. A balance-of-payments deficit resulted in a loss of gold, which theoretically caused a country's money supply to shrink. A balance-of-payments surplus resulted in an influx of gold, which theoretically caused a country's money supply to expand. The supply of money throughout the world also depended on the vagaries of gold discoveries. When gold production did not keep pace with the growth in economic activity, the price level dropped. When gold production exceeded the growth in economic activity, the price level rose. For example, gold discoveries in Alaska and South Africa in the late 1890s expanded the U.S. money supply, leading to inflation.

The Bretton Woods Agreement

During World War I, many countries could no longer convert their currencies into gold, and the gold standard eventually collapsed, disrupting international trade during the 1920s and 1930s. Once an Allied victory in World War II appeared certain, the Allies met in Bretton Woods, New Hampshire, in July 1944 to formulate a new international monetary system. Because the United States had a strong economy and was not ravaged by the war, the dollar was selected as the key reserve currency in the new international monetary system. All exchange rates were fixed in terms of the dollar, and the United States, which held most of the world's gold reserves, stood ready to convert foreign holdings of dollars into gold at a rate of $35 per ounce. Even though the rate that dollars could be exchanged for gold was fixed by the Bretton Woods agreement, *other* countries could adjust *their* exchange rates relative to the U.S. dollar if they found a chronic disequilibrium in their balance of payments—that is, if a country faced a large and persistent deficit or surplus.

International Monetary Fund (IMF)

An international organization that establishes rules for maintaining the international monetary system and makes loans to countries with temporary balance-of-payments problems

The Bretton Woods agreement also created the **International Monetary Fund (IMF)** to set rules for maintaining the international monetary system, to standardize financial reporting for international trade, and to make loans to countries with temporary balance-of-payments problems. The IMF lends a revolving fund of about $250 billion to economies in need of reserves; there are plans to double that. Headquartered in

Washington, D.C., the IMF has 186 member countries and a staff of 2,400 drawn from around the world (half the staff members are economists).

The Demise of the Bretton Woods System

During the latter part of the 1960s, inflation increased in the United States more than in other countries. Because of U.S. inflation, the dollar had become *overvalued* at the official exchange rate, meaning that the gold value of the dollar exceeded the exchange value of the dollar. In 1971, U.S. merchandise imports exceeded merchandise exports for the first time since World War II. Foreigners exchanged dollars for gold. To stem this gold outflow, the United States stopped exchanging gold for dollars, but this just made the dollar less attractive. In December 1971, the world's 10 richest countries met in Washington and devalued the dollar by 8 percent. They hoped this devaluation would put the dollar on firmer footing and would save the "dollar standard." With prices rising at different rates around the world, however, an international monetary system based on fixed exchange rates was doomed.

When the U.S. trade deficit tripled in 1972, it became clear that the dollar was still overvalued. In early 1973, the dollar was devalued another 10 percent, but this did not quiet foreign exchange markets. The dollar, for three decades the anchor of the international monetary system, suddenly looked vulnerable, and speculators began betting that the dollar would fall even more, so they sold dollars. Dollars were exchanged for German marks because the mark appeared to be the most stable currency. Bundesbank, Germany's central bank, tried to defend the dollar's official exchange rate by selling marks and buying dollars. Why didn't Germany want the mark to appreciate? Appreciation would make German goods more expensive abroad and foreign goods cheaper in Germany, thereby reducing German exports and increasing German imports. So the mark's appreciation would reduce German output and employment. But after selling $10 billion worth of marks, the Bundesbank gave up defending the dollar. As soon as the value of the dollar was allowed to float against the mark, the Bretton Woods system, already on shaky ground, collapsed.

The Current System: Managed Float

The Bretton Woods system has been replaced by a **managed float system**, which combines features of a freely floating exchange rate with sporadic intervention by central banks as a way of moderating exchange rate fluctuations among the world's major currencies. Most small countries, particularly developing countries, still peg their currencies to one of the major currencies (such as the U.S. dollar) or to a "basket" of major currencies. What's more, in developing countries, private international borrowing and lending are severely restricted; some governments allow residents to purchase foreign exchange only for certain purposes. In some countries, different exchange rates apply to different categories of transactions.

managed float system An exchange rate system that combines features of freely floating rates with sporadic intervention by central banks

Critics of flexible exchange rates argue that they are inflationary, because they free monetary authorities to pursue expansionary policies; and flexible exchange rates have often been volatile. This volatility creates uncertainty and risk for importers and exporters, increasing the transaction costs of international trade. Furthermore, exchange rate volatility can lead to wrenching changes in the competitiveness of a country's export sector. These changes cause swings in employment, resulting in louder calls for import restrictions. For example, the exchange rate between the Japanese yen and the U.S. dollar has been relatively unstable, particularly because of international speculation.

Policy makers are always on the lookout for a system that will perform better than the current managed float system, with its fluctuating currency values. *Their ideal is a system that will foster international trade, lower inflation, and promote a more stable world economy.* International finance ministers have acknowledged that the world must find an international standard and establish greater exchange rate stability.

The current system also allows some countries to manipulate their currencies to stimulate exports and discourage imports, as discussed in the following case study about China.

CASE STUDY

e activity

The New York Times reviews the basics of the U.S.-China exchange rate at http://www.nytimes.com/2010/09/19/weekinreview/19chan.html. The Bank of China publishes up-to-date exchange rates at http://www.boc.cn/sourcedb/whpj/enindex.html.

WORLD OF BUSINESS

What about China?　The U.S. trade deficit with China of $227 billion in 2009 exceeded America's combined deficits with the European Union, OPEC countries, and Latin America. The deficit with China grew about 15 percent annually between 2000 and 2009. Americans spend four times more on Chinese products than the Chinese spend on American products. Between 2007 and 2010, China's holdings of U.S. Treasury securities more than doubled from $400 billion to $900 billion.

Many economists, politicians, and union officials argue that China manipulates its currency, the yuan, to keep Chinese products cheaper abroad and foreign products more expensive at home. This stimulates Chinese exports and discourages imports, thereby boosting Chinese production and jobs. At the same time, the average Chinese consumer is poorer because the yuan buys fewer foreign products.

As we have seen, any country that establishes a fixed exchange rate that undervalues or overvalues the currency must intervene continuously to maintain that rate. Thus, if the official exchange rate has chronically undervalued the Chinese yuan relative to the dollar, as appears to be the case, then Chinese authorities must continuously exchange yuan for dollars in foreign exchange markets. The increased supply of yuan keeps the yuan down, and the increased demand for dollars keeps the dollar up.

But the charge that China manipulates its currency goes beyond simply depressing the yuan and boosting the dollar. China's trading partners increasingly feel they are being squeezed out by Chinese producers without gaining access to Chinese markets. China seeks every trade advantage, especially for the 125 state-owned enterprises run directly by the central government. For example, China offers some domestic producers tax rebates and subsidies to promote exports, while imposing quotas and tariffs to discourage imports, such as a 25 percent tariff on auto-parts imports.

China has tried to soothe concerns about the trade deficit. Most importantly, Chinese authorities in 2005 began allowing the yuan to rise modestly against the dollar. As a result, the yuan rose a total of 20 percent against the dollar between July 2005 and July 2010. China also announced plans to cut tax rebates paid to its exporters and to lower some import duties. But these measures seem to have had little effect on America's monster deficit with China.

Prior to an international finance meeting in June 2010, a key European Central Bank official said "the rigidity of the Chinese monetary regime had slowed down the recovery in the developed world." Facing political pressure to do something, China announced that it would allow the exchange rate to become more flexible. We'll see.

© Annie Reynolds/PhotoLink/Getty Images

Sources: Lee Branstetter and Nicholas Lardy, "China's Embrace of Globalization," NBER Working Paper 12373 (July 2006); Jason Dean and Shen Hong, "China Central Bank Tames Yuan Appreciation Hopes," *Wall Street Journal*, 22 June 2010; Yujan Zhang, "China Steel Group Accuses U.S. Lawmakers of Protectionism," *Wall Street Journal*, 5 July 2010; and Michael Casey, "Showdown Looms Over China's Currency at G-20," *Wall Street Journal*, 11 June 2010.

Conclusion

The United States is very much a part of the world economy, not only as the largest exporter nation but also as the largest importer nation. Although the dollar remains the unit of transaction in many international settlements—OPEC, for example, still states oil prices in dollars—gyrations of exchange rates have made those involved in international finance wary of putting all their eggs in one basket. The international monetary system is now going through a difficult period as it gropes for a new source of stability four decades after the collapse of the Bretton Woods agreement.

Summary

1. The balance of payments reflects all economic transactions between one country and the rest of the world. The current account measures flows from (a) goods; (b) services, including consulting and tourism; (c) income from foreign assets; and (d) unilateral transfers, or public and private transfer payments to and from foreign residents. The financial account measures international transactions in real and financial assets.

2. Foreign exchange pays for transactions across international borders. In the absence of government intervention, the demand and supply of foreign exchange determines the market exchange rate. According to the theory of purchasing power parity (PPP), the exchange rate between two countries will adjust in the long run to equalize the cost between the countries of a basket of internationally traded goods.

3. Under a system of flexible, or floating, exchange rates, the value of the dollar relative to foreign exchange varies with market forces. An increase in the demand for foreign exchange or a decrease in its supply, other things constant, increases the value of foreign exchange relative to the dollar, which is a depreciation of the dollar. Conversely, a decrease in the demand for foreign exchange or an increase in its supply, other things constant, decreases the value of foreign exchange relative to the dollar, which is an appreciation of the dollar.

4. Under a system of fixed exchange rates, monetary authorities try to stabilize the exchange rate, keeping it between a specified ceiling and floor value. A country may try to hold down the value of its currency, so that exports will be cheaper to foreigners and imports will cost more to domestic consumers. One objective here is to increase domestic production and employment.

5. For much of the twentieth century, the international monetary system was based on fixed exchange rates. A managed float system has been in effect for the major currencies since the demise of the Bretton Woods system in the early 1970s. Although central banks often try to stabilize exchange rates, fluctuations in rates persist. These fluctuations usually reflect market forces but they still raise the transaction costs of international trade and finance.

Key Concepts

Questions for Review

1. BALANCE OF PAYMENTS   Suppose the United States ran a surplus in its balance on goods and services by exporting goods and services while importing nothing.

   a. How would such a surplus be offset elsewhere in the balance-of-payments accounts?

   b. If the level of U.S. production does not depend on the balance on goods and services, how would running this surplus affect our *current* standard of living?

   c. What is the relationship between total debits and total credits in the balance on goods and services?

d. When all international economic transactions are considered, what must be true about the sum of debits and credits?

e. What is the role of the statistical discrepancy?

2. FOREIGN EXCHANGE   What is the difference between a depreciation of the dollar and a devaluation of the dollar?

3. ARBITRAGEURS   How do arbitrageurs help ensure that exchange rates are the same in markets around the world?

4. PURCHASING POWER PARITY   According to the theory of purchasing power parity, what will happen to the value of the dollar (against foreign currencies) if the U.S. price level doubles and price levels in other countries remain constant? Why is the theory more suitable for analyzing events in the long run?

5. Case Study: The Big Mac Index   The Big Mac Index computed by the *Economist* magazine has consistently found the U.S. dollar

to be undervalued against some currencies and overvalued against others. This finding seems to call for a rejection of the purchasing power parity theory. Explain why this index may not be a valid test of the theory.

6. THE CURRENT SYSTEM: MANAGED FLOAT   What is a managed float? What are the disadvantages of freely floating exchange rates that led countries to the managed float system?

7. MERCHANDISE TRADE BALANCE   Explain why a U.S. recession that occurs as the rest of the world is expanding will tend to reduce the U.S. trade deficit.

8. Case Study: What about China?   Why would China want its own currency to be undervalued relative to the U.S. dollar? How does China maintain an undervalued currency?

Problems and Exercises

9. BALANCE OF PAYMENTS   The following are hypothetical data for the U.S. balance of payments. Use the data to calculate each of the following:

a. Merchandise trade balance
b. Balance on goods and services
c. Balance on current account
d. Financial account balance
e. Statistical discrepancy

	Billions of Dollars
Merchandise exports	350.0
Merchandise imports	2,425.0
Service exports	2,145.0
Service imports	170.0
Net income and net transfers	221.5
Outflow of U.S. capital	245.0
Inflow of foreign capital	100.0

10. BALANCE OF PAYMENTS   Explain where in the U.S. balance of payments an entry would be recorded for each of the following:

a. A Hong Kong financier buys some U.S. corporate stock.
b. A U.S. tourist in Paris buys some perfume to take home.
c. A Japanese company sells machinery to a pineapple company in Hawaii.

d. U.S. farmers make a gift of food to starving children in Ethiopia.
e. The U.S. Treasury sells a bond to a Saudi Arabian prince.
f. A U.S. tourist flies to France on Air France.
g. A U.S. company sells insurance to a foreign firm.

11. DETERMINING THE EXCHANGE RATE   Use these data to answer the following questions about the market for British pounds:

Pound Price (in $)	Quantity Demanded (of pounds)	Quantity Supplied (of pounds)
$4.00	50	100
3.00	75	75
2.00	100	50

a. Draw the demand and supply curves for pounds, and determine the equilibrium exchange rate (dollars per pound).
b. Suppose that the supply of pounds doubles. Draw the new supply curve.
c. What is the new equilibrium exchange rate?
d. Has the dollar appreciated or depreciated?
e. What happens to U.S. imports of British goods?

Global Economic Watch Exercises

Login to www.cengagebrain.com and access the Global Economic Watch to do these exercises.

12. GLOBAL ECONOMIC WATCH   Go to the Global Economic Crisis Resource Center. Select Global Issues in Context. In the Basic Search box at the top of the page, enter the phrase "China's exchange rate reform." On the Results page, go to the News Section. Click on the link for the July 30, 2010, article "China's Exchange Rate Reform on Right Track." What is China's exchange rate policy?

13. GLOBAL ECONOMIC WATCH   Go to the Global Economic Crisis Resource Center. Select Global Issues in Context. In the Basic Search box at the top of the page, enter the phrase "foreign exchange." From the past two years, choose one article about a foreign country. What did you learn about international finance in that country?

CHAPTER 21

Global Financial Markets

Stock Exchanges Around the World

Locations of stock exchanges range from Johannesburg to Hong Kong and from Madrid to Lima. More than 130 exist to provide local companies with stock trading services. Emerging market economies in Eastern Europe and parts of Asia and advancements in technology are responsible for new exchanges and new ways of doing business.

The Prague Stock Exchange started in 1993, when Czechoslovakia separated into the Czech Republic and Slovakia. As these countries moved from a centrally planned economy under communist rule to a market economy, citizens were allowed to invest in stocks. Prague is the capital and the center of business activities in the Czech Republic. The Prague Stock Exchange started with transactions for only seven companies. Today, many companies that were previously government-controlled now issue stock. Some of the most popular are hotel and glass manufacturing companies.

In the late 1980s, World Bank consultants from Australia, Britain, Canada, and the United States gathered in Lusaka, Zambia, to create a stock exchange. The process involved reorganizing *parastatals* (government-owned companies during British colonial rule) into privately owned enterprises that sold stock. When the Lusaka Stock Exchange opened for business in February 1994, just two transactions occurred on the first trading day. Now, the exchange is positioned for regional influence attracting foreign investment from other countries in southeast Africa, such as Botswana and Malawi.

Across the continent in western Africa, the stock exchange in Ghana took 20 years to start. After other attempts failed, the stock exchange in Accra began trading in 1990 under the management of the Bank of Ghana. Within a few years, the exchange became a public company. As of 2009, the Ghana Stock Exchange allows *remote* trading, no longer requiring stockbrokers to transact business on the trading floor. The electronic trading system uses a secure Internet network. However, brokers may still conduct business on the trading floor of the exchange.

While many local stock exchanges exist, regional markets are increasing. Euronext was formed when the Paris, Brussels, and Amsterdam stock exchanges merged, and is now owned by the New York Stock Exchange. Recently, NYSE Acra Europe was developed to improve the efficiency of stock trading among eleven European countries.

Think Critically

1. How might the activities of stock exchanges differ around the world?
2. What function did stock exchanges serve as countries changed their political environment?
3. Conduct an Internet search to locate the web site for a stock exchange in another region of the world. Prepare a brief summary of the services offered and recent activities.

21-1 Global Stock Markets

GOALS

- Describe how and where stocks are bought and sold.

- Explain factors that affect stock prices.

- Identify major sources of stock market information.

©mdd, 2009/ Used under license from Shutterstock.com

Major Stock Exchanges

International companies may borrow from financial institutions; however, they also raise funds by selling stock. Stock represents a share of ownership in an organization. Stockholders are the owners of a corporation who elect the board of directors. The board hires the officers who run the company. A stock exchange is a location where stocks are bought and sold. The New York Stock Exchange (NYSE) is the largest and one of the oldest in the world. More than six billion shares of stock are traded (bought and sold) through the NYSE on a typical business day.

Started in 1792, the New York Stock Exchange was created through the efforts of 24 brokers and merchants. Five securities were traded when the NYSE started. Three were government bonds and the other two were bank stocks. Today, more than 2,000 companies are listed on the exchange. The New York Stock Exchange is operated by NYSE Euronext, which was the result of a combination of these two stock exchanges.

The stock of many multinational companies based in other countries (such as British Airways, Nestlé, Royal Dutch/Shell, and Sony Corporation) is bought and sold on the New York Stock Exchange.

In addition to the NYSE, there are other major stock exchanges around the world, including Bombay, Copenhagen, Dusseldorf, Istanbul, London, Milan, Rio de Janeiro, Seoul, Stockholm, Taiwan, Tel Aviv, Toronto, and Zurich. Figure 21-1 shows examples of three stock exchanges and lists some of the companies traded on each exchange.

MAJOR COMPANIES TRADED ON SELECTED GLOBAL STOCK EXCHANGES		
London	**Tokyo**	**Euronext**
• British Petroleum (Oil company)	• Canon (Office Automation)	• Bic (Office Supplies)
• Rolls-Royce (Aerospace/Defense)	• Mazda (Auto—Car/Light Truck)	• Carrefour (Food—Retail)
• Tesco (Food—Retail)	• Nippon Steel (Steel Producer)	• Michelin (Rubber—Tires)
• Unilever (Food-Misc)	• Sony (Audio/Video Products)	• Renault (Auto—Car/Light Truck)

Figure 21-1 Stocks exchanges provide a location where shares of stock are bought and sold.

In total, more than 130 stock exchanges are in operation around the world. These include several in the African countries of Botswana, Ghana, Ivory Coast, Kenya, Namibia, Nigeria, and Zimbabwe. Many of these stock markets started very small, with stock of less than 20 companies traded.

✓ CheckPoint
What does a share of stock represent?

The Stock Market in Action

Every hour of the day, investors buy and sell stocks. On the trading floor of the stock exchange and through computer systems, representatives of buyers and sellers interact to determine the prices of shares of stock. Figure 21-2 summarizes the main steps involved in a stock transaction.

The purchase of stock through a stock exchange commonly involves a stockbroker. A stockbroker is a person who buys and sells stocks and other investments for customers. *Full-service brokers* also provide information about current stock market trends and other types of investments.

Fear of the stock market keeps many people from investing in it. Access the web site shown below and click on the link for Chapter 21. Explore the web site. When you think you understand how the stock market works, click on the simulation link and then the STOCKQUEST link to experience the stock market without the risks. What companies did you choose to invest in? Do you have more confidence to invest?

www.cengage.com/school/genbus/intlbiz

Figure 21-2 Stocks are bought and sold at a stock exchange or online with prices determined by supply and demand.

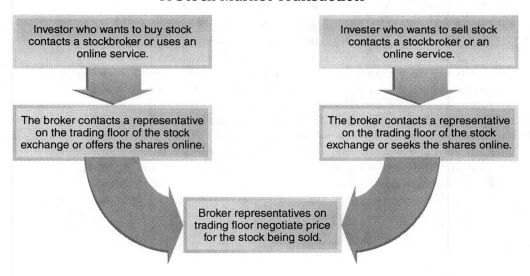

A Stock Market Transaction

Investor who wants to buy stock contacts a stockbroker or uses an online service.

Invester who wants to sell stock contacts a stockbroker or an online service.

The broker contacts a representative on the trading floor of the stock exchange or offers the shares online.

The broker contacts a representative on the trading floor of the stock exchange or seeks the shares online.

Broker representatives on trading floor negotiate price for the stock being sold.

To save money on transaction fees, investors have other choices. *Discount brokers* provide less service than full-service brokers and do not provide as much information and investment research assistance. *Online trading services*, such as E*trade and Ameritrade, charge investors low-cost commission fees.

Completely *computerized* stock trading stock exchanges, without trading floor representatives, are common today. These high-speed, low-cost automated systems are used by most major stock exchanges in Europe and Canada. Some of the world's largest screen-based systems for buying and selling global stocks are based in Europe. Computerized stock trading allows a broker in London to buy and sell stocks of multinational companies listed on stock exchanges in Bombay, Istanbul, Rio de Janeiro, Seoul, or Taiwan anytime, day or night.

✓ CheckPoint

What are the differences between full-service brokers, discount brokers, and online trading services?

COMMUNICATION ACROSS BORDERS

THE CHAMELEON-LIKE SAUDI FINANCIERS

Like chameleons, Saudi Arabian financiers often change their appearance to reflect their surroundings. In other words, they try to blend in with the prevailing dress of their current location. At home, they typically wear traditional Saudi business dress. It consists of a long white robe called a *thobe* and a headcloth called a *ghutra*. Abroad, unless they are in another Arab country, they often wear traditional Western business dress— a dark suit, a white shirt, and a conservatively colored tie. Occasionally, they may choose to dress in the traditional Saudi manner while engaging in business outside of their region. When this happens, Saudi Arabian financiers are trying to stand out from their surroundings.

Think Critically

1. Why is traditional Saudi business dress different from traditional Western business dress?
2. Why might Saudi Arabian financiers choose to wear the traditional business dress of their country within the Middle East?

Stock Market Price Information

Stock prices are affected by many factors. The main influence on stock prices is demand for ownership in a company based on its current and future profitability. If people believe a company is a good investment, demand will cause the stock price to rise. In contrast, as fewer investors buy the stock of a company, its stock price will decline. In addition, economic conditions, the political situation, and social trends can influence stock prices.

After an agreement on price is reached, this information becomes public. Each day millions of stocks are bought and sold. Information about current stock prices, dividends, volume, and past prices are reported online, on television, and in newspapers. Figure 21-3 presents a sample of the stock market information reported every day.

Work as a Team
Create news headlines that could cause stock prices to rise. Then create news headlines that could cause stock prices to decline.

✓ CheckPoint
What is the main influence on stock prices?

Reporting Stock Information

NYSE 52 WEEKS High	Low	Stock	Sym.	Divd.	Yild %.	PE	Vol. 100s	High	Low	Close	Net Chg.
1	2	3	4	5	6	7	8	9	10	11	12
34.85	15.14	Disney	DIS	N/A	N/A	13.7	106628	25.55	24.8	25.33	+0.38
31.14	5.73	General Electric	GE	1.24	9.14	8.6	584600	13.69	13.37	13.56	+0.02
72.01	46.37	General Mills	GIS	1.72	3.17	16.7	56232	54.6	53.91	54.22	+2.06
81.05	5.07	Macy's Inc	M	0.2	1.57	–	71009	12.95	12.39	12.77	–0.04
67	45.79	McDonalds	MCD	2	3.41	15.5	147560	59.18	58.01	58.72	–1.15
63.85	46.25	WalMart	WMT	1.09	2.15	15.2	189752	51	50.4	50.81	+0.26

Column	Explanation
1	Reports the highest price paid for one share of the stock over the past year.
2	Reports the lowest price paid for one share of the stock over the past year.
3	Lists the abbreviated name of the corporation.
4	Identifies the symbol used to report stock prices for the corporations in column 3.
5	Reports the dividends paid per share during the past 12 months.
6	Represents the yield percentage, which is the dividend divided by the current price of the stock.
7	Identifies the price-earnings ratio, which is computed by dividing the current price per share by the company's earnings (profits) per share over the last 12 months.
8	Reports the number of shares traded during the day, based on hundreds of shares.
9	States the highest price paid for one share on the trading day.
10	States the lowest price paid for one share on the trading day.
11	Reports the price paid for a share in the last stock purchase of the day.
12	Represents the difference between the price paid for the last share bought this day and the price for the last share bought on the previous trading day.

Figure 21-3 Current stock prices and other information on stock market activities are reported each business day in newspapers, on television, and online. Notice that the decimal part of the entry is set as superscript.

21-1 Assessment

REVIEW GLOBAL BUSINESS TERMS

Define each of the following terms.

1. stock exchange   **2.** stockbroker

REVIEW GLOBAL BUSINESS CONCEPTS

3. What is a stock exchange?

4. What services does a stockbroker provide?

5. What factors affect daily stock prices?

SOLVE GLOBAL BUSINESS PROBLEMS

For each of the following news items, indicate what types of companies might be affected and how (higher or lower stock prices).

6. A country announces strict regulations to protect the environment.

7. A new food-processing system keeps foods fresh without refrigeration for several weeks.

8. Families are spending more time at home rather than going out for food and entertainment.

9. Scientists discover a device that makes an electric car more practical.

THINK CRITICALLY

10. What are the risks of buying and selling stocks online?

11. Describe how changes in economic conditions (lower interest rates or higher consumer spending) might affect stock prices.

MAKE ACADEMIC CONNECTIONS

12. TECHNOLOGY Go to a web site that provides stock information to obtain the current price of shares for a company of interest to you.

13. MATH Refer to Figure 21-3 to answer the following questions.

a. What was the highest price paid for a share of McDonald's stock during the past year?

b. How many shares of Wal-Mart were traded on this business day?

c. What was the highest price paid for a share of Disney stock on this trading day?

d. What was the closing price of General Electric stock on the previous trading day?

e. If a company pays an annual dividend of $2 per share and the stock sells for $50 a share, what is the yield percentage?

21-2 Bond Markets and Other Financial Markets

©akva, 2009/ Used under license from Shutterstock.com

GOALS

- Explain how investors earn money from corporate bonds.
- Identify different types of government bonds.
- Describe the role of other global financial markets.

Corporate Bonds

A *bond* is a certificate representing money borrowed by a company or another organization to be repaid over a long period of time. The bond market helps organizations raise debt capital.

A corporate bond is a debt certificate issued by a multinational company or another corporate enterprise. Most corporate bonds in the United States are sold in amounts of $1,000. This amount is called the *face value,* or *maturity value.*

Around the world, bonds may be issued with different face values. In the United Kingdom, bonds traditionally are issued for 100 pounds sterling. In Brazil, the standard amount is 1,000 reals, while in South Africa it is 100 rand.

Two types of corporate bonds are commonly issued by companies. A mortgage bond is debt secured by a specific asset or property. The collateral for a mortgage bond may be equipment, a building, or land. A corporate bond without collateral is a debenture bond. These are unsecured debt in which the bondholder is a general creditor of the company.

The interest rate on a bond determines the income for investors. For example, a 10 percent bond would pay $100 a year in interest, calculated as follows.

Face Value × Interest Rate × Time in Years = Interest
$1,000 × 0.10 × 1 = $100

The *rate of return* on a bond is calculated by dividing the income from the investment by the cost of the investment. For example, if the annual income from a $1,000 bond is $72, the annual rate of return is 7.2 percent, as calculated below.

Annual Income ÷ Cost of Investment = Annual Rate of Return
$72 ÷ $1,000 = 0.072

Bond investors should also consider the *maturity date*. This is the point in time when the loan will be repaid. A 20-year bond, for example, means an investor will earn interest each year for 20 years. Then at the end of the 20 years, the investor will be repaid the face value. Remember, when a company issues bonds, it is borrowing money that must be repaid.

> ✓ **Check**Point
> How do investors earn money from bonds?

Government Bonds

Governments also issue bonds for example, the federal government of the United States sells treasury bonds to obtain needed funds for its operations. State and local governments in the United States also borrow by issuing municipal bonds.

FEDERAL GOVERNMENT BONDS

The U.S. government sells bonds to finance the national debt and to pay operating expenses. Three common debt instruments of the federal government are available to investors.

- Treasury bills (T-bills) are short-term borrowing instruments with maturities ranging from 91 days to 1 year.
- Treasury notes (T-notes) are intermediate-length borrowing instruments with maturities ranging from 1 to 10 years.
- Treasury bonds (T-bonds) are long-term borrowing instruments with maturities ranging from 10 to 30 years.

U.S. savings bonds are another type of federal government debt instrument. Individuals who want to save for the future commonly purchase these bonds. U.S. savings bonds are purchased at one-half of their face value (e.g., a $100 bond costs $50). The time it takes for a savings bond to grow to the maturity value will vary depending on the current interest rate paid by the U.S. Treasury Department. For a quick update on U.S. savings bonds rates and other information, visit the TreasuryDirect web site.

STATE AND LOCAL GOVERNMENT BONDS

A municipal bond is a debt certificate issued by a state or local government agency. Since most countries organize their government structures differently from the United States, municipal bonds are not common in other nations.

The major benefit of municipal bonds for U.S. investors is that the interest earned is excluded from federal income taxes. Such income, not subject to tax, is called tax-exempt income. Other types of investments, such as certain types of retirement accounts, earn tax-deferred income, which is income that will be taxed at a later date.

FOREIGN GOVERNMENT BONDS

Foreign governments use bonds to finance roads, schools, and military equipment for their nations. These bonds are categorized as external and internal.

Work as a Team
Describe situations in which governments and businesses might use bonds for financing.

- External bonds are intended for investors in other countries. The interest and principal are paid in the currency of the country in which an investor lives. For example, dollar bonds are intended for investors in the United States.
- Internal bonds are aimed at investors in the country issuing the bond and payable in the native currency. Foreign government bonds payable in several currencies are called multiple currency bonds.

The value of a foreign government bond is affected by the economic and political circumstances of the nation issuing the bond. People who invest in these bonds commonly face risks, such as varied exchange rates, currency stability, and changes in government administrations.

✓ CheckPoint

What are four types of debt instruments sold by the U.S. federal government?

A Question of Ethics

INFORMAL CURRENCY TRADERS

As you are walking the streets of Addis, Ethiopia, you need to exchange some U.S. dollars for birr. At a bank you will get 8.5 *birr* per dollar. If you do business with a street trader you will get 10 *birr* per dollar. What should you do?

Travelers have many options for exchanging currency, including banks, exchange bureaus, and travel agencies. Exchange services frequently are available at hotels, airports, railway stations, and even small shops. In many countries, another alternative exists—informal currency traders.

In some places in Ethiopia, there are money exchange kiosks. Often, they use a legitimate business enterprise, such as selling food items, as a cover for currency

exchange activities. In general, it is illegal for a person to participate in foreign exchange transactions except in banks and other authorized locations.

In Zambia, informal currency traders offer better rates for several currencies, including the U.S. dollar, the British pound, the South African rand, and the Botswana pula. It is common to see individuals offering bundles of Zimbabwean banknotes for sale on the roadside near the Zambia border with Zimbabwe. You might also find freelance currency traders in the marketplaces of larger towns and cities.

Many opportunities exist in Peru to exchange currencies in settings other than banks and other formal financial institutions. Individuals on street corners in large cities change money, mostly

involving transactions between U.S. dollars and Peruvian *sol*.

Informal currency trading is not always possible, especially in countries where strong government controls exist. In Tunisia, you are not allowed to import or export *dinars*. Transactions outside the formal financial system are forbidden. Violation can result in heavy penalties. A similar situation exists in Morocco, where no currency trading of the *dirham* outside of banks is allowed. In Thailand, currency traders must have a license issued by the Bank of Thailand.

Think Critically

Use the three guidelines for ethical analysis to examine the above situations. How does informal currency trading affect businesses, consumers, and society?

Other Financial Markets

In addition to stock and bond markets, other financial markets exist to serve companies involved in global business. These locations allow for the buying and selling of stocks, currencies, and commodities in international settings.

THE OVER-THE-COUNTER MARKET

Large companies that meet financial requirements of a stock exchange and are traded regularly are called *listed stocks*. In contrast, stocks of new and small companies are traded through computer networks.

The over-the-counter (OTC) market is a network of stockbrokers who buy and sell stocks of companies not listed on a stock exchange. The National Association of Securities Dealers Automated Quotations (NASDAQ) is the major computerized trading system for OTC stocks in the United States. Around the world other OTC markets have developed. These unlisted securities markets often involve new, innovative companies with strong potential. In Germany, the Neuer Markt trades the stocks of emerging companies in the European Union.

FOREIGN EXCHANGE MARKET

The foreign exchange market involves the buying and selling of currencies needed to pay for goods and services bought from companies in other countries. A Eurodollar is a U.S. dollar deposited in a bank outside of the United States and used in the money markets of Europe. *Eurodollars* should not be confused with the *euro*, which is the official currency of the European Union.

The term "Eurocurrency" has come to mean any money deposited in a bank outside the country of its origin and used in the money markets of Europe. These funds are used to make payments among countries for foreign trade.

FUTURES MARKET

Farmers want to get a fair price for their grain. Food companies want to avoid paying high prices for grain that will be used to make breakfast cereals and other products. By agreeing to a price now for delivery in the future (usually three or six months from now), a farmer is protected from receiving a lower price for grain. The food company is protected from higher costs.

The futures market allows investors and others to buy or sell contracts on the future prices of commodities, metals, and financial instruments. Futures markets involve contracts on corn, oats, soybeans, wheat, cattle, cocoa, sugar, oil, natural gas, gold, silver, treasury bonds, and currencies—yen, pound, euro, and Eurodollars.

✓ **Check**Point
What are the functions of the OTC, foreign exchange, and futures markets?

ISLAMIC BANKING ACTIVITIES

The influence of Islam on banking is visible today. The Arab word *sakk,* evolved into *cheque,* and today *check.* The plural is *sukak,* Arabic for "financial certificate," is viewed by many as the Islamic equivalent of a bond. After more than 200 years of colonization, most countries with a Muslim majority gained independence by the early 1980s. This resulted in banking activities based on traditions and beliefs consistent with Islamic law in the *Shari'ah.*

A foundation of this system is the prohibition of charging *riba,* the Arabic term for interest. Instead of earning interest, depositors share in the profits. While not guaranteed, savers may receive a premium called *hiba* (gift).

Riba is also forbidden when lending, but gains in the value of capital are allowed. This practice, based on the Qur'an and Hadith (teachings of the Prophet Mohammed), prevents exploitation of borrowers. "Allah will deprive usury of all blessing, but will give increase for deeds of charity" (Qur'an 2: 276). However, profit is viewed as a reward for the use of capital.

Two main financing methods are used. With *mudaraba,* a financier provides funds to the entrepreneur. In this arrangement, the financier may not influence the operations of the enterprise but receives a specified share of the profit or loss. The lender is responsible for all financial losses. The entrepreneur only loses the time and effort invested in the business. In recent years, a two-tiered mudaraba system evolved with three parties. The bank depositors are the financiers. The bank is the financial intermediary, and the entrepreneur uses the funds.

In contrast, *musharaka* involves the entrepreneur supplying a portion of the capital needed to operate the business. Profits and losses are shared based on a percentage agreed in advance. The financier in this situation may be involved in the management and operation of the enterprise.

Another fundamental principle of Islamic banking and financing is an emphasis on socially beneficial business activities. Participants are not allowed to invest in enterprises involved in alcohol, gambling, and other activities prohibited by Islamic law. This social focus, along with an emphasis on wealth creation rather than highly speculative ventures, offers a strong foundation for financial market stability. Islamic banking practices are often recognized by British banks where Muslim investors are permitted to invest funds according to their own preferences.

Think Critically

1. What are some of the basic principles of Islamic banking activities?
2. Conduct an Internet search to obtain information about the use of credit and attitudes toward borrowing in different cultures.

Photodisc/Getty Images

21-2 Assessment

REVIEW GLOBAL BUSINESS TERMS

Define each of the following terms.

1. corporate bond
2. mortgage bond
3. debenture bond
4. municipal bond
5. tax-exempt income
6. tax-deferred income
7. over-the-counter (OTC) market
8. Eurodollar
9. futures market

REVIEW GLOBAL BUSINESS CONCEPTS

10. How is the rate of return on a bond computed?
11. What are two main types of foreign government bonds?
12. What types of stocks are commonly traded on the over-the-counter (OTC) market?

SOLVE GLOBAL BUSINESS PROBLEMS

For the following corporate bond situations, calculate the amounts requested.

13. Earnings for three years of a $1,000 bond with a 7 percent interest rate.
14. Earnings for five years of a $1,000 bond with a 5.65 percent interest rate.
15. Annual rate of return from the purchase of ten $1,000 bonds with a total annual income of $860.
16. Maturity value of a $1,000 bond with a 10 percent interest rate, maturing in 6 years.

THINK CRITICALLY

17. How do changes in interest rates affect the market value of bonds?
18. Why do countries issue both internal and external bonds?
19. What are the benefits of the futures market?

MAKE ACADEMIC CONNECTIONS

20. GEOGRAPHY Create a chart showing the current market value of the natural resources of various countries, such as oil, wheat, corn, and soybeans.
21. TECHNOLOGY Use the Internet to locate online resources for international financial markets.
22. CURRENT EVENTS Use the Internet to identify three recent events around the world that had a significant effect on international financial markets.

21-3 Global Investments

©Stephen Coburn, 2009/ Used under license from Shutterstock.com

GOALS

- Describe the two major goals of investors.
- Analyze international investment opportunities.
- Identify major sources of investment information.

Investment Goals

Changing currency rates, environmental concerns, and political instability are typical in the international business environment. Just as companies attempt to make the right global business decisions, individuals want to make investments that will achieve their personal financial goals.

The long-term financial security of a person or family results from an ability to save and invest for the future. *Saving* is the storage of money for future use. In contrast, *investing* involves putting money to work in a business venture. The risks associated with investing are higher than the risks associated with saving. However, the potential returns from investing are also greater. Investing has two common goals, which are current income and long-term growth.

CURRENT INCOME

Some people depend on investment income for current living expenses. Retired people and others may need investments that provide income. These earnings may be in the form of dividends (from stocks), interest (from bonds), or rent (from real estate).

LONG-TERM GROWTH

In contrast to current income, many people invest for long-term financial security. They want funds for retirement or for their children's college education. Investors who desire long-term growth of their funds will choose investments that they hope will increase in value over time.

The earnings obtained over the long term can provide substantial wealth. A capital gain is the profit made from the resale of investments—such as

REACHING YOUR INVESTMENT GOALS

Current Income	Long-Term Growth
• Stocks paying dividends	• Growth stocks
• Savings certificates	• Raw land
• Corporate bonds	• Gold, silver
• Rental property	• Coins, stamps
	• Art, antiques

Figure 21-4 People with different investment goals select different types of investments.

stocks, bonds, or real estate. For example, land purchased in 2003 for $12,000 and sold in 2011 for $31,000 represents a capital gain of $19,000.

The growth in value of an investment can be projected with the use of future value calculations. Future value involves computations for determining the expected worth of an investment in the future.

The following example shows how future value is calculated. The n represents the number of years the investment will be earning the yield. The future value of $1,000 invested at 7 percent for two years would be calculated as follows.

$$\text{Amount Invested} \times (1 + \text{Annual Rate Earned})^n = \text{Future Value}$$
$$\$1,000 \quad \times \quad 1.07^2 \quad = \quad \$1,144.90$$

Figure 21-4 lists some of the common investments used to meet the two main investment goals of current income and long-term growth.

✓ CheckPoint
What is the difference between the two major goals of investing?

Global Investment Opportunities

Should a person invest in a gold mine in South America, real estate in the Middle East, or a computer company in Nevada? When planning to invest, people must identify potential investments and evaluate those investment opportunities.

IDENTIFYING POTENTIAL INVESTMENTS

Successful investments can result from a variety of business activities around the world. For example, as the demand for health care increases because of illness or an aging population, companies involved in medications, medical supplies, and hospital equipment may become more profitable.

News stories can be used to identify investment opportunities. When you hear a news report, ask yourself what types of companies might be affected by this news. Next, decide what type of investment would be appropriate. Investors may buy stock in the company or even start their own company. Finally, investors must select an action to take—buy, sell, or hold certain investments.

Global investment advisors recommend that investors choose a country before choosing specific companies. A nation's economic conditions and political environment strongly influence business success. Companies in the same industry (automobiles, chemicals, or electrical equipment) often perform differently depending on the country. For example, energy stocks in China may decline during a period in which Brazilian energy stocks rise.

EVALUATING INVESTMENT OPPORTUNITIES

Consider four major factors when choosing between various investments. These factors are rate of return, liquidity, taxes, and safety.

Work as a Team
Prepare a list of factors to consider when buying an international mutual fund.

Rate of Return The annual earnings for an investment are measured by the annual *rate of return,* or *yield.* This rate is the percentage of the investment cost that is earned in a year.

For example, an investment that costs $5,000 and produces an annual income of $450 has an annual rate of return of 9 percent, calculated as follows.

$$\text{Annual Income} \div \text{Cost of Investment} = \text{Rate of Return}$$
$$\$450 \div \$5,000 = 0.09$$

Liquidity Many people want to be able to obtain and use their money quickly. **Liquidity** refers to the ability to easily convert an asset into cash without a loss in value. Certain types of assets are highly liquid, such as stocks, bonds, and mutual funds. These investments have a continuing market of buyers and sellers.

In contrast, real estate, rare coins, and other collectibles have low liquidity. These assets may be difficult to sell quickly. Buyers for these investments are not always available.

A trade-off between liquidity and rate of return is common for investments. In general, assets with high liquidity have a lower return over time. Low liquidity can give you a higher rate of return over the long run.

Taxes The amount earned on an investment is frequently affected by taxes. If an investor has to pay taxes on earnings, that lowers the annual rate of return. A *tax-exempt* investment earns income that is not subject to tax. In contrast, a *tax-deferred* investment earns income that will be taxed at a later date.

Safety When making an investment, people expect their money to be available in the future. Most people want investments that minimize their chance of losing money. Generally, the higher the return expected, the higher the risk involved.

✓ CheckPoint
What four factors are usually considered before making an investment?

Investment Information Sources

Wise investing, as with any business decision, requires reliable, up-to-date information. The main sources of investment information are the news media, the Internet, financial experts, and investment information services.

News Media Business periodicals and the business section of the daily newspaper provide a readily available source of investment news. Many investors find *The Wall Street Journal, Financial Times, Business Week, Fortune, Forbes,* and *The Economist* helpful. In addition to domestic and international business, economic, and financial news, these publications feature articles on companies and product trends. Cable television channels such as CNN Financial and CNBC also provide news and data about financial markets and investment opportunities.

Internet Web sites are very important sources for investment information. The periodicals mentioned above all have web sites with news, articles, and financial data. Also, hundreds of other web sites are available to assist investors with researching, selecting, and monitoring their stocks, bonds,

Photodisc/Getty Images

mutual funds, and other investments. Some of the most useful investment web sites are those maintained by *Money* magazine, Motley Fool, and Yahoo Finance.

Financial Experts A stockbroker advises customers and sells investments. Other financial experts who provide investment recommendations and assist with purchases are bankers, personal financial planners, insurance agents, and real estate brokers.

Before acting on the advice of any investment advisor, wise investors take the following additional precautions.

- Research the investment and company using several sources.
- Talk to others who have this type of investment.
- Contact state and federal government agencies for information about the investment and the seller of the investment.
- Compare costs of the investment broker with others who provide this service.

Each year investors lose billions of dollars on phony investments. These losses are often the result of not completely understanding the investment situations they encounter. Actual losses may be even higher since, after being scammed, many consumers are too embarrassed to report their losses to government agencies. Common investment scams in recent years included fake low-cost stocks, wireless cable television partnerships, Internet services, and paging licenses.

Investment Information Services Information on the current performance and the future of stocks and bonds is published in *Value Line, Moody's Investors Service,* and *Standard & Poor's Reports.* These investment services provide financial data, current stock prices, recent company developments, and recommendations for buying and selling. Investors can find these information sources at libraries or through the organizations' web sites.

✓ **Check**Point
Who are some of the financial experts that can provide assistance with your investment decisions?

GLOBAL BUSINESS SPOTLIGHT

ONLINE INVESTING FOR EVERYONE, EVERYWHERE

The *good news*—you can be your own stockbroker. The *bad news*—you need to be careful! Online buying and selling of stocks is available to anyone with Internet access. However, you can easily make unwise choices or become a victim of a scam. Before trading stocks online, you need to understand the process, costs, and risks involved.

In the past, stock transactions involved calling a broker to place your order. Today, investors can purchase stocks through online brokerage firms such as E*trade and TD Ameritrade. Traditional brokers, such as Charles Schwab and Merrill Lynch, also provide this service for investors around the world. A stock trade that previously would have cost $100 can now be done online for a commission of as little as $5.

Think Critically

1. How do online stockbrokers affect competition and prices in the investment industry?
2. Go to the web site of a traditional broker or an online broker to obtain information about the services offered to investors. Make a list of the services you find.

REVIEW GLOBAL BUSINESS TERMS

Define each of the following terms.

1. capital gain   **2.** liquidity

Study Tools

www.cengage.com/school/genbus/intlbiz

REVIEW GLOBAL BUSINESS CONCEPTS

3. What are two common goals of investing?

4. What is the rate of return of an investment?

5. What are common sources of investment information?

SOLVE GLOBAL BUSINESS PROBLEMS

Calculate the future value of the following investments.

6. The expected value of a stock in three years that grows at 4 percent a year and has a current value of £100.

7. The future value of land in five years that costs Cr$3,000 today with an expected growth rate of 7 percent per year.

8. The future value of an antique automobile after eight years, with a current value of $12,000 and an expected growth rate of 6 percent per year.

THINK CRITICALLY

9. Describe a situation in which a person would be investing for income. Next, describe a situation in which a person would invest for long-term growth.

10. How could a person decide if a web site is a reliable source of investment information?

MAKE ACADEMIC CONNECTIONS

11. TECHNOLOGY Locate a web site that offers investment information and assistance. What types of investments might be wise choices based on the information offered on this web site?

12. MATHEMATICS What is the annual rate of return for these situations?
a. A share of stock in a company in Singapore costs $40 and has an annual dividend of $4.

b. A South African government bond costing $1,000 earns $65 interest a year.

c. An oil investment in the Middle East costs $20,000 and pays an annual income of $4,400.

CHAPTER SUMMARY

21-1 GLOBAL STOCK MARKETS

A The activities of global stock markets include providing a location or computer system for the buying and selling of shares of ownership in corporations. The New York Stock Exchange is the largest of the more than 130 exchanges around the world.

B Stock market transactions involve negotiations between broker representatives or online negotiations to agree on a price settlement between the buyer and the seller of a stock.

C Stock prices are affected by demand based on a company's expected current and future profitability. Economic conditions, the political situation, and social concerns can also affect demand for a stock.

21-2 BOND MARKETS AND OTHER FINANCIAL MARKETS

A A corporate bond is a debt certificate issued by a multinational company or another corporate enterprise. Investors earn interest on bonds.

B Government bonds are issued by the U.S. federal government, state and local governments, and foreign governments.

C The over-the-counter (OTC) market is a network of stockbrokers who buy and sell stocks of companies not listed on a stock exchange. The foreign exchange market involves the buying and selling of currencies needed to pay for goods and services bought from companies in other countries. The futures market allows investors and others to buy or sell contracts on the future prices of commodities, metals, and financial instruments.

21-3 GLOBAL INVESTMENTS

A The two major goals of investors are current income and long-term growth.

B The analysis of international investments involves identifying potential opportunities in other countries. The rate of return, liquidity, tax situation, and safety of the investment should also be considered.

C The major sources of investment information are the news media, the Internet, financial experts, and investment information services.

GLOBAL **REFOCUS**

Reread the Global Focus at the beginning of this chapter, and answer the following questions.

1. Describe global trends that might influence the growth of regional stock exchanges.

2. What actions might be taken to reduce risk when selecting stock investments of companies based in other countries?

REVIEW GLOBAL BUSINESS TERMS

Match the terms listed with the definitions.

1. Income that will be taxed at a later date.
2. A network of stockbrokers who buy and sell stocks of companies not listed on a stock exchange.
3. Income not subject to tax.
4. The ability to easily convert an asset into cash without a loss in value.
5. A corporate bond without collateral.
6. A debt certificate issued by a state or local government agency.
7. A location where stocks are bought and sold.
8. A market that allows investors and others to buy or sell contracts on the future prices of commodities, metals, and financial instruments.
9. Debt secured by a specific asset or property.
10. A U.S. dollar deposited in a bank outside of the United States and used in the money markets of Europe.
11. The profit made from the resale of investments—such as stocks, bonds, or real estate.
12. A debt certificate issued by a multinational company or another corporate enterprise.
13. A person who buys and sells stocks and other investments for customers.

a. capital gain
b. corporate bond
c. debenture bond
d. Eurodollar
e. futures market
f. liquidity
g. mortgage bond
h. municipal bond
i. over-the-counter (OTC) market
j. stockbroker
k. stock exchange
l. tax-deferred income
m. tax-exempt income

MAKE GLOBAL BUSINESS DECISIONS

14. Why are many international companies traded on the New York Stock Exchange (NYSE) as well as on stock exchanges in their home countries?
15. Why do some people use an online stockbroker instead of a full-service broker?
16. What happens when there is no buyer for shares of stock that someone wants to sell?
17. Which type of investment, stocks or bonds, involves more risk for an investor? Why?
18. Which would have less risk for an investor, a mortgage bond or a debenture bond?
19. How does a *Eurodollar* differ from a *euro*?
20. How does the futures market serve the needs of many groups of people in a country?

Photodisc/Getty Images

Photodisc/Getty Images

MAKE ACADEMIC CONNECTIONS

21. GEOGRAPHY Describe how the climate, terrain, waterways, and natural resources of a country might affect the development of a stock exchange in that nation.

22. CULTURAL STUDIES Talk to people from different countries about their attitudes toward investing. Compare your findings about what types of investments people prefer.

23. MATHEMATICS Select a company, and chart the changing price of its stock. Prepare a graph showing the closing price of a share over a three-week period. Use the library and Internet to locate news about the company and economic conditions. Prepare a short report explaining how this news has affected the company's stock price.

24. RESEARCH Locate bond prices using online or print resources. *The Wall Street Journal* or the business section of a daily newspaper are good places to start your research. Report to the class about the information included in the daily bond report.

25. TECHNOLOGY Prepare a spreadsheet or table comparing the features presented on three different web sites that provide investment information.

The GLOBAL Entrepreneur

CREATING AN INTERNATIONAL BUSINESS PLAN

Global Investment Activities

Conduct research on global investment activities based on the company and country you have been using in this continuing project, or create a new idea for your business in the same or a different country. Make use of previously collected information, and do additional research. This phase of your business plan should answer the following questions.

1. If the company is a major corporation, on what stock exchange is the company's stock traded? What is the current price of a share of the company's stock?

2. What recent economic, social, and political factors could affect the company's stock price?

3. What is the current interest rate paid on the company's bonds?

4. How might the company use other financial markets, such as the foreign exchange market or the futures market?

5. Describe actions of the company that would make it an attractive investment choice.

Prepare a written summary or present a short oral report (two or three minutes) of your findings.

Photodisc/Getty Images

Externalities and the Environment

17

- Why do people fish until the fish are gone?

- Why might environmentalists buy rights to pollute the air and water?

- How did barbed wire tame the Wild West?

- In what sense was the biggest environmental disaster in U.S. history not a negative externality?

- And how does someone else's antitheft device affect the chances that your car will get stolen?

These and other questions are answered in this chapter, which looks at externalities and the environment.

The rivers in Jakarta, Indonesia, are dead—killed by acid, alcohol, and oil. Coral reefs in the South Pacific are being ripped apart by dynamite fishing. BP's drilling accident could affect the Gulf of Mexico for years. The tropical rainforest is shrinking because of slash-and-burn claims on the land's resources. The build-up of greenhouse gases threatens to warm the oceans and near-surface air. Some streams in Colorado are still considered toxic from gold mining that ended more than a century ago. These environmental problems are all negative externalities, which result from the actions of producers or consumers that affect many others. Markets can allocate resources efficiently only as long as property rights are well defined and can be easily enforced. But property rights to clean water, air, and soil, to fish in the ocean, to peace and quiet, and to scenic vistas are hard to establish and enforce. This lack of property rights to some resources results in externalities.

Externalities may be either negative, such as air and water pollution, or positive, such as the general improvement in the civic climate that results from better education.

This chapter discusses externalities and explores how public policies can reduce negative externalities and increase positive externalities.

Topics discussed include:

- Exhaustible resources
- Renewable resources
- Common-pool problem
- Private property rights
- Optimal pollution

- Marginal social cost
- Marginal social benefit
- Coase theorem
- Markets for pollution rights
- Environmental protection

Externalities and the Common-Pool Problem

exhaustible resource
A resource in fixed supply, such as crude oil or coal

Let's begin by distinguishing between exhaustible resources and renewable resources. An **exhaustible resource** such as oil or coal does not renew itself and so is available in a finite amount. Technology may improve the ability to extract and utilize these resources, but each gallon of oil burned is gone forever. Sooner or later, all oil wells will run dry. The world's oil reserves are *exhaustible*.

Renewable Resources

renewable resource
A resource that regenerates itself and so can be used indefinitely if used conservatively, such as a properly managed forest

A resource is **renewable** if, when used conservatively, it can be drawn on indefinitely. Thus, timber is a **renewable resource** if trees are cut at sustainable rates and replaced with seedlings. The atmosphere and rivers are renewable resources to the extent that they can absorb and neutralize a certain level of pollutants. More generally, biological resources like fish, game, forests, rivers, grasslands, and agricultural soil are renewable if managed appropriately.

common-pool problem
Unrestricted access to a renewable resource results in overuse

Some renewable resources are also open-access resources, an idea introduced in the previous chapter. An open-access resource is rival in consumption, but exclusion is costly. Fish caught in the ocean, for example, are not available for others to catch, so fish are rival in consumption. Yet it would be difficult, if not impossible, for a person or a firm to "own" fish still swimming in open waters and to prevent others from catching them, so ocean fish are nonexclusive. An open-access good is often subject to the **common-pool problem**, which results because people harvest a resource as long as the marginal benefit exceeds marginal cost. For example, people will fish the oceans as long as the marginal benefit of catching more fish exceeds the marginal cost. Practically speaking, unless otherwise checked, people will fish until the oceans become "fished out." Open-access goods are overfished, overhunted, overharvested, and overused. Because the atmosphere is an open-access resource, it's used as a dump for unwanted gases. Air pollution is a negative externality imposed on society by polluters. The problem is that people exploit any resource as long as their personal marginal benefit exceeds their personal marginal cost. As we'll see, personal marginal cost ignores the costs imposed on others.

In a market system, specific individuals usually own the rights to resources and therefore have a strong interest in using those resources efficiently. *Private property rights*, a term introduced in Chapter 2, allow individuals to use resources or to charge others for their use. Private property rights are defined and enforced by government, by informal social actions, and by ethical norms. As Robert Frost wrote, "Good fences make good neighbors."[1] But because defining and enforcing property rights to open-access resources, such as the air, are quite costly or even impossible, these resources usually are not owned as private property.

Pollution and other negative externalities arise because there are no practical, enforceable, private property rights to open-access resources, such as the air. Market prices usually fail to include the costs that negative externalities impose on society. For example, the price you pay for a gallon of gasoline does not reflect the costs imposed by the greenhouse gases, sootier air, oil spills, and the greater traffic congestion your driving creates. Electric rates do not reflect the negative externalities, or external costs, caused by fossil-fueled power plants. Note that externalities are unintended side effects of actions that are themselves useful and purposeful. Electricity producers, for example, did not go into business to pollute.

Resolving the Common-Pool Problem

Users of the atmosphere, waterways, wildlife, or other open-access resources tend to ignore the impact of their use on the resource's renewal ability. As quality and quantity diminish from overuse, the resource grows scarcer and could disappear. For example, Georges Bank, located off the New England coast, long one of the world's most productive fishing grounds, became so depleted by overfishing that by the 1990s the catch was down 85 percent from peak years. Tuna, once abundant in the Mediterranean, now faces extinction there. The United Nations reports that 11 of the world's 15 primary fishing grounds are seriously depleted.

By imposing restrictions on resource use, government regulations may reduce the common-pool problem. Output restrictions or taxes could force people to use the resource at a rate that is socially optimal. For example, in the face of the tendency to overfish and to catch fish before they are sufficiently mature, the U.S. government has imposed a variety of restrictions on the fishing industry. The laws limit the total catch, the size of fish, the length of the fishing season, the equipment used, and other aspects of the business.

More generally, when imposing and enforcing private property rights would be too costly, government regulations may improve allocative efficiency. For example, stop signs and traffic lights allocate the scarce space at intersections, minimum size restrictions control lobster fishing, hunting seasons control the stock of game, and enforced study hours may calm the din in the college dormitory.

But not all regulations are equally efficient. For example, fishing authorities sometimes limit the total industry catch and allow all firms to fish until that limit is reached. Consequently, when the fishing season opens, there is a mad scramble to catch as much as possible before the industry limit is reached. Because time is of the essence, fishing boats make no effort to fish selectively. And the catch reaches processors all at once, creating congestion throughout the supply chain. Also, each firm has an incentive to expand its fishing fleet to catch more in those precious few weeks. Thus, large fleets of technologically efficient fishing vessels operate for a few weeks until the limit is reached and then sit in port for the rest of the year. Each operator is acting rationally, but the collective effect of the regulation is grossly inefficient in terms of social welfare. Consider the complicated and sometimes confounding fishing regulations in Iceland:

The Icelandic government realized that it would have to curb the capacity of its own fleet. But the fishermen compensated by buying more trawlers. Then the

net bookmark

Read the history of the U.S. Environmental Protection Agency at http://www.epa.gov/history/index.htm. Search on "market-based incentives" to find evidence of the role of incentives in environmental policy. The Acid Rain program is often cited by economists as an example of how such incentives can be implemented. This topic is well documented at http://www.epa.gov/acidrain/. For introductory information about almost any environmental problem, go to the EPA's Student Center at http://www.epa.gov/students/.

---

1. From the poem "Mending Wall" in Robert Frost, *You Come Too* (Holt, Rinehart, and Winston, 1967): 64.

government restricted the size of the fleet and the number of days at sea; the fishermen responded by buying larger, more efficient gear. The cod stocks continued to decline. In 1984, the government introduced quotas on species per vessel per season. This was a controversial and often wasteful system. A groundfish hauled up from 50 fathoms [300 feet] is killed by the change in pressure. But if it is a cod and the cod quota has been used up, it is thrown overboard. Or if the price of cod is low that week and cod happens to come in the haddock net, the fishermen will throw them overboard because they do not want to use up their cod quota when they are not getting a good price.[2]

Ocean fish remain a common-pool resource because firms have not yet been able to establish and enforce rights to particular schools of fish. But advances in technology may some day allow the creation of private property rights to ocean fish, migrating birds, and other open-access resources. Establishing property rights to cattle on the Great Plains once seemed impossible, but the invention of barbed wire allowed ranchers to fence the range. Patented in 1867, barbed wire was advertized as "The finest fence in the world. Light as air. Stronger than whiskey. Cheaper than dirt." In a sense, barbed wire tamed the Wild West.

Optimal Level of Pollution

Though the science is not yet fully resolved, fossil fuel used to power the likes of automobiles and electricity generators produces carbon dioxide, which mixes with other greenhouse gases that may contribute to climate change. Electricity production from fossil fuels, therefore, involves the external cost of using the atmosphere as a gas dump. This section considers a way to analyze such externalities.

External Costs With Fixed Technology

Suppose *D* in Exhibit 1 depicts the demand for electricity. Recall that a demand curve reflects consumers' marginal benefit of each unit. The lower horizontal line reflects the marginal private cost of electricity using fossil fuels. If producers base their pricing and output decisions on their marginal private costs, the equilibrium quantity per month is 50 million kilowatt-hours and the equilibrium price is $0.10 per kilowatt-hour. At that price and quantity, identified by point *a,* the marginal private cost of production just equals the marginal benefit enjoyed by consumers of electricity.

Electricity production involves not only the private cost of the resources employed but also the external cost of using the atmosphere as a dump for greenhouse gases. Suppose that the marginal external cost imposed on the environment by the generation of electricity is $0.04 per kilowatt-hour. If the only way to cut emissions is to reduce electricity production, then the relationship between electricity production and pollution is fixed; the pollution in this case occurs with **fixed-production technology.**

The vertical distance between the marginal private cost curve and the marginal social cost curve in Exhibit 1 shows the marginal external cost of $0.04 per kilowatt-hour. The **marginal social cost** includes both the marginal private cost and the marginal external cost that production imposes on society. Because the marginal external cost here is assumed to be a constant $0.04 per kilowatt-hour, the two cost curves are parallel. Notice that at the private-sector equilibrium output level of 50 million kilowatt-hours, the marginal social cost, identified at point *b,* exceeds society's marginal benefit of

fixed-production technology
Occurs when the relationship between the output rate and the generation of an externality is fixed; the only way to reduce the externality is to reduce the output

marginal social cost
The sum of the marginal private cost and the marginal external cost of production or consumption

2. Mark Kurlansky, *Cod: A Biography of the Fish That Changed the World* (New York: Walker., 1997), p. 172.

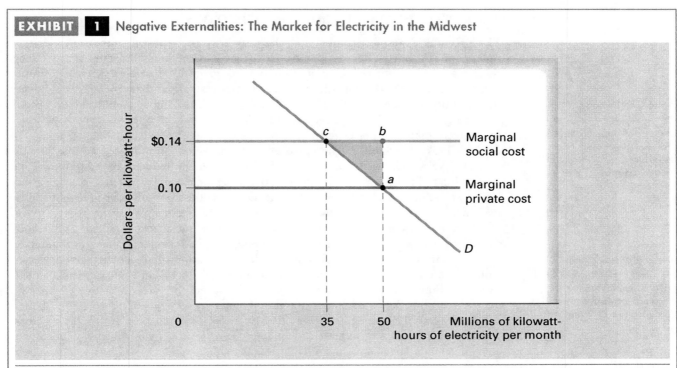

EXHIBIT **1** Negative Externalities: The Market for Electricity in the Midwest

If producers base their output on marginal private cost, 50 million kilowatt-hours of electricity are produced per month. The marginal external cost of electricity is the cost of pollution imposed on society. The marginal social cost curve includes both the marginal private cost and the marginal external cost. If producers base their output decisions on marginal social cost, only 35 million kilowatt-hours are produced, which is the optimal output. The total social gain from basing production on marginal social cost is reflected by the blue-shaded triangle.

electricity, identified on the demand curve at point *a*. The 50-millionth kilowatt-hour of electricity costs society $0.14 but yields only $0.10 of marginal benefit. Because the marginal social cost exceeds the marginal benefit, too much electricity is produced.

The efficient quantity of 35 million kilowatt-hours is found where the demand, or marginal benefit, curve intersects the marginal social cost curve. This intersection is identified at point *c*. How could output be restricted to the socially efficient amount? If regulators knew the demand and marginal cost curves, they could simply limit production to 35 million kilowatt-hours, the efficient quantity. Or, on each kilowatt-hour produced, they could impose a tax equal to the marginal external cost of $0.04. Such a pollution tax would lift the marginal private cost curve up to the marginal social cost curve. Thus, the tax would bring private costs in line with social costs.

With a tax of $0.04 per kilowatt-hour, the equilibrium combination of price and output moves from point *a* to point *c*. The price rises from $0.10 to $0.14 per kilowatt-hour, and output falls to 35 million kilowatt-hours. Setting the tax equal to the marginal external cost results in the efficient level of output. At point *c*, the marginal social cost of production equals the marginal benefit. Notice that greenhouse gas emissions are not eliminated at point *c*, but the utilities no longer generate electricity for which marginal social cost exceeds marginal benefit. The social gain from reducing production to the socially optimal level is shown by the blue-shaded triangle in Exhibit 1. This triangle also measures the social cost of allowing firms to ignore the external cost of production. Although Exhibit 1 offers a tidy solution, the external costs of greenhouse gases often cannot be easily calculated or taxed. At times, government intervention may result in more or less production than the optimal solution requires.

External Costs With Variable Technology

The previous example assumes that the only way to reduce greenhouse gases is to reduce output. But power companies, particularly in the long run, can usually change their resource mix to reduce emissions for any given level of electricity. If pollution can be reduced by altering the production process rather than by simply adjusting the quantity, these externalities are said to be produced under conditions of **variable technology**. With variable technology, the idea is to find the optimal level of pollution for a given quantity of electricity.

Let's look at Exhibit 2. The horizontal axis measures greenhouse gas emissions for a given level of electricity production. Emissions can be reduced by adopting cleaner production technology. Yet the production of cleaner air, like the production of other goods, is subject to diminishing returns. Cutting emissions of the most offensive greenhouse gases may involve simply changing the fuel mix, but further reductions call for more sophisticated and more expensive processes. Thus, the marginal social cost of reducing greenhouse gases increases, as shown by the upward-sloping marginal social cost curve in Exhibit 2.

The **marginal social benefit** curve reflects the additional benefit society derives from greenhouse gas reductions. When emissions are high, an improvement can save lives and thus is valued by society more than when emissions are low. Cleaner air, like other goods, has a declining marginal benefit to society (though the total benefit still increases). The marginal social benefit curve from cleaner air therefore slopes downward, as shown in Exhibit 2.

variable technology
Occurs when the amount of externality generated at a given rate of output can be reduced by altering the production process

marginal social benefit
The sum of the marginal private benefit and the marginal external benefit of production or consumption

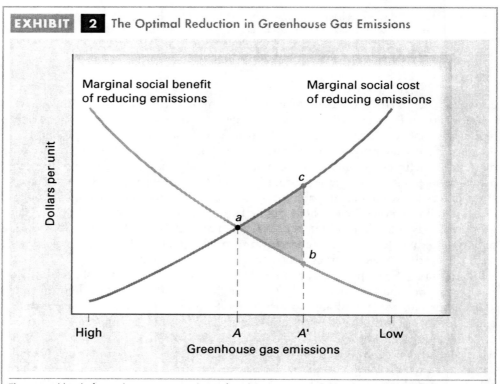

EXHIBIT 2   The Optimal Reduction in Greenhouse Gas Emissions

The optimal level of greenhouse gas emissions is found at point a, where the marginal social benefit of reducing such emissions equals the marginal social cost. If some lower level of emissions were dictated by the government, such as A', the marginal social cost would exceed the marginal social benefit, and social waste would result. The total social waste resulting from a lower than optimal level of emissions is shown by the pink-shaded triangle.

The optimal level of air quality for a given quantity of electricity is found at point *a*, where the marginal social benefit of cleaner air equals the marginal social cost. In this example, the optimal level of greenhouse gas emissions is *A*. If firms made their production decisions based simply on their private cost—that is, if the emission cost is external to the firm—then firms would have little incentive to search for production methods that reduce greenhouse gas emission, so too much production would result.

What if government regulators decree that greenhouse gas emission levels should be no greater than *A'*? For example, suppose a law establishes *A'* as the maximum acceptable level of emissions. The marginal social cost, identified as *c*, of achieving that level of air quality exceeds the marginal social benefit, identified as *b*. The total social waste associated with imposing a greater-than-optimal level of air quality is shown by the pink-shaded triangle, *abc*. This area is the total amount by which the additional social costs of cleaner air (associated with a move from *A* to *A'*) exceed the additional social benefits. Improving air quality benefits society only as long as the marginal social benefit of cleaner air exceeds its marginal social cost.

What would happen to the optimal level of emissions if either the marginal cost curve or the marginal benefit curve shifted? For example, suppose some technological breakthrough reduces the marginal cost of cutting greenhouse gas emissions. As shown in panel (a) of Exhibit 3, the marginal social cost curve of reducing emissions would shift downward to *MSC'*, leading to cleaner air as reflected by the movement from *A* to *A'*. *The simple logic is that the lower the marginal cost of reducing greenhouse gases, other things constant, the cleaner the air.*

An increase in the marginal benefit of air quality would have a similar effect. For example, suppose research indicates that the effects of a one degree increase in the Earth's average surface temperature would be much more devastating than previously believed. This finding would increase the perceived benefits of reducing greenhouse gases. Thus, the marginal benefit of cleaner air would increase, as reflected in panel

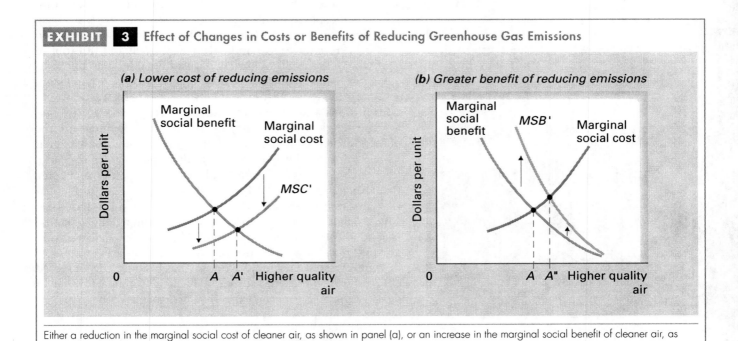

EXHIBIT 3   Effect of Changes in Costs or Benefits of Reducing Greenhouse Gas Emissions

Either a reduction in the marginal social cost of cleaner air, as shown in panel (a), or an increase in the marginal social benefit of cleaner air, as shown in panel (b), increases the optimal level of air quality.

(b) of Exhibit 3 by an upward shift of the marginal social benefit curve to *MSB'*. As a result, air quality would improve, moving from A to A" in panel (b) of Exhibit 3. *The greater the marginal benefit of reducing greenhouse gases, other things constant, the cleaner the air.* As another example, recent research indicates that deaths from heart and lung disease would decrease 0.7 percent in large U.S. cities if suspended particulates in the air decrease by just 1/100,000th of a gram per cubic meter of air.[3] This finding increases the perceived benefits of cleaner air, leading to an increase in the optimal quality of air.

The atmosphere has the ability to cleanse itself of some emissions, but the destruction of the tropical rainforest has reduced this ability, as discussed in the following case study.

PUBLIC POLICY

The Lungs of the Planet   The tropical rainforests have been called the lungs of the planet because they naturally recycle carbon dioxide into oxygen and wood, thus eliminating heat-trapping gases and helping to maintain the world's atmospheric balance. These rainforests cover just 6 to 7 percent of the Earth's land surface but contain over half of the world's plant and animal species. The Amazon rainforest, for example, contains the largest collection of plant and animal life on Earth, along with 20 percent of the world's supply of fresh water.

The world's rainforests are located in countries that are relatively poor, such as Bolivia, Brazil, Colombia, Indonesia, Venezuela, and the Philippines. Landless peasants and settlers burn down these forests to create farmland and pastures. Worse yet, to meet the growing demand for timber, loggers strip rainforests. Because most of the rainforest amounts to an open-access resource, where property rights are not easily established, poor settlers and timber companies usually pursue a slash-and-burn approach. The world's tropical forests have been cut in half in the last 50 years.

Burning the world's rainforests spells trouble for the environment. The fires add greenhouse gases to the atmosphere. Destruction of tropical forests around the world is estimated to be responsible for about 20 percent of global greenhouse gas emissions. The loss of trees reduces the atmosphere's ability to cleanse itself and increases flash flooding and mud slides. Stripped of trees, the land contains huge amounts of carbon subject to oxidization. Soil gets eroded by rains and baked by the sun and runs out of nutrients after only two growing seasons. Such farming is unsustainable. With nutrients lost, the ecosystem is not very resilient—*it takes a century for a clear-cut forest to return to its original state.* The loss of the tropical forests involves other costs. A canopy of trees protects a rich, genetically diverse, ecosystem.

The tropical rainforests, by serving as the lungs of the planet, confer benefits around the globe. But these external benefits are usually ignored in the decision to clear the land. It's not the greed of peasants and timber companies that leads to inefficient, or wasteful, uses of resources. The problem is that the rainforests and the atmosphere are open-access resources that can be degraded with little immediate personal cost to those who clear the land. The costs of deforestation are imposed on people around the globe. As an example of how interrelated the global economy has become, the increased demand for biofuels to replace fossil fuels is a major driver of deforestations. Farmers clear rainforests to grow soybeans, one source of biodiesel fuel.

Jason Edwards/Getty Images

3. Jonathan M. Samet et al., "Fine Particulate Air Pollution and Mortality in 20 U.S. Cities, 1987–1994," 343 *New England Journal of Medicine*, (14 December 2000): 1742–1749.

Poverty in the rainforest countries combined with the lack of legal title to the land encourage people to exploit that timber and soil rather than maximize the long-term value of these resources. For example, a secure property right to the land would reduce the need to clear it in order to claim some value. A farmer with title to the land could even leave a forest bequest to heirs. Research shows that people granted rights to the Amazon rainforest manage their land more conservatively. Property rights promote efficient harvesting of hardwoods and reforestation, allowing the forest to serve as an air filter. For example, the frequency of reforestation among those settlers granted land title was about 15 times greater than among those without title. Without title, the only way to capture some of the land's value is through a slash-and-burn approach. Thus, granting peasants and settlers property rights could help conserve the rainforests.

Sources: Alexai Barrionuevo, "Giants in Cattle Industry Agree to Help Fight Deforestation," *New York Times*, 6 October 2009; R. Godoy et al., "The Role of Tenure Security and Private Time Preference in Neotropical Deforestation," *Land Economics*, 74 (May 1998): 162–170; Charles Wood and Robert Walker, "Saving the Trees by Helping the Poor," *Resources for the Future* (Summer 1999): 14–17; and *State of the World's Forests: 2009*, Food and Agricultural Organization of the United Nations, at http://www.fao.org/docrep/011/i0350e/i0350e00.htm.

The Coase Theorem

The traditional analysis of externalities assumes that market failures arise because people ignore the external effects of their actions. For example, suppose a manufacturer of heavy machinery is next door to a research laboratory that tests delicate equipment. The vibrations caused by the manufacturing process throw off the delicate equipment next door. Professor Ronald Coase, who won the Nobel Prize in 1991, would argue that the negative externality in this case is not necessarily imposed by the heavy machinery— rather, it arises from the incompatible activities of the two firms. The externality is the result of both vibrations created by the factory *and* the location of the testing lab next door. Solutions might include modifying the factory, moving the factory, making the test equipment more shock resistant, or moving the testing lab.

According to Coase, the efficient solution depends on which party can avoid the externality at the lower cost. Suppose it would cost $2 million for the factory to reduce vibrations enough for the lab to function normally. On the other hand, if the factory makes no changes, the lab can't insulate its testing equipment enough to operate accurately, so the lab would have to relocate at a cost of $1 million. Based on this information, the least-cost solution would be for the testing lab to relocate at a cost of $1 million. Coase argues that, as long as transaction costs are low, the parties will reach the efficient solution if one party is assigned the property right. And here's Coase's special insight: *This efficient solution will be achieved regardless of which party gets the property right.*

Suppose the testing lab is granted the right to operate free of vibrations from next door, so the testing lab can force the factory to reduce its vibration. Rather than cut vibrations at a cost of $2 million, the factory can pay the lab to relocate. Any payment greater than $1 million but less than $2 million makes both sides better off, because the lab would receive more than its moving cost and the factory would pay less than its cost of reducing vibrations. Thus, the lab will move, which is the efficient outcome.

Alternatively, suppose the factory is granted the right to generate vibrations in its production process, regardless of the impact on the testing lab. For the factory, this means business as usual. Because the minimum payment the factory would accept to reduce vibrations is $2 million, the lab would rather relocate at a cost of $1 million. Thus, whether property rights are granted to the lab or to the factory, the lab will move, which is the efficient, or least-cost, solution. The **Coase theorem** says that as long as bargaining costs are small, merely assigning the property right will generate an efficient solution to an externality

Coase theorem
As long as bargaining costs are low, an efficient solution to the problem of externalities is achieved by assigning property rights to one party or the other, it doesn't matter which

problem regardless of which party is assigned that right. A particular assignment determines which side bears the externality costs but does not affect the efficient outcome.

Inefficient outcomes do occur, however, when the transaction costs of arriving at a solution are high. For example, an airport located in a populated area would have difficulty negotiating noise levels with all the affected residents. Or peasants contemplating clearing a portion of the tropical rainforest would be unable to negotiate with the millions, and perhaps, billions, of people ultimately affected by that decision. *When the number of parties involved in the transaction is large, Coase's solution of assigning property rights may not be enough.*

Markets for Pollution Rights

According to the Coase theorem, the assignment of property rights is often sufficient to resolve the market failure typically associated with externalities. Additional government intervention is not necessary. If pollution can be easily monitored and polluters easily identified, the government may be able to achieve an efficient solution to the problem of pollution simply by assigning the right to pollute. To see how this could work, let's look at an example. Firms that dump into a river evidently value the ability to discharge waste in this way. For them, the river provides a zero cost outlet for by products that otherwise would have to be disposed of at greater cost. The river provides a disposal service, and the demand curve for that service slopes downward, just like the demand for other resources.

The demand for the river as a discharge system is presented as *D* in Exhibit 4. The horizontal axis measures the tons of discharge dumped into the river per day, and the

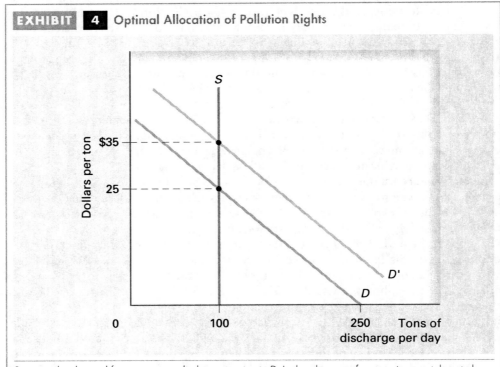

EXHIBIT   4   Optimal Allocation of Pollution Rights

Suppose the demand for a river as a discharge service is *D*. In the absence of any environmental controls, polluters dump 250 tons per day, where the marginal benefit of discharge is zero. If regulatory authorities establish 100 tons as the maximum daily level of discharge and then sell the rights, the market for these pollution rights clears at $25 per ton. If the demand for pollution rights increases to *D'*, the market-clearing price of pollution rights rises to $35 per ton.

vertical axis measures firms' marginal benefit of disposing of each ton of waste in this way. The demand curve thus measures the marginal value to firms of using the river as a disposal service. With no restrictions on river pollution—that is, if all firms were free to dump waste into the river—dumping would continue as long as it provided firms some marginal benefit. This marginal benefit falls to zero in Exhibit 4 when 250 tons per day are discharged. At that point the marginal private cost of dumping, which is zero, equals the marginal private benefit.

The river, like the atmosphere, the soil, and the sea can absorb and neutralize a certain amount of discharge per day without deteriorating in quality. What if voters make the public choice that the river should remain clean enough for swimming and fishing? Suppose engineers determine this level of water quality can be maintained as long as no more than 100 tons are discharged per day. Thus, the "supply" of the discharge service provided by the river is fixed at 100 tons per day, shown by the vertical supply curve, S, in Exhibit 4.

If government regulators can easily identify polluters and monitor their behavior, authorities can allocate permits to discharge 100 tons per day. If polluters are simply given these permits (that is, if the price of permits is zero), there will be an excess demand for them, because the quantity supplied is 100 tons but the quantity demanded at a price of zero would be 250 tons. An alternative is to sell permits for 100 tons of pollution at the market-clearing price. The intersection of supply curve S and demand curve D yields a permit price of $25 per ton, which is the marginal value of discharging the 100th ton into the river each day. To most permit buyers, the marginal value of a permit exceeds $25 per ton.

The beauty of this system is that producers who value the discharge rights the most ultimately end up with them. Producers who attach a marginal value below $25 per ton apparently have cheaper ways of resolving their waste problems, including changing production techniques. And if conservation groups, such as the Sierra Club, want a cleaner river than the government's standard, such as water clean enough to drink, they can purchase pollution permits but not exercise them.

What if additional firms spring up along the river that are willing to pay more than $25 per ton for pollution rights? This greater demand is reflected in Exhibit 4 by D'. This increase of demand would bid up the market price of pollution permits to, say, $35 per ton. Some existing permit holders would sell their rights to those who value them more. Regardless of the comings and goings of would-be polluters, the total quantity of discharge rights is restricted to 100 tons per day, so the river's quality will be maintained. Thus, *the value of pollution permits, but not the total amount of pollution, may fluctuate over time.*

If the right to pollute could be granted, monitored, and enforced, then what had been a negative externality problem could be solved through market allocation. Historically, the U.S. government had relied on setting discharge standards and fining offenders. But in 1989, a pollution rights market for fluorocarbon emissions was established and was followed in 1990 by a market for sulfur dioxide. During the 1990s, sulfur dioxide emissions in the nation fell by more than half, exceeding the goals of the authorizing legislation. The "cap-and-trade" proposal by President Obama aims to create a market for greenhouse gas emissions. So the market for pollution rights is alive and growing.[4] Even China is now experimenting with this approach. Some companies and even celebrities have used a variant of pollution rights to become "carbon neutral"—that is, by estimating their carbon emissions then offsetting this impact by paying for projects

---

4. For a discussion of the market for sulfur dioxide emissions, see Paul Joskow, Richard Schmalensee, and Elizabeth Bailey, "The Market for Sulfur-Dioxide Emissions," *American Economic Review*, 88 (September 1998): 669–685.

to neutralize, or "sop up," equivalent emissions.[5] For example, Delta Air Lines until recently allowed online ticket buyers to pay an extra $5.50 for domestic flights or $11 for international flights for tree plantings to help offset flight emissions. And the band Coldplay funded the planting of 10,000 mango trees in India to help sop up emissions related to the release of a new CD.[6]

Pollution Rights and Public Choice

Unfortunately, legislation dealing with pollution is affected by the same problems of representative democracy that trouble other public policy questions. Big polluters have a special interest in government proposals relating to pollution, and they fight measures to reduce pollution. But members of the public remain rationally ignorant about pollution legislation. So pollution regulations may be less in accord with the public interest than with the special interests of polluters. To win their cooperation, a portion of pollution permits are often *given* to existing firms or offered at below-market prices. For example, under the sulfur dioxide program, the nation's 101 dirtiest power plants were granted credits equal to between 30 and 50 percent of the pollution they emitted before the program began. Because they received something of value, polluters were less inclined to oppose the legislation. Once permits were granted, some recipients found it profitable to sell their permits to other firms that valued them more. Thus, a market emerged that led to an efficient allocation of pollution permits. According to some analysts, the sulfur dioxide program saves up to $3 billion annually compared with the old system. More generally, a system of marketable pollution rights can reduce the cost of pollution abatement by as much as 75 percent.

Before 1990, **command-and-control environmental regulations** were the norm—an approach that required polluters, such as electric utilities, to introduce particular technologies to reduce emissions by specific amounts. These regulations were based on engineering standards and did not recognize unique circumstances across generating plants, such as plant design, ability to introduce scrubbers, and the ease of switching to low-sulfur fuels. But the market for pollution rights reflects an **economic efficiency approach** that offers each electric utility the flexibility to reduce emissions in the most cost-effective manner, given its unique operation. Firms with the lowest costs of emission control have an incentive to implement the largest reduction in emissions and then sell unused pollution permits to those with greater control costs.

Now that you know something about the theory of externalities, let's turn to an important application of the theory—environmental protection.

command-and-control environmental regulations
An approach that required polluters to adopt particular technologies to reduce emissions by specific amounts; inflexible regulations based on engineering standards that ignore each firm's unique ways of reducing pollution

economic efficiency approach
An approach that offers each polluter the flexibility to reduce emissions as cost-effectively as possible, given its unique cost conditions; the market for pollution rights is an example

Environmental Protection

Federal efforts to address the common-pool problems of air, water, and soil pollution are coordinated by the Environmental Protection Agency (EPA). Four federal laws and subsequent amendments underpin U.S. efforts to protect the environment: (1) the Clean Air Act of 1970, (2) the Clean Water Act of 1972, (3) the Resource Conservation and Recovery Act of 1976 (which governs solid waste disposal), and (4) the Superfund law of 1980 (legislation focusing on toxic waste dumps). When the EPA was created in 1970, it began with about 4,000 employees and a budget of $1.2 billion (in 2011 dollars). By 2011, it had about 18,000 employees and a $10.0 billion budget.

---

5. See Andrew Revkin, "Carbon-Neutral Is Hip, But Is It Green," *New York Times*, 29 April 2007.
6. Michael Hill, "Can Planting a Tree Absolve Your Eco-Sins?" *Arizona Republic*, 28 May 2007.

According to EPA estimates, compliance with pollution-control regulations cost U.S. producers and consumers about $300 billion in 2011, an amount equivalent to 2 percent of gross domestic product, the market value of all final goods and services produced in the economy. We can divide pollution control spending into three categories: spending for air pollution abatement, spending for water pollution abatement, and spending for solid waste disposal. About 40 percent of the pollution control expenditures in the United States goes toward cleaner air, another 40 percent goes toward cleaner water, and 20 percent goes toward disposing of solid waste. (These figures are from a typical year, and do not include cleanup costs after the drilling accident in the Gulf of Mexico.) In this section, we consider, in turn, air pollution, water pollution, Superfund activities, and disposing of solid waste.

Air Pollution

In the Clean Air Act of 1970 and in subsequent amendments, Congress set national standards for the amount of pollution that could be released into the atmosphere. Congress thereby recognized the atmosphere as an economic resource, which, like other resources, has alternative uses. The air can be used as a source of life-giving oxygen, as a prism for viewing breathtaking vistas, or as a dump for carrying away unwanted soot and gases. The 1970 act gave Americans the right to breathe air of a certain quality and at the same time gave producers the right to emit particular amounts of specified pollutants. Research shows that people value clean air and are willing to pay more to live in communities with less pollution.[7]

Smog is the most visible form of air pollution. Automobile emissions account for 40 percent of smog. Another 40 percent comes from consumer-oriented products, such as paint thinner, fluorocarbon sprays, dry-cleaning solvents, and baker's yeast by products. Surprisingly, only 15 percent of smog comes from manufacturing. The 1970 Clean Air Act mandated a reduction of 90 percent in auto emissions, leaving it to the auto industry to achieve this target. At the time, automakers said the target was impossible. Between 1970 and 1990, however, average emissions of lead fell 97 percent, carbon monoxide emissions fell 41 percent, and sulfur dioxide emissions fell 25 percent. In fact, an EPA study concluded that because auto emissions and industrial smoke have been reduced so much, *air pollution on average is now greater indoors than outdoors.* For example, in the Los Angeles area, a smog alert, meaning the air reached dangerous levels, occurred on a weekly basis during the 1980s, but the city did not experience a smog alert between 2003 and the heavy forest-fire season of 2008. U.S. air quality is now considered good compared to the air quality in much of the world. For example, no U.S. city ranks among the world's worst in sulfur dioxide. Despite recent improvements in air quality, the United States is still a major source of fossil-fuel carbon dioxide emissions, a major greenhouse gas. As you can see from Exhibit 5, which shows the world's 25 worst nations in annual fossil-fuel carbon dioxide emissions per capita, the United States ranks fourth worst with 5.2 tons per capita.

There have been efforts to address greenhouse gases on an international scale. A report by the Intergovernmental Panel on Climate Change, a group sponsored by the United Nations, was approved in May 2007 by more than 120 nations.[8] The study says, to fight climate change, the world must cut emissions of carbon dioxide and other greenhouse gases by (1) sharply improving energy efficiency in buildings, vehicles, and machines; (2) shifting from fossil fuels to nuclear, wind, solar, and other renewable

---

7. Kenneth Chay and Michael Greenstone, "Does Air Quality Matter? Evidence from the Housing Market," *Journal of Political Economy*, 113 (April 2005): 376–424.
8. For panel reports, go to http://www.ipcc.ch/.

EXHIBIT 5 Fossil-Fuel Carbon Dioxide Emissions per Capita: The 25 Worst Nations

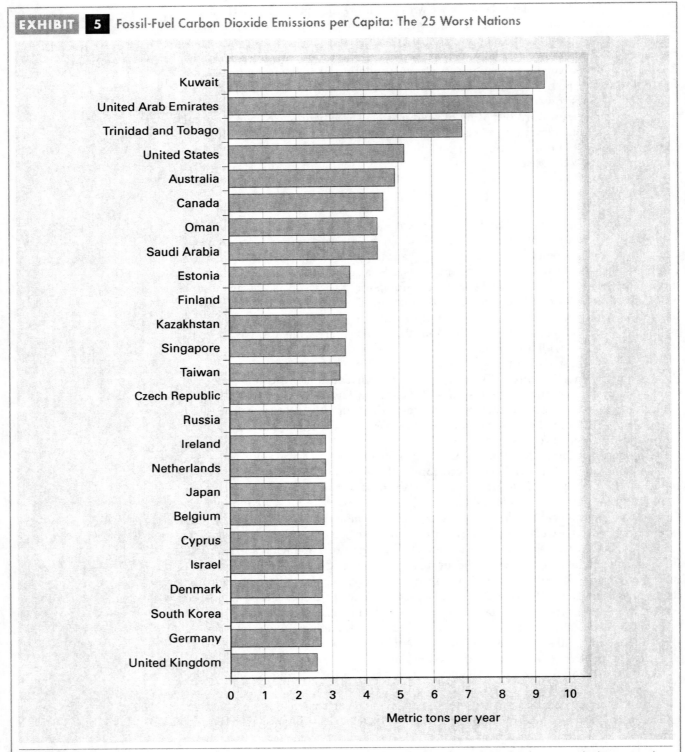

Metric tons per year

Sources: Figures are for 2006 and were estimated by Tom Boden, Gregg Marland, and Bob Andres at the Oak Ridge National Laboratory and can be found at http://cdiac.ornl.gov/trends/emis/top2006.cap. Excluded are nations with fewer than one million people.

energy sources; (3) preserving forests as absorbers of carbon dioxide, or as "carbon sinks"; and (4) capping agricultural emissions. The United States and China, which account for more than 40 percent of the world's emissions, approved the report but offered no indication that they would reverse their opposition to mandatory emission reductions. The report said that such reforms would require lifestyle changes, increased prices for some basics including gasoline and electricity, and greater investment in research and development.

Water Pollution

Three major sources of water pollution are sewage, chemicals, and oil. For decades, U.S. cities had an economic incentive to dump their sewage directly into waterways rather than clean it up first. Water current or tides would carry off the waste to become someone else's problem. Although each community found it rational, based on a narrow view of the situation, to dump into waterways, the combined effect of these local choices was water pollution, a negative externality imposed by one community on other communities. Federal money over the years has funded thousands of sewage treatment plants, which cut water pollution substantially. Nearly all U.S. cities now have modern sewage treatment systems. Hundreds of once-polluted waterways have been cleaned up enough for swimming and fishing.

Chemicals are a second source of water pollution. Chemical pollution may conjure up an image of a pipe spewing chemicals into a river, but only about 10 percent of chemical pollution in the water comes from point pollution—pollution from factories and other industrial sites. About two-thirds come from nonpoint pollution—mostly runoff from agricultural pesticides and fertilizer. Congress has been reluctant to limit the use of pesticides, although pesticides pollute water and contaminate food. Industrial America seems an easier target than Old MacDonald's farm. In 1970, Congress shifted control of pesticides from the U.S. Department of Agriculture to the newly created Environmental Protection Agency (EPA). But the EPA already had its hands full administering the Clean Water Act, so it turned pesticide regulation over to the states. Most states gave the job to their departments of agriculture, which usually promote the interests of farmers, not restrict what farmers can do. The EPA now reports that in most states pesticides have fouled some groundwater.[9]

A third source of water pollution is oil. The cleanup of oil spills on land are overseen by the EPA. About 600,000 underground storage tanks for oil and chemicals pose a potential threat of contamination for groundwater, the source of drinking water for half of Americans. The cleanup of offshore oil spills is overseen by the U.S. Coast Guard. The most notable offshore spill in U.S. history is discussed in the following case study.

PUBLIC POLICY

CASE STUDY

BP's Oil Spill in the Gulf   On April 20, 2010, the Deepwater Horizon oil rig exploded in the Gulf of Mexico in a drilling accident that killed 11 workers and hospitalized many. Both BP and the government initially underestimated the size of the spill, and neither had a response plan in place. Though the oil industry had experienced blowouts at shallower depths, an accident a mile down was new and devastating. Federal regulators seemed lax prior to the accident, perhaps captives of the industry. The size of the Gulf spill combined with live video of the gushing well and photos of oil-soaked birds marked this tragedy in the public's mind. President Obama called it the worst environmental disaster in U.S. history.

9. John Cushman, "E.P.A. and States Found to Be Lax on Pollution Law," *New York Times*, 7 June 1998.

e activity

To get BP's perspective, go to
http://www.bp.com and click
on the tab for Gulf of Mexico
response. For an analysis of
the costs and maybe surprising
benefits of an oil spill, go to
http://www.alaskadispatch.
com/dispatches/energy/5798-
economics-of-an-oil-spill-
cleanup. The *Alaska Dispatch*
article discussed the aftermath
of the 1989 Exxon Valdez spill.

The explosion and resulting oil spill, accidental byproducts of BP's efforts to supply oil, threatened the livelihood of tens of thousands around the Gulf and could impose lasting damage on the habitat. BP spent billions on cleanup in the first three months, but that was peanuts compared to the costs company owners have and will face. More than 150 class-action lawsuits named BP as a defendant. Hoping to attract more clients, law firms purchased domain names such as offshoreinjuries.com and bigoilspills.com and advertised with billboards along the Gulf Coast. Environmental groups filed suits of their own. President Obama warned BP against "nickel and diming" the economic victims of the accident. And the Justice Department opened a criminal probe against BP for possible violations of the Clean Water Act and other environmental laws.

Here's a question: Was this oil spill a negative externality? Was this an unpriced by-product that affected neither buyer nor seller but third parties? The buyers in this case were customers for BP gasoline and the seller was BP. Market competition may make it difficult for BP to pass along its spill-related costs, so BP consumers may not be much affected. How about BP?

If this were truly an externality, then the accident would have had little impact on the supplier, BP, or the company BP hired to drill the well, Transocean. But both have been profoundly affected. Because BP has been reviled by everyone from President Obama on down, the company's brand name will be tarnished for a generation, becoming the poster child of polluters in the public's mind, in the media, even in textbooks. Lawsuits will likely cost the company billions and may take years to settle (some Exxon-Valdez suits from the 1989 Alaska spill took more than two decades to resolve). For its part, Transocean, the owners of the rig, saw 11 workers die in the explosion and many more hospitalized. The drilling rig itself, which cost Transocean $375 million, sank two days after the explosion.

Although lawsuits may be in the courts for years, share owners of BP and Transocean didn't have to wait long to see their losses reflected in stock prices. Within six weeks of the accident, the share price of each company sank 50 percent. In BP's case, that meant a loss in the market value of the company of about $90 billion. Because Transocean was a smaller company, its market value fell about $15 billion. Although the exact amount of the spill may never be known, let's say the total turns out to be about 200 million gallons, a figure higher than any reported estimate. This would imply that BP and Transocean stockholders together lost more than $500 in market value for each of the 200 million gallons of crude oil spilled into the Gulf. There remained some question whether the companies will survive. For example, BP established a $20 billion fund to compensate those affected by the spill. The company was forced to sell rights to some oil fields to pay for the cleanup and was expected to issue bonds to raise more money. No question, many in the Gulf region have been harmed by the spill, and some of the damage could last for years. But many people will be compensated for their losses. The legal system, the government, the media, and the stock market have placed much of the cost of this accident squarely on BP and Transocean, and to that extent, most of what otherwise would have been external costs became internalized.

Sources: Michael Shear and Steven Mufson, "Obama to BP: Take Care of Gulf Victims," *Washington Post*, 5 June 2010; Justin Gillis and Leslie Kaufman, "After Oil Spill, Hidden Damage Can Last for Years," *New York Times*, 17 July 2010; Dionne Searcey, "Attorneys Scramble to Gather the Most Plaintiffs for the Broadest Action Possible," *Wall Street Journal*, 2 June 2010; and Brian Baskins, "BP: 'No Evidence' of Problems with New Caps," *Wall Street Journal*, 17 July 2010.

Hazardous Waste and the Superfund

The U.S. synthetic chemical industry has flourished in the last 50 years, and over 50,000 chemicals are now in common use. But some have harmful effects on humans and other living creatures. These chemicals can pose risks at every stage of their production, use, and disposal. New Jersey manufactures more toxic chemicals than any other state and, not surprisingly, has the worst toxic waste burden. Prior to 1980, the disposal of toxic waste created get-rich-quick opportunities for anyone who could rent or buy a few acres of land to open a toxic waste dump. As an extreme example, one site in New Jersey took in 71 million gallons of hazardous chemicals during a three-year period.[10]

Before 1980, once a company paid someone to haul away its hazardous waste, that company was no longer responsible. The Comprehensive Environmental Response, Compensation, and Liability Act of 1980, known more popularly as the Superfund law, requires any company that generates, stores, or transports hazardous wastes to pay to clean up any wastes that are improperly disposed of. A producer or hauler who is the source of even one barrel of pollution dumped at a site can be held liable for cleaning up the entire site.

The Superfund law gave the federal government authority over sites contaminated with toxins. But to get an offending company to comply, the EPA frequently must sue. The process is slow, and nearly half the budget goes to lawyers, consultants, and administrators rather than to site cleanups. The law did not require that benefits of a cleanup exceed costs or even that such comparisons be attempted. Although billions have been spent so far, a recent EPA study concluded that the health hazards of Superfund sites have been vastly exaggerated. Chemicals in the ground usually move slowly, sometimes taking years to travel a few feet, so any possible health threat is confined to the site itself. People know when they live near toxic waste sites, and they can exert political pressure to get something done, whereas people exposed to polluted air, water, and pesticide residue may develop health problems but never make the connection to their environment. Thus, people see less reason to press public officials for cleaner air and water (though the threat of climate change has focused more attention on greenhouse gas emissions). Toxic waste sites, because of their greater political urgency and media appeal (witness the movies on the subject), tend to receive more attention than air or water pollution. And with the federal government picking up the tab, localities demand all the cleanup they can get. But research indicates that Superfund cleanups have little or no impact on residential property values, property rental rates, the housing supply, total population, or the types of individuals living near the sites.[11] In short, Superfund cleanups seem to be much to do about not much.

Solid Waste: "Paper or Plastic?"

Throughout most of human history, households tossed their trash outside as fodder for pigs and goats. New York City, like other cities, had no trash collections, so domestic waste was thrown into the street, where it mixed with mud and manure (until recently, many residents of Beijing and other parts of China did the same thing).[12] Decades of such accumulation explain why the oldest Manhattan streets are anywhere from 3 to 15 feet above their original levels. Until the last century, people buried their trash near their homes or took it to a local dump. Most localities now forbid trash burning.

U.S. households generate about 4 pounds of garbage per resident per day—more than twice the 1960 level and the most in the world. Much of the solid waste consists

---

10. Jason Zweig, "Real-Life Horror Story," *Forbes*, 12 December 1988.
11. Michael Greenstone and Justin Gallagher, "Does Hazardous Waste Matter? Evidence from the Housing Market and Superfund Programs," *Quarterly Journal of Economics*, 123 (August 2008): 951–1003.
12. Laurence Brahm, "Hygiene? It's a Load of Rubbish," *South China Morning Post*, 1 November 2005.

of packaging. The question is, how do we dispose of the more than 200 million tons of household garbage generated in this country each year? Advanced economies produce and buy more than less developed economies, so there is more to throw away. And because of higher incomes in advanced economies, the opportunity cost of time is higher, so Americans tend to discard items rather than repair or recycle them. For example, it's cheaper to buy a new toaster for $20 than to pay $40 an hour to fix a broken one, assuming you can even find a repair service. (Look up "Appliance Repair, Small" in the *Yellow Pages* and see if you can find even one such service in your area.)

About 70 percent of the nation's garbage is bulldozed and covered with soil in landfills. Although a well-managed landfill poses few environmental concerns, at one time, communities dumped all kinds of toxins in them—stuff that could leach into the soil, contaminating wells and aquifers. So landfills got a bad reputation. Now, the prevailing attitude with landfills is Nimby! (Not in my backyard!). We all want our garbage picked up but nobody wants it put down anywhere nearby.

As the cost of solid waste disposal increases, some state and local governments are economizing, charging households by the pound for trash pickups, and requiring more recycling and returnable bottles. **Recycling** is the process of converting waste products into reusable materials. Nearly half of U.S. households participate in curbside recycling programs. Still, according to the EPA, only about 15 percent of U.S. garbage gets recycled; about 15 percent is incinerated and, as noted already, the remaining 70 percent goes into landfills. Of the recycled material, three-quarters consists of corrugated boxes, newspapers, office paper, and other paper products. Some paper is shipped to Korea, Taiwan, and China, where it becomes packaging material for U.S. imports such as Blu-ray players and computer components. Exhibit 6 ranks the world's top 25 recyclers of paper and cardboard among major economies. Ireland heads the list, recycling 78 percent. The United States is in a five-way tie for 18th, recycling 50 percent (but more than double that of 1985). Poorer countries recycle much less—Mexico, for example, only 7 percent.

Most of the 15 percent of garbage that is incinerated gets burned in trash-to-energy plants, which generate electricity using the heat from incineration. Until recently, such plants looked like the wave of the future, but less favorable tax treatment and environmental concerns over incinerator locations (Nimby strikes again!) have taken the steam out of the trash-to-energy movement.

To repeat, only 30 percent of U.S. garbage is recycled or incinerated, and about 70 percent goes to landfills. In contrast, the Japanese recycle or incinerate 73 percent, sending only 27 percent to landfills. Japanese households sort their trash into as many as 21 categories. Because land is scarcer in Japan—we know this because it costs relatively more—it is not surprising that the Japanese deposit a smaller share of their garbage in landfills.

Some recycling is clearly economical—such as aluminum cans, which are a relatively cheap source of aluminum compared to producing raw aluminum. About two out of three aluminum cans now get recycled, though only 11 states require returnable deposits on such cans. Still, returnable deposit laws increase recycling. Incentives matter. Even if you decide to discard your empties, chances are that someone down the line with a lower opportunity cost than you will find them and claim the deposits. For example, researchers found an average of 47 bottles and cans along a one-block path of city park each day prior to the enactment of deposit law, but one year after the law was introduced, they found an average of only two bottles and cans each day along the same path.[13]

Recycling paper and cardboard is also economical and occurred long before the environmental movement. Such old standbys as paper drives, drop-off bins, and redemption centers collect more tonnage than curbside programs. Most recycling results from salvaging scrap material from business and industry, a practice that dates back decades.

recycling
The process of converting waste products into reusable material

---

13. J. Trinkaus, "A Bottle Law: An Informal Look," *Perceptual and Motor Skills*, 59 (December 1984): 806.

EXHIBIT   6   Paper and Cardboard Recycling: Top 25 Among Advanced Economies

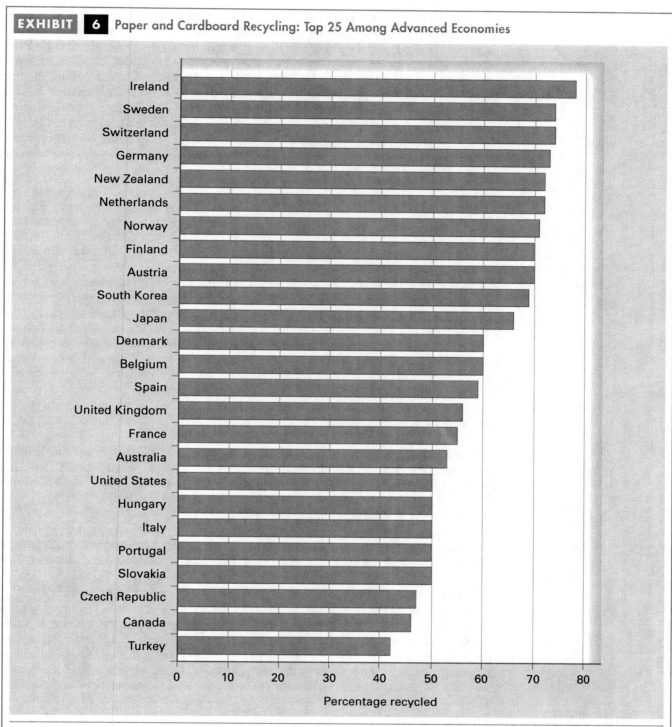

Percentage recycled

Sources: Figures are rankings among members of the Organization of Economic Cooperation and Development as reported in *OECD Environmental Data 2006/2007*, Table 4A, p. 25. This can be found at http://www.oecd.org/dataoecd/60/59/38106368.pdf. Figures are for 2005, except for South Korea, Germany, Sweden, and the U.K., which are for 2004, and for Japan and Turkey, which are for 2003.

Governments have tried to stimulate demand for recycled material—for example, by requiring newspapers to use a minimum percentage of recycled newsprint. Other recycled products are not in such demand. In fact, some recycled products have become worthless and must be hauled to landfills. Recycling imposes its own environmental cost. Curbside recycling requires fleets of trucks that pollute the air. Newsprint must first be de-inked, creating a sludge that must be disposed of. But greater environmental awareness has made consumers more receptive to more efficient packaging. For example, liquid laundry detergent now comes in a concentrated "ultra" form, which cuts volume in half, and Unilever's brand All Small & Mighty cuts volume by two-thirds. Labels for all kinds of products proudly identify the recycled content of the packaging.

Positive Externalities

To this point, we have considered only negative externalities. But externalities are sometimes positive, or beneficial. Positive externalities occur when consumption or production benefits other consumers or other firms. For example, people who get inoculated against a disease reduce their own likelihood of contracting the disease (the personal benefit), but they reduce the risk of transmitting the disease to others (the external benefit). Parents who don't get their children vaccinated risk triggering an epidemic, so the vaccination decision is not simply a private matter. Likewise, society as a whole receives external benefits from education because those with more education become better citizens, can read road signs, are better able to support themselves and their families, and are less likely to require public assistance or to resort to violent crime for income. Researchers found that more schooling significantly reduces the probability of incarceration.[14] Thus, your education benefits you but it also benefits others.

The effect of external benefits is illustrated in Exhibit 7, which presents the demand and supply of education. The demand curve, D, represents the private demand for education, which reflects the marginal private benefit for those who acquire the education. More education is demanded at a lower price than at a higher price.

The benefit of education, however, spills over to others in society. If we add this positive externality, or marginal external benefit, to the marginal private benefit of education, we get the marginal social benefit of education. *The marginal social benefit includes all the benefits society derives from education, both private and external.* The marginal social benefit curve is above the private demand curve in Exhibit 7. If education were a strictly private decision, the amount purchased would be determined by the intersection of the private demand curve D with supply curve S. The supply curve reflects the marginal cost of producing each unit of the good. This intersection at point e yields education level E, where the marginal private benefit of education equals its marginal cost, as reflected by the supply curve. But at level E, the marginal social benefit, identified as point b, exceeds the marginal cost. Social welfare would increase if education expands beyond E. As long as the marginal social benefit exceeds the marginal cost, social welfare increases as education expands. Social welfare is maximized at point e' in Exhibit 7, where E' units of education are provided—that is, where the marginal social benefit equals the marginal cost. The blue-shaded triangle identifies the increase in social welfare that results from increasing education from E, the private optimum, to E', the social optimum.

14. Lance Lochner and Enrico Moretti, "The Effects of Education on Crime: Evidence from Prison Inmates," *American Economic Review*, 94 (March 2004): 155–189.

EXHIBIT **7** Education and Positive Externalities

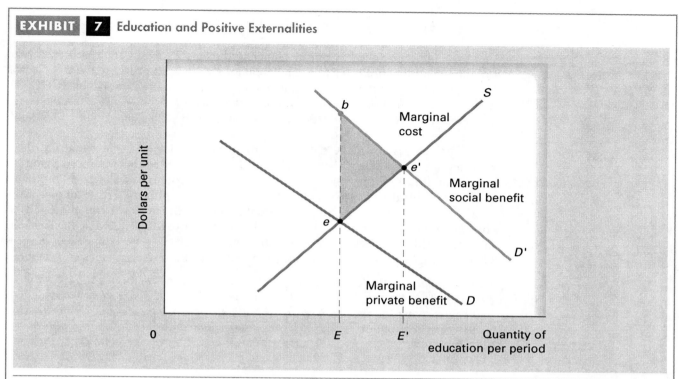

In the absence of government intervention, the equilibrium quantity of education is E, where the marginal private benefit of education equals the marginal cost as reflected by the supply curve. Education also confers a positive externality on the rest of society, so the social benefit exceeds the private benefit. At quantity E, the marginal social benefit, point b, exceeds the marginal cost, point e, so more education increases social welfare. In this situation, government tries to increase education to E', where the marginal social benefit equals the marginal cost.

Thus, society is better off if the level of education exceeds the private equilibrium. With positive externalities, decisions based on private marginal benefits result in less than the socially optimal quantity of the good. Thus, like negative externalities, positive externalities typically point to market failure, which is why government often gets into the act. When there are external benefits, public policy aims to increase quantity beyond the private optimum. For example, governments try to increase education by providing free primary and secondary education, by requiring students to stay in school until they reach 16 years of age, by subsidizing public higher education, and by offering tax breaks for some education costs.

Another source of externalities stems from precautions people take to avoid becoming crime victims, such as LoJack, a device used to track and recover a stolen vehicle. Because the device is completely undetectable by a potential thief, the more LoJacks installed, the more nervous thieves get and the fewer vehicles stolen in general. Thus, car owners without LoJack get a positive externality when others install the device. Researchers estimated that a 1 percent increase in LoJack installations cuts car thefts in general by at least 20 percent.[15] On the other hand, the use of The Club, a very visible lock for the steering wheel, generates a negative externality, because it increases the likelihood that vehicles without The Club will get stolen. In terms of social welfare, there are not enough LoJacks installed and too many Clubs.

15. Ian Ayres and Steven Levitt, "Measuring Positive Externalities for Unobservable Victim Precautions: An Empirical Analysis of Lojack," *Quarterly Journal of Economics*," 113 (February 1998): 43–77.

Conclusion

About 6.9 billion people live on the planet, and over 72 million are added each year. World population is projected to reach 9.3 billion by 2050, according to the U.S. Census Bureau, with most of this growth occurring in countries where most people barely eke out a living. Population pressure coupled with a lack of incentives to conserve open-access resources results in deforestation, dwindling fish stocks, and polluted air, land, and water.

Ironically, because of the tighter pollution controls in industrial countries, these countries are less polluted than developing countries, where there is more pollution from what little industry there is. Most developing countries have such profound economic problems that environmental quality is not a priority. For example, when India's Supreme Court tried to close some polluting factories in New Delhi, thousands of workers torched buses, threw stones, and blocked major roads, demanding the factories stay open. Although New Delhi's pollution masks any trace of a blue sky, workers believe their jobs are more important. Here's one account of New Delhi's air quality:

> *In the heat of the afternoons, a yellow-white mixture hung above the city, raining acidic soot into the dust and exhaust fumes. At night the mixture condenses into a dry, choking fog that envelops the headlights of passing cars, and creeps its stink into even the tightest houses. The residents could do little to keep the poison out of their lungs or the lungs of their children, and if they were poor, they could not even try.*[16]

Market prices can direct the allocation of resources only as long as property rights are well defined. Pollution arises not so much from the greed of producers and consumers as from the fact that open-access resources are subject to the common-pool problem.

Summary

1. An exhaustible resource is available in fixed supply, such as crude oil or coal. A renewable resource can regenerate itself if used conservatively, such as a properly managed forest. Some renewable resources suffer from a common-pool problem because unrestricted access leads to overuse.

2. Production that generates negative externalities results in too much output. Production that generates positive externalities results in too little output. Public policy should tax or otherwise limit production that generates negative externalities and should subsidize or otherwise promote production that generates positive externalities.

3. The optimal amount of environmental quality occurs where the marginal social benefit of an improvement equals its marginal social cost. An upward shift of the marginal benefit curve of environmental quality or a downward shift of its marginal cost curve increases the optimal level of environmental quality.

4. The world's tropical rainforests recycle greenhouse gases into oxygen and wood. Because rainforests are open-access resources, settlers and loggers cut them down to make a living. This destruction reduces the environment's ability to cleanse itself of greenhouse gases, which may contribute to climate change.

5. The Coase theorem argues that as long as bargaining costs are low, assigning property rights to one party leads to an efficient solution to the externality problem. The market for pollution permits reflects the Coase theorem in action.

6. Aside from greenhouse gases, America's air and waterways are getting cleaner. The air is cleaner because of stricter emissions standards for motor vehicles, and waterways are cleaner because of billions spent on sewage treatment plants. Toxic waste sites do not pose as great a health threat as other forms of pollution such as smog and pesticide residue, but toxic waste sites often get more media and political attention.

---

16. William Langewiesche, "The Shipbreakers," *Atlantic Monthly* (August 2000): 42.

Key Concepts

Exhaustible resource   372

Renewable resource   372

Common-pool problem   372

Fixed-production technology   374

Marginal social cost   374

Variable technology   376

Marginal social benefit   376

Coase theorem   379

Command-and-control environmental regulations   382

Economic efficiency approach   382

Recycling   388

Questions for Review

1. **EXTERNALITIES**   Complete each of the following sentences:
   a. Resources that are available only in a fixed amount are _____ resources.
   b. The possibility that a open-access resource is used until the marginal value of additional use equals zero is known as the _____.
   c. Resources for which periodic use can be continued indefinitely are known as _____ resources.

2. **RESOLVING THE COMMON-POOL PROBLEM**   Why have authorities found it so difficult to regulate the fishing catch in the open ocean to allow for a sustainable yield?

3. **OPTIMAL LEVEL OF POLLUTION**   Explain the difference between fixed-production technology and variable technology. Should the government set a goal of reducing the marginal social cost of pollution to zero in industries with fixed-production technology? Should they do so in industries with variable technology?

4. **Case Study: Destruction of the Tropical Rainforests**   Why does a solution to the overharvesting of timber in the tropical rainforests require some form of international cooperation? Would this be a sufficient solution to the deforestation problem?

5. **THE COASE THEOREM**   Suppose a firm pollutes a stream that has a recreational value only when pollution is below a certain level. If transaction costs are low, why does the assignment of property rights to the stream lead to the same (efficient) level of pollution whether the firm or recreational users own the stream?

6. **THE COASE THEOREM**   Ronald Coase points out that a market failure does not arise simply because people ignore the external cost of their actions. What other condition is necessary? What did Coase consider to be an efficient solution to a negative externality?

7. Four federal laws and subsequent amendments underpin U.S. environmental protection. Identify these laws.

8. **Case Study: BP's Oil Spill in the Gulf**   Should the government require deepwater oil companies to spend whatever it takes to reduce the chance of future spills to zero?

9. **POSITIVE EXTERNALITIES**   The value of a home depends in part on how attractive other homes and yards in the neighborhood are. How do local zoning ordinances try to promote land uses that generate external benefits for neighbors?

Problems and Exercises

10. **EXTERNAL COSTS WITH FIXED-PRODUCTION TECHNOLOGY**   Review the situation illustrated in Exhibit 1 in this chapter. If the government sets the price of electricity at the socially optimal level, why is the net gain equal to triangle *abc*, even though consumers now pay a higher price for electricity? What would the net gain be if the government set the price above the optimal level?

11. **NEGATIVE EXTERNALITIES**   Suppose you wish to reduce a negative externality by imposing a tax on the activity that creates that externality. When the amount of the externality produced per unit of output increases as output increases, the correct

tax can be determined by using a demand-supply diagram; show this. Assume that the marginal private cost curve slopes upward.

12. **EXTERNAL COSTS**   Use the data in the table from the next page to answer the following questions.
   a. What is the external cost per unit of production?
   b. What level is produced if there is no regulation of the externality?
   c. What level should be produced to achieve economic efficiency?
   d. Calculate the dollar value of the net gain to society from correcting the externality.

Quantity	Marginal Private Benefit (demand) ($)	Marginal Private Cost (supply) ($)	Marginal Social Cost ($)
0	—	0	0
1	10	2	4
2	9	3	5
3	8	4	6
4	7	5	7
5	6	6	8
6	5	7	9
7	4	8	10
8	3	9	11
9	2	10	12
10	1	11	13

13. **EXTERNAL COSTS WITH VARIABLE TECHNOLOGY** Think of an industry that pollutes the water and has access to variable technology for reducing that pollution. Graphically illustrate and explain the impact of each of the following, other things constant, on the optimal level of water quality:

a. New evidence is discovered about a greater risk of cancer from water pollution.
b. The cost of pollution-control equipment increases.
c. A technological improvement reduces the cost of pollution control.

14. **MARKET FOR POLLUTION RIGHTS**   The following graph shows the market for pollution rights.

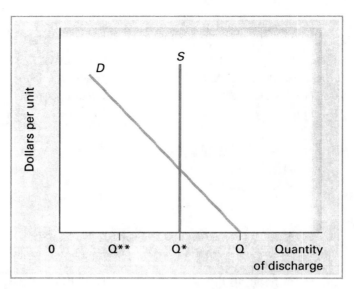

a. If there are no restrictions on pollution, what amount is discharged?
b. What is the quantity supplied and the quantity demanded if the government restricts the amount of discharge to Q* but gives the permits away?
c. Where is market equilibrium if the government sells the permits? Illustrate this on the graph.
d. What happens to market equilibrium if the government reduces the amount of discharge permitted to Q**? Illustrate this on the graph.

Global Economic Watch Exercises

Login to www.cengagebrain.com and access the Global Economic Watch to do these exercises.

15. **GLOBAL ECONOMIC WATCH and** Case Study: Destruction of the Tropical Rainforests Go to the Global Economic Crisis Resource Center. Select Global Issues in Context. In the Basic Search box at the top of the page, enter the phrase "carbon ranching." On the Results page, go to the Global Viewpoints Section. Click on the link for the June 16, 2007, editorial "Home on the Rainforest." Is the program described an example of command-and-control environmental regulation or of the economic efficiency approach?

16. **GLOBAL ECONOMIC WATCH** Go to the Global Economic Crisis Resource Center. Select Global Issues in Context. Go to the menu at the top of the page and click on the tab for Browse Issues and Topics. Choose Environment and Climate Change. Choose one of the topics listed and read the overview for that topic. Analyze the marginal social benefit and marginal social cost involved in your chosen topic.